Reclaiming the Canon

Reclaiming the Canon

Essays on Philosophy, Poetry, and History

Herman L. Sinaiko

Foreword by Joel Beck

Yale University Press   New Haven and London

For Susan and Joel in love and friendship

Designed by Rebecca Gibb.
Set in Perpetua type by The Composing Room of Michigan, Inc.
Printed in the United States of America by Vail-Ballou Press, Binghamton, New York.

Library of Congress Cataloging-in-Publication Data
Sinaiko, Herman L.
Reclaiming the canon : essays on philosophy, poetry, and history /
Herman L. Sinaiko ; foreword by Joel Beck.
p.   cm.
Includes bibliographical references.
ISBN 0-300-06529-9 (alk. paper)
1. Canon (Literature).   2. Literature—History and criticism.
I. Title.
PN81.S5274   1998
809—dc21
97-40723

A catalogue record for this book is available from the British Library.

10 9 8 7 6 5 4 3 2 1

Contents

Foreword

The essays collected in this volume make the work of Herman L. Sinaiko available to a wider public. Twice awarded a prize by the University of Chicago for excellence in undergraduate teaching, he has inspired, prodded, and irritated generations of students. Douglas Unger, a former student, remembers how Sinaiko "paced a room, how he would fill almost every inch of a chalkboard with scatterings of ideas and notes and how he was constantly running his hands through his hair, teaching *at* us, using the Socratic method in a way that permitted, acknowledged, and honored a question."

The author of a highly regarded book on Plato, Sinaiko has devoted much of his teaching career to thinking about and lecturing on what, following Hume, he calls great art. Recently, in the so-called canon wars, we have heard much heated debate about how and why certain texts came to be known as great art. This is not the place to summarize that debate. Suffice it to say that the canon reclaimed by Sinaiko is broad enough to include Confucius, Chinese poetry, and Mary Shelley. But, for reasons that he specifies in Chapter 14, on Hume's "Of the Standard of Taste," he does not deviate too far from the standard canon.

More interesting is that Sinaiko reclaims the canon for philosophy and, in so doing, reclaims something vital about philosophy itself. Philosophy today exists almost exclusively within the confines of the university. Most people encounter it in the form of introductory college courses, which typically include a dialogue by Plato, a treatise by Descartes, a short work by Kant. A few pursue advanced studies in philosophy at a graduate department. Philosophy, in short, has become a profession with its own associations, journals, and conferences. In what follows I shall sketch Sinaiko's retrieval of Plato's conception of philosophy and indicate the use that he makes of the canon.

Philosophy is the search for wisdom. We begin to seek wisdom when we acknowledge that we are ignorant. Plato, in his *Dialogues,* depicts a variety of situations in which Socrates leads interlocutors to acknowledge their ignorance. In the *Republic,* Socrates badgers Thrasymachus into retracting his claim that justice is the interest of the stronger. Thrasymachus' capitulation provokes Glaucon and Adeimantus to challenge Socrates to prove that justice is intrinsically good. The young men talking with Socrates no longer know what is just or unjust, good or evil, or how they should lead their lives. Glaucon's spirited defense of injustice shows that tyranny is a real temptation for him.

The disturbing and disruptive recognition that we are ignorant about the most fundamental things, that we no longer know who or what we are, can originate anywhere, with any problem. Plato's *Dialogues* teaches that philosophy can begin with a headache, with an argument about how to instill courage in our children, with a drinking party, or with a stroll in the country. Philosophy is latent in a life crisis and in an argument about the meaning of a film.

To acknowledge that we are ignorant about the most fundamental things is difficult. Socrates, in the *Republic*'s parable of the cave, compares the experience of enlightenment to being exposed to the light after a lifetime of being bound and forced to face the wall of a dark cave. We want to return to the familiar, to escape the anxiety of not-knowing. Philosophy begins when we persist in questioning, for it is also the quest to replace opinions with knowledge. But the opinions that we seek to replace are about the very fabric of our being. As the search for wisdom, philosophy is concerned with the whole. Where and how do we find the whole? In one sense, it is all around us. Any conversation about any topic can potentially lead to reflection on its foundation and possibility and thereby to reflection on the whole. But there are privileged places that one can visit in the quest for wisdom. For Sinaiko these places are great works of art.

A concern for the whole gives the canon its unique position for philosophy. In Chapter 19, "The Ancient Quarrel," Sinaiko argues that great art presents us with an image of the whole as we experience it as human beings. In the chapter on Hume he spells this out more clearly: "Great art alone provides us with access to that general humanity which we all share, and to that small but select society of civilized men and women whose collective judgment constitutes the true standard of taste. What I am suggesting is that great art, according to Hume, is privileged in that, more than any other human endeavor, it provides us with such knowledge of ourselves as we are able to achieve. For true self-knowledge, we need the canon of classic works." The *Iliad,* for example, discussed in Chapter 19, "presents us with a profoundly tragic vision of human life, but a vision that makes sense of and even exalts the human phenomena as we know them directly from the experience of our own life."

Commenting on *War and Peace* in Chapter 5, Sinaiko shows more clearly what he means by the "experience of our own life." He writes: "Tolstoy has not just told the story of what happened to those people at that time, of the changes that occurred; behind the constant changes and supporting them he has rendered the fabric, the context, of human life, unchanged and eternal. In taking on permanence as well as change, his poetry encompasses philosophy." Conrad, in *Heart of Darkness,* offers a vision of the nature of the whole. Writes Sinaiko in Chapter 9: "What I find most terrifying in his vision is the idea that goodness, morality, decency, whatever one wants to call it, has no foundation in reality. Reality is the darkness, a howling nightmare, the insane desires of the primeval human soul. Civilization, morality, and restraint are fragile constructs. They are the idea at the back of it; not a sentimental pretense but an idea; and an unselfish belief in the idea—something you can set up, and bow down before, and offer a sacrifice to . . . "

Great art, then, does at least three things. It teaches what it means to be human by telling a story. It discloses the unchanging fabric and context of human life. And it offers an account of something like the being of the whole. For Homer the whole is in constant strife. For Conrad it is a howling nightmare of darkness. For Yeats, in Chapter 8, the whole is defined by the appearance of the mysterious "Presences."

To the extent that great art makes claims about the whole, it inevitably raises questions about how its creators arrive at their knowledge of the whole. On this, the poets are silent. Sinaiko, following Socrates, insists in Chapter 19 that there is an ancient quarrel between philosophy and poetry. "Homer is radically corrupting precisely because he makes such a marvelously convincing case for his view. To the degree that we are emotionally convinced by Homer, we deny the possibility of philosophy." We no longer need philosophy because Homer's art persuades us that we already know. The quarrel is ultimately a lover's quarrel, however, because philosophy needs poetry: "Philosophy cannot do without Homer and the other poets, for the poets present with immense power the eternal problems that make philosophy possible and necessary."

In reclaiming Plato's dialogical conception of philosophy, Sinaiko reminds us that the possibility of philosophy is latent in every question that moves the questioner. In reclaiming the canon, he reminds us that there are no better partners in the continuing conversation about who we are than the great poets. I invite the reader to let Herman Sinaiko act as a guide in exploring some great works of art and to begin thereby a journey out of a gloomy cave into the open air, where the Good has not lost its power to illuminate our lives.

Joel Beck

Preface

This book is a collection of essays on major literary and philosophical texts, essays written over a number of years and originally prepared in the form of lectures, each given to a specific audience, ranging from students in an introductory humanities course at the University of Chicago to the members of the Chicago Psychoanalytic Society to the faculty of the Air Force Academy. As a whole, the essays express a single, coherent point of view. They are serious but nontechnical and are intended for a thoughtful, educated general audience without any particular professional qualification.

The essays can also be seen as an implicit polemic against some of the prevalent trends in contemporary academic and intellectual attitudes toward literature and philosophy. They are attempts to rescue a number of major works— from the learned experts who would monopolize access to them; from overprofessionalized academics who often use their scholarly expertise to anchor a work so thoroughly in its historical context that it no longer has relevance for the present; from contemporary theorists who view these works through the lens of a tendentious theory that reveals more about their personal biases than about the works being discussed.

My own view, informed primarily by my reading of Plato, is that these works have something serious to say that can be heard and responded to by any thoughtful reader. My effort in each essay is to open the work under discussion to the sensitive response and informed judgment of the reader.

The essays are arranged into four parts. The first part consists of two introductory essays, one on Socrates and Freud, both of whom believed that conversation is the royal road to truth, and one on Plato's *Laches,* a dialogue about the need for courage not only in war but especially in that always frightening, always threatening search for genuine wisdom. This opening part introduces the notion that philosophy is essentially dialogical—that the strangely unsettling activity of talking to each other—not private meditation or technical analysis—is what constitutes the perennial human search for wisdom.

The second part, the substantive heart of the book, consists of twelve essays on a wide range of texts from Homer to Yeats, Confucius to Frankenstein. Here the aim is to articulate accurately, appreciatively, and with a minimum of preconception the rich diversity of powerful views expressed in these works about our common human condition.

In the third part, consisting of two pieces on education and teaching, I use my experience as a student and as a teacher to reflect further on the centrality of dialogue to that search for wisdom traditionally called philosophy.

The fourth and final part contains four essays on Plato. In the first three I examine passages at the beginning, the middle, and the end of the *Republic* and explore a series of issues involved in the enterprise of philosophy understood as conversation. The fourth and concluding essay, on the relation of dialogue and dialectic throughout Plato's writings, is an attempt to show that although the dialogue that is philosophy never ends, it is not therefore fruitless. We may never be fully wise, but we can become wiser.

Because these essays have grown out of my repeated efforts to teach these texts over the years, I owe a special debt of gratitude to all those students and audiences who by their friendly but penetrating questions and criticisms forced me to rethink and deepen what I had to say. To my friend Joel Beck I owe an unpayable debt; his editorial patience and tact are largely responsible for whatever grace these essays may have.

Gladys Topkis and Mary Pasti, both of Yale University Press, helped pare down the inevitable wordiness of a veteran classroom teacher. Benjamin Schalet tracked down and checked the references, and Jonathan Aronoff handled the permissions.

Finally, for Ben and Jane my hope is that in their time they enjoy and learn as much from these books as I have.

Earlier versions of five of the chapters were previously published and are reproduced by permission of the publisher: "Plato's *Laches:* Courage, Expertise, Psychotherapy, and Adolescence," in *Adolescent Psychiatry: Developmental and Clinical Studies,* vol. 13, ed. Sherman C. Feinstein (Chicago: University of Chicago Press, 1986), pp. 44–61, © 1986 by the University of Chicago, all rights reserved; "Dialectic in the *Republic:* The Simile of Light and Elenchus," chapter 3 in *Love, Knowledge, and Discourse in Plato: Dialogue and Dialectic in Phaedrus, Republic, Parmenides,* by Herman L. Sinaiko (Chicago: University of Chi-

PART I   THE SEARCH FOR WISDOM

1 Socrates and Freud
Talk and Truth

Socrates and Freud—a strange pair! The ancient Athenian philosopher and the modern medical scientist—what do they have in common? In what reasonable sense could they be said to be the joint subject of a lecture? Of course, in view of the modern mania for comparing and contrasting anything and everything, Socrates and Freud are as good a pair to examine as any other. Both are major figures in the intellectual history of the West. Both were great innovators, protean thinkers whose influence has been deep and pervasive far beyond the limits of the issues they explicitly addressed. Both were deeply interested in the human psyche. But as soon as I say that, as soon as I move from abstract points of comparison to concrete subjects, the profound differences between them begin to emerge. For Socrates *psyche* seems to mean "soul" in all its diverse theological, poetic, and even commonplace meanings, whereas for Freud *psyche* takes on its characteristic and definitive contemporary sense of something like "the inner self."

Rather than detailing the differences between the two figures, what I want to do is focus on a single, central feature of their activity as thinkers, a feature that they share with each other and that distinguishes them from all—and I mean all—other major thinkers across the whole span of Western thought. I am referring to the peculiar emphasis both of them place upon talk, discourse, conversation, dialogue. The extraordinary focus both give to this everyday activity is well known but has been too little contemplated. Indeed, it is frequently the basis for sharp criticism of the thought of both men. You can read in many textbooks on the history of philosophy how Socrates naively thought that it was possible to arrive at true definitions of the virtues or to discover the nature of moral principles simply by talking to people. Similarly, when Freud's method of psychotherapy is called the talking cure, that description is not always neutral or complimentary; it often contains a slight note of contempt and derision at the absurdly self-limiting discipline of psychoanalysis.

What is interesting and important to note is that both Socrates and Freud were well aware that the ends to which they devoted themselves were not usually achieved simply by talking. In Socrates' case, the pre-Socratic tradition of Greek thought included many thinkers who were profound observers of natural phenomena as well as of human social and political affairs. Freud, too, engaged in a great deal of scientific research, in the laboratory and clinical practice, in his early career as a neurologist and psychiatrist. The truth seems to be that both men, as they matured into the great thinkers we admire, deliberately restricted their respective pursuits of philosophy and psychoanalysis to the single activity of talking. It was Socrates who brought philosophy "down out of the heavens into the marketplace" and thus defined his method of philosophical investigation as *dialectic*—that is, as "conversation." It was Freud who rejected hypnosis, the laying-on of hands, and the empirical investigation of the objective facts of a case in favor of the rigorous and exclusive use of talk as the method of psychoanalysis.

Freud was so fanatical in his emphasis on talk, nothing but talk, that he invented the technique of having patients lie on a couch while the analyst sits behind them, so that they can't see the analyst's face and try to read its expression. In classical psychoanalysis, except for the unavoidable few seconds at the beginning and end of each session when the patient is in the process of lying down on or getting up from the couch, the analyst is essentially a disembodied voice. The effect is very similar to what many readers feel when they read Plato's *Dialogues*. Frequently a dialogue begins with a lively, highly dramatic scene; but as Socrates takes hold of the conversation the dramatic hustle and bustle fades away, and soon all that is left is the sound of two or more voices talking back and forth in a kind of temporal and spatial void.

Socrates and Freud both knew, without doubt, that in restricting philosophy and psychoanalysis to mere talk, by excluding the other possible resources available to them, they were paying a heavy price. They knew this, and yet they did it. So far as we know, neither of them ever regretted it or reversed himself.

In these remarks I want to follow their lead; I want to transform talk from a commonplace phenomenon that we take for granted into an open question to be seriously reflected on. I will do so by looking at what Socrates and Freud each discovered about talk and what each did with and through talk. I hope thereby to begin to explore the power of talk, the way it can become not merely an important or even the primary technique but the sole instrument by which philosopher and psychoanalyst can pursue their ends.

For both Socrates and Freud the only end that counts, the end to which both of them bend their efforts, is the discovery of the truth—not a trivial truth about this or that but truth with a capital *T,* the truth about the nature of things.

Were they serious? Can mere talk be the privileged, the only, means to significant truth?

Let me begin with Socrates. He himself apparently wrote nothing; we know about him only through the reports of others, reports whose pictures of Socrates are not always consistent with each other. I will develop my account of his understanding of discourse primarily from a few well-known, noncontroversial facts about him.

He grew up in the fifth century B.C. during the heyday of the Athenian empire, in what used to be called the golden age of Greece. In his youth he earned his living as a stonemason, like his father, and he probably worked on the Parthenon. At some point, probably when he was quite young, he became fascinated with philosophy, and from then on he seems to have spent almost all his time talking in the agora, the marketplace, of Athens. He seems to have given up stonemasonry and, as a consequence, become poverty-stricken. We do not know how he supported himself, but it seems likely that he was partly supported by some of his wealthy friends and followers.

Socrates lived in this fashion for many years. He married a woman named Xanthippe, whom later tradition portrays as a thoroughly unpleasant shrew. (This may be an injustice, for the contemporary evidence tells us very little about her.) Socrates had three sons with her, the last of whom was still a nursing infant when Socrates was tried and executed at the age of seventy for impiety and for corrupting the young.

Socrates, like all other able-bodied Athenians of his day, served in the army during military campaigns, and we know he fought in at least three battles. Like many other Athenians, he was highly critical of the extreme democratic government of Athens. But when that government was briefly overthrown by a despotic junta of wealthy aristocrats, Socrates, at direct risk to his life, refused to comply with their attempts to involve him in their murderous regime.

A member of the intellectual and cultural elite of Athens, he was a personal friend of Euripides, the tragic poet, and an acquaintance of Aristophanes, the comic poet, who publicly ridiculed him in his play *The Clouds.* He was a friendly rival and colleague of all the philosophers and sophists of his time— Protagoras, Parmenides, Anaxagoras, Gorgias. He may even have been a friend or an acquaintance of Pericles, the leader of the Athenian democracy at its height. He certainly knew intimately several members of Pericles' family, including Alcibiades and Plato. Though impoverished, he seems to have been regularly invited to the homes and dinner parties of the rich and powerful. Apparently he also spent much time conversing with ordinary citizens and visitors to Athens—businessmen, artisans, politicians, performers, doctors.

A fascinating, compelling figure, he wrote nothing, established no schools or other institutions, engaged in no significant political activities, and associated himself with no particular intellectual or philosophical doctrine or movement. He was an interesting local figure, idiosyncratic, even eccentric, nothing more; like many other such figures throughout history, fated to be remembered for a while in amusing or sentimental anecdotes and then fade into obscurity.

But Socrates did not fade into obscurity. He became one of the most influential figures in ancient Greek thought, then Roman thought, then medieval Christian, Jewish, and Muslim thought, and finally modern thought. Every single school of philosophy in the ancient world directly or indirectly traced its origins to Socrates. Platonists, Aristotelians, Stoics, Epicureans, Cynics, Skeptics—all claimed Socrates as their founder. In the generation before Socrates and during his lifetime there was a flourishing group of thinkers in Greece called sophists. Socrates opposed them (although, through one of those ironies so common in the world, many of his fellow citizens in Athens apparently thought he himself was a sophist). By the time of his death Sophism as a distinctive intellectual movement had more or less disappeared—apparently because of Socrates' critique.

Already in antiquity, Greek thought was conventionally divided into two periods: pre-Socratic and post-Socratic. Unfortunately, we know very little about the pre-Socratic thinkers—Heracleitus, Parmenides, Democritus, among others. The impact of Socrates' thought upon his contemporaries and succeeding generations was so powerful that they seem to have stopped reading the works of his predecessors. The result was that their works became exceedingly rare within a few generations, and many disappeared altogether. Today we know the works of the pre-Socratics only in fragments, in odd passages quoted by later authors whose works did survive. Students of ancient Greek thought, myself included, mourn the loss of those pre-Socratic works. But I believe we must take seriously the judgment of those who knew Socrates that he effected a fundamental revolution in thought, a revolution so compelling that it rendered those earlier thinkers obsolete and established the intellectual tradition within which we still live today.

What did Socrates do or discover that so impressed his friends and followers? He is a mysterious, puzzling, even paradoxical figure, hard to grasp not because his thought was so complicated but because it was so simple, not because it was hidden or esoteric but because it was so obvious, so public. The greatness, the profundity, of his thought lies in his discovery of what Alfred

North Whitehead describes as "first principles almost too obvious to need expression, and almost too general to be capable of expression. In each period there is a general form of the forms of thought; and, like the air we breathe, such a form is so translucent, and so pervading, and so seemingly necessary, that only by extreme effort can we become aware of it" (*Adventures of Ideas*, p. 14). We still live in the period of thought initiated by Socrates, and that is why he remains so hard to perceive.

Scattered through Plato's *Dialogues* there are a number of images of Socrates that help to catch the extraordinary quality of the man and his thought. In the *Meno*, Meno, a young Thessalian aristocrat—sophisticated, well educated, thoroughly lazy, stupid, and thoughtless—likens Socrates to a stingray, which paralyzes everything it touches (80a). Until he talked to Socrates, Meno says, he had always thought of himself as an articulate, knowledgeable, self-confident young man. After half an hour's conversation with Socrates he finds himself tongue-tied, confused, frustrated, unsure of himself and of his opinions. Socrates, he says, paralyzed his mind the way the stingray paralyzes the body.

In the *Theaetetus,* Socrates describes himself to Theaetetus, a young mathematician, as an intellectual midwife, analogous to his own mother, a physical midwife. The ordinary midwife, he says, has two functions: to preside at the birth of a child or, if the woman is suffering from a false pregnancy, to relieve her of the illusion that she is going to have a child. Socrates says that he performs the same function for ideas, helping those whose souls are pregnant with ideas to give birth to those ideas or, if they are not pregnant, showing them that there are no ideas ready to emerge. And like the midwives who help with the birth of babies but are themselves infertile, Socrates says that he can help others give birth to their ideas even though he himself is intellectually sterile, with no ideas of his own (149a–151d).

In the *Apology,* in which he unsuccessfully defends himself against the capital charges of impiety and corrupting the young, Socrates likens the city of Athens to a noble horse, very beautiful but a little stupid and slow-moving. He describes himself as a gadfly, sent by God to irritate and rouse the city from its mindless slumbers (302e). An intellectually paralyzing stingray, a midwife for the offspring of the soul, a stinging gadfly for his community—these catch something of what it meant to encounter Socrates.

But there is a fourth image of Socrates in Plato's writings. It occurs in the *Symposium,* an account of a dinner party at which the host and his guests give speeches in praise of love. Alcibiades, perhaps the most brilliant and talented of Socrates' young men (with the exception of Plato himself), comes late to the party, and he comes drunk. He gives the last speech of the evening, and he discusses, not love, but Socrates. Socrates, he says, is like the figurines of the satyr Marsyas that are sold in the shops of Athens. Outwardly these are statues of a short, potbellied, bulging-eyed, ugly little man, but, says Alcibiades, they are cleverly hinged so that they can be opened, and inside there are beautiful images of divinity. Socrates and his words are like these statues: outwardly ugly and ordinary; inwardly, containing rare treasures and images of the divine (215a–215c). I think Alcibiades' image of Socrates best captures the quality of the man and his talk that I am trying to evoke.

What were Socrates' words like? What did Socrates say that was so compelling to those who could see beyond the prosaic surface? What was there in those conversations with local politicians, artisans, poets, visiting philosophers, and wealthy young men that revolutionized Western thought?

In the *Tusculan Disputations,* Cicero described Socrates as "the first to call philosophy down from the heavens, establish her in the cities of men, and introduce her even into private houses, and compel her to ask questions about life and morality and things good and evil" (V.4.10). The remark has been repeated so often that it has become a cliché, but what did Cicero mean?

The great task for the so-called pre-Socratic thinkers was to find the fundamental ground and principle of all things. Typically, those thinkers asked questions about the nature of the cosmos, what we call the universe—the whole of everything that is. They wanted to understand being itself, to grasp with their minds the nature of things; and they called their enterprise philosophy.

According to Cicero, Socrates was interested in the same thing, engaged in the same enterprise, but he decisively shifted the locus of investigation. He sought knowledge of the nature of things, not in the universe around us, but in the opinions of men. Or, to put it differently, he apparently thought that the key to understanding the nature of things lay, not in the external world of material things, but in that world as it includes human beings and as it appears to the human soul. More precisely, Socrates seems to have argued that the key to understanding the nature of things lies in the world as it appears to the one particular soul that is most important to each of us—our own. He never tired of quoting the injunction of the god Apollo that was inscribed in stone over the entrance of his temple at Delphi: "Know thyself." Socrates said many times that everything he did was devoted to fulfilling that single task—gaining self-knowledge—and until he had done so, he had no time for any other pursuit or activity.

What does it mean to know thyself? And why does every other human activity pale to insignificance beside it? To begin with, self-knowledge is different in kind from all other knowledge. In the search for self-knowledge we are both the object of the search and the one who does the investigating. But can we fail to know ourselves? Are we not more intimately knowledgeable about ourselves than about anything else in the world? Is not the very notion of seeking knowledge of the self intrinsically absurd or at least paradoxical?

This Socratic quest for self-knowledge is perhaps the single most difficult and problematic of all human endeavors. Probably the most difficult aspect of the enterprise is to understand that, appearances to the contrary, we are not knowledgeable but profoundly ignorant of ourselves. It is this profound ignorance of ourselves that was Socrates' great discovery.

When the god Apollo said "Know thyself" to those humans who came to ask questions of the oracle at Delphi, he originally meant something specific and achievable. The wise and immortal god says to each of us, "Know yourself as a mortal, finite, limited human being; know yourself to be ignorant of what the future will bring, to be forgetful of the past, to be weak and more or less incompetent to deal with the demands of the present. Most of all, know yourself to be a human being and not a god. Know that you are an actor in a drama of which you are not the author or director, a drama that is sometimes tragic and more frequently comic, and that the best you can achieve in life is to understand and accept your fundamental limitations." Fully articulated, this understanding of human existence is the one embodied in classical pre-Socratic Greek culture, in the statues of the gods, in the serene and harmoniously ordered architecture of the great temples, and, most of all, in the lucid and brilliant writings of the poets—Homer and the Attic tragedians.

What Socrates discovered in his search for self-knowledge goes far beyond this traditional Greek understanding of what it means to be human. In our everyday lives, in our actions and reactions, and especially in our deeply held beliefs about the world, Socrates discovered that we are in touch with things whose existence we absolutely take for granted but whose nature remains mysterious. Let me illustrate what I mean. If I ask you, "Is it true that two plus two equals four?" you will undoubtedly answer, "Of course, Everyone knows that." But if I then ask you, "Since you are so sure it is true to say that two plus two equals four, perhaps you would be so good as to tell me what truth is?" You will not, I think, answer this question without some hesitation and uncertainty. If you are sophisticated and learned in these matters, you may be able to tell me what Aristotle or Heidegger or Descartes said about truth, but whether you are sophisticated or not, if I continue this line of questioning, you will eventually fall into confusion.

This problem—and it is a problem—is not confined to questions about truth; it holds equally for such notions as beauty, goodness, justice, and knowledge and even for such seemingly obvious terms as *equal, like,* and *one.* Every general term that we use in ordinary conversation becomes opaque when we stop using it as if we understood it and instead subject it to direct examination.

Not only does each of us use these terms all the time, in whatever language we happen to speak, but when we use these terms we mostly seem to understand one another. It is by the use of these mysterious but commonplace terms that we articulate our understanding of ourselves and the world in which we live.

Without these terms and the uses we put them to, we would instantly revert to the condition of the mute beasts; we would lose our humanity. "Man," says Aristotle, a spiritual grandson of Socrates, "is the animal who talks," but by "talk" Aristotle doesn't mean the grunts or barks with which animals communicate fear or desire or other information. By "talk"—the Greek word is *logos*—Aristotle means the words, the statements, the arguments about our opinions—opinions about what we should do, why we should do it, what the true facts in a situation are, and so forth. Talking is what we humans are doing when we use these mysterious terms that we understand and do not understand. Socrates seems to have investigated these terms, to have tried to explore with his interlocutors what they meant by them.

Let me be very clear here. I do not mean to suggest, as many scholars have done, that Socrates was only interested in finding definitions for general terms, particularly the terms of moral discourse, such as *goodness, courage, moderation,* and *virtue*. He was primarily concerned with the realities they point to, the phenomena they articulate. That is, he explored those terms as they are used by human beings in the contexts of their lives. Socrates talks about truth and knowledge, for example, with Theaetetus, who has just made a significant mathematical discovery. He talks about the teachability of virtue—that is, human excellence—with Protagoras, a famous sophist who claims to be able to educate young men and to make them better people. He talks about justice with the jurors at his trial—jurors who will shortly be making a decision about whether he, Socrates, has committed an injustice.

Hence, a Socratic conversation is never idle talk about ideas or concepts; it is always deeply serious, though frequently laced with wit and humor. The talk is serious because it is about issues central in the lives of the people with whom he is talking. Socrates engages us in conversation in the context of the fundamental concerns and commitments of our lives and, through conversation, undertakes his investigation of himself and helps his interlocutors, if they are willing, to investigate their own lives—that is, to seek jointly with Socrates for self-knowledge.

And what comes of this investigation of the self? What is the result of this lifelong search for who and what we are, for what we are doing and why, for what we should be doing and how we should do it? Throughout his career, up to the very last day of his life, if Plato's testimony is accepted, Socrates made only one substantial claim to knowledge of himself. "I know," he said, "that I know nothing." This claim in all its arrogance and modesty, with its perfect irony, embodies the whole of Socrates' wisdom—a wisdom, he himself suggests, that is the most we humans can attain.

I wish we had the space to explore the full ironic meaning and import of this claim to wisdom. But let me mention some of its implications for Socrates' relationships with his friends and students. He denied having any substantial knowledge, so he clearly had nothing to teach and therefore could hardly be said to have students. All that he had, all that he could have, were associates, friends, fellow travelers on the journey toward self-knowledge.

Notice, too, that the Socratic enterprise is essentially communal—conversational, dialogical, if you will. The image of Socrates engaged in the search for wisdom is not that of the solitary thinker meditating alone in his study or on a mountaintop; it is that of a man living in a human community passionately engaged in conversation with his fellow men. Even that most solitary and silent of human activities—thinking—is defined by Socrates in one of Plato's *Dialogues* as "the dialogue of the soul with itself." So Socrates' friends and associates are not there with him simply because they want to be or because he allows them to be present; they are with him because his enterprise is communal. He needs them as much as they need him. The plurality of voices, the clash of opinions, the attempt to persuade others of what you think you really know, the rigorous and unstinting scrutiny of every opinion, the common search for fallacies, weaknesses, ambiguities, self-deceptions, unfounded certainties—all these and more are essential to that search for self-knowledge.

The young men who followed Socrates about, listening to and conversing with him, were not his students but his associates, and it is as such that he deals with them. The respect that Socrates displays toward his young friends is genuine, not a matter of technique or a form of etiquette; he takes his fellow conversationalists seriously because they are, in the face of the profound ignorance of all of us, his genuine equals in the search for self-knowledge.

This does not mean that Socrates treats them with kid gloves. The gravity of their common enterprise requires that the truth, the knowledge they are all seeking and all need, must take precedence over feelings of inferiority and embarrassment. To engage in the quest for self-knowledge with Socrates may be exciting, but it is not always pleasant or fun, for the questors have to be prepared to admit error publicly, to accept correction from anyone, and to follow the argument wherever it leads, regardless of personal wishes or felt needs. The self-discipline required for participation in the Socratic quest for self-knowledge is exacting and unyielding. Failure to accept and obey that discipline entails the failure of the whole enterprise. Thus, if Socrates is respectful of his friends, he is also extremely demanding of them, both for his sake and for theirs.

Along with offering respect and making demands, Socrates allows his fellow participants complete freedom within their common activity. There is a stringent discipline to observe, but no rules or regulations are laid down in advance to govern the relationship between the parties to the conversation. Both Socrates and his fellow discussants are free to do what they will, to set such rules as they agree on, and to mutually enforce them until they agree to change or ignore them. They jointly decide what is and is not relevant to the conversation as they proceed. Even the question of what is and is not a valid argument is open to discussion. In short, participation in a Socratic conversation is an exercise in freedom.

With this last point I have begun to shift my focus from what Socrates does to and for his interlocutors to what those interlocutors acquire for themselves from participating in that search for wisdom. What they emphatically do not get from him are any definitive answers to their questions, not because he withholds what he knows but because he genuinely does not know. Of course, many of those who talk with Socrates are convinced that he does know the answers but for some reason refuses to impart them.

It takes considerable insight and maturity to see that Socrates' professions of ignorance are the literal truth. But if his interlocutors don't get answers, what do they gain from talking with him? As interlocutors come to see that Socrates, for all his irony, always means what he says, they come to see that they themselves are participating as equals with Socrates in a genuine quest for knowledge. To realize that is to begin to discover one's own power—to ask, to answer, to judge the adequacy of an answer, to admit error, to rethink a position, to search for the necessary but elusive new insight.

In short, in talking to Socrates one may discover one's own power to do what Socrates does—that is, to think for oneself. This is perhaps the greatest gift Socrates or any genuine teacher can offer, although it is only in part a gift. Necessarily, the discovery of our own freedom and power as thinking beings must be one we make for ourselves. And this, I think, is the secret of Socrates' extraordinary authority and influence, the reason so many of his young friends went on to become eminent and powerful thinkers in their own right, the reason he has served as a source of inspiration to generation after generation of thinkers, the reason we still live in the Socratic era two thousand years after he died.

Before I conclude my remarks about Socrates, let me interject a word about terminology. Socrates generally called his enterprise philosophy. The word, which may have existed before him but which he probably was the first to use with any regularity, means "the love of wisdom." He uses it in part to distinguish himself from the sophists, whose name means "wise ones." Socrates wished to emphasize that he did not claim to have wisdom, as they did; he claimed only to desire it.

But he had another name for his enterprise, a name that he may also have originated. In several of Plato's *Dialogues,* Socrates likens his activity to the work of doctors. But whereas doctors treat the body, correcting its deficiencies and malfunctions, Socrates wishes to treat the soul and correct its disorders. The Greek phrase he used is *psyche therapein,* literally, "therapy for the soul." For Socrates the sickness of the soul that psychotherapy was designed to cure was ignorance—not ignorance of this fact or that body of information, but the essential ignorance from which we all suffer, ignorance of ourselves. This ignorance, this sickness, in its most common and virulent form is so deep that we do not know how ignorant we are; we do not even know that we are ignorant. We may not be able to overcome our ignorance of ourselves, but we can overcome our ignorance of our ignorance. That is, we can come to understand that we do not know most, perhaps all, of what we think we know.

Thus, although we may never be able to achieve full knowledge of ourselves, we can be released from the shackles of false knowledge. The discovery of our ignorance of ourselves is identical with the discovery of our freedom. The possibility of human wisdom, according to Socrates, may indeed be severely limited, but from Socratic psychotherapy we can at least learn just how ignorant and free we are.

It is no accident that I concluded my remarks about Socratic discourse with a reference to Socratic psychotherapy. In shifting our attention to Freud and his version of psychotherapy, we shift from a metaphorical to a literal use of the term. Freud was trained as a physician, and it was as a physician that he made his discoveries, developed his ideas, gathered a group of followers and disciples around himself, and organized the international psychoanalytic movement.

If Socrates had no discernible profession, Freud, by contrast, is in large measure defined by his relation to the profession of modern scientific medicine. If Socrates wrote nothing, Freud, by contrast, must have spent a very large proportion of his adult life writing. The standard English translation of his collected works runs to twenty-four sizable volumes, and his correspondence with various figures, if it were ever collected and published, might bulk as large or larger than the published works.

If Socrates founded no single school of thought, Freud explicitly, deliberately, and with enormous success spent years organizing and establishing the international psychoanalytic movement. If Socrates claimed to know nothing, Freud at times seems to claim to know everything, or at least everything important, or, to put it more modestly, to have discovered a method and founded a science that makes it possible to discover everything worth knowing that can be known. If Socrates is noted for his ironic modesty in admitting his ignorance, Freud, by contrast, proudly places his discovery of psychoanalysis alongside Copernicus' heliocentric theory and Darwin's theory of evolution—

the three great fundamental discoveries that, Freud says several times in his writings, define our understanding of ourselves, our world, and our place in it.

Freud was not tried and executed by his community as Socrates was, but he was and remains a no less controversial figure. He openly attacks all religious belief as basically neurotic or childish, and he is notorious for finding sex and sexual significance in every aspect of human life, even the most seemingly innocent—one might almost say, *especially* the most seemingly innocent. On the one hand, he defends all sorts of despised perversions as more or less natural, and, on the other hand, he argues that much of our morality is perverse and that most of our claims to rationality, integrity, disinterestedness, and objectivity are self-serving and false. He feels free to dismiss most philosophy as insignificant; to interpret art, literature, politics, anthropology, and economics in his own terms; to attack those of his followers who disagree with him as knaves and fools. He changes his mind and then denies that he has done so. And he is often ambiguous; he sometimes talks as if psychoanalysis might someday be reduced to the neurology and physiology of the brain and central nervous system, and at other times he talks as if every condition of our bodies, even death, is to be understood as a psychological phenomenon. Yet Freud's influence is enormous; we live in a world definitively marked by Freud's thought.

I do not want to enter into the controversies about Freud or to question his stature as one of the foundational thinkers of our time. Instead I want to take his influence for granted and remind you that all of Freud's thought has its source in a single peculiar activity, that activity in which the patient comes into the doctor's office, lies down on a couch in front of the seated doctor, and begins to follow the first and only law of psychoanalysis: to say whatever comes into your mind. Freud's discoveries about dreams, slips of the tongue, neurotic behavior, the several structures of the mind, the existence of the dynamic unconscious—all these and more emerged from his observations of his patients when they engaged with him in that strange conversational activity of free association.

Paradoxically, although everything significant in psychoanalytic thought flows from that process, Freud himself has told us very little about it beyond a few generalities and a large number of anecdotes. Even his famous case studies tell very little about what goes on in a psychoanalytic session. Furthermore, Freud's general discussions of psychoanalytic theory and practice often provide a misleading picture of what such a session is like. I am not going to present such a picture here, but I would like to discuss several features of psychoanalytic discourse.

In the first place, as is generally known, psychoanalysis is very long, very expensive, very time and energy consuming, and very, very difficult for the patient. Freud was quite clear that unless patients were in considerable pain, unless their lives were more or less intolerable, they would not be willing to invest the money, time, and energy and accept the pain that psychoanalysis requires. Why should this be so? Why should saying whatever comes into your mind be so difficult and painful? To make a long story very short, it is because we conceal a great deal that we think and feel, not only from others but from ourselves. For one reason or another, we do not want to admit to ourselves that we have such thoughts or feelings.

In effect, Freud discovered that the range of thought, action, and passion in the human psyche is far larger and far more difficult to get at than was previously understood. He found, further, that much human misery was due to conflicts within the psyche, although sufferers usually failed to realize this and normally thought their unhappiness was due to an external cause they could not control. Like Socrates, Freud found that we are far more ignorant of ourselves than we realize.

Psychoanalysis, then, is the slow, painful process that Freud discovered by which patients, with the help of the analyst, come to understand themselves better. What is important for my purposes is that for Freud this process of self-discovery is essentially dialogical, a conversation between the analyst and the analysand. We cannot discover the truth about ourselves by ourselves; we need to do it with someone else.

This dialogical necessity is built into the human situation. If we could admit to ourselves what we really felt and thought about ourselves and the people around us, we wouldn't be so conflicted that we needed to suppress and hide significant portions of ourselves from ourselves. The very structure of the human psyche is such that the truth about ourselves is accessible only with the direct aid and support of someone we trust more than we trust ourselves. Such people are very hard to find. In fact, Freud thinks that such people cannot be found; they must be made through the long, arduous process of analytic training. What is interesting from my point of view is that the central, irreplaceable element in the training of a psychoanalyst is the training analysis: every psychoanalyst, in order to become one, has to go through the analytic process as a patient.

As I noted earlier, in a conversation with Socrates the discussion always tends to grow less and less private and particular and more and more generic. The idiosyncratic concerns of the interlocutor tend to drop away as the more fundamental features of the problem under discussion come into view. In psychoanalysis almost the exact opposite tends to happen. When patients start talking about themselves and their problems, they usually talk in generalized, cliché-ridden terms that reflect common opinion, not their actual experiences. It takes a long time of allowing oneself to reflect on one's feelings to be able to feel and describe them accurately in all their highly individualized reality. Almost always in this process the analysand discovers that a given feeling, which might be named embarrassment or guilt or anger, is based on very specific experiences, frequently from the early years of his or her life. Not until these original experiences are recovered in memory can many of the idiosyncratic, strange, or puzzling features of the general feeling make sense to the person on the couch. In effect, the psychoanalytic dialogue becomes more gossipy as it proceeds, not less so.

Socrates almost never engaged in gossip, in that endless iteration of who did what to whom, when, where, how, and why. For Freud, the gossip we tell about ourselves is not an indulgence but the key to discovering the fundamental features of who and what we are. It is, I think, one of Freud's great discoveries that there is a proper use of gossip that can lead to the perception of significant general truths about what it means to be human.

The truths that emerge from psychoanalytic discourse are discoveries as much for the analyst as they are for the analysand. This point is an important one and is not always appreciated, even by those sympathetic to psychoanalysis. Freud himself is largely responsible for the misunderstanding because he frequently writes as if the analyst understands everything about the patient on the couch and has only to determine the strategy by which the analyst will, step by step, always at exactly the right moment, bring the patient to see the truth.

This image of the all-knowing, all-competent psychoanalyst also feeds conveniently into the fantasies of many analysands, who need, or prefer, to think that their analyst has all the answers. The reality is quite different. Analysts do have at their command a great deal of psychoanalytic theory and experience; they know all about the Oedipus complex and pre-Oedipal object relations, about repression and regression, about transference and countertransference, about dream theory and parapraxes, and the rest. But when confronted by a particular analysand describing a particular painful experience, the analyst must set aside all that acquired knowledge and simply listen to what is being said. Otherwise the analyst, like the patient, runs the risk of mishearing what is being said and of assimilating it to concepts and categories that are inappropriate and inaccurate.

Analysts, like patients or anybody else, can jump to wrong conclusions, can systematically distort evidence, unintentionally suppress essential data, and so forth. And there are analysts who do these things, who listen for a few minutes and then are completely confident that they know exactly what is wrong with the patient and exactly what needs to be done. There is even a certain understandable tendency among analysts who do not act this way to talk as if they did.

The true situation is an uncomfortable one for analysts as well as their patients. For all their training (or perhaps because of it) psychoanalysts do not know what is wrong with their patients or what to do about it. They don't even know whether the analytic theory and practice are right, whether this patient might not be the one who tests the rule, the patient to whom the theory doesn't apply, the patient for whom the theory needs to be rethought, reexamined, reformulated. In the reality of a psychoanalytic encounter, the analyst is quite ignorant and needs, with the analysand, to rediscover and work out the theory all over again from the beginning. Anything less is likely to result in a less than satisfactory analysis.

What I am arguing here is that every psychoanalysis is a genuine voyage of discovery for both the analyst and for the analysand. But this voyage is not merely an exploration of analytic theory for the analyst; it is and must be a voyage of self-discovery as well. After all, if analysts cannot simply rely on theory to guide and shape the discourse with analysands, because that theory is always—and must always be—uncertain and unreliable, they must fall back on nontheoretical resources. This means, I think, that analysts must rely on their own personal responses to the people with whom they are dealing. The more effectively analysts can individualize their patients, the more personalized their responses will be to each one. In that intimate encounter between two unique individuals, the analyst, like the patient, must encounter himself or herself, as well as the other, in new and surprising ways.

This brings me to a final point about the psychoanalytic process that I find difficult to express accurately and without distortion. A number of features of psychoanalytic practice were thoroughly fixed in analytic dogma for many years. Analysis required that the patient recline on a couch with the analyst sitting out of sight. Analysis required at least three or four or five sessions a week. Analytic sessions all had to be forty-five or fifty minutes long. The patient had to establish a transference neurosis toward the analyst, and so on.

There has been much argument in the psychoanalytic community in recent years about the relative importance of these various doctrines and how they are to be understood. There have also been many changes in theory and in practice. Specifically, serious attention has been given to the nonverbal dimensions of the analytic process and the analytic relationship. But even here, the desired therapeutic outcome of treatment requires that the nonverbal components eventually be reflected, and at least partially articulated, in discourse between analyst and analysand.

If I have been accurate in my sketch of the psychoanalytic process, then the essence of psychoanalysis lies in the character of the talk between the analyst and the analysand. That talk, as I have argued, is difficult to achieve and to sustain, but it is what psychoanalysis is all about. Everything else, all those practices, beliefs, doctrines, and dogmas, are just means to achieve that extraordinary conversation. There is considerable evidence that Freud himself constantly broke the rules—that he had his patients over for dinner, took them on vacations with him, and behaved in all kinds of seemingly unanalytic ways. My point is simply that because these customary practices and doctrines of psychoanalysis are means to an end, they can and should be violated if they do not serve the purpose for which they were intended.

Socrates, too, did many things that seem strange or inappropriate for a philosopher—unless you hold on to the central fact that his aim was to initiate and sustain that extraordinary conversation that constituted his search for self-knowledge. If he had to use bad arguments, tell outrageous stories, and act in strange ways to serve his ends, so be it. Only an arrogant fool who believed he knew the answers beforehand would have been so foolish as to limit the means used to achieve an end he did not yet know how to reach.

With this last remark I have pushed these reflections to the point of suggesting that the strange kinds of talk that Socrates and Freud discovered and pursued with such single-minded devotion were not, finally, merely means to the end of self knowledge but were intrinsic to the end they pursued. This, in turn, suggests that the end—self-knowledge—is already present in the activity.

The tradition of Western philosophy as we know it begins with Socrates and his discovery that the search for wisdom entails a certain kind of discourse. The tradition started by Socrates has largely ignored his discovery, and for the past twenty-five hundred years philosophers have pursued wisdom in a wide variety of ways, but none that I can think of has attempted to follow the Socratic example by rigorously engaging in Socratic conversation. Maybe the enterprise has not been understood, maybe it is too difficult, or maybe even the philosophers could not bring themselves to believe that Socrates meant what he said.

Whatever the reason, Freud may well be the first thinker since Socrates to take talk as seriously as Socrates did. And that recognition poses both a challenge and an opportunity for us. With Freud as a model, we may be the first thinkers since antiquity who are able to grasp the experience of discourse with which Socrates initiated philosophy. Philosophy, the desire and the search for wisdom, is, in the end, the desire and the search for self-knowledge. We might, I suggest, rediscover philosophy for ourselves. That is the opportunity. The challenge is to accept the opportunity.

2 Plato's *Laches*
Psychotherapy and the Search for Wisdom

The *Dialogues* written by Plato in the fourth century B.C. are for the most part narrative or dramatic accounts of conversations of Socrates, who was tried and executed in Athens for impiety and corruption of the young when he was seventy and Plato about twenty-seven. After Socrates' death it became quite the fashion for philosophers to write "Socratic" dialogues. Almost all of these writings have been lost through the centuries; only the dialogues of Plato and his contemporary Xenophon have survived intact, and much of what we know about the intellectual life of Athens at the time we know only from their works.

I want to make several points here. First, it seems clear that Socrates was an original thinker of enormous importance for the whole history of Western thought, although we know very little about him apart from what Plato wrote. Second, Plato's *Dialogues* have been recognized since antiquity as philosophical and literary masterpieces of the highest order: Plato is to philosophy what Shakespeare is to drama and what Tolstoy and Dostoyevsky are to fiction. He is the master whose works set the standard against which other works are judged. Third, Plato's *Dialogues* are rooted in the history of a particular time and place, the city of Athens in the last quarter of the fifth century B.C.

With perhaps one or two exceptions, every character in the *Dialogues* seems to have been a real historical figure, but we have no evidence on whether any of the dialogues occurred or whether Plato's literary accounts are historically accurate. My private judgment is that none of the dialogues could be a fully accurate rendering of a historical event; they are too perfect as literary works to be historically accurate. No event in the real world is so well formed or devoid of irrelevancy and accident as a Platonic dialogue. It must be said, however, that Plato's artistic powers are so great, his control of his material so complete, that his works frequently seem artless, even clumsy. Shakespeare's plays are similar in this respect: To unsophisticated audiences or critics they often seem shapeless, full of digression, filled with unnecessary detail. It takes a good deal of experience to see how perfectly formed the plays are. The same is true of Plato's *Dialogues,* and the *Laches* is a perfect example of this effect.

In many respects the *Laches* is a typical Platonic dialogue: it is short, it seems to be an attempt to define a virtue—in this case, courage—and it fails in that attempt and thus ends inconclusively. But Plato was fully in command of his material. If the *Laches* is inconclusive, Plato, a consummate artist, wanted it that way. If readers find this feature puzzling, he wanted it that way, too. He intended his audience to be genuinely puzzled by the dialogue.

Let me summarize the action of the dialogue. It opens with Lysimachus explaining to Nicias and Laches why he and Melesias have invited them to watch an exhibition by Stesilaus, a reputed expert on fighting in armor. Lysimachus and Melesias each have an adolescent son who has reached the age at which he needs formal training to equip him for adult life and an active career. Lysimachus explains that he and Melesias need help in deciding what training to give their boys because they themselves feel inadequate to the task.

These two rather elderly fathers are themselves the sons of two of the most eminent figures of the previous generation, the generation that fought and defeated the Persians in defense of Greek freedom and went on to found the Athenian empire and initiate the golden age of Greece. Lysimachus explains that their two statesmen-fathers were so busy founding an empire that they had no time for their sons, and as a result, he and Melesias have had unusually mediocre and undistinguished careers. Now they want their sons to have distinguished careers like their grandfathers' and not mediocre ones like their fathers'. So they have asked Nicias and Laches, two eminent generals, for their advice. Nicias agrees to help, and so does Laches, who remarks that they should invite Socrates, who happens to be at the exhibition, to join the conversation.

Mentioning that the two boys have recently been talking about their conversations with someone named Socrates, Lysimachus invites Socrates to join the group. Socrates defers at first to the views of the older, more knowledgeable Laches and Nicias. Nicias presents a careful, ordered argument that learning to fight in armor is the first step toward the ultimate goal of mastering the art of the general, besides which it will also make the boys braver and give them a fine martial appearance. Laches then argues, in opposition, that the Spartans, acknowledged masters of the art of war, have nothing to do with this newfangled skill. He adds that Stesilaus, the expert on fighting, made a laughingstock of himself in a battle with some absurd new weapon that he had invented, and that the so-called art which Stesilaus now teaches will serve to make cowards more rash and brave men more cautious.

With the two experts in flagrant disagreement, Lysimachus turns to Socrates to cast the deciding vote. Socrates, surprised, asks whether Lysimachus intends to go with the majority. Lysimachus asks what the alternative is. Socrates turns to Melesias and, in the only part of the dialogue where Melesias joins in, leads him through an argument that is almost a commonplace of Socratic conversation.

If the question is whether Melesias' son should practice a particular kind of exercise, asks Socrates, should Melesias follow the advice of the greater number of those who happen to be on hand or the advice of one who has been educated under a good trainer? Melesias designates the latter authority. Thus, says Socrates, one ought to make such decisions on the basis of knowledge, not majority rule. Melesias agrees.

Having established the superiority of the knowledgeable expert over the ignorant multitude, Socrates points out that what they are talking about is not a small matter but perhaps the greatest of all their possessions—their sons. The question is whether their sons will turn out to be worthwhile or the opposite, and on that outcome the whole of the fathers' reputations and estates are staked. So the question becomes: Who is an expert? Who has studied and practiced the art under discussion?

Before they can take up this question, Socrates asks what the art is that they are looking for someone to teach. Now Nicias joins the conversation. He asserts that they are discussing the art of fighting in armor and that they are trying to decide whether young men ought to learn it. Using the example of medicine, Socrates asks whether, if the eyes are diseased and one takes counsel, one should take counsel about the medicine or about the eyes. Nicias responds, the eyes. Therefore, says Socrates, in the case they are discussing, the question is not about fighting in armor but about the reason for learning to fight in armor. What they are looking for is not an expert in the art of fighting in armor but an expert in the care of the souls of young men. What they need is a doctor of the soul, not a trainer of the body.

Now that the general subject matter of the dialogue—the care of the soul—has been defined, the question becomes one of methodology: How should one find an expert who understands the care of the soul and who can instruct the fathers about the education of their sons? To mark the shift in subject, Laches replaces Nicias as Socrates' interlocutor. The sign of a good craftsman, says Socrates, is not the touting of his skill but the well-executed product of his art. Thus, what Laches and Nicias and he should do for Lysimachus and Melesias is to point out the teachers who have tended the souls of the young and taught them well.

If Laches, Nicias, or he claims to have a skill without having had a good teacher, says Socrates, let that person show which Athenian or which foreigner, which freeman or which slave, became good through his teaching. Socrates regrets that he had no money to pay for a teacher for himself, but he notes that Nicias and Laches, who are wealthy men, have had plenty of opportunities to get educated. So, says Socrates, Lysimachus and Melesias should not let Laches and Nicias go until they reveal who among the teachers is cleverest at educating young men and from whom the teachers learned the art of teaching, unless they taught themselves. In that way, if Nicias and Laches are too busy, the two fathers can go to their teachers and solicit advice from them.

The question of who is expert in the art of improving the young has turned into an investigation of Nicias' and Laches' strong, but conflicting, claims to be experts. Lysimachus, following Socrates' suggestion, requests that Laches and Nicias answer Socrates' questions. This matter, he points out, is important not only to Melesias and himself but also to Nicias and Laches, because they, too, have sons who are nearly of an age to be educated. Socrates has subtly managed to transform the conversation from one in which two humble laymen request advice from experts to one in which he, Socrates, as the agent of the humble laymen, will examine the acknowledged experts on an issue in which, as it happens, they themselves have a direct personal stake but about which they deeply disagree.

Nicias explains to the two older men that they are obviously unacquainted with Socrates; they know him only as the child of his father, not as an adult. Socrates, explains Nicias, conducts conversation in an unusual way. A person who converses with Socrates is led by his arguments to answer questions about himself until his whole life is subject to investigation. Socrates does not let his respondent go until he has been tested in every detail.

Nicias professes to know Socrates well; He says that he himself has been put through this treatment before, and he knows what he is about to submit to. He claims that he likes Socrates and doesn't run away from such examinations because, as Solon once said of himself, he values lifelong learning. But Nicias cautions the older men that in an examination by Socrates the conversation will not be about the boys but about themselves.

Laches chimes in with his views about discussions. In some respects he loves discussions, and in others he hates them, depending on the character of the man with whom he is talking. If he is talking with a man about virtue and other such matters and there is a harmony between the speaker and his words, then Laches is a lover of discourse and delights in the conversation. But if there is a deep disjunction between his interlocutor's words and deeds, he becomes a hater of discussion. Laches is not, he says, familiar with the words of Socrates, but his deeds have been such as to ensure the fairness of his words. Laches claims that he, too, like Solon, wishes to grow old learning many things—but only, he adds, from good men. The fact that Socrates is younger than he is makes no difference to Laches. Because of his respect for Socrates' valor, he is prepared to allow Socrates to cross-examine him.

Pleading a failing memory, Lysimachus now turns the entire conversation over to Socrates. From here on, the dialogue is basically a conversation between Socrates, Nicias, and Laches. Characteristically, Socrates begins by redefining the question. Instead of asking about teachers, he pushes back to a more fundamental issue using his medical metaphor.

If we do not know, he says, that sight added to the eyes improves the eyes, we would hardly be good doctors or worthy counselors about the health of the eyes. We have to know not only that sight improves the eyes but also what sight is. Analogously, he says, is it not virtue or human excellence that we wish to add to the souls of the young? Do we not therefore have to know what virtue is?

Laches quails at this task, so Socrates eases it. Perhaps we do not have to explore the whole of virtue, he says; perhaps we can gain sufficient knowledge by examining a part. Laches eagerly agrees, and Socrates asks which part of virtue they should choose. Isn't it obvious, he remarks, that the virtue involved in fighting in armor is courage? So, says Socrates, let us undertake to state what courage is.

With this remark—halfway through the dialogue—Socrates has finally gotten around to defining the subject of investigation. The rest of the dialogue consists mostly of arguments alternating between Socrates and, first, Laches, then Nicias, then Laches again. Each general tries his hand at defining courage but finds himself unable to withstand the rigors of Socrates' cross-examination. It may be instructive to look at their unsuccessful attempts at definition.

Laches starts by defining courage in a simple, straightforward way: A courageous man is a man who remains at his post to defend himself against the enemy. Socrates attacks this view by citing a certain tactical situation. He notes that in battles against the Persians, the Scythians, instead of remaining at their posts, feigned retreat to draw the Persians after them. When the enemy was disarrayed in pursuit, the Scythians turned, attacked, and defeated them, thereby gaining a great reputation for valor. Even Laches' much admired Spartan hoplites, Socrates points out, behaved in a similar manner at the battle of Plataea.

In sum, says Socrates, we are trying to discover what constitutes the courage of not just a hoplite or a horseman but every warrior. We also want to know what constitutes the courage of people who are not warriors but who are in danger at sea; of those who show bravery in illness and poverty and affairs of state, and in the face of pain or fear; and of those who fight desire and pleasure. In all these aspects of life, says Socrates, we want to find out what makes some people brave and others not.

With help Laches grasps the point and redefines courage in a fully generalized way: Courage is not standing one's post in the physical sense; it is an endurance of the soul. Socrates examines the notion of endurance. Is it any and every kind of endurance or only some instances of endurance that are courageous? Is it not always endurance accompanied by wisdom that is the virtue, the human excellence, that they are looking for? Not simply endurance but "wise endurance" becomes the definition of courage. Socrates explores this new definition. What about the man in battle who wisely calculates that he is better armed and better trained than his enemy? Would the endurance of this man, based on this wisdom, be courage? Or, asks Socrates, is it the man in the other camp, the man who is willing to take on a superior opponent, who is the brave one?

Laches, predictably, prefers the man in the opposite camp. Not wise endurance but foolish endurance becomes the measure of courage. At this point Laches understandably grows confused and discouraged, but Socrates urges that they continue the investigation—that they not become ridiculous by being cowardly in their search for courage itself. Laches responds with enthusiasm. He insists that he knows what courage is but cannot quite pin it down in words. The disjunction in Laches, according to himself, is not between words and deeds but between understanding and words.

Socrates asks Nicias if he can help. Nicias says that their whole approach has been wrong. He repeats a remark that he has heard from Socrates on previous occasions: Every one of us is good in respect to the things about which he is wise, and bad in respect to those things about which he is ignorant. This means, says Nicias, that if a man is courageous, he is wise, so courage is not endurance but some kind of wisdom. What kind of wisdom? asks Socrates. Nicias replies that courage is knowledge of what is to be feared and hoped for in war and in every other situation.

Laches breaks in. Nicias, he says, is talking nonsense; wisdom is quite different from courage. Nicias retorts that Laches accuses him of talking nonsense merely because Laches has been shown to be talking nonsense himself. Laches now briefly takes on the role of Socrates and attempts to demonstrate to Nicias the absurdity of his definition. He points out that farmers know what to fear in farming and that craftsmen know what to fear in their crafts. But farmers and craftsmen are not thereby courageous. Nicias responds that doctors know what can make a person sick or healthy, but they cannot tell when a person might be better off sick than healthy. Laches, confused by this answer, accuses Nicias of twisting about to avoid contradicting himself. With Laches' approval, Socrates takes over the questioning again to see if they can find out what Nicias is really saying.

According to Nicias, says Socrates, courage is knowledge of the grounds of fear and hope; Nicias agrees. Socrates observes that this knowledge can be possessed by very few. Nicias must deny courage to wild beasts or else admit that beasts have a kind of knowledge that very few men can attain. Laches joins in, delighted by what he sees as Nicias' difficulty. He says that if that were so, all the wild beasts accepted as courageous—lion, boar, leopard—would also have to be described as wise, which would be absurd. Sophisticated Nicias again avoids the trap. They lack understanding, he says, so they are not courageous; they are merely rash or mad. Children, who fear nothing because they have no sense, can hardly be called courageous. Laches objects and accuses Nicias of logic-chopping.

Socrates takes up the argument. First he persuades Nicias to agree that courage is only one part of virtue, the other parts being such things as justice and moderation. Then he explores further the definition of courage as knowledge of the grounds of hope and fear. Fearful things are things that produce fear; hopeful things are things that do not produce fear. Fear, says Socrates, comes not from evils that have happened or are happening but from evils that are anticipated, because fear is the expectation of evil. Knowledge of these things is what is called courage. Socrates argues that there is not one kind of knowledge about the past, another about the present, and a third about the future. Knowledge of what is fearful and what is hopeful is the same whether the thing has already happened, is happening, or will happen. In the case of health, there are not separate arts related to the present, past, and future; medicine is a single art of what was, what is, and what is likely to be.

But if fearful and hopeful things are future goods and evils, knowledge of these things must also be knowledge of present and past goods and evils. To define courage, says Socrates, as knowledge of the grounds of fear and hope about future goods and evils is thus to define only a part of courage, for the whole of courage, according to Nicias, is knowledge of all goods and evils, past, present, and future. The man with this kind of knowledge would seem to have virtue in every respect. What Nicias defines as courage is really the whole of virtue, so his definition also fails to convince. They have not yet discovered what courage is.

Laches cannot restrain himself from taking another dig at Nicias, and Nicias reciprocates. Both men agree, however, that Lysimachus and Melesias would do well to retain the services of Socrates rather than the services of either of them. Nicias further says that he would be delighted to entrust his own son to the care of Socrates if Socrates didn't seem unwilling and didn't always recommend someone else for the job.

Lysimachus returns to the discussion and joins in a general appeal that Socrates help make the young men good. The trouble is, Socrates says, that he is no better than Nicias and Laches. He, too, is essentially ignorant of what they are searching for. He suggests instead that they all search for the best possible teacher for themselves and then look for a teacher for the young men. Even if to be searching for a teacher at their age makes them ridiculous in the eyes of others, they should do so anyway. Lysimachus invites Socrates to come to his house the following day in order to plan this search; Socrates accepts, and the dialogue ends.

I have summarized this dialogue at such length not only to draw attention to the mass of detail and the complexity of the arguments packed into a short space but also to make as vivid as I can the fact that the *Laches* is, like all Plato's works, a genuine dialogue and not a disguised treatise. Remember that the dialogue is half over before Socrates even arrives at the question on the nature of courage. The inconclusive arguments about courage that take up the second half of the dialogue thus occur in a larger context—that of the conversation between Socrates and the two elderly fathers. Let us look a little more closely at these older men and their situation.

The men define their own condition with a certain poignancy and irony. Lysimachus is the son of Aristides, nicknamed the Just, who was a peer of Miltiades, the hero of the battle of Marathon, and of Themistocles, the hero of the battle of Salamis. Melesias is the son of Thucydides, the admiral who, among other Athenians, converted the Delian league of Greek cities into the Athenian empire. What, then, are we to make of the attitudes of Lysimachus and Melesias toward their illustrious fathers?

On the one hand, it is clear that they resent their fathers, who were so busy doing great deeds that, according to their sons, they had no time to give their sons the attention they needed to have glorious careers of their own. The resentment and anger that Lysimachus and Melesias feel are still palpable. At the same time, they want nothing more than that their own sons—namesakes of their famous grandfathers—should grow up to have glorious careers. On the other hand, if the two boys grow up to be like their illustrious grandfathers, will they in turn neglect their sons? By seeking to give their children careers like those of their grandfathers, are Lysimachus and Melesias re-creating in the next generation the pain and resentment that has marred their own lives? By their own admission, Lysimachus and Melesias are mediocre men who have led lives that are largely wasted.

Yet why should we accept their judgment of themselves? In the brief passage in which Socrates talks to Melesias, he persuades him to agree that his son is the greatest of all his possessions and that Melesias' estate, what he bequeaths to posterity, will be managed well or poorly depending on how his son turns out. By that standard, Aristides the Just and Thucydides the admiral, the fathers of Lysimachus and Melesias, were failures because they did not do well by their sons, whereas Lysimachus and Melesias, despite their mediocrity by conventional standards, are devoting their lives to the care of their children. By Socrates' standards they may be better than they think—a good deal better, in fact, than their illustrious fathers.

All the ambivalence and irony reflected in Lysimachus' and Melesias' relationships with their fathers and their sons are mirrored in the next generation by the attitudes of Nicias and Laches. Laches and Nicias are, as it were, the Aristides and Thucydides of the present generation. They are the current experts on valor, the winners of battles, the builders of empire. They are also so concerned with public affairs that they seem to be neglecting their own children; they seem prepared to turn them over to teachers without further thought.

For all the ironies implicit in the situation, the generations do not merely repeat the patterns of the past. The situation is far more complex than that. Plato was born and grew up in the last quarter of the fifth century B.C. He lived the bulk of his adult life and wrote his dialogues during the first half of the fourth century B.C. The immediate audience for the *Laches,* therefore, would have been about as distant from and as familiar with the events to which the *Laches* refers as we are distant from and familiar with the events from the First World War up to the debacle of Vietnam.

The century opened with the conflict between Greece and the mighty empire of Persia. The Greece of that day was largely confined to the southern half of the peninsula occupied by modern Greece and consisted of many small independent city-states. The Persian empire, by contrast, consisted of what is today all of Turkey, Lebanon, Syria, Israel, Egypt, northern Saudi Arabia, Iraq, Iran, Afghanistan, Ukraine, and parts of northern India. It was perhaps the largest empire in the history of the world up to that time.

The Persians attempted two invasions of Greece, the first in 490 B.C., when they sent a naval expedition across the Aegean Sea to land at the small village of Marathon, about twenty-five miles from Athens. The Athenian army, commanded by Miltiades, marched out to meet the Persians, who had an unblemished record of military success. Greatly outnumbered, the Athenians waited a few days for additional troops from other Greek cities, notably Sparta. When that support was not forthcoming, the Athenians, more or less on their own, attacked the Persians and against all odds won a complete and glorious victory. Throughout the fifth century the men who fought at Marathon were known as the flower of Athenian martial valor; the tombstone of Aeschylus, perhaps the greatest playwright of the age, identifies him, not as a tragedian, but as one of the men of Marathon.

Ten years after Marathon, in 480 B.C., the Persians returned to Greece, this time with an enormous land army and a fleet that was certainly the largest ever collected in the Mediterranean up to then. This force swept down the coast of Greece, overwhelming everything in its path. In a narrow pass between the mountains and the sea, three hundred Spartans stood and faced the assembled might of the Persians. The Spartans held the pass for several days, until they were outflanked by the Persians, who crossed a mountain pass and came at them from the rear. Tradition has it that every one of the Spartans fell in the battle at Thermopylae.

Like the Athenians at Marathon, the Spartans at Thermopylae represent a shining moment in the Greeks' national history. Following the battle of Thermopylae, the Persians marched south into Greece, burned Athens, and engaged in a monumental naval battle off the island of Salamis near Athens, where they were decisively defeated by the combined fleets of all the Greek maritime cities, whose combined power amounted to only a fraction of their foe's.

The following spring, at Plataea, in one last massive land engagement, a Greek army of fifty thousand under the command of a Spartan general met and utterly defeated the remaining Persian army, which numbered perhaps a third of a million men. Thus ended the Persian threat to Greece. In the next fifty years the confederation of mainland Greek cities fought to free many of the Greek cities in Asia Minor from Persian control. In the course of the campaign the alliance of free Greek cities was converted into the Athenian empire. It was in the heyday of that empire, under the rule of Pericles, that Athenian literature and art flourished in a golden age.

Throughout the fifth century, Athens and the other major city of mainland Greece, Sparta, fell steadily into competition and conflict. In 432 B.C. the two cities and their respective allies finally went to war. This war—known as the Peloponnesian War—lasted for nearly the rest of the fifth century—for twenty-seven years in all. It ended in 404 with the total defeat of Athens and the dissolution of the Athenian empire.

The dramatic date of the *Laches*—the date at which the dialogue presumably occurs, not the date when it was written—can be determined with fair accuracy. We know from Thucydides' *History of the Peloponnesian War* that Laches and Nicias played major roles in that war. We know from the dialogue itself that Laches (along with Socrates) was present at the battle of Delium, where the Athenians suffered a defeat at the hands of the Thebans. The battle of Delium occurred in 424 B.C.. Three years later, in 421 B.C., Athens and Sparta concluded a truce, called the Peace of Nicias, because Nicias negotiated it. It lasted only three years.

In 418 B.C. a mixed force of Athenians and Argives fought the Spartans in the Peloponnesus, near the town of Mantinaea. The Argive-Athenian force was decisively defeated. The Athenian detachment under the command of Laches met with many casualties. Laches himself was killed. The many admiring references that Laches makes to the Spartans and their martial valor are not without considerable irony.

Three years after the battle at Mantinaea, the Athenians mounted the largest naval expedition that they ever attempted, sending forty thousand troops and hundreds of ships fifteen hundred miles from Athens to the east coast of Sicily to conquer the island and subdue the city of Syracuse. The expeditionary force besieged Syracuse for over a year. After a series of reverses in which the supporting fleet was lost, the entire Athenian force was captured, and the soldiers were either killed or sold into slavery.

The commanding general of that expedition was Nicias, and he died in the Athenian defeat. His death has a special poignancy, because according to the account by Thucydides, Nicias originally opposed the Sicilian expedition as unwise. The Athenian assembly, feeling that the general who commanded such an enormous undertaking should be moderate and careful, therefore appointed Nicias to be in charge. Furthermore, according to Thucydides, during the struggle between the Athenians and Syracusans, the Athenians could see that their affairs were going badly and that they should retreat. But at that moment there was an eclipse. Nicias, overcome with superstitious fear, refused to order a retreat for twenty-seven days. During that time the Syracusan army moved to block the Athenian retreat, thus ensuring their final defeat. Athens never really recovered from the disastrous failure of the Sicilian expedition. Eleven years later, Athens surrendered to Sparta, and a Spartan army occupied the city. So ended the Athenian empire.

Much of the irony that informs the *Laches* should now be apparent. Both Laches and Nicias—portrayed as eminent, confident, successful generals—were known to the original readers of the dialogue as the generals who presided over two of the most costly defeats that Athens ever suffered. Laches, the uncritical admirer of Spartan valor, came to know the full force of that valor. Nicias, the man who defined courage as a kind of wisdom, died at Syracuse because he observed the superstitious custom of not moving an army after an eclipse.

Yet perhaps we should not make such harsh judgments—after all, if Lysimachus and Melesias can be wrong in their evaluations of themselves, who is to say that Laches and Nicias, who died in defeat, were not courageous? Courage can be found in defeat as well as in victory. But before we tackle the question of courage, let me point out that Nicias' and Laches' defeats resulted ultimately in the destruction of the Athenian empire.

When the young sons of Lysimachus and Melesias reached manhood, there was no empire left for them to maintain with glorious deeds. To the original audience of the *Laches,* then, all of the ironies and ambiguities attendant on the rise and fall of the Athenian empire in the fifth century B.C. were encapsulated in this charming, inconclusive conversation about courage. The mythical glories of the founding generation; the mediocrity of the succeeding generation; the pompous certainty of the third generation that will lead Athens to defeat; and the sad realization that the eager anticipation of the coming generation will come to nought—all this is built into the very structure of the *Laches*.

Almost everyone we have been discussing in the *Laches* is a member of a pair: the two founding fathers, the two mediocre elderly men, the two young sons, and the two eminent generals. Each pair represents a different polarity. Of the founding fathers, Aristides was a land general, Thucydides an admiral. Of the two mediocre men, Lysimachus talks at great length, Melesias hardly at all.

The two military commanders stand in the sharpest possible contrast to each other in character, in conversation, in their relationship to Socrates, and in their understanding of courage. Laches believes in deeds more than words; Nicias has a love of argument. Laches believes in the old-fashioned virtues of obedience and endurance; Nicias is a follower of the newfangled study of strategy and modern weapons development. Laches admires the Spartan style of warfare, Nicias the Athenian. Laches is quick to anger; Nicias is calm and sophisticated. Laches knows the deeds of Socrates the warrior; Nicias knows the words of Socrates the supersophist. Laches identifies courage with endurance—a stolid, even foolish or mindless holding-on—and is prepared to claim that wild beasts may be courageous; Nicias identifies courage with a special kind of arcane knowledge, available only to the elite who can grasp its rational principles.

Two figures in the dialogue do not appear to be a pair but stand out as singular, even unique individuals. I refer to Stesilaus, the man who gave the exhibition of fighting in armor, and to Socrates. Stesilaus seems to be something of an inventor; he develops new weapons and new techniques of fighting. Unfortunately, the weapons do not work very well, and his method of fighting in armor may not have anything to recommend it either. But Socrates, too, is a controversial innovator—not in warfare but in ways of arguing and searching for the truth.

The original occasion for the dialogue is Stesilaus' exhibition of a martial skill that the fathers think may help their sons to become brave. But the dialogue itself consists of an exhibition by Socrates of his art of investigation through argument. Ironically, the two boys have already discovered this new art for themselves; they have known Socrates for some time. We go to watch Stesilaus, but we stay to listen to Socrates. And what we hear from him is that we do not understand courage.

What is that Socratic art? In his first exchange with Nicias, Socrates says,

"Then the question whether any one of us is skilled in the treatment of the soul and is capable of caring for it well and has had good teachers is the one we ought to investigate" (185e). That sentence is where Socrates defines once and for all the fundamental issue of the dialogue. The phrase in Greek that is translated by the English "treatment of the soul" is *psychotherapy*. To my knowledge, this is the oldest use of the term *psychotherapy* in Western literature. This dialogue may well represent the moment at which the very notion of psychotherapy was born in the Western philosophical tradition. Significantly, the term occurs for the first time in a discussion of courage, in a conversation in which two fathers express a deep concern for the education and training of their adolescent sons. This dialogue, with its ironies and ambiguities, absurdities and pathos, has a great deal to do with the very notion of psychotherapy, particularly for adolescents.

The recurrent pairs of contrasting figures in the *Laches* suggest the equivocal character of courage itself. From antiquity to the present, courage, bravery, valor, manliness, intestinal fortitude, whatever it is called, has been a strange and problematic virtue. In its conventional form it seems to require war and killing to be realized. Whatever one's attitude toward war, there always remains the uneasy sense that the price of Achilles' distinction and excellence as a warrior was the death of Hector, one of the few genuinely lovable people in Homer's *Iliad*.

What can we make of such a virtue? There are those—perhaps including Socrates—who would like to extend the range of courage so that it can also be realized outside the martial arena in every area of life. But if Achilles and Hector display courage in their fight to the death, each knowing the other is a deadly fighter of enormous skill and power, what are we to say of the person on a diet who resists the temptation to have a hot fudge sundae? Can we compare that mundane exercise of willpower to risking one's life to defend one's home or family or to avenge the death of a friend?

Many people speak of courage in terms of risk taking. But the risk that someone takes by going into military combat seems very different from the risk someone takes in starting a new job, marrying, or going off to college, not to speak of the small risks that we all take every day of our lives as we pursue our daily affairs. The scope of courage, then, remains profoundly ambiguous. Are we, like Aristotle, to restrict it largely to those situations in which we literally risk our lives (*Nicomachean Ethics*, III.6, 1115a30)? Or can courage extend to the whole of life?

Finally, if courage is a virtue, it is a morally ambiguous one. What are we to make, for example, of those dedicated Nazis who fought resolutely and well in the last days of World War II, when their cause was lost and they knew it? Are they, the murderers of Auschwitz and Buchenwald, to be called courageous, meaning virtuous? We feel much better when what seems to be courage occurs in the service of an unambiguously good cause. But those who fight in the name of other values, even bad ones, may also fight well and risk just as much. Is courage a morally neutral value? This is a puzzling and disturbing possibility.

If the contrasting pairs of figures around which the *Laches* is structured suggest the problematic character of courage, the same dualities also suggest that each member of a pair has a defect that is to some degree corrected by the other member of the pair. Thus, if Lysimachus says more than he should, Melesias says too little.

This suggestion is particularly interesting if we think about it in relation to the views of Laches and Nicias. Might the problem with each general lie in the incompleteness of his view, an incompleteness that would be corrected by incorporating the view of the other? Thus, Laches, with his notion of courage as brute endurance, may rightly emphasize the way courage is rooted in character. But he may seriously underestimate the role of intelligence and choice. Nicias, with his notion of courage as knowledge, may in turn underestimate the significance of character. If this suggestion is valid, the problem with Laches' and Nicias' divergent views of courage is not that either is wrong but that each is only partially right. The truth about courage would thus be found not by rejecting both views, nor by accepting one or the other, but by finding a way to synthesize the views into a coherent whole.

The two views, however, are presented by their spokesmen as diametrically opposed. Each general sees the other general's view as an account not of courage but of a vice with which courage is ordinarily contrasted. Nicias thinks of Laches' conception of courage as rashness, and Laches thinks of Nicias' notion of courage as cowardice. It was Aristotle—that most thoughtful and moderate of thinkers—who located courage as the mean between the two extremes of rashness and cowardice (*Nicomachean Ethics,* III.7, 1115b6–1116a15).

Should we, with Aristotle, think of courage as an aspect of character that enables us to endure in the face of fearful things and thereby permits us to use our reason to discover the good thing to do in a given situation without being moved more than we should by the possible fearful consequences of our choice? This notion of courage has two advantages. First, it resolves the inconclusiveness of the *Laches* by producing a unified understanding of courage. Second, it conforms very closely to the view presented by Aristotle in book III of his *Ethics*—and any conception that is close to Aristotle's has a lot to be said for it.

Unfortunately, this conception begs the question that the dialogue so startlingly raises about courage. Whether courage is endurance, knowledge, or a synthesis of the two, for courage to be operative must we not know what is truly fearful and what is truly hopeful? But isn't this exactly what we do not know—or, better, what we wrongly believe we do know? Is it not precisely the role of Socrates to bring home to us the comprehensive and fundamental ignorance that we so desperately attempt to deny or ignore? Is it not this ignorance that renders the efforts and careers of Aristides and Thucydides, in founding the empire; of Lysimachus and Melesias, in their concern for their sons; of Nicias and Laches, in their martial eminence—is it not the basic ignorance of all these pairs of men that renders the dialogue pathetic and ironic?

We, with the hindsight of history, can look upon these men with amused superiority. But are we not, in our own lives, in relation to our careers and families and each other, in exactly the same predicament? Living in the world as we do, courage is the virtue that we all need and the one that none of us seems to be able to achieve. But I think I have gone too far. I have turned Socratic ignorance into a counsel of despair. Let us pause for a moment.

In *The Human Condition* (pp. 43–45), Hannah Arendt proposes a distinction between behavior and action, a distinction rooted in the classical thought of Plato and Aristotle but almost extinct in the modern world. Most of the time, in the ordinary course of our lives, we are engaged in behavior. The things we do are predictable and in character. But once in a while, Arendt thinks, we stop behaving and begin to act. From the point of view of the neutral observer or the objective scientist, the difference may be hard to see. But to those of us who undertake to act, the difference is clear. We act when we cease to be determined by the past, when habit no longer defines what we do in the present and no longer reliably predicts what we will do in the future. We act, Arendt thinks, when we initiate, when we break the chain of causation that binds the present and the future to the past; when we start a new line of causation, create a situation that is inherently *un*predictable.

Behavior is fundamentally repetitive; action, by contrast, is original and unique and individual. Animals behave; humans can act. Action, the occasion of creating something new, carries with it the possibility of greatness. That is why we celebrate actions in song and story and record them in history and not the everyday behavior of people who do today and will do tomorrow what they did yesterday. In both poetry and history we celebrate those unique initiating events that somehow make our world different.

Courage, it seems to me, is the specific human excellence that makes action possible. How, without courage, could we ever bring ourselves to take the overwhelming risks involved in acting? Courage is a problematic, ambiguous virtue because action itself is always problematic and ambiguous. To act, to start a chain of events the outcome of which is unknown and is in principle unknowable, is to admit a fundamental ignorance about the things that matter most and yet not to be paralyzed by that ignorance or deny it. To act is to risk failure. The only way to avoid failure is never to act, never to initiate anything new, but always to behave in predictable patterns.

Just as there can be no action without courage, so, too, there can be no philosophy without action. I am thinking here of philosophy not in the sense of a body of doctrine but rather in its root, Socratic sense, as the love of and search for wisdom. The Socratic career, the philosophical endeavor, the active search for wisdom, requires as its first step the acceptance of a fundamental human ignorance. The discovery of our own ignorance—the realization that we do not know what we so desperately want and need to know—is, furthermore, not just the first step toward self-knowledge. It is a permanent truth about the human condition, not a fact that will change as we gather wisdom.

Socratic ignorance is beautifully illustrated in the failure of the *Laches* to come up with a clear and distinct answer to the question of what courage is and what those two boys should be taught in order that their souls be properly cared for. Our awareness of this ignorance and our acceptance of this failure are what make it possible for us to achieve and maintain our excellence, our virtue, as human beings.

I am arguing that philosophy—the love of knowledge and the search for wisdom—is a kind of action and, as such, is impossible without courage. I suggest that philosophy and courage are linked by the unique human capacity to act. The Socratic search for wisdom, moreover, is not just one action among many but perhaps the most daring one of all, because it requires that we be willing to risk everything, that we be prepared to fail at what we care about most. Nicias and Laches, with ignorant self-assurance, believe that possessing the skills of a general gives them a guarantee against failure. Lysimachus and Melesias, on the other hand, have no such guarantee; they know that they lack the competence to educate their boys right. They know from their own experience—or so they think—that their boys might turn out to be mediocre like themselves.

Perhaps the deepest irony of the *Laches* is that the question so worrisome to the two older gentlemen—what shall we do about our boys' education, how shall we care for their souls?—arose before the dialogue begins, because both boys on their own have already made the acquaintance of that master psychotherapist Socrates. We know from watching Socrates in action as he deals with the two fathers and the two generals that he will not teach the boys anything.

He is unique, but he is no Stesilaus who would train the boys in a newfangled skill that might or might not prove useful. Through their acquaintance with Socrates, the two boys, if they listen and talk seriously, may learn to confront their own fundamental ignorance. They may learn that they can act, they can start something new, and not be the passive victims of their own and their parents' pasts. Through their acquaintance with Socrates, the two boys may experience the joy and the terror of thinking for themselves and taking responsibility for their lives. That experience may or may not lead to eminent public careers, but it is the necessary first step in the life of an excellent human being. This is where caring for one's soul and courage begin.

PART II   THE HUMAN CONDITION

3 Reading Homer's *Iliad*

The *Iliad* is the oldest work in Western literature and the quintessential canonical classic. Still, many readers don't bother to read the poem, thinking that they already know Homer's epic account of the Trojan War: how it started with the abduction of the beautiful Helen, how Achilles, the mightiest Greek warrior, was killed by an arrow in his vulnerable heel, and how Troy was finally taken through Odysseus' stratagem of the Trojan Horse. Unfortunately, none of these events occurs in the *Iliad*. But I aim in these remarks not to correct misperceptions so much as to persuade you to read it.

Let me be clear at the outset: I am convinced that Homer may be the only artist who measures up to Shakespeare. I would like to suggest some of the grounds for my fascination with the *Iliad* and show why, even in translation, Homer has had the reputation for over two and a half millennia of being the wisest and best of poets. I propose to sketch out the kind of poet he is and then take up some specific aspects of the *Iliad:* the use of epithets and similes; the peculiar structure and unity of the work; the contrast between the Greeks and the Trojans—especially in the figures of Achilles and Hector; the nature and role of the Olympic gods in the story; and, finally, the whole problem of the Homeric conception of virtue, morality, and tragic stature.

To discuss the poetic character of Homer's works requires addressing the Homeric Problem. The Homeric Problem is the name given to an enormous debate that has engaged the attention of classicists for two full centuries. The debate began in 1795 with the publication, in Latin, of a work by a German scholar, Friedrich August Wolf. Wolf maintained that the *Iliad* and the *Odyssey,* as they have come down to us, were not composed at one time by a single man but were built up by many generations of rhapsodes and bards who added to, developed, and refined the poems. I won't go into the details of this controversy; it is enough to say that it revolved around the question of whether poems as long, as complex, and as sophisticated as the *Iliad* could have been created at the time when Homer was supposed to have lived, when Greece had a rude, disordered, and possibly illiterate society.

After 125 years of acrid debate the problem of the authorship of the *Iliad* was revolutionized by a few articles published in the late 1920s and early 1930s by an American classicist named Millman Parry. Parry had the brilliant idea of dealing with the scholarly controversy about the epic and bardic traditions in Archaic Greece by investigating a living oral epic tradition. He went to the former Yugoslavia, not far from present-day Greece, and studied the oral verse tradition that still exists there. His discoveries by no means ended the controversy about Homer, but they did shift the focus of the argument.

Parry discovered an entirely new kind of poetry, or perhaps I should say that he rediscovered an extremely old kind. Until Parry, scholars had assumed that the author or authors of the *Iliad* were poets like Donne, Keats, and Wordsworth—men who, in deciding to write a poem, also decided what verse form they would use, what line length, what words and images. Parry discovered that this conception of the independent, freely creating poet did not exist in the mountains of Yugoslavia or, by extension, in ancient Greece either. In place of the independent romantic poet, Parry found a bardic tradition in which boys were apprenticed to a master bard and then spent ten or twenty years mastering the tools of their trade.

Parry found that these oral poets, these bards, not only committed to memory traditional epic poems that approximated the *Iliad* and the *Odyssey* in length but also mastered techniques and skills that enabled them to produce new epics extemporaneously. The epic line, for example, is of a fixed length and metrical pattern. The Yugoslavian bards had, over the generations, worked out a large number of formulaic phrases with which, through combination and permutation, they could produce new lines at will. Furthermore, they knew standard plots or forms for all epic occasions, so that at the appropriate moment—say, the military victory of a local hero—the bard could almost immediately produce a new epic celebrating the event. They also learned set pieces that had been worked out for almost all major occasions—the scene, for example, of the warrior girding himself for battle, or the following scene, in which he bids farewell, perhaps for the last time, to his family. For these moments in the highly formalized story, the epic bard would have not just a fixed line or two but perhaps a whole piece of thirty or forty lines that would hardly vary, except for the names, from one epic to the next. Set pieces that can be fitted into the developing structure of an epic are a great convenience to the bard, for he can perform them automatically while giving his attention to the portion of the story to come.

The closest thing in contemporary American experience to this sort of oral epic tradition is the folksong. There are folksingers today who have an enormous repertory of songs, verses, pairs of rhyme words for ending lines, and so forth. With a simple melody and lyric, like the tune and words for "Blow the Man Down" or "Skip to My Lou," a skilled folksinger can endlessly improvise clever and appropriate verses for any occasion. This is the kind of poetry that Parry found in the Yugoslavian mountains and that he argued existed in Greece at the time of Homer.

Parry's discovery of what he called the epic technique of oral verse-making provides a context in which we can make sense of the poetry found in the *Iliad*. For example, the repetition from time to time of individual lines and often whole groups of lines merely indicates that they are set lines or set pieces that Homer had available to him from the epic tradition and that he used whenever appropriate. Similarly, the battle scene that each major Greek hero has in which he is the center of attention and is shown to be a warrior of enormous skill and courage merely attests to the national character of the *Iliad*: the hero of each city has his big moment. I could go on like this, taking each aspect of the *Iliad* and showing how its inclusion in the work and its peculiar treatment by the poet can be understood by reference to the techniques and demands of the epic tradition. In effect, I could show that every element, aspect, and scene in the *Iliad* that outrages or annoys our modern sensibility and taste is excusable. It is not difficult, using Parry's discovery, to make excuses for Homer or the several dozen men who go by that name.

Yet I think Homer needs no excuses, and for me the value of Parry's discovery is of a different order. A moment ago I said that the poetry in the *Iliad* is completely different from the independent, freely creative lyric poetry with which we are largely familiar. I made the distinction between Homer and a poet like Keats to emphasize my point, but now I would like to qualify the difference as one of degree, not kind. After all, every poet has always written under some form of restraint or discipline. A poet today may freely choose to write a sonnet, but once she makes that choice she must express herself in fourteen lines or else she has not written a sonnet. When Keats wrote his sonnets, he accepted a discipline of the same general sort as Homer did when he wrote the *Iliad*. The glory of Keats' sonnets is precisely the perfection with which Keats fused his innate lyricism with the cruel, externally imposed discipline of the traditional sonnet form. Compared to the discipline imposed on Homer, however, that imposed on Keats was minimal; no poet has ever worked with more intractable material and a crueler discipline than Homer. The value of Parry's discovery is that it permits a modern reader to appreciate the formal, externally imposed forms employed by Homer and, more important, to see how Homer dominated those forms to write what may be the greatest single poem ever composed.

Before I take up the various examples with which I shall defend my contention, let me make one more point, about one's emotional response to the events and characters portrayed in the *Iliad*. All of us have undoubtedly picked up in our early schooling various ideas and notions about the epic tradition, the nature of Greek religion, and the figure of the tragic hero. When we read the *Iliad* for ourselves, most of us were probably dismayed. That great, noble adventure—the expedition of the Greeks to recover the beautiful Helen from the Trojans—doesn't seem noble at all. It looks far more like a raiding expedition by a gang of crude, brawling pirates who are always fighting among themselves over the spoils. Achilles, the greatest of epic heroes, appears to be a spoiled, willful, bloodthirsty fighting machine who would rather see his friends and allies slaughtered than give an inch in a petty quarrel over a slave girl. And the Olympic gods who hover over the battlefield deciding the fate of individuals, armies, and cities are like petty, bickering humans without wisdom, courage, grace, or dignity.

Most of us assumed that our initial response was wrong, that Homer and the Greeks for whom the poem was intended never responded to it in this way because they admired Achilles as a great hero and worshiped the Olympic gods. From this assumption it is a short step to the invention of all kinds of nonsense about the relativity of values and the need to read the *Iliad* from the point of view of the intended audience rather than from our own modern, sophisticated viewpoint. My belief is that the first response was correct, that if we want to see what the *Iliad* is about, we must not reject our initial feelings of bewilderment and disgust; we must accept them fully and go forward from there to grasp what Homer is saying.

That initial dismay was, however, only partly right. Achilles *is* the greatest of all epic and tragic heroes, but we can see the heroic dimensions of his humanity only if we accept that he is, indeed, a spoiled, willful, bloodthirsty fighting machine. Zeus and Hera are figures of awe, and they are worthy of a kind of religious devotion, but to feel their divinity we must first recognize Zeus as a henpecked husband and Hera as the shrewish, suspicious wife who tries to dominate him.

With this by way of introduction, I turn now to some of the details of the poem. I will begin with the epithets. All Homeric figures have epithets—formulaic phrases or words that are always associated with them. Odysseus is "brilliant," Hector is "glorious," Aphrodite is "laughing," the Achaians are "flowing-haired." As Richard Lattimore points out in his excellent introduction to his even better translation of the *Iliad,* these epithets are probably not Homer's invention; they are traditional and are determined by the metrical requirements of the dactylic hexameter line used by Homer and other epic bards. While reading the *Iliad* the epithets can become hackneyed, so that one becomes unconscious of them. But readers must guard against this, for the way Homer employs the conventional epithet can galvanize an entire character or episode, transforming it from a simple, straightforward narrative into great dramatic poetry.

One of the epithets for Hector, for example, is "the slayer of men." In book VI there is a marvelous scene in which Hector, having left the battle, returns to the city, urges his brother Paris, Helen's abductor, to leave Helen and join the fight, and goes looking for his wife, Andromache. He does not find her at home or in the streets. Finally, just before he is to leave the city gates, she comes running to meet him, carrying their infant son. Andromache pleads with Hector to have pity on her and their child and not go out to battle. She reminds him that Achilles slew her father and seven brothers, that she has no family but her husband, and that he means much to her. Hector answers her plea by talking of his honor and the shame he would feel if he were to shrink from the fighting (remember, he has just left Paris). He foresees his own death, and he tells Andromache to be brave. His infant son then cries out, afraid of his father's shining helmet, and Hector, taking off the helmet, tosses the child in his arms, kisses him, and prays to Zeus.

> *Zeus, and you other immortals, grant that this boy, who is my son*
> *may be as I am, pre-eminent among the Trojans,*
> *great in strength, as I am, and rule strongly over Ilion;*
> *and some day let them say of him: "He is better by far than his father,"*
> *as he comes in from the fighting; and let him kill his enemy*
> *and bring home the blooded spoils, and delight the heart of his mother.*

(VI.476–481)

Returning the child to Andromache, Hector sends his wife back to her household work with a final word about the uselessness of trying to avoid one's fate.

> *And as she came in speed into the well-settled household*
> *of Hektor the slayer of men she found numbers of handmaidens*
> *within, and her coming stirred all of them into lamentation.*

(VI.497–499)

This scene needs no defense by me or anyone else; it is one of the most beautiful vignettes in the *Iliad*. Yet for me, when Homer uses the conventional epithet and has Andromache return to the "household of Hektor the slayer of men," he adds that final brilliant touch that makes for great art. At that moment the epithet is no longer merely conventional; it defines Hector in all his glory, pathos, and blindness.

Hector carries the whole responsibility for the defense of Troy, and he knows that he is fated to perish in battle and all Troy along with him. This he makes clear when he tries to comfort Andromache. Then, with incredible blindness, he plays with his son for a moment and prays that the boy will grow up to be a better man than his father—that is, a better and bloodier warrior. Hector is here called a slayer of men not simply because of the requirements of the dactylic hexameter line but because that is what he is. Homer must have known exactly what he was doing in this little domestic scene when he used this most terrible and warlike of epithets to describe Hector.

My next example of the use of epithets is in book XXII, which opens with Achilles bearing down on Troy in a towering rage. All the Trojans except Hector have fled into the city. Hector alone remains outside the walls, awaiting his fate. From the top of the wall Priam, king of the city and Hector's father, sees Achilles in the distance and pleads with Hector to withdraw. Hecuba, his mother, pleads in her turn. But Hector remains transfixed outside the gate, aware that if he stays he will die but, at the same time, unable to face the shame and dishonor of retreat. When Achilles closes in on him, even great Hector quails and takes to his heels. Three times Achilles chases him completely around Troy, until Athena comes to Achilles and tells him to rest while she persuades Hector to stand and fight. Then, disguised as Hector's brother Deiphobos, Athena appears next to Hector and says,

> Dear brother, indeed swift-footed Achilleus is using you roughly
> and chasing you on swift feet around the city of Priam.
> Come on, then; let us stand fast against him and beat him back from us.

(XXII.229–231)

Hector is deceived; he stops to fight with the help of Deiphobos, and when he discovers his error, it is too late—he is doomed.

Notice Athena's use of the epithet "swift-footed" in reference to Achilles, a term applied to Achilles many times in the preceding twenty-one books. Yet here, at the crucial moment of the entire war, when Achilles is about to kill his antagonist, the one man who might lay claim to being as great a hero as he is; here, at the moment when Achilles' stature as the greatest of heroes is about to be demonstrated, the heroic epithet "swift-footed" becomes a hollow and ironic mockery. Achilles may be the greatest of heroes and he may indeed be swift-footed, but he cannot catch Hector without the help of the gods. It is, of course, a measure of Hector's terror that he can match Achilles' speed. The deliberate use of the traditional epithet in contrast to the facts of the situation casts a peculiar light on Achilles. Homer does not exactly undercut Achilles' greatness. But he does suggest through the ironical use of the epithet that even the greatest of heroes is not omnipotent and that Achilles' greatest victory is not without its slightly shady and unheroic aspects.

For my third and last example of the way Homer, by the skillful use of the traditional epithet, transforms a scene into great and creative poetry, I turn to book XXIV, the scene in which Priam, king of Troy, comes as a helpless suppliant to the dwelling of Achilles to beg from him the dead body of his son Hector. With the help of the god Hermes, Priam slips into the Greek camp.

> *Tall Priam came in unseen by the other men and stood close beside him*
> *and caught the knees of Achilleus in his arms, and kissed the hands*
> *that were dangerous and manslaughtering and had killed so many of his sons.*

(XXIV.476–480)

Again, it is traditional to speak of Achilles' hands as "manslaughtering"—the epithet belongs to the epic tradition and is not Homer's invention. But the natural place to use the term is in a scene of battle and bloodshed, where those hands are doing their terrible work. As with "swift-footed" in the previous scene, the use of the epithet in this particular context lends irony and surprise. But this time the irony is not the corrosive sort that expresses doubt, that deflates and minimizes. Rather, it is the irony of high tragedy: Priam in supplication must kiss the very hands that slew his son. There is much more in this scene, for it is the climactic moment of the *Iliad*, and Homer returns again and again to those terrible manslaughtering hands. They are the physical expression, the symbol, of the link that binds Achilles and Priam together. It is precisely because the epithet is conventional and has been used so many times before in the poem that it works in this scene as the poetic vehicle for the full expression of tragedy.

Moving away from the traditional epithets, I want now to take up a closely related phenomenon in the *Iliad*: Homer's use of poetic imagery and detail. The greatest examples are his similes, but let me first give an example of the way Homer employs descriptive details. I have chosen a tiny example because I want to show just how attentive a reader of the *Iliad* has to be. The scene occurs in book VI, just prior to the scene in which Hector bids farewell to Andromache. Hector has just come from the battle "with blood and muck all splattered upon him" (VI.268), and he goes to the house of Paris.

> *There entered Hektor, beloved of Zeus, in his hand holding*
> *the eleven-cubit-long spear, whose shaft was tipped with a shining*
> *bronze spearhead, and a ring of gold was hooped to hold it.*
> *He found the man in his chamber busy with his splendid armor,*

the corselet and the shield, and turning in his hands the curved bow,
while Helen of Argos was sitting among her attendant women
directing the magnificent work done by her handmaids.

(VI.318–324)

In the exchange that follows Hector rebukes Paris for his cowardice; Paris, as pliant as ever, apologizes and says that Helen was just urging him to go, and he was about to put on his armor and leave. Helen speaks sweetly to Hector while cursing Paris and her own fate in being married to such a miserable man. Hector concludes the scene by rejecting Helen's offer to sit and rest for a minute; he impatiently leaves to find Andromache and return to the battle.

As a picture of Helen, the woman for whom the entire war is being fought, the scene is perfect; but let me call attention to the way Homer sets up the scene in the quoted passage. Hector enters carrying his enormous spear with its shining bronze spearhead and the hoop of gold that holds the spearhead to the shaft. That is all we see of Hector, although we know from a few lines earlier that he is bloody and weary from the battle.

Paris, in contrast, is sitting quietly polishing his splendid armor, surrounded by Helen and her attendants, who are doing their fancy embroidery. Homer doesn't bother to tell us anything explicit about the characters in the scene, but he doesn't have to, for by an extraordinarily economical selection of detail he has told us what we need to know. Think of that shining bronze spearhead with its single, useful hoop of gold in contrast to the splendid armor of Paris; think of Hector standing upright grasping his enormous spear and Paris sitting down idly turning his curved bow in his hands; think of Hector rushing alone from the battle while Paris relaxes among the women.

The scene is of great importance in the *Iliad*, not so much for what happens in it but for the picture it gives of the Trojan side of the war, a picture in which honor and shame, cowardice and bravery, absurdity and tragedy are all intermingled. The scene itself is perfectly prepared for and prefigured in those few narrative lines describing Hector's entrance. I myself came to feel the significance of the scene only when I was reading it with some friends and someone idly asked why Homer bothered to mention that shining spearhead with its ring of gold. It was in reflecting on that tiny detail that we came to see the drama of the ensuing scene and its meaning for the whole structure of the *Iliad*.

Homer's lyric powers are perhaps most immediately evident in his famous similes, those passages in which he describes something indirectly by likening it to something else. As every reader senses, however, the similes are more than a mere technique of description. Lattimore, in his introduction, analyzes the formal structure of a Homeric simile: "A is like B: B has such and such a history, progresses in such and such a manner: and (we repeat) it is like A" (p. 42).

Yet, as Lattimore realizes, this abstract formula hardly does justice to the similes, for many of them almost take on the character of independent lyric poems inserted in the text, poems that start from a point of likeness to the event or thing being described but rapidly leave that single point of likeness and take on a life of their own. Frequently, as Lattimore says, the simile ends by "contradicting the effect which it was introduced in order to achieve" (p. 42). How extraordinary—a simile contrasts with or contradicts the thing it was meant to illustrate. And such a simile is by no means rare in the *Iliad:* it is almost the prevailing type.

I could go further and point out that the material of the similes is largely drawn not from the heroic, aristocratic strife-torn world of the Trojan War but from the homely, commonplace, peaceful world of Greek rural life. Lattimore says that "such passages represent in part an escape from the heroic narrative of remote events which is the poet's assignment and the only medium we know of through which he could communicate his craft" (p. 42). This may well be true. Homer may have chafed under the restrictions of the traditional epic forms and materials; and the many similes that are not like the things they are supposed to be like may be a spontaneous breaking-through of Homer's lyric urge. But, as Lattimore himself suggests, whether or not the similes were a relief to Homer, they are certainly a relief to the modern reader, who does grow a little weary of bloodshed and slaughter. But I think that the similes do much more than afford a momentary lyric relief from the rigors of heroic warfare.

I suggest that the similes play a crucial role in the *Iliad*. They have an extremely subtle effect, so subtle that very few readers are consciously aware of it, and yet the effect is almost always felt. To put it bluntly, the almost continual fighting, bickering, and bloodshed that make up the story of the *Iliad* would by themselves fail to produce the intended epic and tragic effect that Homer seeks to achieve. It is not so much that we would weary of unrelieved warfare, although that can happen; rather, we would lose our sense of perspective.

The Trojan War, after all, is not a commonplace, everyday event, and the incidents that make it up, particularly the chain of happenings that lead to the battle between Achilles and Hector, are meant to have genuine epic proportions. Yet how can Homer convince us that the deaths of Patroklos and Hector are significant when we have been sated by page after page of fighting and killing? This problem is not unique to Homer. It is, in fact, a refrain of modern critics, who explain that there are no genuine tragedies or epics written today, because the horror and magnitude of modern nuclear war have outstripped the ability of poets to represent them, and, anyway, in the face of such enormous events the individual has shrunk to insignificance. This view, in my opinion, is nonsense; the Trojan War was no more or less susceptible to artistic treatment than any other. War is always inhuman, brutal, and impersonal, and it is

Homer's genius, not the character of the Trojan War, that makes his account of it tragic.

The similes, moreover, are the primary device by which Homer constantly reminds us of the true nature of the war. By introducing scenes of commonplace domestic life, he provides us with the general human context within which all high tragedy occurs. Without that context, tragedy itself becomes commonplace and emotionally fatiguing, thereby losing the very qualities that make it tragedy. Tolstoy was fully aware of this, and in *War and Peace* the rhythm of alternating scenes of war and peace defines emotionally the great battle sequences that would otherwise be humanly incoherent. Homer couldn't do this, for the traditional story that he worked with had no place for extended scenes of peaceful life. The brief scenes of domestic life in Troy do not serve because of the doom that hangs over the city. But with his terribly limited material Homer was even more skillful than Tolstoy, for he does not alternate between scenes of war and peace. Rather, through his similes he integrates moments of domestic and pastoral tranquility right into the heart of his battle scenes.

Let me, by way of illustration, take two of the similes that Lattimore quotes in his introductory remarks. The first occurs in book IV when the massed forces of the Greeks and the Trojans meet in battle.

> Now as these advancing came to one place and encountered
> they dashed their shields together and their spears, and the strength
> of armoured men in bronze, and the shields massive in the middle
> clashed against each other, and the sound grew huge of the fighting.
> There the screaming and the shouts of triumph rose up together
> of men killing and men killed, and the ground ran blood.
> As when rivers in winter spate running down from the mountains
> throw together at the meeting of streams the weight of their water
> out of the great streams behind in the hollow stream-bed,
> and far away in the mountains the shepherd hears their thunder;
> such, from the coming together of men, was the shock and the shouting.

(IV.446–456)

Overtly this simile is meant to illustrate the magnitude of the shock and noise in the meeting of the two armies. Beyond this, however, as Lattimore says, such a simile is a "landscape, direct from the experience of life, and this one is humanized by the tiny figure of the shepherd set against enormous nature" (p. 42). Lattimore is quite right, but he apparently does not see the wonderfully complex relation between the simile and the event that it illustrates. The image, drawn from nature, of the two streams meeting in spring flood is Homer's way of expressing the immensity and raw power of the clash of the two armies. The image of the lonely shepherd who hears the noise far away in the mountains does far more than humanize the landscape evoked in the simile; it also reflects back on the event being described. That lonely shepherd is the only human in the simile, and he is far away from the thunderous meeting of the two streams. By poetic association the clash of the two armies is thus dehumanized; it becomes an overwhelming natural event in which individuals disappear.

In dehumanizing the clash of the armies, Homer does not forget his audience's humanity, so we watch and listen to the meeting of the armies from a distance, just as the shepherd listens from afar to the thunder of the convergent streams. Thus we are reminded of our own humanity at the moment that we witness the senseless violence of the battle, and our awareness of ourselves heightens its inhuman magnitude. Yet we also know that the battle is not a natural event; the simile is only a simile. Those armies are made up of individuals like ourselves, human beings who are fighting and dying horribly. The simile not only illustrates and sharpens the event but also contrasts sharply with it, vividly reminding us of the ordinary, untragic world of pastoral tranquility where an awesome noise is merely two streams coming together.

For the second example, let us consider another simile cited by Lattimore, this one from book XI. The Trojans and Greeks have been fighting furiously all morning, and with the help of Zeus, the Trojans have been getting the better of their adversaries.

> So long as it was early morning and the sacred daylight increasing,
> so long the thrown weapons of both took hold and men dropped under them.
> But at that time when the woodcutter makes ready his supper
> in the wooded glens of the mountains, when his arms and hands have grown
>   weary
> from cutting down the tall trees, and his heart has had enough of it,
> at that time the Danaans by their manhood broke the battalions
> calling across the ranks to each other.

(XI.84–91)

Here again, as Lattimore says, the simile has a simple function: it is an elaborate way of indicating when the tide of battle shifted in favor of the Greeks. The image of the woodcutter taking a break for lunch after working hard all morning is touching and shows us Homer's lyric sensitivity to everyday events.

Homer could have saved himself the trouble of writing five lines of poetry by saying instead, "And then at noontime the Danaans by their manhood broke the battalions / calling across the ranks to each other." Yet how much we would have missed—not only the beauty of the five lines but, more important, what they tell us about the battle and about what a real fighter is made of. When the woodcutter is tired, he takes a break. But that is exactly the moment when the Greeks, after losing all morning, exert their manhood and begin to drive back the Trojans. Note, too, that the woodcutter, like the shepherd who heard the streams meeting, is alone, but this time the army is made up of individuals, men who call to each other across the ranks, exhorting, encouraging, and exulting in their manhood.

I could reflect on Homer's similes almost indefinitely, but I will stop here. In general, I think it would be fair to say that the similes are, on the surface, some of the simplest and most straightforward poetry ever written; the images are clear, and the language is not the least bit fancy. Yet, looked at in context, they also constitute some of the most subtle, complex, and beautiful poetry ever written, poetry that depends for its effect on only one thing: Homer's ability to see and to render concretely the full human meaning of the event he is describing. His similes alone provide sufficient evidence for calling Homer the wisest and best of poets.

I want now to move to a much larger level of analysis and point out a peculiarity of the overall structure of the *Iliad*. The poem tells the story of the anger of Achilles from its inception to its final tragic purgation. This could be called the plot of the work. But because large chunks of the *Iliad* have only the most tenuous of connections with the particular events that compose the anger of Achilles, it would not be difficult to edit the *Iliad* by leaving out that extraneous matter and thus reduce the work to about a quarter of its present length. One might produce a tighter, better-organized, faster-paced story, but only by giving up just that leisurely and humane pace that I have been trying to evoke by my discussion of tiny details. The story of the anger of Achilles is delayed and expanded by the insertion of all kinds of unnecessary material. But in a deeper sense, the *Iliad* is composed of numerous tiny building blocks: epithets, images, similes. These tiny blocks are arranged to form larger blocks: incidents, events, scenes. And from these larger blocks Homer builds the monumental epic structure called the *Iliad*.

In taking this second view of the structure of the work, I would be justified in saying that the *Iliad* does not have one line or one word too many. Anyone who reads the work from this point of view rather than from the other, simpler perspective will let the larger structure emerge naturally and leisurely from the welter of incredibly rich poetic detail.

I cannot, here, even begin to discuss that larger structure, but I would like to take up two elements of it: the contrast and conflict between Achilles and Hector and the role of the Olympic gods. As I mentioned earlier, Hector is, in many respects, far more admirable and endearing than Achilles. Hector, after all, is defending his home and city against attack, whereas Achilles is the hero of those who have come to pillage and destroy Troy. Hector is a brave fighter, a considerate son and husband, and a responsible leader. In contrast, Achilles has no family about him, he quarrels with his commanding general about a captive slave girl, and in his pique he allows many of his Greek comrades to be killed. When he finally leaves off sulking, he does not fight out of a conviction that he has been wrong or out of a sense of honor; he fights instead out of personal anger at the death of his friend, and he has only one desire—to take revenge on the man who killed Patroklos. When he secures his revenge by killing Hector, he is not satisfied, but almost like a brute he insists on dragging the body about as if he could exact some further revenge from the corpse. Homer's audience must have felt even more disgusted by Achilles' behavior than we do, for by mistreating Hector's corpse Achilles was outraging not only the human feelings of the Greeks but also some of their strongest religious sanctions.

How, given all this, can Homer expect us to admire Achilles as the greater hero? To answer this question, or at least suggest an answer, it is necessary to consider the Olympic gods. There are three levels on which divinity is present in the *Iliad*. At the lowest level are those gods with the names of generic human passions: Hate, Fear, Terror. These divinities are said to hover over the battlefield instilling their nature into the struggling mortals below. They have no personalities or even any existence except as semisymbolic expressions of those human passions and drives that seem to have a force or life of their own and that are not readily controllable by our conscious selves. At the highest level of divinity there is what Homer calls Fate or Destiny, and this, too, seems to be an impersonal force, but one that governs the outcome of events. Between the purely symbolic gods of the human passions and the misty force of destiny that decrees the outcome of all lives and events there are the Olympic gods: Zeus, Hera, Athena, and all the rest. They constitute a community ruled by Zeus, and individually and collectively they have enormous power over humankind and the world. They seem to control the depersonalized symbolic gods of the passions, and in turn they seem to be controlled, or at least limited, by the overriding power of Fate. Unlike all the other divine forces, however, the Olympic gods have personalities, and it is this aspect of them that we shall consider.

Taken all in all, the Olympic gods are a despicable lot: they are cruel, selfish, quarrelsome, unpredictable, deceitful, and open to bribes. They take some interest in the affairs of humans and, indeed, split into factions in their disputes over the war between the Trojans and the Greeks, on rare occasions even taking a direct hand in the fighting. Yet they are also peculiarly detached, and when the fighting gets too bloody or when they are wounded, they run back to the safety of Olympus.

In sum, they are exactly like most people and would in fact be indistinguishable from ordinary human beings except for one difference. They are immortal, they live forever. I don't know whether the Greeks of Homer's day worshiped the gods as Homer portrays them, but his gods bear some resemblance to the gods worshiped in all the temples and sanctuaries of Greece. Yet I suspect that Homer's personal attitude toward the gods had a strong skeptical streak. I can easily imagine him saying, "It is uncertain whether the gods really exist, but if they do, this is probably what they are like, and if the picture I paint is not very pretty, it is at least reasonable, given the nature of the world we live in."

It is not Homer's theology but his poetic use of the gods that is relevant here, however. I said earlier that the world of tragedy, if it is to affect us as it should, must be set within the broader context of the everyday world. Without the contrast afforded by that larger context, the intensity and magnitude of the tragic events are attenuated. Analogously, there is also a need for a figure or figures against whom the tragic hero, his stature and suffering and dignity, can be measured.

Shakespeare, for instance, frequently has in his tragedies subordinate figures who resemble the hero in one respect or another. The contrast between the hero and the lesser figure helps to define the greatness of the hero. Hamlet's tragedy is seen against the lesser tragedies of Laertes and Fortinbras, and Lear's suffering is reflected in the suffering of Gloucester. The Olympic gods serve this function in the *Iliad* with respect to the heroic tragedy of Achilles, but with a difference: With Shakespeare and all the other tragedians I know of who have employed this device, the hero's suffering is always reflected in someone who is lower than he is. The full dimensions of the hero's fate are seen in contrast to the smaller dimensions of his reflection. Homer is the only poet I know of who had the audacity and the genius to define his hero's tragedy from above rather than from below. Achilles must ultimately be contrasted not to Hector or any of the other humans in the *Iliad* but to the Olympic gods.

Let me illustrate what I mean with two examples. The first is based on a contrast between two juxtaposed scenes in book I. After a quarrel with Agamemnon in which Athena restrained Achilles from attacking that frequently stupid, arrogant king, Achilles returns to his shelter and allows the heralds of Agamemnon to take Briseis, the slave girl, away. Briseis unwillingly leaves, and

Achilleus

weeping went and sat in sorrow apart from his companions
beside the beach of the grey sea looking out on the infinite water.
Many times stretching forth his hands he called on his mother:
"Since, my mother, you bore me to be a man with a short life,
therefore Zeus of the loud thunder on Olympus should grant me
honour at least. But now he has given me not even a little.

Now the son of Atreus, powerful Agamemnon,
has dishonoured me, since he has taken away my prize and keeps it."

(1.348–356)

Thetis, his divine mother, comes to comfort Achilles and agrees to intercede with Zeus on his behalf.

Almost immediately after this scene we are given our first full picture of the Olympic gods. Thetis comes to Zeus on Olympus and entreats him to favor the Trojans so that the Greeks, needing Achilles, will restore his rights and honor. Zeus hesitates, fearing his wife's displeasure, but agrees. Hera, however, sees Zeus and Thetis whispering together and, like the shrewish wife she is, accuses Zeus of keeping secrets from her. A domestic brawl ensues, and Hephaistos, the half-crippled son of Hera, tries to calm her down. He reminds her of how he once helped her against Zeus and was thrown off Olympus for his disobedience and lamed. Then he takes a goblet of nectar and pours out drinks for the assembled gods, and

> *among the blessed immortals uncontrollable laughter*
> *went up as they saw Hephaistos bustling about the palace.*

(1.599–600)

Think of these two scenes together for a moment: Achilles, the proudest of men, sits alone weeping by the infinite sea, bitter at the fated shortness of his life and helplessly frustrated by the stripping-away of his honor and dignity. By contrast, when Hera is humiliated by Zeus she lightly accepts the bumbling warning of Hephaistos, drinks a cup of nectar, and roars with laughter at the pathetic limp of her own son. Mortals weep alone, gods laugh together. Achilles, deeply aware of his mortality, is stung to the quick by the insult of Agamemnon, but why should the immortal Hera seriously quarrel with her divine husband over anything so trivial as the fate of a few mortals? In the juxtaposition and contrast of these two scenes, Homer has presented in miniature a complete poetic definition of the human condition, a condition he reminds us of throughout the *Iliad*.

My second example comes much later in the work, at the beginning of book XIX. Thetis comes to Achilles bearing his new armor and finds her son mourning over the corpse of Patroklos. She gives him his arms, and

> *he was glad, holding in his hands the shining gifts of Hephaistos.*
> *But when he had satisfied his heart with looking at the intricate*
> *armour, he spoke to his mother and addressed her in winged words:*
> *"My mother, the god has given me these weapons; they are such*

as are the work of immortals. No mortal man could have made them;
therefore I shall arm myself in them. Yet I am sadly
afraid, during this time, for the warlike son of Menoitios,
that the flies might get into the wounds beaten by bronze in his body
and breed worms in them, and these make foul the body, seeing
that the life is killed in him, and that all his flesh may be rotted."
In turn the goddess Thetis the silver-footed answered him:
"My child, no longer let these things be a care in your mind.
I shall endeavor to drive from him the swarming and fierce things,
those flies, which feed upon the bodies of men who have perished;
and although he lie here till a year has come to fulfillment,
still his body shall be as it was, or firmer than ever.
Go then and summon into assembly the fighting Achaians."

(XIX. 18–34)

Thetis loves her son, and she tries hard to please and comfort him. When Achilles in his grief says that he is worried lest his friend's body rot, his mother, with the very best intentions, promises to keep the flies away and to preserve the corpse for a year if necessary, so that, as she says, it "shall be as it was, or firmer than ever." What a wonderful comfort that must be to Achilles when he goes forth to fight Hector, to know that the corpse of Patroklos will remain as firm and lifelike as before—or even more than when he was alive! In that little touch, that extra bit of comfort that immortal Thetis gives to her mortal son, Achilles, can be felt the whole range of agony and cruelty that attends the intercourse of gods with humans, of immortals with mortals.

The gods, I have said, are just like ordinary people except for their immortality. But what an enormous difference that is; being freed from the curse of death, from the finite existence that is the fate of human beings, the gods are deprived of the great qualities that make a human fully human. They can never feel deeply about anything because for them nothing really important is ever at stake. They can never feel genuine love or hate, joy or sorrow, because they know that they will always have another chance—the future stretches limitlessly before them.

Thus the emotional life of the gods is peculiarly attenuated. They do not love and hate—they like and dislike; they do not fight—they bicker; they cannot rejoice—they can only enjoy themselves. For all their power the gods have neither dignity nor integrity, which are precisely what Achilles has to an extent that overshadows anyone else in the *Iliad*.

Homer was careful to make this clear. Hector has a wife and child and parents; he has brothers he loves, enemies he hates, and a city to defend. Achilles has none of these; he is virtually isolated, with the exception of his friendship with Patroklos and his love for Briseis. When Briseis is taken from him in a petty quarrel with Agamemnon, he sulks in his tent with Patroklos, and when Patroklos is killed by Hector, Achilles is left totally alone.

Achilles is not merely angry with Agamemnon for taking Briseis from him, nor is he simply enraged at Hector for killing his friend. Achilles' full rage is directed against his mortal condition. The ultimate fate of Achilles, death, is the ultimate fate of all of us. But Achilles lives his life and faces his fate with incredible directness and intensity, because he has nothing in the form of a family or a city to divert his attention. Achilles is almost a monster, given his violence and brutality, but most of all he is human. In the figure of Achilles, Homer created the first tragic hero. Achilles' tragedy is based not on any particular qualities of his character, nor on what he does or what is done to him, but on the sheer fact of his being human, and mortal. Achilles is not only the first but the greatest of all tragic figures.

The *Iliad* is an exciting work, but not the way a boy's adventure story is. It is probably the most adult poem ever written, and we must read and respond to it as adults. It is beautiful, but it is neither pretty nor pleasant. If we are mature enough to face and accept its terrible beauty, we will, in reading and discussing and rereading it, be embarking on what may be one of the memorable experiences of our lives.

4 Homer's *Odyssey*
The Adolescence of Telemachus

The *Odyssey* is the second oldest poem in the European literary tradition, second only to the *Iliad*. A sequel to the *Iliad*, it is a much smaller work, written, according to an ancient account, many years after the *Iliad*, when Homer was extremely old. Yet if the *Odyssey* is a lesser work, it is, and probably always has been, more accessible, more popular, and far more loved. The *Iliad* is a massive, grim, austere tragedy set in the Archaic world of heroic warfare. The *Odyssey*, although it recounts events occurring only ten years after those in the *Iliad* and involving many of the same characters, seems to occur in a very different world, one with which we are much more familiar—a world of households and families, of husbands and wives, of parents and children, of courtship, parties, quarrels and reconciliations, everyday domesticity and exotic, romantic adventure. In short, the *Odyssey* bears a striking resemblance to much modern popular fiction, and it has frequently and rightly been called the first novel.

But if the *Odyssey* needs no excuse to be read and discussed beyond the delight it provides, is there not something reminiscent of adolescence in its position as a sequel to the *Iliad* and the precursor of the modern novel? Is not adolescence itself a stage of life that looks forward and backward, forward to that wonderful development into independent adulthood, a development that seems to be agonizingly slow, filled with terror, and uncertain in outcome, and backward to the deeds of the previous generation, the generation of the parents, which always appears both great and despicable, providing models to be imitated and standards against which no one ever quite measures up? There is within the *Odyssey* itself an image of adolescence that reflects these themes. I am referring to Telemachus, Odysseus' late-adolescent son, who plays a major role in the story of Odysseus' return home. Before I take up the details of Telemachus' role, let me remind you of the main events of the story.

After a ten-year siege, the city of Troy finally falls to the Greeks—not through the heroic efforts of such mighty warriors as Achilles and Ajax but through the clever stratagem of the Trojan Horse, conceived and executed by Odysseus. When the city has been sacked and the loot distributed, the Greek heroes set sail for home. For a variety of reasons, including a storm sent by the gods, the Greek fleet is scattered, and Odysseus and his contingent of ships are separated from the other Greeks.

Odysseus and his men embark on a series of adventures that form the most famous and intriguing part of the *Odyssey*. There are eleven adventures, which take place over the course of ten years. During this time Odysseus' men die off until only Odysseus himself is left. Some of the adventures are encounters with monsters like the cannibalistic Lastrygonians and the Cyclops. Others are with alluring peoples like the Lotus-Eaters and the pleasure-loving Phaeacians, and still others are with attractive, and attracted, women like the witch Circe, the goddess Calypso, and the lovely young princess Nausicaa.

Between the dangers, the temptations, and the dalliances Odysseus visits Hades, the land of the dead, where he alone among living men meets and talks to the spirits of the dead. Later he alone hears the enchanting song of the Sirens. At long last he returns alone, with the help of Athena, to his native Ithaca. There he discovers that in his prolonged absence 110 local and foreign swains have moved into his house and are courting his wife, Penelope, on the assumption that he has died. She has been stalling them for several years with stratagems of her own but time has run out, and the suitors are about to force her to choose among them.

Odysseus' son Telemachus, a nineteen- or twenty-year-old boy, rages helplessly about the house but can do nothing. A few weeks before Odysseus returns to Ithaca, Telemachus, at the covert urging of Athena, goes off on a journey to glean news of his father, of whom nothing has been heard for ten years. Telemachus visits several old war comrades of his father, including Menelaus and his wife, Helen. Shortly after he returns home, he is reunited with Odysseus, and together the father and the son, with the help of two faithful retainers and Athena, plot to rid the house of the suitors and set things right in Ithaca.

Odysseus successfully reenters his house disguised as a beggar, takes part in a competition to shoot the famous bow of the long-lost Odysseus, and, when he gets his hands on the bow, proceeds, with his son and the two servants, to slaughter all the suitors. He is then reunited with circumspect Penelope, who has remained faithful for the entire two decades of his absence, and with his aged father, who has been living alone and in squalor in the country. In the end Odysseus has gloriously reclaimed his wife, his son, his father, his home, and his kingdom; he has survived, and can recount, the most fascinating series of adventures that any man has ever experienced; and he can look forward to a peaceful old age, a prophesied last adventure in a faraway land, and a death "from the sea."

This is a reasonably accurate, if foreshortened, account of the events of the *Odyssey*, but Homer chose to tell the story another way, not in chronological order. For example, Odysseus tells the bulk of his adventures to the Phaeacians in a long flashback just before they bring him back to Ithaca in their magic boats. Even more fascinating, Homer does not begin his story with Odysseus at all. We do not even meet the hero of the tale until book V. The first four books of the *Odyssey* are centered on Odysseus' son, Telemachus. It is on him that I want to concentrate my remarks.

Picture the situation on Ithaca. Odysseus, the king, has been gone for twenty years, ten of them fighting in Troy, the last ten simply gone. No one has seen him; there are vague rumors that he has been killed or marooned in some faraway place. All the other Greek leaders have returned from Troy. We the readers know that Odysseus is alive and that the day of his homecoming is at hand, but no one on Ithaca knows. Those who knew him best—his wife and close retainers—cannot believe he is dead; they know he is too resourceful, too clever, to be defeated by circumstances. Everyone else in Ithaca—the suitors, the ordinary servants, the citizens of the town—believes that Odysseus is dead after all these years. By refusing to accept this quite reasonable view, by failing to transcend the past and accept the new situation, Penelope has made Ithaca into an ungoverned, faction-ridden, lawless, visibly disintegrating community. This is the setting for Telemachus' adolescence.

A prince, the son of a great hero, Telemachus has no memory of his father, yet his daily life is dominated by the man, or at least by the absence of the man. For the past three years the palace has been taken over by a horde of boisterous men eating, drinking, wenching with the servant girls, insulting Telemachus, while competing for his mother's hand. Telemachus himself can do nothing. He eats and drinks with the suitors but is clearly apart from them.

At the beginning of the *Odyssey*, when the gods are deciding that it is time for Odysseus to return home, Athena turns her thoughts to Telemachus. She says:

> But I will make my way to Ithaka, so that I may
> stir up his son a little, and put some confidence in him
> to summon into assembly the flowing-haired Achaians
> and make a statement to all the suitors, who now forever

slaughter his crowding sheep and lumbering horn-curved cattle;
And I will convey him into Sparta and to sandy Pylos,
to ask after his dear father's homecoming, if he can hear something,
and so that among people he may win a good reputation.

(1.88–95)

This remark, at the beginning of book I of the *Odyssey,* neatly lays out the events of the first four books: in book I Athena visits Telemachus in disguise and persuades him to go off on a voyage seeking news of his father; in book II Telemachus calls an assembly of the citizens of Ithaca, denounces the suitors, and announces his trip; in book III he visits Nestor, king of Pylos; and in book IV he goes on to visit Menelaus and Helen in Sparta. He does to some extent win a good reputation by taking the trip, but, far more important, his experiences on the trip effect in him a transformation, a development toward adulthood that will permit him to play his appropriate role in the stirring events that climax Odysseus' return.

We first see Telemachus in book I when Athena, disguised as an old friend of Odysseus', comes to the palace at Ithaca.

Now far the first to see Athena was godlike Telemachus,
as he sat among the suitors, his heart deep grieving within him,
imagining in his mind his great father, how he might come back
and all throughout the house might cause the suitors to scatter,
and hold his rightful place and be lord of his own possessions.

(1.113–117)

The image of Telemachus, helplessly dreaming of his mighty father come back to right the wrongs of his young life, seems to sum up his adolescence. But Telemachus does not simply miss his father. When the disguised Athena asks if he is the son of Odysseus, he replies,

See, I will accurately answer all that you ask of me.
My mother says indeed I am his. I for my part
do not know. Nobody really knows his own father.
But how I wish I could have been rather son to some fortunate
man, whom old age overtook among his possessions.
But of mortal men, that man has proved the most ill-fated
whose son they say I am: since you question me on this matter.

(1.214–220)

The note of resentment toward his father and whining self-pity for his own predicament gets sharper in his next remark.

My guest, since indeed you are asking me all these questions,
there was a time this house was one that might be prosperous
and above reproach, when a certain man was here in his country.
But now the gods, with evil intention, have willed it otherwise,
And they have caused him to disappear, in a way no other
man has done. I should not have sorrowed so over his dying
if he had gone down among his companions in the land of the Trojans,

. . .

he would have won great fame for himself and his son hereafter.

. . .

Nor is it for him alone that I grieve in my pain now, no longer.
For the gods have inflicted other cares on me.
For all the greatest men who have the power in the islands,

. . .

all these are after my mother for marriage, and wear my house out.
And she does not refuse the fateful marriage, nor is she able
to make an end of the matter, and these eating up my substance
waste it away; and soon they will break me myself into pieces.

(I.231–251)

A little later in the evening, after dinner, the local bard entertains the suitors by singing of the Greeks' bitter homecoming from Troy. Penelope hears the song in her chamber, comes down, and in tears asks the bard to sing some other song, for this one painfully reminds her of her husband who has *not* come home from Troy. At this point Telemachus turns on his mother.

Why, my mother, do you begrudge this excellent singer
his pleasing himself as the thought drives him? It is not the singers
who are to blame, it must be Zeus who is to blame, who gives out
to men who eat bread, to each and all, the way he wills it.
There is nothing wrong in his singing the sad return of the Danaans.
People, surely, always give more applause to that song
which is latest to circulate among the listeners.
So let your heart and let your spirit be hardened to listen.
Odysseus is not the only one who lost his homecoming
day at Troy. There were many others who perished, besides him.
Go therefore back in the house, and take up your own work, the loom
and the distaff, and see to it that your handmaidens
ply their work also; but the men must see to discussion,
all men, but I most of all. For mine is the power in this household.

(I.346–359)

The authentic voice of the late adolescent is unmistakable here, and it is, I think, reassuring to know that twenty-seven hundred years ago it sounded the same as it does today. In any event, after some prodding by Athena, Telemachus rouses himself. The next day he calls the assembly of all Ithacans, and although he has an imposing appearance and makes a fine speech, he can do no more than stand his ground when the suitors threaten and jeer at him. That night he collects supplies and a crew and sneaks off on his journey. He leaves stealthily, fearing not the suitors but his mother, who he correctly perceives will stop him if she knows of his plan to depart.

The trip, though brief and only slightly adventurous, is the first time Telemachus sees the big world that he knew previously just through stories. He meets Nestor, one of the heroes of the Trojan War, an old, pious, garrulous bore who talks about the war, the exploits of Odysseus, and the homecoming of the Greek heroes, especially Agamemnon, who was murdered by Aigisthos, his wife's lover, when he returned in triumph from Troy. With a deplorable lack of tact Nestor even tells Telemachus how Agamemnon's son, Orestes, avenged his father's death by killing Aigisthos. Nestor says,

> But Aigisthos paid for it, in a dismal fashion;
> so it is good, when a man has perished, to have a son left
> after him, since this one took vengeance on his father's killer.

(III. 195–197)

The parallel between Orestes and himself can hardly be lost on Telemachus; but it is one thing to come home in disguise after eight years and assassinate your father's murderer, altogether another to take on 110 armed men who have occupied your house and want to marry your mother.

Telemachus makes friends with one of Nestor's sons who is his own age, and together the two young men go off to Sparta, where they meet fatuous Menelaus and beautiful Helen. At Menelaus' luxurious and elegant palace, Telemachus has his first glimpse of opulence and sophistication. When Menelaus, with the grace of the very wealthy, presents him with some horses, Telemachus politely turns them down, explaining that Ithaca is too small and rocky to provide adequate pasturage for horses; only goats can live on its steep, stony hillsides. Small, provincial, and poor though Ithaca is, however, Telemachus realizes that it is lovely and his home.

Just as Telemachus is preparing to return home, the scene shifts back to Ithaca, where word has spread that Telemachus has left. The suitors respond to the news by plotting to kill him on his way back, and Penelope, his mother, weeps bitter tears. "For if I had heard," she says,

> that he was considering this journey,

> then he would have had to stay, though hastening to his voyage,
> or he would have had to leave me dead in the halls.

> (IV. 732–734)

And a little later as she falls asleep she thinks:

> Now again a beloved son is gone on a hollow
> ship, an innocent all unversed in fighting and speaking,
> and it is for him I grieve even more than for that other one,
> and tremble for him and fear, lest something should happen to him
> either in the country where he has gone, or on the wide sea.

> (IV. 817–821)

   Penelope's groundless fear is the measure of Telemachus' growth. Although he has not yet grown much, he has developed enough maturity to manage the trip and to return safely. When he returns to Ithaca, his father is already there, and when the two are reunited in book XVI, Telemachus becomes his father's major supporter in Odysseus' campaign to reclaim all that is rightfully his. Telemachus' great test comes in book XXII, when he and his father, with the two loyal servants, stand against the suitors.

   Two moments in that climactic confrontation define what Telemachus has and has not achieved. The first comes near the end of the slaughter. The great hall is filled with the bodies of the dead suitors; Odysseus, Telemachus, and the two servants are covered with blood and gore. Phemius, the bard who sang for the suitors, is standing off to the side. Now he throws himself at the feet of Odysseus, clutches him by the knees, and pleads as a suppliant for his life.

> Odysseus. Respect me, have mercy.
>   . . .
>
> Telemachus too, your own dear son will tell you, as I do,
> that it was against my will, and with no desire on my part,
> that I served the suitors. . . .
>
>   . . .
>
> They were too many, and too strong, and they forced me to do it.

> (XXII. 344–353)

Up to this point Odysseus has sternly rejected all pleas for mercy or forgiveness. But now Telemachus, who has so far done whatever his father has asked of him, intercedes:

> So he [the bard] spoke, and prince Telemachus heard him.
> Quickly then he spoke to his father, who stood close by him:

> "Hold fast. Do not strike this man with the bronze. He is innocent.
> And let us spare Medon our herald, a man who has always
> taken care of me when I was a child in your palace."

(XXII.354–360)

Medon, who has been hiding under a chair, comes out and also begs for his life.

> Then resourceful Odysseus smiled upon him and answered:
> "Do not fear. Telemachus has saved you and kept you
>   alive."

(XXII.371–373)

The moment is magical. Scarcely a week before, Telemachus barely managed, for the first time in his life, to stand up to his mother by going away without her permission, and now he stands shoulder to shoulder with his heroic father, a companion in arms, and, most wonderfully of all, he is capable of autonomous judgment with a slight but definite touch of hostility. Odysseus would have killed both men. Telemachus knows this and makes his demand anyway. And Odysseus gives to his son the gift of deferring to that demand. Telemachus has arrived at manhood, and Odysseus acknowledges it.

Yet there are limits to his growth. The second telling moment comes when the killing is done, the house has been cleansed, and Odysseus and Penelope meet again after twenty years. Penelope, who has been sleeping in her room, can hardly believe the servant who tells her that Odysseus has returned and killed the suitors.

> She spoke, and came down from the chamber, her heart pondering
> much, whether to keep away and question her dear husband,
> or to go up to him and kiss his head, taking his hands.
> But then, when she came in and stepped over the stone threshold,
> she sat across from him in the firelight, facing Odysseus,
> by the opposite wall, while he was seated by the tall pillar,
> looking downward, and waiting to find out if his majestic
> wife would have anything to say to him, now that she saw him.
> She sat a long time in silence, and her heart was wondering.
> Sometimes she would look at him, with her eyes full upon him,
> and again would fail to know him in the foul clothing he wore.
> Telemachus spoke to her and called her by name and scolded her:
> "My mother, my harsh mother with the hard heart inside you,
> why do you withdraw so from my father, and do not
> sit beside him and ask him questions and find out about him?
> No other woman, with spirit as stubborn as yours, would keep back,

> *as you are doing from her husband who, after much suffering,*
> *came at last in the twentieth year back to his own country.*
> *But always you have a heart that is harder than stone within you."*

(XXIII.85–103)

Telemachus has gone too far, and for the first time in his life both his parents talk to him. First his mother.

> *Circumspect Penelope said to him in answer:*
> *"My child, the spirit that is in me is full of wonderment,*
> *and I cannot find anything to say to him, nor question him,*
> *nor look him straight in the face. But if he is truly Odysseus,*
> *and he has come home, then we shall find other ways, and better*
> *to recognize each other, for we have signs that we know of*
> *between the two of us only, but they are secret from others."*

(XXIII.105–110)

And Odysseus adds a very mild rebuke.

> *and much-enduring noble Odysseus*
> *smiled and presently spoke in winged words to Telemachus:*
> *"Telemachus, leave your mother to examine me in the palace*
> *as she will, and presently she will understand better."*

(XXIII.111–114)

Telemachus is now a full adult, he is a blooded warrior who has taken lives and granted mercy, but in the presence of his parents' marital intimacy he is still, and will always be, a boy.

There is one further point to make. I have suggested that Telemachus' growth into adulthood crucially begins when he undertakes a journey away from home into the wide world, ostensibly seeking news of his father. I have also suggested that the journey, with its little adventures, is a preview of the great adventures of Odysseus, not yet recounted in Homer's tale—the adventures that have captured the imaginations of readers for more than twenty-five hundred years. But if Telemachus' adventures constitute an adolescent rite of passage in preparation for his adult combat alongside his father, then what do the great adventures of Odysseus constitute?

Let me sketch the outlines of an answer. I begin by noting that Odysseus does not "learn" anything from his adventures in the ordinary sense of the term. He is already an adult when he leaves Troy on his journey home, and he is already prudent, crafty, resourceful, curious, and enduring. He already knows everything that Telemachus starts to learn during his brief journey, and much more besides. In fact, the two journeys are very different from each other. Telemachus' journey is from a narrow, disordered, provincial home out into the world of adult life, a world in which he has to deal with many different people, friends and enemies alike, and difficult situations, requiring him to make choices and take responsibility. When Odysseus undertakes his voyage homeward from Troy, he is fully familiar with and competent in the world into which Telemachus journeys.

By contrast, strangely enough, the world into which Odysseus travels looks very much like the fantasy world of childhood, a world of monsters and marvels, of dangers and temptations, a world that is completely unpredictable. The world that Telemachus ventures into is the world of adults as it appears to adolescents. The world that Odysseus travels through is, in fact, the real world, but a real world that very few of us are privileged to visit. Odysseus' world is much larger than the cut-and-dried realm that Telemachus sees. Telemachus needs self-confidence and experience to negotiate his world. Odysseus needs these qualities in abundance to survive his adventures—but he needs other qualities as well.

Odysseus is fascinated with the real world. He never rejects an opportunity to explore or investigate the new and unknown. The world he explores has a folktale and fantasy quality, as if made for children, and Odysseus requires a childlike quality to explore it. In his adventures he explores the far limits of the world, a dangerous and painful undertaking. In consequence he has come to understand the far limits of himself. The payoff is not in that fantasy land of seductive goddesses and six-headed monsters but right at home in an Ithaca that looks very different to Odysseus than it does to Telemachus.

To Telemachus, Ithaca is home, that familiar place he has always known and has had to leave even to begin to appreciate. To Odysseus, Ithaca is also home, but it is the destination of a very long journey, a prize to win, not a place to take for granted. Moreover, everything Odysseus has done and experienced during his incredible journey turns out to be present in Ithaca as well: the cannibalism, the treachery, the friendship, the love, the monstrous and the beautiful, the need for poetry and the meaning of human existence. Beyond that general recognition there is the tangible, unique reality of Ithaca, poor by the standards of Sparta and Phaeacia but rich in particular, irreplaceable things: Odysseus' house, his dog, his bow, his son, his scar, his wife, their bed, his story and hers—all the contingent, individual things that are his own.

The Greeks called Homer the best and wisest of poets. Among many other things, he seems to have understood that the journey from adolescence to adulthood is, for all its difficulties, just a necessary preparation for the greater journey to come, the journey from adulthood to wisdom.

5 History, Poetry, and Philosophy in Tolstoy's *War and Peace*

Tolstoy's *War and Peace* is both my favorite novel and the novel I most enjoy talking about. Everything about it is big. It has more pages, more characters, and more events than any three normal great novels, and, as if that weren't enough, not one epilogue, but two.

Just as Tolstoy had a pronounced tendency to go to extremes, so have critics of his work. Henry James, a great novelist himself and a great critic of the art of the novel, remarks in "Loose and Baggy Monsters": "A picture without composition slights its most precious chance for beauty, and is moreover not composed at all. The painter knows *how* that principle of health and safety, working as an absolutely premeditated art, has prevailed. There may in its absence be life, incontestably as Tolstoy's *War and Peace* has it; but what does such a loose and baggy monster with its queer elements of the accidental and the arbitrary, artistically mean?"

Few readers take James's adverse judgment of *War and Peace* seriously. His condemnation is usually cited as an example of just how wrong a great artist may be in his judgment of other great artists. It is frequently paired, for example, with Tolstoy's equally wrongheaded and far more savage attack on Shakespeare. The overwhelming consensus is that *War and Peace* is a great novel, probably the greatest written—it is, indeed, almost always included in lists of the ten greatest books. When E. M. Forster wanted to indicate his profound appreciation of Proust's artistic achievement, the highest accolade he could find for *Remembrance of Things Past* was to call it "our second greatest novel"—second, of course, to *War and Peace*.

Yet if most ordinary readers would agree with Forster's estimation of *War and Peace,* critics tend to agree with James's. They are not indisposed toward *War and Peace* so much as they are baffled by it. It is, they grudgingly admit, a delightful book to read, but everything about it is wrong. It has twice as many characters and events as an economical and well-ordered novel ought to have, and yet it lacks the one character every novel has to have—a hero. It is filled with long digressions about Freemasonry, medicine, and military strategy—topics that fascinated Tolstoy but that can hardly be said to titillate most readers. Tolstoy has scattered a great deal of unnecessary factual historical material about the Napoleonic Wars throughout the book, and both within the book and in the second epilogue he spells out a general theory of history and free will. To top it off, the omniscient narrator of the novel is a garrulous and opinionated, though genial, old moralist who insists upon telling us at every possible juncture exactly why Napoleon was no genius, why Moscow is a better place to live than Saint Petersburg, and why fathers should not take their innocent young daughters to improperly chaperoned parties.

No ordinary novel could survive these or the many other defects that abound, yet *War and Peace* flourishes on them. Is it any wonder that the critics, in their frustration, either adopt a querulous tone like Henry James's or gush about how the novel is like life itself and thus transcends the usual critical canons?

It is my hope, not to find a compromise between the critical extremes, but to combine them into a coherent viewpoint. I have every intention of praising *War and Peace* as our greatest novel, but I want to do so on the basis of sound critical analysis, not sentimental outpourings. I shall take as the text of the critical sermon I am going to preach a famous remark of Aristotle's. In his *Poetics* he says, "Poetry is something more philosophic and of graver import than history" (9.1451b6). Aristotle thus locates poetry, or art, between history and philosophy.

I shall argue that *War and Peace* achieves such magnitude that it expands beyond the normal limits of art to encompass within itself both history and philosophy. But that is the end of my story; let me begin by considering *War and Peace* as art in the conventional sense—with a discussion of Tolstoy's artistry, starting with the overall plot and gradually working down to the smaller parts and technical details.

Most critics have a good deal of trouble perceiving the dramatic center of *War and Peace.* They tend to describe it in one of two ways: either the novel is the story of the Napoleonic invasion of Russia in 1812, or it is the story of one or another of the major characters, Pierre and Natasha being the favorite choices. Neither view seems adequate to the novel as a whole. The Napoleonic invasion of Russia, despite its importance for the story, doesn't begin until the novel is half over. And even though Pierre and Natasha are very important figures, neither of them bulks large enough to be considered the hero of the work. The book is not a national epic, nor is it the story of an individual.

This does not mean that the novel has no plot. It does, but it is a plot unique in literature. I propose the following formulation. *War and Peace* deals primarily with the unfolding and interrelated destinies of *five* dominant characters: Pierre, Natasha, Andrew, Mary, and Nicholas. We must understand the fate of each of the five as essentially affecting and being affected by the other four. There are not five stories, but one story of five tightly connected individuals. Not only does each character interact with each of the other four, but Tolstoy has with consummate skill managed to contrast dramatically each of the five with all of the others.

Many artists have written works with a double plot or a double protagonist. Thackeray did in *Vanity Fair* with contrasting stories of Becky Sharp and Amelia Sedley; Shakespeare did in *Antony and Cleopatra;* and Tolstoy himself, in *Anna Karenina,* tried his hand at a double plot built around the contrasting stories of two balanced characters, Anna and Levin. But in *War and Peace* he outdid himself by producing a quintuple protagonist.

War and Peace is divided into four major parts. The first part, which consists of the first three sections of the novel, covers the period from the summer of 1805, when Russia first goes to war with Napoleon, through December of that year, when the Russian army is destroyed at the battle of Austerlitz. This first part might be titled "Beginnings," for in it the five protagonists are launched. The novel begins with each character poised on the brink of a career. They are of different ages and are about to take different paths in life, so the parallels between them are neither obvious nor mechanical.

At the start Pierre is a young man of twenty-one vaguely looking for a career. The illegitimate son of a nobleman, he is a charming, passionate, bumbling liberal intellectual. By December 1805 he has inherited his father's fortune and title and been willingly shoved into a disastrous marriage with the beautiful Helene.

In sharp contrast to Pierre is his friend Andrew, a brilliant, sophisticated, enormously talented and ambitious man of twenty-seven. Andrew is married to a woman whom he has already ceased to love when the story opens. For him, life begins with his decision to go off to war in search of fame and honor. When the battle of Austerlitz ends, Andrew lies wounded and perhaps dying on the battlefield.

Thirteen-year-old Natasha is on the verge of her career as a passionate and active woman. Characteristically, she first appears when she bursts into the room where adults are chatting. Just as characteristically, she is laughing uncontrollably and being followed by a young man, Boris, her first conquest, whom she shortly thereafter kisses and promises to marry.

Her eighteen-year-old brother Nicholas is a passionate, romantic young man about to leave for the army and a military career. Six months later he has been thoroughly indoctrinated into the military life, has been in combat several times, has been wounded, and has suffered the double disillusionment of seeing the Russian army destroyed and his beloved Emperor Alexander retreating like an ordinary human being.

Meanwhile, Andrew's sister, Mary, lives a quiet, miserable life of religious devotion and filial duty in the country. Intelligent, clumsy, innocent, moral, and, in her way, beautiful, Mary is confirmed in this life by the brief but disastrous courtship of Anatole Kuragin, a degenerate rake who cannot keep his hands off Mary's French companion.

During the same period of time Russia enters violently into the life of Europe and suffers a violent defeat. In a sense, then, this whole first part details nothing but false starts, for neither the individual characters nor Russia will succeed so long as they continue to act as they have done so far. Yet each protagonist has taken an irrevocable step and set in motion a train of incidents that will eventually lead to the fully successful climax and conclusion; but success will require radical changes in everyone's point of view and way of life. All, including Russia, must suffer a great deal before the destinies they have begun to work out will be achieved.

The second major part of the novel covers the period from just after the battle of Austerlitz to the end of 1811, right before Napoleon invades Russia. Through these seven years everything proceeds in fits and starts from bad to worse. Nicholas plays the man-about-town, gets involved with Dolokhov, loses forty-three thousand rubles, returns to the army, is disillusioned, tries his hand at running the family estates, and finally retreats back into the army as the Rostov family fortune declines further.

Andrew returns from Austerlitz determined to make his marriage work, but he arrives home only to see his wife die in childbirth. Immersing himself in the country for years thereafter, he is gradually brought out of his depression by speaking with his friend Pierre and by overhearing Natasha and her cousin Sonia talking at night. He goes to Petersburg, enters politics, and meets and falls in love with Natasha. He leaves her to recuperate from his old battle wound and then is shattered by the news of her attempted elopement with Anatole Kuragin.

During the same period Natasha grows into a woman, winning proposals first from Denisov, then from Boris again, and finally from Andrew. Left alone by Andrew at exactly the moment when she needs to be a wife and mother, she falls for Anatole, tries to elope but fails, tries to commit suicide but fails, and ultimately is saved from complete despair by Pierre's declaration of love.

During these years Pierre, gradually disillusioned in his marriage, is provoked into a pointless duel with Dolokhov. He separates from Helene in remorse at having almost killed a man, retreats into Freemasonry and typically vague attempts to do good, slowly settles into an existence as a worthless man-about-town, and finally, in a desperate attempt to save Natasha's life, declares his utterly hopeless love for her.

Mary continues to suffer under her father's tyranny, giving herself more and more to a religious devotion she does not quite believe in and slowly turning into a rigid spinster strikingly like her father.

Russia, meanwhile, engages in a number of indecisive battles with Napoleon and then concludes an insincere peace. By the end of 1811, at the midpoint of the novel, all five of the human protagonists have, like Russia, come to rest at a low point of misery, helplessness, bafflement, and despair. All are deeply frustrated, and none seems able to work his or her way out of difficulty and hopelessness. Life appears to have ended in failure for all of them—although the portentous comet of 1812 suggests differently.

In the third part of the book the storm of the Napoleonic invasion breaks over Russia and engulfs our protagonists. Whereas the first two parts of the novel are the complication of the plot, this part and the next are the denouement. Specifically, the third part is the climax, the part in which historical events meet and coalesce with the small, personal events that constitute the private lives of our protagonists. In this merging of the historical macrocosm with the personal microcosm, both Russia and our heroes find themselves and their destinies through suffering and defeat.

The third part starts with Napoleon's invasion, which changes the course of everyone's life. The first climax is at the battle of Borodino, where Andrew is mortally wounded, as is Napoleon's army, although at the time no one, including the French army, is aware of it. The second climax is at the burning of Moscow, when the Rostov fortune is finally destroyed, although Andrew and Natasha are briefly reunited, and Pierre, on his way to assassinate Napoleon, stops to rescue a child from a burning building and is arrested as an incendiary.

In the fourth and final part of the novel, the appearance of events begins to catch up with the inner reality. Nicholas and Mary, having met during the Russian retreat, meet again and cement their relationship. Pierre faces death, meets Platon Karatayev, and, during the French retreat from Moscow, comes for the first time to a firm grasp of life. Together Natasha and Mary watch Andrew die. When Natasha hears the news of her brother Petya's death, her vitality, her enormous capacity for suffering and sympathy, saves her mother's sanity and life. Meanwhile, the French retreat becomes a rout, and thus both Russia and the five protagonists are purified.

In the first epilogue, which takes place eight years later, the remaining loose ends are tied up. After some difficulties Nicholas and Mary, and Natasha and Pierre, are married, settle down, and have children.

This is what happens in *War and Peace*. Tolstoy has shown us a diverse group of characters during the critical period in their lives—the time between youthful immaturity with all its vagueness, potentiality, and indetermination, and full maturity, which is marked by the determination, if not yet the fulfillment, of one's personal destiny. Life with its joys and sorrows is not over for Natasha and Pierre, for Nicholas and Mary, at the end of the first epilogue, but key choices and events are clearly in the past.

At the end of the novel the five protagonists are in the same situation vis-à-vis their children as their parents were in relation to them at the beginning. In the interim, everything has changed: individuals have grown up, loved, suffered, learned, and died; families have lost and recouped their fortunes, dissolved, and merged; historical events have come crashing down and ebbed away. For those who did not live through the events, who did not share these people's lives, what happened can never be more than a tale, can never be really understood. But young Nicholas Bolkonski, Andrew's adolescent son, sits quietly listening to the recollections of his elders and vows that he, too, will one day do great things. So the epilogue is not the end of the story of our five friends; it is the beginning of the story of young Nicholas.

In this part-by-part account of the novel I have sketched what might be called its plot to show the discernible and, to quote Henry James, absolutely premeditated art at work here. By that art the immensely complex characters and situations are shaped into a unified composition. The trouble with Tolstoy is not that he produced a loose and baggy monster full of queer elements of the accidental and the arbitrary but that he worked on such a monumental scale that most readers do not consciously perceive the extraordinary precision and artistic discipline with which the novel was composed—but every reader feels that composition subliminally.

Structurally, *War and Peace* is to an ordinary great novel, like *Madame Bovary*, what Aeschylus' *Oresteia* is to one of Ibsen's tragedies. There is nothing wrong with *Ghosts* or *Enemy of the People;* they are brilliant plays. But viewed from the limited dramatic perspective of a well-made nineteenth-century play, the *Oresteia* can hardly fail to look primitive, sprawling, and uneconomical. My point is that Tolstoy conceived and composed a novel on an unprecedented scale in both size and complexity. And here lies some of the explanation for the divergence between the baffled judgment of the critics and the enthusiastic response of most readers. Tolstoy's structure does not need to be perceived intellectually to be effective. On the contrary, it functions most efficiently on the level of emotional affect. The complex interweaving of lives creates a sense of coherence that most readers feel with exhilaration, and this feeling represents a more accurate perception of Tolstoy's intention than the critics' inability to see a conventional plot or identify a conventional hero.

The discrepancy between emotional response and intellectual analysis is one of the pervasive features of *War and Peace*. At almost every level, there is a peculiar disjunction between thought and feeling. Intellectually we are constantly confused, distracted, or insulted by the novel while emotionally we are deeply and delightfully involved in it. This effect is what has led critics to talk of the work as a direct representation of life, as if Tolstoy were some sort of idiot savant who managed to write the world's greatest novel without having the slightest understanding of what a novel is or how it should be put together. As I have tried to show with respect to its overall architecture, that is simply not true—no novel is more artfully composed than *War and Peace*.

Nevertheless, it *is* true that Tolstoy's artistry is not very evident in the work. In reading *Madame Bovary,* by contrast, one is always aware of reading a great novel and, beyond that, of being in the hands of a great artist who has skillfully arranged and manipulated characters and events to achieve exceedingly precise and subtle effects. It is, I think, one of Tolstoy's most admirable artistic achievements in *War and Peace* that he is able to efface his own presence in the novel to such an extent that the work seems to achieve its effects without the help of a guiding hand, or perhaps even despite the presence of that unlettered genius. *War and Peace* is so artfully composed that ordinary readers and learned critics alike find it artless.

This artful artlessness is difficult to penetrate because Tolstoy has covered his tracks so well. But once we look, the full range of Tolstoy's astounding artistic skill becomes apparent. A stage magician chats constantly to the audience, explaining what he has done, telling them what he is going to do, carefully and rather obviously directing their attention, thus creating the image of a pleasant, reasonably competent, not too bright performer. Meanwhile, his hands flutter about vaguely and almost imperceptibly, and astounding things keep happening almost as if by accident or of their own accord. Rabbits and bowls of goldfish appear out of hats, beautiful ladies appear and disappear, dogs talk, empty glass jars produce buckets of gold coins. So it is with Tolstoy. Let me illustrate what I mean with a few examples from the early parts of the novel.

The opening section consists of three sequential episodes: an evening in Petersburg, a name-day party in Moscow, and Andrew's visit to his father's home in the country, where he says good-bye to his wife before heading off to the army. I have already described what happens during these episodes. Let us now consider what Tolstoy is doing behind the facade of events: establishing his characters—with only one or two exceptions, every major character in the entire book is presented to the reader in these first scenes—and rendering certain settings that are crucial for the novel, Petersburg, Moscow, and the country-side.

The distinct qualities of Petersburg and Moscow are established largely in contrast to each other, and both together serve as a contrast to life in the country. Petersburg and Moscow are cast into relief by the parties held there: the evening at Anna Pavlovna's, with which the novel opens, and the name-day party at the Rostovs'. Both parties are dominated by talk of Napoleon and the impending war. But everything else is different. At Anna Pavlovna's party the nobles and bureaucrats who run Russia gossip excitedly about Napoleon's terrible crimes, the health of the empress, and phony schemes for establishing universal peace. The talk is clever, the women are beautiful, the atmosphere is sophisticated. The spirit of the party is captured by the mechanical image of a spinning mill with the hostess as the plant overseer who keeps it running smoothly. Just how mechanical and artificial Anna Pavlovna's soirée is becomes apparent when the scene shifts to Moscow.

The Rostovs' guests are not particularly important people; they are friends, relatives, and acquaintances. Although the talk here, too, is of Napoleon and the war, the quality of the talk is altogether different from the chatter in Petersburg, because these people have a direct stake in the war. Boris and Nicholas and Berg are going off to fight, perhaps to die, and they leave behind parents, brothers, sisters, and sweethearts. More than that, children and young people dominate the party.

Not everybody at Anna Pavlovna's party is the same age, but the generational differences in Petersburg are not important, whereas in Moscow they are. In Petersburg the mechanical and unnatural quality of social life is accented by Pierre, who is so naive that he actually attempts a serious discussion in which he expresses his own genuine opinions. Anna Pavlovna has to work very hard to shut him up and smooth over the disruption he causes. In Moscow, by contrast, the party comes alive exactly at the moment when the children, led by Natasha, break in on the gossiping adults.

In Petersburg, policy is made and decisions are reached that affect the whole of Russia, yet life there is superficial, trivial, and finally of no consequence. In Moscow, on the other hand, no one has much power, yet these are the people who actually do things. They enjoy themselves, as apparently no one in Petersburg knows how to do, and they also seem capable of suffering. Petersburg people give orders and Muscovites obey them, but when the battles are fought, Muscovites are the ones who fight them. In Petersburg patriotism is the latest fashion; in Moscow patriotism is a matter of life and death and honor. Petersburg is permeated by French culture; Moscow has a strong grain of native Russian culture beneath the thin veneer of French affectation.

All this information emerges in the implicit contrast between the two parties, a contrast that Tolstoy never makes explicit. The whole destiny of Russia and of the five protagonists is tied up in the difference between the cities. Furthermore, the opening scenes show that it matters whether a particular event takes place in Moscow or Petersburg. It is no accident, for example, that the ill-fated love of Natasha and Andrew begins in Petersburg—that city seems innately hostile to all genuine human feeling.

Some of the crucial elements of Tolstoy's theory of power and authority are part of the contrast between the cities. The theory, explicitly developed later in the book, posits that power and authority are inversely proportional, that as one's authority increases, one's actual ability to do anything decreases, and vice versa. Tolstoy embodies the theory in the contrast between the cities long before he ever mentions it explicitly. This is true of every other theory he develops in the course of the novel, including his theory of history and free will, treated in the second epilogue.

The countryside is represented in the first section of the novel by Andrew's home, Bald Hills. Compared to Bald Hills, life even in Moscow seems rather stilted and artificial. Only at Bald Hills is talk about the war completely honest, direct, and informed. And as with the overall strategy of the war, so also with its personal implications: only at Bald Hills when Andrew talks with his father and sister does anyone mention the possibility that in going off to war a man might get killed. Even the best of cities, Moscow, cannot compare to the countryside.

Taken together, Petersburg, Moscow, and Bald Hills constitute geographical Russia. But Russia is also composed of families, and each locale has it own characteristic family. Tolstoy's skill is perhaps nowhere so evident as in his portrayal of families. He manages to give each family a distinctive quality that both binds its members together and differentiates and individualizes them. Tolstoy is famous for creating three-dimensional characters, and much of his success is due to his ability to locate each character within the matrix of a family.

In Petersburg the Kuragins are the characteristic family. If nothing else was wrong with the capital city, that would be enough to condemn it. Prince Vasili, the father, is a high government official—poised, influential, sentimental, and corrupt (the mother has only the shadowiest kind of existence). His daughter, "the beautiful Helene," has nothing whatever to say. Of the two sons, Hippolyte and Anatole, one is an unpleasant imbecile and the other a notorious rake. The very success of Helene, Hippolyte, and Anatole in Petersburg society is suggestive of the corruption at the center of authority.

The full extent of the Kuragins' immorality emerges during the novel, but in these opening scenes in Petersburg something of their nature can be perceived. The Kuragins could almost be described as a family only in the biological sense, since they have no genuine family life, and not once in the entire novel are they shown together as a family. Beyond a veiled hint of an incestuous relationship between Anatole and Helene, love and family affection are absent. Most significantly, there are no children in the Kuragin family. Tolstoy even hints that Helene dies of an attempted abortion.

In contrast to the Kuragins are the Rostovs, appropriately associated with Moscow, the old and holy and true capital, the ultimate objective of Napoleon's invasion, the Russian city *par excellence*. Their qualities as a family—their gaiety, spontaneity, naturalness, and lack of sophistication—match their city of residence. The Rostov household is filled with children, ranging from Petya, who is still a child, to Vera, who is on the verge of marriage. Between them are Natasha and Nicholas. The Rostovs are a family in the full sense—they share not only a common way of life but that bond of understanding and sympathy peculiar to a family.

Tolstoy, however, makes no attempt to idealize the Rostovs. On the contrary, their shortcomings and problems are almost painfully emphasized. Vera, the oldest, is a failure as a person; Natasha is spoiled by her father, and Nicholas by his mother; the count is a weak, ineffectual man; and the countess has neither the desire nor the strength to become the family authority. But the Rostovs do have an extraordinary capacity for feeling both joy and misery. They may not be particularly intelligent, but they know how to live.

The Bolkonskis stand apart from both the Rostovs and the Kuragins. Andrew, Mary, and the old prince are torn apart by the deepest possible antagonisms: Mary is a devout Christian, Andrew a freethinking admirer of Napoleon and all he stands for, and the old prince a skeptical, caustic man of the Enlightenment. They agree on almost nothing, yet they, like the Rostovs, constitute a genuine family, and each of them displays the Bolkonski character. They are all intelligent, obstinate, and strong-willed, each holding powerful convictions. Beyond this, however, there are the strongest bonds of mutual love and respect between them, although they are all quite incapable of expressing their feelings with anything like the spontaneity and naturalness of the Rostovs. The constant tensions and lacerations of their relationships are, paradoxically, the strongest possible sign of the genuine affection they have for each other. Living in the country as the old prince does, he is isolated both from the center of authority in Petersburg and from the typically Russian life of Moscow. Individuality, independence, and isolation are the trademarks of the Bolkonskis.

Pierre, the last of the protagonists, has no family, and this is perhaps his main characteristic. Unlike the others, Pierre has no place of his own. He lives in a vague world of female cousins, servants, and friends. Tolstoy emphasizes Pierre's lack of a solid human context. He is an illegitimate son who has never really known his father. Pierre was reared abroad, and when he inherits his father's wealth, he is no less isolated than before. Only Pierre's inner life, his hopes, ambitions, ideas, and dreams, has solidity. His external life lacks the concreteness that only a genuine family can give it. Because of his wealth and his lack of family ties, Pierre is freer than any of the other major characters. His decisions and actions affect only himself, and he need not take anyone else into account.

By establishing Pierre as a man without a family, Tolstoy contrasts, on the one hand, the emptiness of Pierre's life with the fullness of the others' and, on the other hand, his freedom from obligations to the others' immersion in them. When Andrew goes off to war, he leaves behind an unloved, frightened, pregnant wife who dies in childbirth. The remorse that Andrew suffers later is of a kind that Pierre in his freedom can never know. Such feelings are both the price and the privilege of having a family.

Let me turn now to the section of the novel in which the Russian army arrives in Austria. Nicholas sees his first action when the Russian rear guard burns the bridge over the River Enns; Andrew is sent on a diplomatic mission to the Austrian court; and both Nicholas and Andrew take part in the battle of Schon Graben, where Nicholas is slightly wounded. This second section of the novel is totally devoted to the army. It now becomes apparent that the first section, with its emphasis on parties, localities, and families, is an introduction to Peace, whereas the second section introduces the mysteries of War. Together, they define the basic polarity of the novel. If spatial location, whether in a particular place or within the matrix of a family, is the key to understanding the peaceful life, time and movement are the essence of war.

To an army, spatial location is a matter of indifference; for the soldiers the only difference between Russia and Austria is that the buildings, fences, and gardens look a little different. Tolstoy initiates readers into the nature of war step by step. We first see the army preparing for inspection after marching all day. Orders arrive to prepare for a review the following day. The soldiers stay up all night polishing and cleaning for the review, only to discover that General Kutuzov wants them to look ragged and ill-kempt so that he will have an excuse not to join forces with the Austrians. Because such snafus are typical of an army under the best of circumstances, we can begin to imagine what mistakes will be made in battle.

The next incident concerns Nicholas and his quarrel with the quartermaster Telyannin over a missing purse. Telyannin has apparently stolen the money, and Nicholas, to protect his own honor, unthinkingly accuses him of theft. When the colonel tries to hush up the affair, Nicholas is further insulted. Only later, through a heated argument with his fellow officers, does he learn that in the army honor belongs to the regiment, not to the individual.

Tolstoy next introduces us to war itself. He does so by way of an incident of almost no military significance—the burning of the bridge across the River

Enns. Typically, the bridge was not burned when it was supposed to be, so Nicholas's company is ordered to burn it while they are under fire from the French artillery.

The entire Tolstoyan theory of battle is dramatically rendered in this tiny scene. We experience the immense human gap between the generals on the hills in the rear who watch the action, and the men under fire in the valley below who perform it. We feel—with Nicholas—the psychological effect of knowing that the fellows across the field are trying to kill you even though you have never met them and even though they don't know who you are—and even though your mother and everyone else who knows you loves you. We discover the utter impossibility of knowing what actually happens during a battle, and we see the falsification that occurs later. In this minuscule episode one Russian hussar is killed and two are wounded; in comparison, at the historically decisive battle of Borodino there are fifty thousand casualties. Yet both are equally battles, and the truth of them is the same. Tolstoy's theory of battle is dramatically established here long before he starts delivering explicit lectures on it later.

In *War and Peace* the same kind of artistic control and economy govern the handling of the small incidents—and even the language used to describe them—as determine the overarching form of the novel. This is true even on the level of individual images and similes. During the battle of Schon Graben, for example, Nicholas' horse is shot from under him. When he regains his feet in the middle of a field and sees the French infantry coming toward him, he turns and runs "with the feeling of a hare fleeing from the hounds." Several years later, during the wolf hunt, Nicholas and two of his neighbors set their borzois onto a hare. Like Nicholas at Schon Graben, the hare does not realize his danger at first, but when he does he "laid back his ears and rushed off headlong." Later, during the French invasion of 1812, Nicholas leads a small cavalry charge in which he knocks a French officer off his horse. With one foot caught in a stirrup the unfortunate officer hops about helplessly with a terrified look in his eyes until Nicholas captures him.

In the course of the book, then, Nicholas runs from the French like a hare from the hounds, then sets his hounds on a hare during a hunt, and finally plays the part of a successful hound in capturing a French officer. Nicholas is vaguely disturbed and dissatisfied by this last incident, for which he is awarded a medal. When he gets to be a hero, it doesn't quite meet his expectations. Nicholas never figures out why he is upset; but by the use of the recurrent image Tolstoy poetically demonstrates that it is not pleasant to play the hound once you have been cast in the role of the hare. Furthermore, at this point he shatters the basic distinction between War and Peace, because there is now no human difference between a peacetime hunt and a wartime cavalry charge. Generally speaking, this merging of the previously distinct realms of War and Peace character-izes the whole Napoleonic invasion of Russia, when the earlier settings of peace become the battlegrounds of war.

Taken together, the complex presentation of settings, families, and images provides the context for the story of Andrew, Natasha, Pierre, Mary, and Nicholas. In the language of criticism that context is frequently called epic. But the epic of *War and Peace* is unusual not simply in magnitude but also in quality, for Tolstoy takes as background the history of the period in which the story oc-curs. More than that, he insists, over and over again, that his novelistic version of that history is truer than the version of any professional historian, whether French or Russian.

This claim is a strange one and requires special attention. Tolstoy appar-ently did a great deal of historical research in preparation for writing *War and Peace*. The foundation of his often-repeated claim that his novel tells the truth about what happened is his theory of history, presented in bits and pieces throughout the book and given a systematic statement in the second epilogue.

Basically Tolstoy's theory consists of a radical denial of human free will in favor of an iron determinism. Free will is an illusion, however necessary for hu-man consciousness. Events are simply the vector sums of preceding events. Tol-stoy takes pains to deny the "great man" theory of history—the theory that cer-tain important individuals decisively affect the course of events. He also insists that no individual—not the tsar and not Napoleon—is more powerful than anyone else, that power is simply the sum total of the actions of individuals. In effect, Tolstoy radically denies the reality of the large-scale historical events usually treated by historians. Such events, he claims, are fictions that historians have created. The so-called great historical events must be resolved into an infinity of infinitesimal events. By depicting a large, representative sample of infinitesimal events, such as the actions of Pierre and Andrew at the battle of Borodino, Tolstoy can, he claims, tell the truth about what really happened on that battlefield and can dismiss the historians' researched studies of French and Russian strategy as fabrications. The trouble with this claim is that Pierre and Andrew are themselves fictitious characters. Common sense might suggest that one cannot use fictitious characters and events to prove that the profes-sional historians do not comprehend history. Yet that is exactly what Tolstoy does.

To understand Tolstoy's claim to historical truth we need to look a little more closely at three features of his theory of history and examine what he ac-tually does in the novel. First, the theory of history is all-encompassing; it ap-plies to peacetime as well as wartime and to purely private human acts as well as larger events. Thus, if Napoleon's defeat was inevitable, so, too, was Pierre's marriage to Helene, and Natasha's attempted elopement with Anatole.

Second, in treating large-scale historical events as nothing more than the sum total of all the individual events that make them up, Tolstoy is in fact denying the intelligibility of the large-scale events. He believes that there was no such thing as the battle of Borodino, only an immense number of acts by individual men that occurred at that place on that day.

Third, Tolstoy implies that although there are no great men who shape and cause great events, there are genuine heroes. No one man can control a multitude of other men. But, Tolstoy shows, whenever the issue is in doubt in an armed conflict between two more or less evenly balanced groups of men, the slightest difference in the behavior of even one man, if he is in exactly the right place, can change the final outcome. If the man suddenly shouts, "Look out, we're surrounded," he may touch off a panic that leads to utter defeat, like the one the Russians suffered at Austerlitz. But if he shouts, "Hurrah, boys, follow me," he may spark a charge that unexpectedly overwhelms the enemy.

There is, however, one serious difficulty with respect to a hero. Because of the chaotic and rapidly changing conditions of a battlefield, no one ever knows who the hero of a battle is or even that a man behaved heroically. Even the hero is inevitably ignorant of the role that he plays in the battle. And as we might expect, given Tolstoy's delight in deflating great men, he deliberately picks heroes who don't look the part.

At the battle of Schön Graben, for example, there is a modest little captain of artillery named Tushin. When the battle begins, Tushin's infantry support is withdrawn, but because the French assume that an artillery battery will not remain in place without such support, they do not attack. Tushin meanwhile fires on the French without orders and gets caught up in commanding his men, aiming his guns, and puffing on his pipe. Tolstoy says that Tushin does what many men in physical danger do: he constructs a little fantasy in which his cannon become pipes, and each time they fire, it is as if he is taking a puff. The result of Tushin's absorption in his fantasy is that the French, despite their enormous superiority in numbers, are held up for several hours by Tushin, allowing the bulk of the Russians to withdraw. That evening, after the battle, Tushin is reprimanded by the general for abandoning some of his guns, and Tushin himself is embarrassed by what he thinks was his failure to do his duty.

The role of Tushin, the secret hero of Schön Graben, foreshadows Tolstoy's version of the battle of Borodino. Long before the battle, Pierre has been playing anagrams with his name and has discovered that its numerical value is 666, the same as Napoleon's. He thus believes that he is destined to destroy Napoleon. Later, when the battle of Borodino is being prepared for, Pierre accompanies the army for no particular reason. On the day of the battle he wanders around looking for the battle. Not knowing what a battle looks like, he never quite finds it. However, in the course of his search he comes to the Raevski redoubt and stays there for some time, being accepted by the soldiers as a kind of mascot. Later he leaves, and that is all that happens.

Tolstoy's own large-scale narrative account of the entire battle is very strange. He quarrels with all military historians by asserting that the key to the battle was the Raevski redoubt and the French inability to take it. He insists, against all military tradition, that even though the Russians retreated after the battle, the victory was nevertheless theirs, that even though the French army continued to advance on Moscow, after Borodino it was a mortally wounded beast.

The inference is clear. Pierre Beshukov, the bumbling civilian who ambled about looking for the battle, was the secret hero of Borodino, that slight boost to Russian morale at the critical point in the battle that tipped the balance. Pierre never knows, not even the historians know, that the Raevski redoubt was the center of the battle, and most people, including the Russians, don't know that the French didn't win the battle. Still, their army never recovered, and the invasion of Russia turned into a disaster for Napoleon, a disaster from which *he* never recovered. Thus Tolstoy claims in his deeply hidden way that Pierre did have the beast's number, he did destroy Napoleon!

But, you may complain, isn't the whole notion of a hero, secret or otherwise, self-contradictory from Tolstoy's point of view? He argues that the outcome of the battle was the vector sum of individual acts. Every participant played a part, and the result was inevitable from the beginning. That may be true, but if so, then the battle, along with all other events, loses its human meaning, for each event merely follows necessarily from the preceding one. This, at any rate, is what the theory of history seems to imply.

If the theory implies that all events are merely consequences of prior events, and therefore no event has any more or less meaning than any other, the novel most emphatically does *not* exemplify the theory. Every sensitive reader agrees that one of the glories of the novel is the luminous human meaning and significance that Tolstoy infuses into particular events. The theory, like all the other devices employed by Tolstoy is just that, a device—in this case, a device by means of which he can invest the events of his novel with the strict necessity and epic proportions they require.

Let us look again at the battle of Borodino and ask what happened there. Pierre may well have played a role in the destruction of Napoleon, but that is hardly the most important occurrence. Far more important is the conversion of Prince Andrew to the Christian love of God and man. The conversion is prepared with meticulous care: ever since Andrew saw the sky as he lay wounded after the battle of Austerlitz, he has seemed destined for some sort of transcendent vision. Yet every major event of his life after that serves mainly to reinforce and strengthen his native skepticism and cynicism. The culmination of this series of events is the affair between Natasha and Anatole. When he discovers it, Andrew abandons his plans and reenters the army determined to find Anatole and kill him in a duel. He waits patiently for his opportunity, and during the battle of Borodino, while his regiment is in reserve, he is mortally wounded. Taken to the hospital tent to be operated on, he looks over at the next operating table and sees Anatole Kuragin having his leg amputated. Because of the pain and the fever, it takes Andrew some time to recognize him. But then "he remembered everything, and ecstatic pity and love for the man overflowed his happy heart. Prince Andrew could no longer restrain himself and wept tender loving tears for his fellow men, for himself and for his own and their errors. Compassion, love of our brothers, for those who hate us, love of our enemies; yes, that love which God preached on earth and which Princess Mary taught me and I did not understand. . . . I know it."

The conversion of Andrew is, by ordinary standards, wholly improbable, not to say impossible. Furthermore, it occurs through the most outrageous coincidence. Yet anything less miraculous would not have produced Andrew's conversion. How does an author make a miracle probable? Aren't miracles intrinsically improbable? Of course they are, except in a world where every single incident is said to be a necessary consequence of innumerable prior incidents. In such a world, no event is more or less probable than another; every event is absolutely necessary. Tolstoy uses the theory of history to make Andrew's conversion probable. He deliberately picks Borodino, the climactic event of his history of Napoleon's invasion, as the setting for Andrew's conversion to Christianity. Only a historical event of that magnitude would provide a suitable context for Andrew's discovery, and at no other time is the web of necessity felt more tightly than at that moment.

The significant *human* truth about the battle of Borodino is that it is the setting for Andrew's conversion to Christianity. Against that truth, the discovery that the battle marks the beginning of the end of Napoleon Bonaparte fades into insignificance. What is true of Andrew in relation to the battle of Borodino is also true of Mary in relation to the devastation of Russia during the advance of Napoleon's army, of Natasha in relation to the burning of Moscow, of Pierre in relation to the retreat of the French from Moscow, and of Nicholas in relation to the patience and fortitude of the Russian army in defense of the homeland.

So it is that ultimately Tolstoy's story achieves a truth that encompasses and transcends history. History is the realm of change, of transience, of mortality. *War and Peace* is historical in that Tolstoy tells the story of how five people together found their destiny. But Tolstoy has not just told the story of what happened to those people at that time, of the changes that occurred; behind the constant changes and supporting them he has rendered the fabric, the context, of human life, unchanged and eternal. In taking on permanence as well as change, his poetry encompasses philosophy.

6 Tolstoy's *Anna Karenina*

In *The Craft of Fiction,* Percy Lubbock remarks that *Anna Karenina* is almost completely dramatic in presentation, that it is composed of a multitude of dramatic moments with minimal direct narration of events. In fact, the novel is divided into about 250 chapters, some no more than three or four pages long. Each of these chapters, or dramatic moments, has the character of a complete and unified whole, even if it portrays only a portion of an event or conversation that extends over several such chapters. These dramatic moments are the building blocks of the novel. Tolstoy so arranges them that they form clusters or groups, each of which constitutes a larger episode in the development of the action. The larger episodes are themselves grouped together into the eight major parts of the work. I shall return to the arrangement and interrelations of the parts, but for the present, I wish to concentrate on Tolstoy's handling of his smallest units, the dramatic moments.

Whatever else one may think of the novel, it seems to me almost inconceivable that a sensitive reader would not feel the genius with which Tolstoy has rendered the individual scenes. Clearly, all the vignettes are not on the same level dramatically; some are more intense and of greater importance than others. But almost any chapter chosen at random will repay a thoughtful rereading by taking on new depth and luminosity.

Among the most beautiful, though not necessarily most significant, scenes in the book are the following: chapter 22 of part I, in which Kitty arrives at the ball glowing with beauty because of her love for Vronsky and is crushed with shame when he fails to respond to her; chapter 4 of part III, in which Levin joins the peasants in mowing the fields in order to work off the frustration he feels toward his brother, and gradually becomes absorbed in the labor; chapter 4 of part V, which records, seemingly at random, the comments of the spectators at Kitty and Levin's wedding.

I have tried to analyze how Tolstoy achieves his effects in scenes such as these, and I must confess that I have no clear or adequate answers. He does employ several devices in a variety of ways throughout the novel. First, and perhaps most obvious, is his use of a shifting point of view. There is not, I believe, a single scene in the entire novel that is technically dramatic in the sense that the author is himself silent and that only his characters speak. Tolstoy is almost constantly speaking in his own proper person, but the vantage point from which he speaks is almost constantly changing. In the course of the novel practically every character of any significance has at least one scene or part of a scene rendered from his or her point of view. In the episode of the bird-hunting trip taken by Levin, Stiva, and Vassenka in part VI there is a single chapter (12) in which Levin, frustrated the previous day in his attempts to bag a bird, goes out by himself very early in the morning and manages to have a successful hunt. The greater part of that scene is told from the point of view of his dog.

One effect of this constantly shifting point of view is that it gives the reader a vantage point superior to that of any character in the book. Although a single scene may be told from a particular perspective, the reader, from previous chapters, is intimately aware of how the other participants are viewing the situation. No character shares this knowledge. As the novel progresses, the reader's omniscience becomes increasingly important. It culminates in the last part, where Vronsky goes off to die in a senseless war, thinking that Anna committed suicide to spite him and quite unaware of her real state of mind. Levin, on the other hand, undergoes a complete change of heart and mind, which is imperceptible to those around him. The use of shifting and multiple points of view enables the reader to see and to understand the human reality of a given scene, the truth underlying the opaque surface of commonplace conversations and events.

Think, for example, of the dinner party at Stiva's in part IV, where Kitty and Levin see each other for the first time since she refused him and Vronsky jilted her. The guests discuss the role of the family in the political destiny of Russia, women's rights, and the proper response of a husband to his wife's infidelity. The conversation is pleasant and conventional; apart from the details of the latest gossip, everybody present has had the same discussion innumerable times. But at the table, while all this talk is going on among the guests, Kitty and Levin are establishing a new intimacy and confessing their love for each other; Anna's husband, Alexei, is considering his humiliation and cowardice and his plans for a divorce from his unfaithful wife; and Dolly and Stiva, whose marriage is a sham, play the genial hosts. As the narration shifts back and forth between the surface events of the party and the inner life of some of the guests, the scene takes on a concreteness and vividness that no other author I know of, except Dostoyevsky, can create, and he only for moments of the greatest significance. It is Tolstoy's special genius to achieve this effect with the ordinary events of human life.

Within a given chapter, a single point of view is usually established right off, setting the tone and providing the major perspective for what is to follow. Tolstoy, however, frequently shifts to another person's point of view in the middle of the chapter or adds a second point of view to the first and employs both simultaneously. This is done so often that it almost appears as if Tolstoy was unaware of the problems involved. His artfulness is so perfectly controlled that it takes on the appearance of artlessness and simplicity.

Here is another example. We see the famous horse race in the second part of the novel twice—first with Vronsky as he rides in the race and second with the spectators, particularly Anna. Yet during our second viewing, we do not see the race directly through Anna's eyes, nor do we quite see the race itself. The point of view is that of Anna's husband, and he follows the progress of the race indirectly by watching Anna's face as she watches it. Alexei not only sees the race this way; he also learns beyond a shadow of a doubt that his wife is having an affair with Vronsky. Near the end of the race Anna becomes aware that her husband is watching her and that she is betraying her emotions. Her husband realizes that she knows she is being observed and that she does not care whether he knows of her infidelity. Without a word being said between them, without their even meeting each other's eyes, they make a great decision, and their marriage is doomed. All this takes about half a page.

This incident also illustrates a second device that Tolstoy uses throughout the book to give his scenes their peculiar density and concreteness. His characters not only respond to one another with delicate sensitivity but become aware of one another responding. It is in terms of their awareness of the responses of others that they act and feel and talk. With subtlety, Tolstoy shows that action, in the broadest sense of the term, presupposes interaction.

In part III, for instance, sometime after the mowing scene, Levin goes to visit Dolly and her children, who are staying in the country. When he arrives, he almost immediately starts to say that he received a letter from Dolly's husband, Stiva, suggesting that Dolly was having difficulty getting settled in the country, and needed help. After Levin begins to speak of the letter, he stops in embarrassment, for he realizes that Dolly is herself embarrassed that her husband is foisting his domestic duties on someone else. The moment Levin ceases to speak, Dolly realizes why he stopped. She then reflects that it is because Levin has such a fine sense of perception that she likes him so much. This little exchange, almost instantaneous and silent, is not very important to the whole novel, yet it lives as much as any other scene in the book. This dramatic moment, with its obvious and yet profound human truth, and innumerable others like it give the work that intangible but perfectly real quality that makes for great art.

The brilliance with which each of these scenes is represented depends on Tolstoy's perception of human intercourse. All his devices and tricks would be insignificant if he did not have the ability to see what is involved in the ordinary experiences of life. Although we have all gone through similar experiences every day, it is not until we see Tolstoy's rendering that we realize how dense and opaque they normally are to us.

When Stiva and Levin have dinner together near the beginning of the novel, we watch two friends discuss a variety of matters and discover that they have nothing whatsoever in common besides their mutual affection. This lack does not destroy or significantly alter their friendship, but it does make the conversation slightly unpleasant to both men because with respect to marriage they are in precisely opposite situations. Stiva's marriage is on the point of dissolving because his wife has found a letter from a mistress of his, and Levin is hopefully looking forward to marrying Kitty. I know of no other novelist who is capable of representing with such perception the relationship between mature men who are old friends as they draw apart owing to the differences in their situations and ways of life. The same could be said of his treatment of the relationship of brother to brother, sister to sister, husband to wife, and so on indefinitely. Before this kind of genius, we can ultimately do no more than point out and elaborate as best we can the enormous amount of human understanding compressed into each apparently simple and artless vignette. No form of technical analysis that I know of can explain their incredible power and truth. In the hands of almost any other novelist the matter of *Anna Karenina* would probably have taken at least twice as many pages to represent with anything like the same degree of clarity and precision. Far from being a sprawling, padded novel, it rivals a Hemingway work in economy of writing.

I turn now to the problem of Tolstoy's morality or, to put it more precisely, to the moral position expressed in the novel. This aspect of *Anna Karenina* is of critical importance. To speak bluntly, Tolstoy, in this novel at least, is in favor of virtue and opposed to vice. His sense of right and wrong is, moreover, absolutely clear: he does not admit extenuating circumstances, pragmatic tests, or social conditioning. What is right is right, and what is wrong is wrong, no matter what—and, if this were not so, he seems to imply, there would be no such thing as morality at all.

Such an uncompromising, puritanical moral attitude hardly seems conducive to the creation of great art. In this case, however, where it is coupled with an ability to render individual scenes and persons, it serves as a fixed point from which the author can arrange and give meaning to the multitude of places, events, and relationships with which he deals. In effect, he combines the greatest possible understanding of the diversity and uniqueness of people and things with the toughest sort of Christian ethic. He understands all but forgives nothing.

Stiva, for example, emerges as a genial and well-meaning man with the morals of a mink. It is impossible not to like Stiva—even Anna's pathetic and narrow-minded husband cannot resist him. Yet he is not a decent person. This is not to say that Tolstoy ultimately condemns him as evil. Stiva in his amoral and sentimental way inadvertently does good things as well as bad. But he does not hear the voice of his own conscience, and he wants only to have a good time.

Anna's husband is a more complex and difficult case. He is a thoroughly pathetic man who is incapable of much genuine feeling. Yet in the second part of the novel when Alexei waits alone for Anna to come home from Betsy's party, his reflections move us. Unlike Stiva, he tries to be a decent man and a good Christian. He paces back and forth, trying to formulate what he will say to Anna when she returns. As Tolstoy says, he stands face to face with "life" and the real possibility that his wife might be unfaithful to him. At that moment, one cannot help feeling both pity for the man in his misery and contempt for his unfeeling, foolish, fruitless attempts to understand and respond adequately to his situation.

At the opposite pole is the scene in which Levin throws Vassenka out of the house because his manner toward Kitty, who is pregnant, is vaguely improper. Levin, unlike Alexei, always lives face to face with life. He does admit the possibility that his wife could be unfaithful to him. As a result, he is easily jealous and incapable of hiding the suffering that it causes him even as he tries to be an affable and discreet host. Levin knows instinctively what is primary to him and what is secondary. His wife, his honor, and the sanctity of his home are inviolable, and the opinions of his friends and society are not. Tolstoy wants us to think that Levin's jealousy and his decision to throw Vassenka out are admirable and that Alexei's disdain for jealousy and his decision to close his eyes to reality are despicable and pathetic.

The epigraph to the novel comes from Romans, chapter 12, verse 19: "Vengeance is mine; I will repay, saith the Lord." Tolstoy can hardly be accused of small-minded vindictiveness. Anna suffers in full measure for her transgressions, but her sensitivity, her honesty, and her capacity for suffering make her fate genuinely tragic. We cannot help pitying and admiring her intensely. But Tolstoy never gives even the slightest hint that her behavior or the many choices she freely makes are either morally admirable or justifiable. In her search for happiness she destroys her husband and Vronsky, and she does so knowingly. She is not a bad woman, but neither is she a helpless innocent destroyed by circumstances beyond her control. Anna deserves her fate because she has brought it upon herself; to say anything less would diminish the tragic stature that is rightfully hers.

Levin, too, deserves his fate, although, in the sharpest contrast to Anna, he follows the strait path of virtue. Even when he occasionally departs from it, as when he goes to visit Anna for the first and only time, he is painfully aware that he has not acted correctly, and he admits it. His life during the course of the novel is no easier or more pleasant than Anna's. Tolstoy cannot be accused of sententiously proclaiming that virtue pays in any easy or straightforward way. But in the end, Levin is capable of finding significance in his life, whereas Anna is not.

I would maintain that Tolstoy's morality in all its simplicity and directness must *not* be qualified, treated as sophisticated, or brought up to date. Even if its content seems hopelessly old-fashioned to contemporary readers, the responsibility of the critic is to help them appreciate Tolstoy's utter realism and lack of sentimentality. The more familiar we become with these qualities, the more clearly we see that even though Tolstoy's moral judgments may be simple, they are never simplistic. Only if we deal with the morality of *Anna Karenina* face on, with all its unpalatable black-and-white distinctions, will the amazingly complex structure and profound humanity of the novel become clear. In other words, our ability to appreciate its form depends on our ability to grasp its ethical content.

In structure the novel is built on a double plot, with both Anna's and Levin's stories occupying equal positions in spite of the title. This double plot succeeds. In *Vanity Fair,* to the contrary, regardless of Thackeray's best intentions, the story of Becky Sharp is inherently more interesting and engrossing than the story of the insipid Amelia Sedley. It is perhaps one of Tolstoy's greatest achievements that he was able to make a fully virtuous life, as embodied in the career of Levin, as intrinsically interesting as he did. Put crudely, the novel deals with the tragic fall of Anna and the commensurately serious rise of Levin.

The two stories are, admittedly, connected causally in only the slightest way. Although Anna and Levin have friends and even family in common, they meet only once. That encounter, which occurs near the end of the book, is significant in that nothing whatever comes of it. Anna and Levin are related to each other indirectly through their relationships with Kitty and Vronsky. On the whole, however, they pursue their own lives and seek their own fates independently of each other.

Yet if their lives are causally unrelated, they are artistically interdependent. This interdependence is based on a close and systematic contrast between Anna and Levin, which runs through the novel. The parallelism is so tight and pervasive that the two stories may be said to define and illuminate each other; that is, the two stories are what they are and have the effects they do largely by virtue of their juxtaposition and dramatic counterpointing. On a rather simple level, they are dramatically related more or less in the fashion of the stories of Becky Sharp and Amelia Sedley, for, as Levin's fortunes decline, Anna's rise, and vice versa.

Far more important than this routine and uninteresting contrast is the parallelism of their inner lives. Both characters are far more complex than the others in the book. Unlike Becky and Amelia, they have a great deal in common and show a striking similarity in their responses to similar situations. But even though their careers are tightly parallel in this subtler sense, Tolstoy is still careful in his handling of the two stories to prevent the double structure from appearing mechanical or clumsy.

As I mentioned before, the dramatic moments or chapters of the novel are grouped together to form larger episodes, and these episodes are themselves arranged in eight major parts. Through an examination of these parts, with an emphasis on the parallel development of Anna's and Levin's lives, I would like to show how Tolstoy has ordered the enormous mass of dramatic detail and incident into an artistic whole, of which his moral position is an integral and essential element. Tolstoy has not given titles to the eight parts, so for purposes of identification I shall supply them.

Part I may be called "Beginnings." It deals with the simultaneous trips to Moscow by Anna and Levin, and it ends when they return to their respective homes. The trips in themselves are inconclusive, and Anna and Levin go home in the same external condition in which they came to Moscow. Psychologically, however, both trips produce significant changes. Most important, the two visits to Moscow initiate chains of events that will be decisive in determining the destinies of both protagonists.

Anna comes to Moscow to help her brother Stiva and stays to find love, while Levin comes to propose to Kitty and unexpectedly finds his sick brother Nicholas, whom he decides to help. In both encounters Anna is eminently successful and Levin a complete failure. Although Anna and Levin do not meet, Kitty and Vronsky act as intermediaries. Thus Levin and Vronsky compete with each other for Kitty's affections, and Vronsky wins out. Anna and Kitty compete for Vronsky in the scene at the ball, and Anna is successful. The Oblonskys, both Stiva and Dolly, are also established as intermediaries, a role they fill throughout the book.

When Levin and Anna leave Moscow, both reflect on their trips, their past lives, and the future. Levin, when he arrives home, decides to change his way of life and then, as he looks around him and sees all the old familiar things, feels the weight of the past and the impossibility of shifting the course of the future in any significant way. Finally, he settles down with a scientific book and reflects that "all's well."

Anna, while returning home on the train, also reads a book, in her case an English novel. But instead of finding peace, she becomes annoyed at its artificiality and experiences a sudden and intense desire to live. In contrast to Levin's relaxation, her nervous state is tense, and, as she dozes, she dreams of a pleasant catastrophe. When she arrives in Petersburg, the first familiar things she notices are her husband's protruding ears. At home even her beloved son disappoints her by not being as perfect as she remembered him. She, too, finally settles back into her customary life, but with twinges of regret and disturbing memories of Vronsky. This first part of the novel ends with Vronsky returning to his home and preparing his campaign to win Anna.

Much more could be said of this first part, but in general terms its function in the novel can be summed up as follows: the parallelism between Anna and Levin is made clear, the probabilities for the whole course of the novel are established, the major characters are introduced, and the contrasting images and themes that mark the two lines of action are developed.

Part II covers the spring and summer following the winter trips to Moscow. Dramatically, it is divided into five episodes. The first episode is a short section dealing with Kitty's illness, which is due more to a bruised psyche than to a sick body. In the second, the scene shifts to Petersburg, and Vronsky's pursuit of Anna is described. This episode, which counterpoints the growing love between Anna and Vronsky with the widening rift between Anna and her husband, culminates with Anna's seduction. The scene then shifts to the third episode, which portrays Levin's quiet, solitary, and almost static life in the country. Following this pastoral interlude, we return to Petersburg for the horse race; this fourth episode reaches its climax when Anna, after the race, tells her husband of her affair with Vronsky. The part ends with an episode centering on Kitty's experiences in Germany, where she recovers her health by making a discovery about her own character.

The whole part thus moves from Kitty to Anna to Levin, back to Anna, and, finally, back to Kitty. The two episodes with Kitty frame the whole part, and in them Kitty's condition undergoes a complete reversal owing to the insight achieved at the German spa. Anna's career moves forward in two big steps separated by the Levin episode: she transgresses the rules of society by beginning her illicit affair, and she makes the fateful decision to reveal her transgression to her husband. Levin, whose episode occupies the center of the part, develops the least of all; he learns of Kitty's illness with mixed feelings of pleasure and sorrow and achieves sufficient distance from his pain and wounded pride to admit to Stiva that he proposed to Kitty and was rejected by her. Kitty and

Levin, who are separated both in actual and in dramatic space, are contrasted in this part—Kitty develops a lot, whereas Levin remains practically unchanged—yet Kitty's growth and Levin's stability are requisite steps toward their realization of a life of mutual love and significance. On the other hand, Anna and Vronsky, who physically and spiritually come together, begin their now inevitable journey toward isolation, individual loneliness, and senseless death. I call this part "First Complications."

Part III covers the rest of the summer and fall and thus completes the first year following Anna's and Levin's trips to Moscow. It is broken into three major episodes and balances the preceding part in that Levin's career moves forward during these six months whereas Anna's is quite static. The first episode deals with Levin's life in the country and his visit to Dolly and culminates with his glimpse of Kitty driving by in a carriage at dawn. In the second episode we watch Anna, her husband, and Vronsky during the days immediately after the horse race. In the third episode the scene shifts back to Levin; we hear about his trip to see his friend Sviazhsky and the short visit of his brother Nicholas. Soon Levin is to leave for Europe to do research for his projected book on agriculture. For lack of a better title I call this part "Crucial Developments."

In the first episode there seem to be two decisive events for Levin: the day he spends mowing the fields with the peasants and the glimpse he catches of Kitty after he has spent the night in a hayfield meditating on his future. Before he goes mowing, Levin has been ineffectually arguing with his brother Sergei, the philosopher. On the evening after the mowing, Sergei admits that Levin's position has some value, and he is charmed by Levin's energy and freshness. Levin wins the argument without opening his mouth. Yet it is clear that he has learned something during his stint in the field, something truer and more persuasive than all his brother's too-clever rationalizations. Self-interest, which Levin defended unsuccessfully against his brother's praise of dedication to the common good, involves not the pursuit of selfish hedonism but immersion in necessary work and through that the discovery of inner endurance and capacity.

The second crucial event in the episode, Levin's momentary sight of Kitty, follows his visit to Dolly—from whom he learns that Kitty is still not engaged—and the night spent in the hayfield. There, Levin decides to change his whole manner of existence, to lead a good, simple life, and perhaps even to marry a peasant girl. When he sees Kitty unexpectedly, all his plans vanish instantly. He realizes that he still loves her and that she is somehow a necessary part of his life.

Immediately after this, the scene shifts to Petersburg, where Anna, her husband, and Vronsky all vainly attempt to come to terms with their positions. Alexei methodically thinks through all possible alternatives and decides to accept the existing situation. Anna considers leaving Petersburg for Moscow with her son but instead goes off to a party given by her corrupt and charming friend Betsy. There she sees with frightening clarity the kind of behavior and the sort of acquaintances the future seems to hold for her. Vronsky spends the day reckoning up his position and ends by believing that he has resolved his difficulties in strict accordance with his noble code of honor. But when he and Anna meet, they give in to each other; they have failed to come to a reasonable decision after all. The result is that the husband's plan, which is the least satisfactory, stable, or realistic, more or less wins the day.

At this point the scene shifts back to Levin. He goes to visit Sviazhsky, at whose house he conceives his plan for cooperative profit-sharing with the peasants. When he returns home, he puts the plan into effect. As he is preparing to leave for Europe to do research on agriculture, his brother Nicholas comes to see him. Levin realizes that Nicholas is dying and that he, too, will die one day. The inevitability of his own death completely overwhelms him, and he leaves for Europe having given up all thought of ambition and glory.

At the end of this part the complications arising from the two earlier trips to Moscow have been played out. Both Levin and Kitty have recovered from the shame of rejection and have made significant self-discoveries in the process, while Anna and Vronsky, having made several decisive choices, have reached a state of uneasy equilibrium. Levin's discovery of the inevitability of his own death has created a problem for him that transcends his love for Kitty and cannot be solved simply by marrying her and settling in the country. Similarly, Anna's genuine love for her son poses a difficulty for her that transcends her love for Vronsky.

Part IV takes place during the winter, one year after the start of the novel. In this part there are no distinct episodes, and each event merges almost imperceptibly into the one after it. After an initial episode in which Vronsky spends a week with a foreign prince and both he and Anna have almost identical dreams, the dominant point of view is that of Anna's husband. When Vronsky comes to see Anna after his absence of a week, he inadvertently meets Alexei leaving the house, which triggers Alexei's decision to get a divorce. From this moment on, we follow the movements of Alexei. He stops in Moscow on his way east and there goes to a dinner party at Stiva's, which I discussed earlier. After the party he receives a telegram from Anna and returns to Petersburg just in time to catch her apparent deathbed scene, after which she recovers. The part ends with Anna and Vronsky leaving together for Europe after Vronsky has failed in a suicide attempt.

As a whole, this fourth part, which I call "Decisions," contains the crucial turning points for both Anna and Levin. Levin proposes to Kitty and is accepted, and Anna leaves her husband and son to go off with Vronsky. These are the two choices that largely determine their starkly different futures. Stiva plays a crucial role in both cases; it is he who invites Kitty and Levin to his party—presumably hoping for them to get together—and it is he who persuades Anna that she should try to regularize her position with Vronsky.

Part V covers the remainder of that winter and spring and might conveniently be titled "Life Together." Of all the parts, it and the next part have the most articulated structure. It is divided into four episodes: Levin and Kitty's wedding; Anna and Vronsky in Italy; the death of Nicholas, attended by Kitty and Levin three months after their wedding; and Anna and Vronsky's return to Petersburg, where Anna sees her son for the last time and is humiliated during an evening at the opera. The first two episodes are predominantly happy ones for Anna and Levin, and the second two are mainly unhappy. Again, the contrast between their lives is clear, but for Kitty and Levin every shared experience, whether joyous or sad, brings them closer together, whereas for Anna and Vronsky every event drives them into a more acute separation from society and a deeper isolation from each other.

On the basis of my summary of this part, one might conclude that Tolstoy's uncompromising moral vision leads him to draw the contrast between the virtuous and adulterous lovers too strongly. In all four episodes, however, he is careful to give depth and complexity to the happy occasions by including an element of suffering and to leaven the unhappy ones with moments of joy. Even the gloom of Nicholas' impending death provides the context for an instant of the most intense pleasure for Kitty when Levin admits to her that he was wrong in not wanting her to be present. At that moment she realizes that he no longer thinks of her as a pampered child but as a mature person who understands things he does not, and that she has his respect.

Part VI deals with the following summer through October, and I call it "Life in the Country." It has three distinct though closely linked episodes. The first depicts the life of the Levins in the country, with visiting in-laws, futile attempts at matchmaking between Levin's brother Sergei and Kitty's friend Varenka, and the hunting trip that Levin takes with Stiva and Vassenka. That episode concludes with the scene in which Levin throws Vassenka out of the house. The next episode treats of Anna and Vronsky's life in the country; it, like the previous one, is largely seen through the eyes of Dolly, who goes from Levin's estate to pay Anna a visit. The last episode concerns the provincial elections, which both Levin and Vronsky attend.

The contrast between the first two episodes may be described in terms of the apparent and real conditions of the Levin and Vronsky households. Kitty and Levin have one crisis, argument, or misunderstanding after another, but these surface ripples are signs of the solidity of their common life, with all its intimacy and happiness. Beneath the luxury, the social welfare projects, and the playfulness at the Vronsky estate, Anna and Vronsky suffer from a combination of isolation and misery that is close to total despair. The episode of the provincial elections heightens this contrast, for Vronsky is a success and Levin, who is out of tune with the times, is only one among many insignificant landowners.

Part VII deals with the following winter and spring, and most of the action takes place in Moscow. It has two distinct episodes. The first constitutes a description of Levin's aimless life in Moscow during the last weeks of Kitty's pregnancy and the birth of their son. The second is concerned with Stiva's attempts to get a better job and to persuade Anna's husband to give her a divorce. Then there is a shift to Anna's growing despair, which culminates in her suicide. I call this part "Fulfillment I."

The concluding part of the novel, "Fulfillment II," takes place three months later and inversely parallels the previous part. It also has two main episodes. The first centers on Vronsky pacing the station platform as he suffers from a toothache and waits for the departure of the train that will take him to the Serbian war and death, and the second records Levin's spiritual crisis and its resolution. The contrast between the final episode in Anna's life and this Levin episode, which ends the book, is perhaps the most striking in the entire novel. All the similarities and differences that have been developing throughout reach their culmination here. These episodes contain Anna's and Levin's visions of life and reality, which are the bases for their ultimate choices—death for Anna and life for Levin.

Anna chooses to die after being presented with a comprehensive picture of the world as ugly, sordid, full of hate and envy, and meaningless. Levin chooses to live when he comes to see that life—*his* life with his wife and child, his farm, his work, and his soul—is meaningful, beautiful, and worthy of dedication to God. Anna never quite hears or understands what the peasant she has dreamed of for so long actually mutters at the moment of her death. Levin, on the other hand, just barely catches the offhand remark of the peasant working in his barn, "Fokanitch is a righteous man. He lives for his soul. He does not forget God." Anna has her vision as she is characteristically in motion, driving about Moscow in her carriage and sitting on the train; Levin, after he has heard the peasant's comment and lies down in the field to think. Anna is surrounded by people; Levin is completely alone. Anna barely thinks at all—she merely looks around her and comments on fleeting surface impressions. Levin thinks through his problem almost methodically once he has been presented with the key to its solution.

Everything in the book leads to these two intensely dramatic moments; at no other point is the contrast between Anna and Levin so sharp and their common humanity so apparent. That each of these scenes is the inevitable consequence and summation of all the preceding events and choices in the lives of the two protagonists, that the contrast and correspondence between these scenes is well-nigh perfect—these are the marks of the novel's structural beauty and the primary source of its immense power. Both Anna and Levin have made moral choices, and these choices have determined their fate. In the novel, form and content mutually determine each other.

7 Theme, Structure, and Meaning in Herodotus' *History*

Herodotus' *History* is a remarkable work. It is immensely long and stuffed with enormous quantities of material. We find anecdotes, myths, geographical descriptions, accounts of strange customs of exotic peoples, backstairs gossip about the love life of the great king and his queen, scientific and pseudo-scientific accounts of natural wonders, reports of the battles of great armies, speculations about the remote origins of peoples, the public speeches and private dreams of historical figures, dogmatic assertions about the relation between the divine and the human, and much more.

Its author has both charmed and irritated his perplexed readers since antiquity. Cicero called him the father of history; Plutarch thought he deliberately lied. "Moderns," T. R. Glover said fifty years ago, "vie in declaring that his breadth of sympathy and his interest in human things place him nearer to Shakespeare than to Thucydides and next to Homer as the exponent on a generous scale of the thought and life of his people." Note how neatly Glover's remark manages to capture the current ambivalence toward Herodotus by damning him with extravagant praise. If it is a compliment to be put in the company of Homer and Shakespeare, it is surely a put-down to be removed from the company of that quintessential historian Thucydides. The comparison with Thucydides, generally made to the detriment of Herodotus, points to the central question that I want to address: What did Herodotus accomplish? Or, How are we to describe, classify, assess his work?

Herodotus was apparently the first writer in the Western tradition to use the term *history* as a title for his work. Originally, and perhaps for Herodotus as well, the term meant "research," "exploration," or "information." But the term could not carry for him the particular meaning that it carries for those who came after, particularly those of us who live two and a half millennia later. If Herodotus is the father of history in modern terms, he is also the father of geography, anthropology, natural history, travel literature, comparative religion, and political science.

More to the point, we must remember that when he wrote, none of these disciplines or literary genres existed. In the field of history there were no departments of history with learned professors and eager graduate students, no courses on historical methodology, no learned journals, no bibliographies of the books and articles published in every known language on every conceivable topic. When Herodotus did his researches, he seems to have known of a few other works by near contemporaries, works that no longer exist but that were probably accounts of travel to faraway, exotic places. No, if Herodotus is the father of history, he had few, if any, significant predecessors or models from which to work. In effect, he invented what he called history all by himself. If we wish to understand and appreciate his achievement, we must resolutely purge ourselves of anachronisms and imagine ourselves living in a world in which history does not exist.

To begin to grasp the magnitude of Herodotus' creation, it may be helpful to reflect that, so far as I know, history as a mode of thinking about the significance of human experience has been independently invented or created only three times in the whole of recorded human existence. In addition to Herodotus' book, there are only the Hebrew Bible (apparently produced by many different scribes and editors over many centuries) and, at the other end of Eurasia, the Chinese tradition of historiography, which began with the classic *Book of History* (an ancient collection of even more ancient documents), developed through a number of chronicles of various states and periods, and culminated in the first century B.C. with Sima Qian's monumental universal history of China, the *Shi ji* (Historical record). In both Israel and China the discipline of history evolved over a long period of time through the efforts of many individuals. In Herodotus, by contrast, it seems to have emerged full-blown with the creation of a single book.

Herodotus, who evidently knew nothing of these other traditions, nevertheless has some interesting affinities with both of them. The biblical account of the divine history of the world, with its special focus on the emergence and vicissitudes of the people of the Covenant, bears some significant similarity to Herodotus' notions about the role of the divine in human affairs. Although Herodotus is far more skeptical and restrained in his treatment of these matters than the authors of the Bible, the divine occupies an important place in his work as well.

With respect to the Chinese tradition, the material in Sima Qian's work is similar in sheer scope to what Herodotus included in his *History*. Sima Qian divided his work into five major parts. The first part contains a chronicle, year by year, sometimes day by day, of all the emperors of China from remote antiquity down to his day. The second consists of chronological tables showing year by year developments in politics, literature, and the arts, plus events of local importance, the birth and death of important figures, and so on. The third is a series of treatises on rites and customs, astrology, music, flood control engineering, and other special topics. The fourth contains annals of each of the major feudal domains and their ruling houses. And the fifth contains biographies of famous and eminent figures from every field of endeavor and from every period of history up to his time.

This material, which Sima Qian in his neat, scholarly, and rather modern manner divided into separate categories and sections, Herodotus integrates into a single complex narrative. Apart from an interest in natural events, like eclipses and earthquakes, that portend future human disasters, Sima Qian's work, like Herodotus', is remarkably secular and scholarly in tone, with considerable attention paid to sources, documentation, and the need for objectivity. Like Herodotus' history, Sima Qian's work, which was heavily criticized and largely dismissed by modern scientific historians of the nineteenth and early twentieth centuries, has turned out to be far more reliable, accurate, and objective than those critics believed.

Herodotus, then, with little, if any, significant historiographical tradition behind him, seems to have created out of his own personal researches a work that combines both the Hebrews' concern for the ultimate divine meaning and pattern discernible in human events and the early Chinese concern for accuracy, objectivity, and comprehensiveness in historiography.

But before we can assess Herodotus' achievement, we need to look more closely at what he did. He wrote a single book, considerably shorter than either the Hebrew bible or the *Historical Record* of Sima Qian but monumental in its own right. Herodotus apparently thought of it as a universal history, so he titled it simply "Inquiries," but almost everyone else, starting with Thucydides, has considered it primarily a history of the Greco-Persian war, which occurred near the beginning of the fifth century B.C. Herodotus himself says that he wrote his book to preserve "those great and wonderful deeds, manifested by both Greeks and barbarians, and . . . the reason why they fought one another" (I.i). The text that follows this introductory remark is divided into nine books, and Herodotus does not get around to the war between the Greeks and the Persians until about two-thirds of the way through book VI. The war began in 490 B.C. when Darius, emperor of Persia, sent a naval expedition to enslave Athens and Eretria as punishment for their participation nine years earlier in the sacking and burning of Sardis. David Grene's translation runs to 664 pages, and it is not until page 446 that Darius decides to send his forces against mainland Greece. To understand how Herodotus could write a history of the Persian War and yet not address the war itself until more than halfway through, we need to stop reading Herodotus wearing the anachronistic lens of our modern understanding of history; that is, we must stop viewing him as a liberal, broad-minded, multidisciplinary, charming, but essentially confused, muddle-headed, pious, naive, gullible, provincial, and Archaic, not to say primitive, Greek. We also need to look more closely at what he says in his book—what he wrote about and in what order.

After his famous introductory statement, Herodotus presents various Persian and Phoenician stories about how the quarrel between the Greeks and the Asians began. These stories concern escalating incidents, which are very ancient, even mythical, with first one side and then the other abducting the other's women. Herodotus doesn't deny or discount these stories. He presents them and then says that he will tell the story of the first man who, by Herodotus' own knowledge, "began unjust acts against the Greeks." This is Croesus, king of Lydia, who subjugated the Greek cities of Ionia.

Herodotus recounts the history of Lydia, particularly the dynasty to which Croesus belonged, from the time of his ancestor Gyges five generations earlier. The story of Croesus reaches its climax in his disastrous war against the Persian emperor Cyrus, a war in which Croesus loses both wealth and kingdom. He manages to save his life by becoming the dedicated, faithful servant first of Cyrus and later of his son Cambyses.

Croesus' fateful encounter with Cyrus leads Herodotus to give an account of the rise of the Persian empire. Typically, he starts not with Persia but with the Medes and their rise to power, which provides the occasion for Cyrus' and the Persians' emergence from obscurity into world prominence. Book I ends with the death of Cyrus in a campaign against the Massegetae somewhere in the far reaches of central Asia. But the Persian empire has been established, and it includes among its subjects numerous Ionian Greeks living in cities along what is now the Aegean coast of Turkey.

Book II begins with the accession of Cambyses to the throne of Persia and the statement that he undertook an expedition against Egypt. The rest of book II is an account of the history, customs, and wonders, both natural and constructed, of Egypt, from the most ancient times to the reign of Amasis, the king who ruled Egypt at the time of Cambyses' attack. In form, the treatment of Egypt is identical with the treatment accorded to each of the peoples who become key actors in his story. He tells us about their strange customs, good and bad, the most impressive geographical and manmade features of their country, their religious beliefs, and their history. Since Egypt is so ancient—the second oldest nation in the world according to an experiment conducted by King

Psammetichus—and so different from anyplace else, Herodotus' account takes up an entire book.

Book III begins with Cambyses' successful campaign against Egypt and his unsuccessful campaigns against Ethiopia and Ammon. A Carthaginian campaign is planned but never comes off. The expeditions against Ethiopia and Ammon are disastrous failures. Readers are then treated to the roughly contemporaneous stories of Cambyses' growing madness, Polycrates and his ring, and Periander's revenge on the Corcyreans. Following the death of Cambyses, the usurpation of the Persian throne by the false Smerdis, the coup by seven Persian nobles, and an extraordinary debate on the future political structure of Persia, Darius becomes king and reorganizes the empire into satrapies. Appended to Herodotus' account of the satrapies and their revenues is a survey of the regions beyond: Arabia, which is farthest to the south, Ethiopia, farthest to the southwest, the Tin Islands (the British Isles), farthest to the west, and Asia, farthest to the east.

Democedes, a Greek doctor from southern Italy, became the occasion for the first tentative Persian thrust toward Greece. Democedes proceeds from Polycrates, the tyrant of Samos, to Oroetes, satrap of Sardis, to Darius, in Susa, whose twisted ankle he cures. He also cures a growth on the breast of Atossa, Darius' queen, in return for which, and also in aid of his return home, Atossa manipulates Darius to send a spying expedition to Greece in preparation for a full invasion sometime in the future. The Persians conquer Samos, an Aegean island with one of the major Ionian Greek cities, but are temporarily distracted from their interest in Greece by the need to suppress a large-scale revolt in Babylon.

Book IV describes two major thrusts by the Persians under Darius: one to the north, across the Hellespont and the Danube into and across Scythia, and one to the south and west into Libya. The expedition against Scythia is a complete failure. The Scythians, to preserve their freedom, pick up their community, lock, stock, and barrel, and move across the steppes away from the Persians. In fact, the Persian army, including Darius, narrowly escapes disaster when the Ionian Greeks left in charge of the bridge across the Danube refuse to destroy it and thus cut off the Persians, as they are urged to do by the Scythians, who have circled around behind the Persians. According to the Scythians, "as free men" the Ionian Greeks "were the basest and most unmanly of anyone; but . . . as slaves, they were the most subservient and staunchest in their loyalty" (IV.142).

The Persian expedition to Libya is more successful, but it, too, seems inconclusive. Herodotus takes the occasion of these far-reaching expeditions to describe the geographic structure of the known world, which is divided into the three continents of Europe, Asia, and Africa. He discusses the country beyond Scythia, stretching across many lands to the Hyperboreans, the people beyond the north wind; he mentions the Phoenician circumnavigation of Africa.

Book V begins with the Persians consolidating their hold on Thrace and moving into Macedonia. At this point, around the start of the fifth century B.C., Aristagoras of Miletus leads a revolt of the Ionian cities. He goes to Sparta for help but is thrown out when Cleomenes, the king, discovers that the capital of Persia is three months' journey from the sea. So Aristagoras persuades the Athenians to send a fleet to help the Ionians, and with Athenian support, he and his fellow Ionians attack and burn Sardis. This act arouses Darius' anger against Athens. From that point on, events go against Aristagoras: the Persians successfully counterattack, the Athenians abandon him, the Cypriots fail in a revolt. Aristagoras himself is killed in battle in Thrace. Herodotus uses the visits of Aristagoras to Sparta and Athens as the occasion to narrate the history of these two cities before and during this time.

Book VI continues the story of the Ionian struggles against Persia, although the leadership now falls to Histiaeus, a cousin of Aristagoras and the real instigator of the Ionian revolt. The Ionians gather in council and unite their forces into a single navy of 350 ships under the command of Dionysius of Phocaea. He spends a week training the sailors in coordinated naval tactics, but then the sailors, exhausted by all the work, refuse to drill any more. Shortly thereafter, when they meet the Persian fleet, despite displays of courage by several individual ships, the Ionians are decisively defeated, Miletus is devastated, and Histiaeus is captured and killed.

Seizing the victory, the Persians send an army accompanied by a fleet to march across Thrace and down the coast of Greece to Athens. A great storm at Mount Athos in Thrace destroys the fleet, and the army returns to Asia. A few years later, the Persians send another fleet against Athens. This time the expedition sails directly across the Aegean to Attica. At Marathon, the Athenians, under the command of Miltiades and with the help of only a contingent of Plataeans, attack and defeat the much larger Persian force.

In book VII the narrative becomes focused. First, the Egyptians revolt, then Darius dies, and his son Xerxes ascends to the throne determined to avenge the defeat of his father's expedition at Marathon. After putting down the Egyptian revolt he undertakes the greatest military expedition seen to date. An army is collected from across the Persian empire, a gigantic fleet is assembled, a canal is dug across the peninsula so that the fleet can avoid Mount Athos, and a bridge of ships is built across the Hellespont. The army is so vast that the soldiers drink the rivers dry. The fleet is so large that no harbor can hold all the ships. As the army moves through Thrace and Macedonia, accompanied at sea by the mighty fleet, cities and nations surrender to the overwhelming power of Xerxes.

The main Greek cities strive for a common defense and a common strategy. A small force is sent north to block the pass at Thermopylae under the command of the Spartan king Leonidas, and a fleet is sent to protect its flank. A storm destroys a substantial part of the Persian fleet, but not enough to stop its advance. The Persians attack at Thermopylae, and the Greeks defend their position for several days against incredible odds. Finally, through a local collaborator, the Persians find a path over the mountains and outflank the Greeks. Leonidas sends the allied forces away, and his force of three hundred Spartans fights to the last man in one of the most glorious chapters of Greek history.

Book VIII begins with an account of the sea battles around Artemesium during the battle of Thermopylae. After the failure to stop the Persian army at the pass, the Greek fleet retreats to Athens. As the Persian army approaches, the Athenians evacuate the city dwellers to the island of Salamis. After debating what course to pursue, the Greeks find that the Persians, secretly instigated by Themistocles of Athens, have blocked their retreat. So, with the Athenians taking the lead, the combined Greek fleet fights the much larger Persian fleet and wins. Xerxes hastens back to Asia, leaving Mardonius with 300,000 troops to complete the conquest of Greece.

In book IX Herodotus describes the final episodes of the Persian invasion. After wintering in the north, Mardonius comes south and captures Athens again. The Greeks meanwhile continue their endless debate over what to do and where to do it, but at last the Spartans are persuaded to give up their plan to defend the narrow isthmus connecting the Peloponnesus to the mainland when they grasp that without the Athenian fleet to block the sea they can be outflanked by the Persians. Mardonius pulls back to a fortified position in Boeotia, and the Spartans advance toward him with their army under the command of their king, Pausanias. Most of the unoccupied Greek cities send contingents to join Pausanias so that he has between 30,000 and 60,000 hoplites at Plataea against Mardonius' 300,000 men. In spite of the odds, the Greeks win a glorious victory, ending the Persian threat to Greece. On the same day as the battle of Plataea, a Greek expedition, dispatched to help the Ionian cities, defeats a Persian army at Mycale on the Asian mainland.

During this period Xerxes, who fled to Sardis, conceives a passion for his brother's wife. When she persists in resisting his advances, he marries his son to her daughter with the thought that this will bring them together. Instead, Xerxes falls in love with the daughter and, in an attempt to please her, gives her a beautiful cloak woven for him by his wife. When his wife finds out, she blames the girl's mother, and after wringing a consent from Xerxes, mutilates the poor woman. Xerxes' brother, enraged at what has happened to his wife, leaves for Bactria to start a revolt, but Xerxes finds out and sends an army to assassinate his brother.

Book IX, and the whole history, ends with a story told of Cyrus. Just after he founded the empire, a Persian noble urged him to move the Persians from their arid, rocky land to a more watered, arable place. He agrees but says that if the Persians move, they should be prepared to be ruled by others rather than to rule. "From soft countries come soft men," he says. "It is not possible that from the same land stems a growth of wondrous fruit and men who are good soldiers" (IX.122).

This, simplified, is what Herodotus included in his *History*. He wrote an account of the Persian War, but also a good deal more. I have suggested the sweep of the book as well as the diversity and richness of the stories told along the way. To see what Herodotus is doing, we must see the book as an overarching, all-encompassing structure, as an account of the causes and events of the Greco-Persian war, and as a collection of fascinating stories.

Each story that Herodotus tells is complete in itself, although the stories are commonly stitched together as episodes in the larger story of the life of a man or a community. Normally each of the larger narrative sequences is introduced into the work when a figure whose career Herodotus is following encounters someone who has a story of his own or goes to a place with a distinctive history. The whole of book II on Egypt, for example, is written because Cambyses, the king of Persia, who is the primary subject of Herodotus' narrative at that point, decides to invade the land of the Nile. Once Herodotus picks up Croesus as the man who first enslaved Greeks, every other story in *The History* emerges in its proper place. Each story, or sequence of stories, connects with the stories before and after it like the links of a chain—a standard device of traditional storytellers. Yet the effect of the whole is not like the linked but essentially unrelated chain of stories that constitute the *Arabian Nights,* for example. The stories in Herodotus' book seem to be more integrally related, more like the elements of a comprehensive vision.

We find the archetypal Herodotean story, the one that stands out in every reader's memory, very near the beginning of book I. The tale of Arion and the dolphin (I.23–24) is hooked into the narrative sequence more arbitrarily, more loosely, than almost any other story in the work. Herodotus is talking here about the ancestors of Croesus. The last of these, Alyattes, Croesus' father, is involved in a war with Miletus. Thrasybulus, prince of Miletus, gains good advice and help in his conflict with Alyattes from his friend Periander, prince of Corinth. It was during Periander's reign that the wonderful story takes place.

Arion, the most renowned singer of his day, having made his fortune in Italy, is returning to Corinth by boat when the sailors decide to rob him and throw him overboard. Arion asks to perform one last time. Dressed in robes, he sings for the sailors and then throws himself overboard. A dolphin carries him to shore near Corinth. When the ship docks and the sailors are questioned by Periander, they lie about Arion. He then steps out from hiding and confronts them with the truth. The story is certainly farfetched, so Herodotus, well aware of the skepticism of his audience, points out that both the Corinthians and the Lesbians agree on the story. There is, besides, a dedicatory offering of Arion's at Taenerum, the statue of a man riding a dolphin.

This story is crucial to Herodotus' whole history. It is miraculous, wholly improbable; it is a myth or a tall tale. However interpreted by the rational, skeptical reader, it can hardly be taken as literally true. Yet I think that is exactly what Herodotus asks us to do. He wants us to take this story seriously despite our natural tendency to reject his evidence that Arion really was saved by a dolphin. To believe the story we would have to suspend our normal rational frame of mind. The story, after all, is not absolutely impossible, but it is unlikely.

The child in each of us would like such happy endings to be true. But the experienced adult knows full well that if sailors decide to rob and kill a traveler at sea, that traveler is doomed to feed the fishes. Herodotus, who is as experienced and adult as anyone, would, I think, agree that nine times out of ten what is usual is exactly what happens. But he is also saying, "Not every time, not necessarily. One time, maybe, in a million (who can calculate the odds?) the wholly improbable occurs, the dolphin comes, Arion is saved. The ending is happy, just, right. The miracle is real."

That, says Herodotus, is the frame of mind to maintain in order to understand his book. The central story that he tells, the narrative frame around which the entire work is built—the war between the Greeks and the Persians—is exactly the same kind of miracle as Arion and the dolphin. The Persian invasion should have ended with the conquest and enslavement of the Greeks. Every reasonable reader must realize that the Greeks had no more chance to win than Arion had to survive. But they won, and not just by a hairsbreadth; against all odds, they won overwhelmingly.

Herodotus' history is the story of a miracle. As with all miracles that confound our ordinary sense of probability, the meaning is destroyed if we try to reduce it to a probable everyday event. Miracles need to be accepted as such; they call forth our wonder. Herodotus tells us in his opening sentence that his history is devoted to preserving just such wondrous events in all their original color. The story of Arion and the dolphin is the archetypal Herodotean story precisely to the degree to which it elicits our sense of wonder that it actually happened.

Once the story of Arion induces the right frame of mind, it becomes apparent that every story in Herodotus, if we read it right, is worthy of our wonder. None tells of an ordinary, probable event. Not that ordinary events fail to occur during the period whose events Herodotus is recording—there are many, but he does not bother to report them.

Think, for example, of how many times in the course of the book he reports that an army attacked and captured a city. Then remember the extraordinary story of how Zopyrus helped Darius recapture Babylon, which was in revolt and was prepared to withstand a very long siege. Zopyrus, having cut off his own nose and ears, pretended to defect to the Babylonians, telling them that Darius had mutilated him unjustly. With the connivance of Darius, he gained the Babylonians' confidence by killing large numbers of Persians, eventually taking charge of Babylonian defenses, only to betray the city to his king. Now, *that* story of the taking of a city is worth telling and worth remembering, it is something to wonder at, and that is exactly why Herodotus tells it to us.

When the modern critical historian complains that all the events described in Herodotus' history are unusual, he is missing the point. Of course they are unusual—that is why Herodotus tells them. Why bother to record, to remember, a usual event that will be endlessly repeated with slight, insignificant variations over and over again? Do you remember what you had for breakfast on March 17, 1993? Why should you? But do you remember meeting the first person you fell in love with? Of course! How can anyone forget the wonder of falling in love for the first time? There is here, in this notion of the wonderful event, of the occasion worth remembering, the germ of a conception of history quite different from the modern notion that everything that happens is, and should be, part of the historical record.

The history of humankind is replete with wars, big and small, important and insignificant, but there never was a war like the one Herodotus describes. But how does he know that? The story of Arion and the dolphin has another meaning in the context of Herodotus' history. It is not just a wonderful story but specifically the story of a singer, the greatest singer in the world, the inventor of the dithyramb. Possibly Arion was saved because he was a great artist. In any event, the dolphin saw to it that the world was not deprived of the pleasure of listening to Arion. Herodotus' book is like Arion's singing: it is marvelous in itself, to be wondered at. To explain what I mean requires that we shift our focus from the individual stories that fill the book to its larger structure and to the research that went into its making.

We know very little about Herodotus' life. According to tradition, he was born in Halicarnassus, a city on the coast of Asia Minor, about 484 B.C., lived for some time in Athens, and went as a colonist to help found the city of Thurii in southern Italy in the 440s B.C. Herodotus seems to have been attracted to Thurii because it was Panhellenic, that is, founded by citizens from many cities rather than just one. In any event, while living in Athens, Herodotus is reported to have read part or all of his book in public, the way the rhapsodes performed Homer. We know from references in the book that he was alive through the first few years of the Peloponnesian War and that he traveled widely in the eastern Mediterranean, to Egypt and many other places still under Persian rule.

He was born and probably grew up a Persian subject. Did he speak and understand Persian? He certainly had some access to Persian records and to highly knowledgeable Persian informants. Most important of all, he was able to present both Greek and Persian points of view. I think it is also quite clear from a careful reading of his book that Herodotus understood how profoundly the Greeks and the Persians *failed* to understand each other.

Over and over he shows that the Persians, and their conquered peoples as well, failed to grasp the Greek understanding of freedom. Croesus cannot fathom Solon's story of Tellus the Athenian. Darius doesn't understand the Scythians, much less the Greeks. Xerxes, although he admires Demaratus, the defecting Spartan king, cannot understand him or the Greeks whom his army and navy encounter in battle. This means that the Persians never realize how grossly they miscalculate in their attempt to conquer Greece.

The Greeks, for their part, have no precise idea of who the Persians are, where they come from, how far their empire extends, or how vast their resources are. The Greeks see the camels in the Persian forces—do they know how distant Arabia is from Persia? Cleomenes, king of Sparta, kicks Aristagoras out of Sparta for making the absurd suggestion that the Spartans undertake a ninety-day march from the sea to conquer Susa (V.49–55). Does he understand that the Persians can and will march from that far on the other side of Susa to come to Sparta?

One of the staggering implications of Herodotus' account of the Greco-Persian war is that none of the participants understood who their opponents were or what the meaning of the conflict was. They fought the war, but they failed to grasp its significance. Herodotus' account strongly suggests that although the Greeks knew the Persians had a big army and navy, they had no idea *how* big. The Persians had no idea just how deadly those minuscule Greek forces were in combat. It is Herodotus, through his researches, who "discovered" the two combatants and preserved the memory of them for the Greeks of his day.

But Herodotus discovered much more. He is frequently accused of exaggerating or inventing or gullibly believing every story he was told by Egyptian priests or Scythian shamans. But this criticism presupposes that he was like a modern archival historian who, zealous to make a case, is not as scrupulous in handling sources as truth requires. But that is the wrong image of Herodotus.

We don't know how or when he conducted his researches and wrote his book, but for many years he evidently traveled widely through the eastern Mediterranean and the lands of the Persian empire and talked to many, many people, some of them of considerable authority. He learned many unusual things and heard many extraordinary stories wherever he went. But what is entirely his own is his discovery that the things he learned in all those places were pieces of one enormous, complex pattern.

For example, he learned that toward the periphery of the known world, toward the edges, things tend to become exaggerated. Animals are bigger, customs are more extreme. When he went south to Egypt, he found a settled people in the valley of the Nile, whose land was literally a creation of the river. The Egyptians, he learned, were an immensely old people, tremendously clever, the builders of huge monuments, but they were incapable of maintaining their own autonomy or freedom. When, by contrast, he went north to Scythia, he discovered a place that is the exact opposite of Egypt: a land of flat, undifferentiated steppes inhabited by a nomadic people with no settled cities, with few wonders, with little history, quite stupid, but possessed of one extraordinary virtue—they were brave and free, and they knew how to preserve their freedom. The Persians could not conquer them because they could not even find them. Isn't it interesting that directly between the Egyptians and the Scythians are the Greeks, smart and settled like the Egyptians, but brave and free like the Scythians?

To take another example, the Persians, as Herodotus found them, were a brave and warlike people who worshiped gods reigning over the whole earth. The Persians, unlike other peoples, could worship their gods wherever they went and could even emulate them by conquering the world. Having conquered Asia, more or less, we see them continue in their restless quest for dominion by conquering Egypt. They probe south toward Ethiopia; they probe southwest toward Ammon and Carthage; they probe north into Scythia. After encountering difficulty but not disaster with each of these false starts they discover what has been right in front of them ever since they conquered Lydia: Greece. But what looks like the obvious next target for their aggressive imperialism turns out to be their nemesis. If the Persians were looking for trouble in Ethiopia, Ammon, and Scythia, they were fated to find it only in Greece.

As if to tighten the bonds of fate, the Persians have extensive and intimate contacts with the Ionian Greeks before they invade Greece, so they know their enemy well. Or so they think. From the very beginning of the Lydian conquests the Ionians know that their safety and freedom lie in uniting their forces, but they never can manage to join together. During the Scythian expedition, when the Ionians protect the Persian bridge over the Danube, the Scythians rightly call the Ionians the worst of men and the best of slaves—that is how they act. When they do stage a concerted revolt against Persia, they cannot manage to train their united fleet for more than a week before the lazy sailors revolt at so much hard work. In effect, every single experience the Persians have with the Ionian Greeks leads them to misunderstand and misjudge the character of the mainland Greeks they will encounter so fatefully. Through the behavior of the Ionian Greeks, the Persians are lulled into the overconfident arrogance that will make them sitting ducks for the mainland Greeks.

For example, recall Croesus when he is about to go to war against Cyrus (book I). The Delphic oracle tells him that he should make friends with the most powerful of the Greek peoples. So, having verified the accuracy of the oracle, he makes inquiries and finds that the Spartans and the Athenians are the preeminent Greeks. Which should he chose as his allies? At exactly that moment, the Athenians, reputed to be the most intelligent Greeks, behave in an uncharacteristically stupid way by falling for Pisistratus' trick of dressing up a tall woman and claiming that she was the goddess Athena restoring Pisistratus to despotic power. At exactly the same time, an uncharacteristically clever Spartan figures out the meaning of the Delphic oracle's words in another case and, with the cooperation of the whole city, contrives to fool the Tegeans, return the bones of Orestes to Sparta, and thereby ensure permanent Spartan superiority over Tegea. Croesus, when he hears these stories, concludes an alliance with Sparta believing that Spartans are more resourceful than Athenians. The predictable consequence of his error is that when Croesus hurriedly calls for help, the Spartans are, typically, involved in a complicated and foolish war with Argos, so Sardis falls to Cyrus before the Spartans manage to come to Croesus' aid.

In these examples, which could be multiplied tenfold, a pattern emerges from the conjunction of several stories or narratives drawn from widely separated times or places. It is as if Herodotus went to Sardis and heard one story, to Athens and Sparta, where he heard some more, and, when he compared notes, realized that these independent stories were coordinated in such a way as to make sure that Croesus would make exactly the wrong choice. Over and over again, intricate patterns emerge from the welter of story and description that constitutes Herodotus' linked chain of narration. Furthermore, despite his garrulousness, he is surprisingly reticent about these patterns. He says almost nothing about them explicitly. They are left to us to discover for ourselves and to wonder at.

All these particular patterns of significance interconnect to form the single, overarching pattern or vision. This vision is all-encompassing. In time, it stretches from the existence of the earliest human races, the Phrygians and the Egyptians, through the Persian War and even beyond it to the beginnings of the Peloponnesian War, when the two heroic cities of the Persian War have turned on one another in a fratricidal conflict. In space, it is worldwide, for Herodotus' vision extends outward in every direction to the limits of human habitation.

Thus The History is, in fact, a world history from the beginning of civilization to his own time. To tell the full story of the Persian War is to tell the history of humankind. Amazingly, that history turns out to be a single, coherent, though complex, story, which Herodotus discovered piece by piece as he traveled about, engaged in his researches. In this sense, Herodotus' History is itself like the story of Arion: an unexpected miracle, the articulated discovery that despite the surface appearance of disorder and overwhelming heterogeneity, the human world is coherent and significant in both space and time.

This forms the core of what Herodotus found out through his researches. But I do not want to overstate his claim. He was a modest man, careful to leave unsaid and merely implied those things about which he was not—and could not be—certain. Like the predictions of the oracles in whose truth he believed but whose meaning was ambiguous until after the event, the story he tells is significant, but the exact significance remains to be seen. There is here a hint that the shape of the story, like the stories told by the oracle, may be divine in origin, but it is only a hint, and Herodotus explicitly tells us that he will not deal directly with the divine. His subject is human beings.

One last aspect of the story needs to be mentioned. The struggle between the Greeks and the Persians, marked though it is by mutual incomprehension, is only the last in a long series of struggles for supremacy. Lydia, Media, Persia—each in its turn emerged as an empire with a global reach. Croesus, Astyages, Cyrus, Cambyses, Darius, Xerxes—each of these men in turn occupied the throne of empire and grasped at absolute power. Like their empires, these men failed to achieve total rule. But through Xerxes and the Persian empire the pattern is clear, though subject to local variation.

What is most striking about Herodotus' history is that with the Persian War and the emergence of Greece and the Greeks onto the center stage of world history, the pattern no longer holds. Herodotus portrays Greece as unique in many ways. In the first place, the Greeks are a polyglot people compounded from many races and collected from many diverse places. Second, they never cohere into political unity. The multiplicity of Greek cities is unique, not only in number but also in the diversity of regimes, customs, and characteristics that distinguish the cities from each other. I am almost tempted to say that the diversity from polis to polis in Greece matches the diversity from people to people in the rest of the world. It is as if Greece is a microcosm of the world. But finally, what distinguishes Greece from all the rest of the world is its experience of freedom.

On this point Herodotus is, as usual, not very explicit but, instead, complex. In the sense of not being ruled by another people, every nation seems to understand freedom, although some people, like the Persians, treasure it more than others. Here, the key to freedom is courage, the willingness to fight, if necessary to die, to preserve national autonomy. The Scythians understand this. For the Greeks, the meaning of freedom includes national self-determination and the willingness to fight for it, but it includes more.

Solon proffers that further meaning to Croesus in the story of Tellus the Athenian, who, Solon says, was the most blessed of men. Tellus dwelt in a well-ordered city and, even though he lived to be very old, never had to mourn a child or a grandchild. In his moderately prosperous old age he fought and died gloriously in battle against Eleusis, and the Athenians buried him with great honor on the battlefield where he fell. Croesus does not understand the story, and the reason seems obvious: besides the good fortune that Tellus enjoyed during his lifetime, he had the special blessing of being honored and respected by his fellow citizens after his death. Croesus for all his money, power, and exalted position will never experience the blessing of posthumous honor and respect, because they can be given and received only by equals and must be given freely with no ulterior motives. Croesus, emperor of Lydia, has no equals. Instead, he has multitudes of subjects over whom he has absolute power of life and death. How can he get respect from them? How can their praise of him be free of ulterior motive? How can he be honored by his own slaves? Lydians, Persians, and other peoples outside Greece may be brave, decent, and virtuous, but they can never experience the blessedness of Tellus because they do not live as free and equal citizens under the law in a free city.

Herodotus is clear that the Greeks might not always be unique in this respect. During the debate by the seven conspirators over the fate of the Persian Empire in book III, Otanes' speech in favor of equality under the law gives us a magical moment. At that point the possibility of freedom hovers over Persia, only to be stupidly rejected by the other six conspirators, who can see nothing better to do than to replicate the imperial despotism they just overthrew. In book VII, Demaratus tries to explain Spartan courage to Xerxes at Thermopylae and, of course, he fails. Later in the same book, Sperthias and Bulis, two eminent Spartans who offer themselves to the Persians to expiate the Spartan sin of killing two Persian heralds, try to explain to Hydarnes, a powerful Persian general, that he is a slave and does not understand freedom. And they are right; he does not.

In spite of these failures, and in spite of the Greeks' ignorance of the uniqueness of their political freedom, at the end of Herodotus' story an extraordinary thing has happened: the defeat of Persia by the combined Greek forces under the joint command of the Athenians and the Spartans. For the first time in the history of the world a free people in the fullest sense has advanced to center stage. Not another universal empire but a coalition of diverse free cities may now dominate the world.

Herodotus knew that because of internecine warfare, particularly the conflict between Athens and Sparta that was just beginning as he wrote his book, the Greeks might well miss the chance to do something better than establish one more universal empire. In the twenty-five hundred years since Herodotus wrote, we have seen many more great empires come and go. From time to time we have seen—and some of us have experienced—real political freedom. But

I am not sure that those two and a half millennia have added essential knowledge to what we can already see in Herodotus.

Is it possible that in his researches, culminating with his account of the triumph of the free Greeks, Herodotus discovered and articulated for us the full range of human historical possibilities? Human beings have enacted, and historians have recorded, many wonderful stories since Herodotus wrote, but have those historians made any further discoveries of significance beyond those made by Herodotus? He invented the art of history, and he may also have perfected it.

These remarks about Herodotus were originally written in October 1987, a scant few months before the extraordinary events in Tiananmen Square, eastern Europe, and the Soviet Union. After those unexpected, unpredicted, and unpredictable happenings, we can, I think, reread and rethink Herodotus with more sympathetic understanding than was possible during the years of the Cold War, when the formal, polarized structure of the world seemed obvious, and the range of historical possibilities seemed limited, clear-cut, and self-evident. In 1987 everybody had it all wrong—the academic specialists and the intelligence analysts, the ideologues, hard and soft, on both sides, the political players at all levels of government and administration, and ordinary citizens. No one foresaw what was going to happen; none of us even saw what was happening beneath the surface. But interestingly, now that these events are a matter of record, the experts, the scholars, the diplomats and politicians, the pundits, and the reporters all act as if the collapse of the Soviet empire and the Soviet Union itself at the end of the Cold War were like any other events in the past forty or fifty years. They were not.

In the past decade we have witnessed, perhaps are still witnessing, a massive historical earthquake that has radically transformed the landscape of our world. On the wall above my desk I have a small square of cardboard with four pieces of concrete glued to it: they are authentic pieces of the no-longer-extant Berlin Wall. I look at the pieces and ask, However unlikely the prospect, might not our children live in a world without the threat of nuclear war? I ask, How do you define a miracle? I rest my case for Herodotus as a serious historian.

8 Yeats's "Among School Children"
Analyzing a Lyric Poem

AMONG SCHOOL CHILDREN

William Butler Yeats

I

I walk through the long schoolroom questioning;
A kind old nun in a white hood replies;
The children learn to cipher and to sing,
To study reading-books and history,
To cut and sew, be neat in everything
In the best modern way—the children's eyes
In momentary wonder stare upon
A sixty-year-old smiling public man.

II

I dream of a Ledean body, bent
Above a sinking fire, a tale that she
Told of a harsh reproof, or trivial event
That changed some childish day to tragedy—
Told, and it seemed that our two natures blent
Into a sphere from youthful sympathy,
Or else, to alter Plato's parable,
Into the yolk and white of the one shell.

III

And thinking of that fit of grief or rage
I look upon one child or t'other there

And wonder if she stood so at that age—
For even daughters of the swan can share
Something of every paddler's heritage—
And had that color upon cheek or hair,
And thereupon my heart is driven wild:
She stands before me as a living child.

IV

Her present image floats into the mind—
Did Quattrocento finger fashion it
Hollow of cheek as though it drank the wind
And took a mess of shadows for its meat?
And I though never of Ledean kind
Had pretty plumage once—enough of that,
Better to smile on all that smile, and show
There is a comfortable kind of old scarecrow.

V

What youthful mother, a shape upon her lap
Honey of generation had betrayed,
And that must sleep, shriek, struggle to escape
As recollection or the drug decide,
Would think her son, did she but see that shape
With sixty or more winters on its head,
A compensation for the pang of his birth,
Or the uncertainty of his setting forth?

VI

Plato thought nature but a spume that plays
Upon a ghostly paradigm of things;
Solider Aristotle played the taws
Upon the bottom of a king of kings;
World-famous golden-thighed Pythagoras
Fingered upon a fiddle-stick or strings
What a star sang and careless Muses heard:
Old clothes upon old sticks to scare a bird.

VII

Both nuns and mothers worship images,
But those the candles light are not as those
That animate a mother's reveries,
But keep a marble or a bronze repose.
And yet they too break hearts—O Presences

That passion, piety or affection knows,
And that all heavenly glory symbolise——
O self-born mockers of man's enterprise;

VIII

Labour is blossoming or dancing where
The body is not bruised to pleasure soul,
Nor beauty born out of its own despair,
Nor blear-eyed wisdom out of midnight oil.
O chestnut-tree, great-rooted blossomer,
Are you the leaf, the blossom or the bole?
O body swayed to music, O brightening glance,
How can we know the dancer from the dance?

In analyzing lyric poetry, what should be a joy often becomes a wearisome task, a job to be done, and one done badly at that. I do not know why it is so difficult to analyze lyric poetry, nor why so many of us avoid it. Because I have no general method or specific techniques to propose, let me instead discuss a single lyric poem, "Among School Children," to exemplify a useful approach. The substance of the poem is itself relevant to my purpose. I hope that by reflecting on William Butler Yeats's words we may realize how to more effectively make poetry a significant part of our lives.

"Among School Children" is not about children but about an old man who visits them. More precisely, it presents the educational and philosophical reflections of the old man, triggered by his visit to a schoolroom. Educators and philosophers have long talked about poetry, its nature, its powers, and its deficiencies. Yeats is one of the very few poets with the temerity to return the compliment, to write poetry about education and philosophy.

From the beginning up to the prayer in the last stanza and a half, the poem maintains a prosy, colloquial, rambling, meditative, and somewhat self-consciously poetical tone. This tone gives an air of immediacy and effortlessness to the speaker's reflections in perfect keeping with the character of the speaker and the dramatic situation so precisely evoked in the first stanza. Yet the poem is anything but rambling and prosaic; it is charged with passion, and it builds to a magnificent climax in the last stanza. The climax achieves its intensity in large measure from the way it both results from and gives full expression to all of the images and themes of the earlier stanzas. Just how Yeats achieves this fusion of intense lyrical passion with a tone of reflective and slightly ironic meditation is mysterious to me, although I shall try to articulate what the fusion signifies in the poem.

Yeats seems to have devoted most of June 14, 1926, the day after his sixty-first birthday, to the poem's composition, although as late as September 24 of that year he was apparently still working on it. On that autumn day he wrote in a letter: "I read Croce and write verse, and as a result have nothing to say. Here is a fragment of my last curse upon old age. It means that even the greatest men are owls, scarecrows, by the time their fame has come. Aristotle, remember, was Alexander's tutor, hence the taws (a form of birch rod)." There follows in the letter a very slightly different version of the sixth stanza about Plato, Aristotle, and Pythagoras. Yeats continues: "Pythagoras made some measurement of the intervals between notes on a stretched string. It is a poem of seven or eight similar verses."

At this period in his life, Yeats was already a famous poet and one of the leading figures of the young Irish Republic; he was, in fact, a member of the Irish Senate. A member of a Senate investigating committee concerned with primary education in Ireland, he once made an official school inspection tour, and in a letter he describes a charming experience. At a progressive girls' school, of which he speaks approvingly, especially of what he calls its modern curriculum, he visited a recitation class. The ensuing situation was obviously contrived by the principal and the teacher: A little girl, asked to recite the last narrative passage that she had studied, stood up and recited verbatim the section about the great contemporary Irish poet and patriot William Butler Yeats in *Who's Who,* clearly without knowing the identity of the smiling elderly visitor to her class. This incident led to "Among School Children."

The story is amusing, and unlike most such stories about the genesis of great works of art, it is true. The value of this historical material lies not so much in the illumination that it sheds on the poem; rather, the material shows the enormous distance between an ordinary, even trivial, experience and the significance that such an experience has when it is shaped into poetry of the first order. An aesthete or purist might say that Yeats's experience in that classroom and the experience of the poem are wholly different. I am not sure, for it seems to me that Yeats's poem is about what happened to him in that schoolroom, about that charming, trivial incident—that it is not a description, an analysis, or an explanation of what happened.

The poem, as I have said, is educational and philosophical, but in a sense proper to poetry. Yeats does not talk about education or lecture to us about his philosophy; rather, he renders directly for us the extraordinary educational and philosophical experience he underwent when he visited that schoolroom. When we read and experience the poem, we are not merely being given the fruits of Yeats's experience; we participate in and relive that experience.

Philosophy and education, as rendered in the poem, are not what we have when we finish a book or complete a school program. Philosophy and education are the actual processes of thinking and learning while reading books and while attending school. The dramatic character of the poem means that readers must engage in the processes of thinking and learning while reading it. To the extent that we reenact Yeats's experience we must become poets thinking philosophically, and we must become adults acquiring an education.

The first stanza sets the scene. The speaker is being conducted on a tour of a primary school for girls by one of the teachers—a nun. As they walk through the rooms she describes the curriculum, aims, and methods of the school, and he listens politely and with interest. The dramatic situation (and the starting point for the meditation) is suddenly but fully realized when at the end of the stanza he notes that "the children's eyes / In momentary wonder stare upon / A sixty-year-old smiling public man."

At that precise moment the situation shifts from the flat into the round, for the speaker catches a glimpse of how the children are looking at him. He sees himself as they see him. As he is inspecting them, they are inspecting him. And just as they see only that strange creature a sixty-year-old smiling public man, so, too, he has seen, not the real children, but a group of little creatures going through the paces of learning to become human adults.

The dramatic shock of recognition is enormously rich in latent possibilities. The public man making a public inspection of the public selves of the children is confronted with the outward invisibility of his own private self. This self-awareness is produced, ironically, by the children's failure to see his inner life. That is to say, he suddenly sees himself when he realizes that they cannot really see him. Simultaneously, the fact that the children, too, have a private life, as hidden from him as his is from them, becomes obvious as well.

The public inspection has led to the discovery of the mystery of the inner and private self. Outwardly, almost nothing has happened; as before, the speaker and the children are poles apart. But inwardly the situation has undergone a radical transformation; now the children and the speaker are on a perfectly equal footing because both are fully human. If a reader objects that this view is sentimental and romantic, that the children are, after all, only children and not yet complete persons, the speaker could point out—as he does in stanza IV—that he is, after all, only an old man, a scarecrow, and no longer a complete person himself.

The philosophical content of the meditation that follows this first stanza is already present here in dramatic form. The philosophical problem of time, for example, is present in the immediate confrontation of the old man and the children. It is as if living embodiments of the past and the future are meeting in the present. In other words, Yeats has assembled dramatically the three elements of time. The metaphysical problems of actuality and potentiality, of generation and corruption, are equally embodied in this dramatic moment. What is embodied, however, is latent. It is there in the old man's moment of insight, but we do not yet know what he will make of it.

One further point about the first stanza concerns the "momentary wonder" in the children's eyes that triggers the old man's reflection. There is an ancient tradition that philosophy, the love of and search for knowledge, begins with wonder. Here, *wonder* does not mean "curiosity" or "a desire for information," but "awe, amazement at what is." The old man has suddenly gone back to school, and his teachers, the children, have taught him that he is something to wonder at.

The second stanza begins the meditation proper, and although it emerges naturally from the first, it also stands in the sharpest possible contrast to it. Having been reminded of his own inner life, the old man retreats to it in a reverie. The scene abruptly shifts from the completely public, impersonal tour of inspection of the children who are being shaped into adults to the completely private, personal memory of his own beautiful beloved. Once, in a moment of loving intimacy, she remembered an instance of the educational process as seen from a child's point of view. What is, to the adult, a "harsh reproof" or "trivial event" was to her, as a child, a source of tragedy.

Yet the reverie does not merely provide the old man with sympathy for the children; his beloved's story, when she told it, evoked similar memories in himself of his own childhood and thus produced a feeling of sympathy between them that was so intense that momentarily, at least, they realized the age-old desire of all lovers to achieve complete and perfect union. Thus the separation of old and young caused by the public, impersonal appearance of things in the first stanza is precisely balanced in the second stanza by the total unity realized by the mature lovers in the context of an intimate and personal reality.

Leda, who was seduced by Zeus in the form of a swan, was the mother of Helen of Troy. This reference to the story of Leda and the swan, along with the reference to the shell, introduces a swan motif that will be expanded in the next two stanzas. The description of the unity of the lovers through the images of both an egg and a sphere further suggests a connection between the swan motif and the philosophical concept of becoming. If a sphere is the perfect symbol of complete, changeless, eternal being, an egg is the perfect symbol of the entire mystery of creation, of coming-into-being, of the temporal, spatial phenomenon of becoming.

But the shift from the image of the sphere to that of the egg does more than suggest a philosophical theme. It also emphasizes powerfully that the unity achieved by the lovers in that moment of sympathy was spiritual as well as carnal. In this respect, the old man is recalling and modifying the story of human history related by the comic poet Aristophanes in his speech in Plato's *Symposium*. According to Aristophanes, human beings were originally four-handed, four-legged, and two-faced, but because of their overweening pride they were split in half by the gods. Ever since, according to Aristophanes, they have been incomplete and have been searching for their other half. In Yeats's poem, unlike in Aristophanes' myth, the lovers found their unity through memory; and the spiritual unity is likened to an egg—that is, to a prenatal condition.

The role of memory here is crucial. The old man, after being reminded of the inner life of the children in the first stanza, does not recall one of his own childhood experiences. He recalls instead how his beloved once remembered and told him of her childhood experience. Thus childhood and old age are linked by a memory of a memory. The experience recounted in the second stanza is the memory of a perfect moment of love when the old man was in the prime of life, at the peak of his manhood. Maturity, childhood, and old age—or if you will, "the leaf, the blossom and the bole" (stanza VIII)—are indissolubly linked through memory. The importance of memory is not limited to the old man; the young lovers, too, achieved their perfection through a remembered event. Finally, that perfect union was itself no more than a recapitulation or memory of an even more remote past—the perfect prenatal union of the lovers' souls.

In the third verse the speaker turns from his reverie back to the scene in the classroom. But again he does the unexpected. Instead of using his memory to illuminate and give substance to the children before him, he does the opposite. The children in the schoolroom become the instruments for a new imaginative creation. For the first time in his life he is able to see his beloved as she must have been in childhood.

The effect of this stanza, particularly the concluding couplet, is startling. The immediacy and concreteness of Yeats's vision is completely convincing, and his passion is indubitable. The immense gulf separating the inner lives of the children and that of the old man in the first stanza is now fully bridged. The "living child" who stands before him at the end of the stanza is at one and the same time his beloved as she must have been and a real child in the schoolroom. The distant past and the immediate present are united by an imaginative act charged with passion. Such passionate images cannot be created to order by the speculative intelligence—they are genuine "Presences" that only "passion, piety or affection knows."

Throughout stanza III the speaker's concern is with the past, and the children whom he sees are a means to the realization of the past. He is not concerned with them. Yet by subordinating the outward public reality to his inner musings he manages to invest the children with far more reality than if he had simply claimed that the children, because they are like his beloved as she used to be, are already fully developed persons capable of human suffering. By the end of the third stanza his once-perfect, semidivine beloved has been seen as a clumsy child, and the ugly-duckling children in the schoolroom are all potential Helens.

By insisting, paradoxically, on the priority of the private over the public and the past over the present, the old man has managed to add depth to the public realm and the present moment. Furthermore, the meditation has now proceeded far enough for us to discern both the direction it is taking and the dimensions it is assuming. That amusing but trivial moment in the schoolroom has prompted in the old man a meditation on the fundamental nature of his existence. To that meditation nothing human is irrelevant.

The fourth stanza follows the third with perfect plausibility, although it balances and contrasts with it as the second did with the first. The intense, immediate, and concrete union of the past with the present calls to mind his beloved's present reality; after all, the union of past and present in the preceding stanza was only imaginative. Whereas the imaginative vision of his beloved as a child was presented earlier as an intense perceptual experience, now she is an "image" that "floats into the mind." Her appearance is ghostly and immaterial; she never, in this stanza, becomes more than an image—an "it" lacking even sex. Her image floats like a swan, providing not only a contrast to the immediacy of his vision of her in the preceding stanza but also an immaterial, ethereal, ghostly contrast to the living child who stands so solidly in front of the old man.

Her present reality is so fantastic and unbelievable in comparison to her "Ledean body" that she seems to be the creation of an artist, not a natural creature of flesh and blood. So immaterial is she that her life, if it can be called that, seems to be sustained by a diet of wind and shadows. Yet if the contrast between her Helenesque youth and her ghostly old age is great, she is nevertheless as beautiful as ever. She has lost the semi-divine beauty of a Helen, but she has achieved the beauty that can be conferred only by a da Vinci, Botticelli, or Fra Angelico—a "Quattrocento finger."

The image of his beloved presented in the first four lines of stanza IV thus serves to balance, though not counter or deny, the culminating experience of the previous stanza. The exultant, passionate intensity with which the old man saw the living child is matched by the still-beautiful but almost grotesque quality of her present image. The magnificent effort to subordinate the hard reality of the present to the imaginative vision of the past is also balanced and complemented by the wry awareness of his own present reality expressed in the last four lines of the stanza.

The association is obvious: the changes wrought in her by time remind him that he, too, is now old, and unlike her, he was never quite as magnificent as all that. The reverie has apparently come full circle by the end of this fourth stanza, when the old man accepts his public image as the better part of discretion. No matter how intense his inner life or how vital his memories or how passionate his imagination, he is an old man, and his real life is already in the past. He now has a public role to play, and the best he can do is to do what is expected of him as gracefully as possible.

The poem has reached a natural ending point—the speaker has become aware of a problem and has, in a sense, resolved it so far as his personal life is concerned. His solution is genial acceptance of his old age. He has learned something new about his beloved and about the relation of the past to the present. A lesser poet might well have stopped here; but not Yeats. The resolution and acceptance at the end of the fourth stanza are not sufficient. The old man may have come to accept his present state, but the mysteries hidden and revealed in the sequential development from childhood to maturity to old age, the paradoxes implicit in the contrast between memory and expectation, between appearance and reality—all these remain. The old man, now that he sees them clearly in both his imagination and his direct experience can deal with them. The resolution of his personal problem has freed him to explore the larger generic human issues implicit in his situation.

This shift from the personal to the generic is marked in the beginning of the fifth stanza when he muses on the significance of old age for the mother of a child. Would any mother consider her birth pangs or the miseries of motherhood worthwhile if she could see her son at sixty, when he has become, like the old man, a living scarecrow, albeit a genial one? Is there not, in the life history of the boy as he grows to manhood and descends into old age, an inevitable betrayal of the mother by the boy? She had such hopes for him, and look what he became.

But if the child betrays the mother by growing old, the mother also betrays the child, or so we can read the first half of the stanza to say. After all, the child did not ask to be born, and, the old man hints, the mother did not really want him. That honey of generation, the sweetness of love, creates a child and throws it into existence—a painful existence from which the drug of sex and the search for transcendent reality are the only escapes.

There is, I think, a kind of old man's nastiness in the way the speaker implies that the child's existence is an accidental result of the mother's desire for the honey of generation. Because of the mother's search for the anodyne of sex, the child, in his turn, is condemned to suffer existence—and to escape suffering only by immersion in the opiate of sex or through a struggle for Platonic recollection of prenatal freedom. The traditional, sentimental picture of the mother and child has here become an image of mutual betrayal.

This mutual betrayal is softened if we recall the second stanza. There the momentary blending of lovers into a sphere, a primeval egg, suggests that sex or, better, love, on the one hand, and recollection, on the other, may not be disjunctive alternatives. Recollection, even if achieved only momentarily, may be the fruit of moments of genuine love and passion. In any event, the extremely indeterminate and plastic nature of the infant is sharply emphasized by calling the child a "shape"—not once but twice.

Another irony in this stanza deserves noting. The three moments of human life—childhood, maturity, and old age—are here again, but in a new combination. Now childhood and old age are related through the mother. To the mother the future seems to hold infinite possibilities for her infant son, while in fact he will end up like other men. He will age into a withered scarecrow, destined to destroy her hopes and expectations. The genial acceptance of old age by the speaker in the previous stanza is now seen as a denial and betrayal of all that was once expected of him.

I find the emotional tone of this fifth stanza difficult to articulate: it seems to be compounded of almost equal parts of sympathy and pity, on the one hand, and irony and nastiness, on the other, all directed toward both the mother and the child. On the whole, the nastiness seems more of an undertone. What predominates is the poignancy of the mother and child, each loving and yet inevitably betraying the other, both unwittingly caught up in the passionate cycle of human existence.

The sixth stanza is justly famous. The three images describing Plato, Aristotle, and Pythagoras are wonderfully precise epigrammatic summations of their thought, and they are perfectly integrated into the poem. We are presented with three great philosophers who have given answers to the universal problems raised in the poem. All three are polished off and rejected in a single bitter line: "Old clothes upon old sticks to scare a bird."

Like the other stanzas, this one is connected to and contrasted with the preceding. The three philosophers can be seen as examples of the highest and best achievements of humankind. They were everything a mother's heart could hope for, and yet they ended, like the speaker and like all men, as scarecrows. But this barely scratches the surface.

For Plato, nature, as one critic has described it, is a fountain of mist or foam "playing over the divine forms, half revealing, half concealing them." Nature is unreal, and the eternal reality behind it is equally unreal—"a ghostly paradigm of things." Solider Aristotle is shown in his characteristic manner "imposing form on more or less tractable material, forming the mind, so to speak, of the schoolboy Alexander." Pythagoras is shown measuring on a string the intervals of the harmonic scale which he is attempting to derive from the music of the spheres.

All three, according to the old man, think that they have found the explanation of reality and human life in some form of abstraction. Their final state in its concrete and grotesque reality—old clothes upon old sticks to scare a bird—is a living refutation of their philosophies of abstraction. For all three philosophers, in fact, reality is merely play in one form or another. When the world is seen abstractly, it seems to be playful. This stands in the sharpest contrast to the fifth stanza, where both the mother and the child are pathetically caught in suffering and misery. Although the sixth stanza follows naturally enough from the fifth, it is this contrast between the inescapable suffering of human life and the playful, abstract reality of the philosophers that leads to the seventh stanza and to the culminating image of the entire meditation.

In stanza VII Yeats returns to the images of the fifth stanza—that is, to the mother and child—but in the terms developed in the sixth stanza, where reality is viewed in abstract images. The whole movement from stanzas V to VIII is parallel to the movement from I to IV. In the first four stanzas the movement is from a common or trivial experience suddenly seen in a new and unusual way, to a private reflection that serves as a balancing contrast. This leads in the third stanza to a fusion of the first two in the image of the living child. Finally, this leads in the fourth stanza to the present images of the beloved and the old man, images that balance and contrast with those of stanza III and also effect a return to the external situation of the first stanza.

The fifth stanza is based on the experience of the first four stanzas. In it the traditional mother-and-child relationship is considered one of mutual betrayal, pathos, suffering, and inevitable disappointment. From here the old man moves to an ironic, descriptive reflection on the three great philosophers who seem at first to answer in their persons and their philosophies the question asked in the fifth stanza, but who ultimately fail in both respects.

The seventh stanza returns to a reconsideration of the problem of the fifth stanza as the third does to the first. Just as in the third stanza the children are used only to illuminate the imaginative experience of the second stanza, so, too, in the seventh the mother (and now the nuns as well) is used primarily to illuminate the philosophical problem of the relation between concrete reality and abstract images—the problem raised in the sixth stanza. This synthesis in stanza VII of the experience and thought of the two preceding stanzas leads to the concluding verse, which contrasts with the seventh as the fourth does with the third, and also unifies and completes the entire reflection.

The smooth, almost effortless way each stanza follows its predecessor by a clear chain of association is only part of Yeats' structuring of the poem. Beneath the surface flow of passionate psychological assertions there is a precise formal pattern of statement, counterstatement, synthesis, and resolution that gives the poem special intellectual rigor.

With this formal structure in mind, let me now take up the last two stanzas. The seventh stanza breaks into two parts: the explicit comparison of the images worshiped by nuns and mothers and then, suddenly, the invocation of the Presences. The difference between the images worshiped by nuns and those worshiped by mothers is that the former are static and inanimate—crucifixes and icons—whereas the latter are presumably in flux—the mothers' changing conceptions of what their children should become.

Surely it could be objected that nuns do not worship images. They worship the living God symbolized by the images. Similarly, mothers do not worship images of their sons. They worship the living children whom they have given birth to, nursed, and raised. Yet the old man says that both nuns and mothers worship images, and he indicates the difference between their respective images. This difference, however, turns out to be trivial compared to what the images have in common—"yet they too break hearts."

The suffering nuns and mothers, in contrast to the playful philosophers, seem to owe their suffering to precisely the same concern that unites Plato, Aristotle, and Pythagoras. All are concerned with lifeless, perfect abstraction. The nuns and mothers worship images of perfection, and because the concrete reality that they face cannot possibly measure up to or realize these images, the images cannot fail to break their hearts. So much seems clear. But at this point the old man himself suddenly addresses the images directly, and for the rest of the stanza he describes them in a passionate, paradoxical invocation.

When he starts his address with "O Presences" it at once becomes apparent that the old man, too, is a worshiper of images. The shift from images to Presences, with all the personal involvement that is implied, renders absurd any notion that this portion of the poem is an impersonal statement of a philosophical position. It is, rather, a philosophical meditation on a generic human problem that is of great and immediate concern to the old man. His worship of Presences becomes explicit when he says that "passion, piety or affection knows" them.

If the nuns know the images, or Presences, through piety, and the mothers through affection, then the old man knows them through passion, as we saw in the second and third stanzas. Lovers, no less than nuns and mothers, are subject to the inevitable suffering and disappointment attendant on the worship of images. By saying that the Presences are known by passion, piety, or affection, the old man also implies that the philosophers do not and cannot know them.

Ironically, the seekers after abstract knowledge do not know the Presences. The Presences show themselves only to those who are most intimately concerned with the reality of God, children, and lovers. The philosophers search for the abstract but cannot know it. Only the nuns, mothers, and lovers, who are passionately involved with concrete reality, know, worship, and have their hearts broken by the images, which are for them not shadows but awesome Presences.

The next line of invocation, "And that all heavenly glory symbolise," is an apotheosis of the images. They now become symbols of the divine aspirations of human beings—aspirations apparently felt and known only by such passionately committed sufferers as nuns, mothers, and lovers. The stanza concludes with a final paradoxical twist, "O self-born mockers of man's enterprise." The images are self-born in several senses. Philosophically they are self-born in the sense that they are not within the natural order and therefore do not suffer the cycle of birth, growth, decay, and death that is the lot of mortals. The images that mock us are changeless and immortal, and that is the source of their mockery. They are also self-born in a somewhat more immediate and less intellectual sense. The images or, better, the Presences that we worship, are not consciously created by us; they present themselves to us as perfect realities to be worshiped.

A psychologist or a philosopher might say that a mother's image of her boy as she hopes he will be, a nun's image of a perfect, merciful, just, and loving God, or a lover's image of his divinely beautiful beloved are images created by the nun, mother, or lover, psychological projections or fantasies or something of that sort. But the mother, the nun, and the lover know better. What they worship and know is, to each of them, the realest of realities and the purpose toward which their energies are directed.

When the old man calls these presences mockers of man's enterprise he speaks neither as a philosophical realist nor as a philosophical idealist nor as someone caught between and balancing the claims of both the natural and supernatural. He speaks, rather, as a worshiper of the Presences, as one who has suffered and is suffering at their hands, and who at the end of his life is trying to understand what they are and what they mean. Whatever his final answer, at the end of this seventh stanza we can say that the Presences are the source both of human greatness and of tragic human suffering. They are images, abstractions, but they can be known only concretely, not abstractly. The Presences are the most serious things in our life, and yet it would seem that the more seriously they are pursued, the more they mock us, their pursuers.

The last stanza is the old man's statement to the images. In the first four lines he summarizes and affirms to them what he has learned during his life and in the course of this meditation in the schoolroom. In the last four lines he addresses two questions to them for which he receives no answers. These two parts, the affirmation and the questions, are intimately related because the metaphorical terms of the affirmation, *blossoming* and *dancing,* take on a literal meaning within the context of the questions addressed to the chestnut tree and the dancer.

There is a grammatical ambiguity in the first line of the stanza where *blossoming* and *dancing* could be either gerunds or participles—that is, either descriptions of what labor is or descriptions of what labor is doing. I am not sure that it makes any difference or that we are meant to choose between the alternatives, for in the last half of the stanza the distinctions between act, agency, and potency; quality, form, and matter; past, present, and future; being and becoming—all are unknowable, if not unreal.

At any rate, the speaker affirms that labour is blossoming or dancing except under three conditions. The marvelous and mysterious word here is *labor*. It means "work, toil, exertion," but it also means "childbirth." In this sense, labor is a metaphor for the whole process of becoming that is the central motif of the poem. By using labor as a metaphor for becoming the speaker also unavoidably reminds us of the contrast between the playful philosophers and the suffering worshipers of the Presences. *Labor* in both senses, as work, toil, and exertion and as a bringing to birth or creation, is the fate of the worshipers, a fate that they seemingly can never escape since they can never realize or make actual the images.

Yet in a complete and unexpected reversal, the old man now says that labor can achieve perfection, glory, and fulfillment and even a kind of grace or ease or effortlessness. During his visit to the schoolroom the old man has learned that the human enterprise is necessarily doomed to tragic failure because the final aspiration is impossible to achieve. Yet the enterprise itself is not meaningless and may even achieve a transcendent value of its own. But there are conditions. This will happen only

> where
> The body is not bruised to pleasure soul,
> Nor beauty born out of its own despair,
> Nor blear-eyed wisdom out of midnight oil.

These three negative conditions represent, respectively, ways of achieving goodness, beauty, and truth, the great trinity of human aspirations. They also suggest, ironically, the play of Aristotle, Pythagoras, and Plato. The use of *born* as the verb for the last two conditions produces yet another ironic reversal. The birth of beauty or wisdom in the wrong way will prevent labor from blossoming or dancing and thus will be self-negating. In these four lines, then, the old man tells the Presences the conditions under which human fulfillment is not possible. In the last four lines, by asking two unanswered and unanswerable questions, we are shown dramatically how it is possible.

The chestnut tree is described as a "great-rooted blossomer"—it has a long past and an urge toward the future. If this describes the tree, asking whether it is "the leaf, the blossom or the bole"—whether it has present existence, potentiality for the future, or residue from the past—is almost meaningless. All three elements are integral to the being of the tree. The being of the tree includes, and is indistinguishable from, its becoming.

The dancer also is addressed in a way that makes the question asked of her meaningless. Instead of addressing her directly, the old man speaks to two abstract aspects of her, the "body swayed to music" and the "brightening glance"—that is, matter in motion and the spirit or soul that animates and informs the body. The form and matter of the dancer are thus identical with the form and matter of the dance itself, and the two cannot be distinguished, much less separated. The questions are unanswered and unanswerable not only because of the form in which they are asked but also because dancers completely immersed in their dancing, like chestnut trees, do not answer questions. In their concrete reality, the chestnut tree and the dancer indissolubly fuse all the distinctions and abstractions of the philosophers.

The chestnut tree and the dancer are living examples of labor that is blossoming or dancing without any of the destructive elements that frustrate the human enterprise. In this, it seems to me, lies the final mystery of the poem. By virtue of the very perfection of their concrete reality the chestnut tree and the dancer are also, and of necessity, Presences, presences that symbolize heavenly glory and that mock the human enterprise.

Implicit in this final affirmation and questioning are all of the polar opposites through which the entire meditation has moved from the moment the old man and the children confronted each other: (1) being and becoming, (2) knowledge and ignorance, (3) act and agent, (4) past, present, and future, (5) concreteness and abstraction, (6) frustration and fulfillment, (7) suffering and joy, (8) pathos and play, (9) the ideal and the actual, (10) appearance and reality, (11) public and private, (12) coming to be and passing away, and (13) the playful and the serious. None of these is denied; all are affirmed, but together as a whole, implying and defining each other as the elements of that whole.

This is what the sixty-year-old smiling public man learned when he walked through the long schoolroom questioning. To spell out in prosaic detail all that is contained in this ultimate vision would be tedious and a little impertinent. Suffice it to say that the vision is authentic and palpable, that it is genuinely philosophical, that the old man really did learn something when he went back to school, and that Yeats has given his experience full poetic expression for us to experience.

9 Conrad's *Heart of Darkness*
Art and the Artist

I propose to tackle the general problem of the relationship of the artist to the artist's work through an examination of Joseph Conrad's *Heart of Darkness*. The relationship is, I think, central to an understanding of the story and its significance for modern readers.

Let me first give some information about Conrad's life and experience that is directly relevant to the story, then discuss the story itself. I shall concentrate on four points: (1) setting and mood, (2) Marlow's character as narrator and as actor, (3) Kurtz at the culminating point of Marlow's experience, and (4) the significance of the final scenes in Brussels, where Marlow disposes of Kurtz's personal effects, and on the yawl *Nellie,* where years later Marlow tells the story to a small group of friends. Finally, I will suggest some of the implications of the work for the modern understanding of literature and for the peculiar modern version of the notion that the artist is the only serious claimant to the age-old title of seer, prophet, sage.

Conrad, Poland's gift to English literature, was born Joseph Korzeniowski in 1857. He left home at an early age, went to sea at sixteen or seventeen, and by 1889, at the age of thirty-two, had become a captain in the British Merchant Marine. In September of that year, after spending several fruitless months in London seeking a new command, on an impulse one morning he began to write his first novel, *Almayer's Folly*.

About the same time he conceived the equally spur-of-the-moment notion of taking a job as captain of a river steamer on the Congo. The notion had roots in Conrad's early life, as he recounts in his autobiography, *A Personal Record:* "It was in 1868, when nine years old or thereabouts, that while looking at a map of Africa of the time and putting my finger on the blank space then representing the unsolved mystery of that continent, I said to myself, with absolute assurance and an amazing audacity which are no longer in my character now: 'When I grow up I shall go *there*.' And of course I thought no more about it till after a quarter of a century or so an opportunity offered to go there—as if the sin of childish audacity was to be visited on my mature head." In saying that an opportunity offered to go there, Conrad is not being quite honest, despite his reputation for that virtue, or perhaps his fabulous memory slipped a little. The facts seem to be that he made his own opportunity. In late September 1889 he had a friend send a letter of recommendation about him to the managing director of the Joint Stock Company for Commerce in the Upper Congo in Brussels. Early in November he went to Brussels, presented himself at the company, and, because of his knowledge of French, was promised a position as soon as one was available. He waited several months and then, uncharacteristically, pulled strings. Through his family in Poland he made contact with an uncle whom he had not seen since boyhood. He also met his uncle's wife for the first time, and apparently they became close friends. When his uncle died suddenly, Conrad returned to eastern Europe for the first time in sixteen years. During the winter of 1889–1890 his recently widowed aunt wrote a good deal not only to him but also to her influential friends.

In April 1890, Captain Korzeniowski was awarded his coveted riverboat command. After a final visit to Brussels he shipped from Bordeaux in May 1890 for the Congo. The trip took about six weeks because the boat called at Teneriffe, Dakar, Kanakri, Sierra Leone, Grand Bassam, Kotonu, Libreville, Loango, Banana, and Boma. In a letter to a cousin written during this voyage, Conrad says: "As far as I can make out from my service letter, I am destined to command a steamboat belonging to Mr. Delcommune's exploring party, which is now getting ready; but I know nothing for certain as everything is supposed to be kept secret. What makes me rather uneasy is the information that 60 percent of the company's employees go back to Europe before they have completed even six months' service. . . . There are others who are sent home in a hurry at the end of the year so that they should not die in the Congo. God forbid it! In a word, it seems that there are only 7 percent who can do their three years' service."

From Boma, Conrad took a boat thirty miles up the river to Matadi, called the Company Station in *Heart of Darkness*. There he waited some time before undertaking an overland trip of several hundred miles upriver to Stanley Pool—called Léopoldville later, Kinshasa on today's maps, and the Central Station in the story. There is a close correspondence between the events narrated by Marlow in the story and the facts of Conrad's own experience. Conrad himself says in his "Author's Note" that "*Heart of Darkness* is experience, but it is experience pushed a little (and only very little) beyond the actual facts of the case for the perfectly legitimate, I believe, purpose of bringing it home to the minds and bosoms of the readers."

Conrad kept a diary during part of his stay in the Congo. Here are a few excerpts. During his stay at Matadi, the Company Station, where the Grove of Death is located, he says,

> Feel considerably in doubt about the future. Think just now that my life amongst the people (white) around here cannot be very comfortable. Intend to avoid acquaintance as much as possible.
>
> Sat. June 28—Left Matadi with M. Harou and a caravan of 31 men.
>
> Mond. June 30—Long ascent. Harou giving up. Bother, Camp bad. Water far. Dirty. At night Harou better.
>
> Thurs. July 3—Met an officer of the State inspecting. A few minutes afterwards saw at a camping place the dead body of a Backongo. Shot? Horrid smell.
>
> Fri. July 4—Saw another dead body lying by the path in an attitude of meditative repose.
>
> Sat. July 5—Today fell into a muddy puddle—beastly. The fault of the man that carried me. Getting jolly well sick of this fun.
>
> Tues. July 29—At 9 met Mr. Louette escorting a sick agent of the company back to Matadi. Looking very well. Bad news from up the river. All the steamers disabled—one wrecked. . . . On the road today passed a skeleton tied up to a post. Also white man's grave—no name—heap of stones in the form of a cross.
>
> Wed. July 30—Expect lots of bother with carriers tomorrow. Had them all called and made a speech, which they did not understand.
>
> Thurs. July 31—Great difficulty in carrying Harou. Too heavy—bother.

The diary ends the next day. Conrad arrived at Stanley Pool on August 2. On August 4 he left as second officer, not captain, of the *Roi de Belges* on a twenty-eight-day trip up the Congo to Stanley Falls, the site of Stanleyville. The purpose of the journey was to relieve one of the company's agents whose health was failing. The agent's name was Georges-Antoine Kleine. In German *klein* means "small," and kurtz, the name of Conrad's protagonist, means "short." Unfortunately, nothing is known of Mr. Kleine except that he embarked on the *Roi de Belges* for the return trip downriver, died during the trip, and was buried along the way.

In letters written at the time, Conrad reports that he himself was ill during the trip upriver and was feeling homesick for the sea. He hoped, however, to remain in the Congo and to secure the command of another, larger steamer that was to carry the exploring expedition headed by Alexander Delcommune, the brother of the manager of the Stanley Pool station. Conrad apparently had some sort of falling out with the manager of the station, who would not give him command of the steamer. This, in addition to his fever and dysentery persuaded him to leave for the coast in early November—thereby lowering the average length of time the company's agents stayed in the Congo. He returned to Europe to recover from what he himself described as "a long, long illness and a very dismal convalescence."

More than ten years later, in 1902, he wrote *Heart of Darkness* in about thirty days. Many years after that, he told a friend, "Before the Congo, I was just a mere animal." Conrad did not say that before the Congo he was naive, or a child, or an innocent. Given the experience related in *Heart of Darkness,* the term *animal* takes on a special meaning. In any event, whatever Conrad was *before* the trip up the Congo, he was certainly an artist after he returned. Furthermore, that he sat on the experience for more than ten years and then wrote it down, transmogrified, in thirty days suggests strongly that *Heart of Darkness* is not merely one of the many exotic stories and novels that he produced. It played a special role in his own development as an artist, and it requires a special effort of understanding on our part.

So much for the biographical background. The point is clear: in attempting to penetrate the experience rendered in *Heart of Darkness,* we the readers are coming to grips with the formative experience in the life of a great modern artist.

Readers of the novel are struck first by the setting and the peculiar mood that it evokes. We do not go up the river with Marlow; we are not even present when he tells his story to his friends many years later. Instead, we are at three removes from the original experience: an unnamed narrator tells us the story of what happened one night when he and four friends were on a small sailboat in the Thames waiting for the tide to turn. The bulk of the narrator's story is a verbatim account of Marlow's own story. In effect, *Heart of Darkness* is the story of a story.

This storytelling technique is admittedly hackneyed. But in Conrad's hands it is transformed into a vital element of the experience. There is apparently an enormous gap between our everyday, civilized, urban, bourgeois life and the experience that Conrad is about to describe. The five men on the *Nellie* share, as the narrator says, "the bond of the sea." They have a personal link with Marlow that permits him to make contact with them and so to tell his story. Yet the four listeners no longer follow the sea. They are successful landlubbers now, more or less like us. And like us, they are skeptical of Marlow's storytelling style, his "adjectival insistence," his delight in paradoxes and enigmas, his point-less anecdotes that yet create a mood. Still, as former sailors, they share enough of his sense of the world to listen with some patience and sympathy and to help us do the same.

At the same time, the removal of the story from raw experience by so many years and so many intermediaries gives it a certain distance, which insulates us from the literally indescribable and morally unspeakable events in the Congo. Conrad, we know, went through those events himself, and he knows full well how shockingly dangerous they can be to the unprotected soul. The complex narrative frame thus helps to protect the reader from a direct encounter with a potentially destructive experience.

Paradoxically, then, in one respect the narrative frame connects readers with Marlow's story, but in another respect it insulates readers from it. Conrad wants us to face and to understand what happened to him up the Congo, yet he is also afraid of what will happen to us if we do. This ambiguity of the narrative frame is crucial and is emblematic of the whole story: Conrad is constantly forcing us to face the shattering truth and at the same time protecting us from it.

He was too good an artist not to feel this tension and has constructed the story to let each reader resolve it personally. The result is that different readers understand the tale in very different ways. Midpoint in the story, during the trip upriver, Marlow describes the howling of the savages in the bush and admits that he was "thrilled" by the thought of their humanity and his kinship with them and by their "wild and passionate uproar." At this point, one of his auditors mutters some comment, and Marlow angrily replies:

> Ugly. Yes, it was ugly enough; but if you were man enough you would admit to yourself that there was in you just the faintest trace of a response to the terrible frankness of that noise. . . . Let the fool gape and shudder—the man knows, and can look on without a wink. But he must at least be as much of a man as these on the shore. He must meet that truth with his own true stuff—with his own in-born strength.
>
> Principles? Principles won't do. . . . An appeal to me in this fiendish row—is there? Very well; I hear; I admit; but I have a voice too, and for good or evil mine is the speech that cannot be silenced. Of course, a fool, what with sheer fright and fine sentiments, is always safe.

Fools are safe not only from the passionate uproar of the bush but also from the truth expressed, for good or evil, in Marlow's story.

For several decades after *Heart of Darkness* was published (in 1902), it was apparently taken as a root-and-branch attack on the evils of Belgian imperialism and used by critics of King Leopold's Congo policies as a basis for stirring up international sentiment against them. There are still readers who think this is the point of the story. After the First World War and the dissolution of European optimism, some critics saw that Conrad may have been more than a good teller of exotic tales, more even than a slashing critic of injustice and inhumanity. He began to look like a prophet. Conrad accomplished no small thing in seeing as early as 1902 with such incredible clarity the rottenness and corruption of European civilization that became publicly apparent only during and after the horrors of the war of 1914–1918.

We who live in the post-Auschwitz and post-Hiroshima age can see even more, for history at last has more or less caught up with Conrad, and his private vision of 1902 has become the public vision of most perceptive people. To put it bluntly, Conrad learned in the Congo and expressed in *Heart of Darkness*, for those who can face it, the truth that all civilization, all morality, all decency, everything human beings hold dear, is our own fragile creation; it was not laid down by some benevolent creator.

With his ideas abstractly stated like this, Conrad seems to be akin to the postmodernists—and I think he is. But far more than postmodernists usually do, he thought through the moral implications of his vision and came to terms with it. He was not merely a prophet who, having been blessed (or cursed) with a vision of the future, trumpeted it to the world. He was a seer, a sage, an artist who tried to make his vision meaningful to others. But his own sense of the significance of his vision also led him to veil the truth as he revealed it, so that only someone "man enough" could see it. The instrument that he chose both to reveal and to obscure that truth is Marlow, the old sailor who still followed the sea.

Notice how Marlow is introduced. The five men are lazily sitting on the *Nellie* at sunset; the flood tide has come and there is nothing to do for several hours until the ebb tide, when the ship can head downriver. The narrator looks about him, impressed by the serenity of the scene and the "benign immensity of unstained light." As the sun goes down he muses to himself on the setting: "The old river in its broad reach rested unruffled at the decline of day, after ages of good service done to the race that peopled its banks, spread out in the tranquil dignity of a waterway leading to the uttermost ends of the earth. We looked at the venerable stream not in the vivid flush of a short day that comes and departs for ever, but in the august light of abiding memories."

He thinks of all the ships that have sailed up and down the river carrying the knights-errant of the sea, the wielders of the sword, the bearers of the torch of civilization, lit by a spark from the sacred fire. The sun goes down, and as the last light touches the unnamed, immense metropolis upstream the first spoken words of the story are uttered: "'And this also,' said Marlow suddenly, 'has been one of the dark places of the earth.'" It is a dramatic, even melodramatic statement. But with these few words Marlow reveals himself as a seer, for without a word being spoken by the narrator, Marlow knows exactly what he has been thinking.

More than that, with one sentence Marlow has undercut and rendered dubious the optimistic, self-satisfied, narrow perspective of the narrator, the other men on the boat, and the reader. "I was thinking," continues Marlow, "of very old times, when the Romans first came here, nineteen hundred years ago—the other day. . . . Light came out of this river since—you say Knights? Yes, but it is like a running blaze on a plain, like a flash of lightning in the clouds. We live in the flicker—may it last as long as the old earth keeps rolling! But darkness was here yesterday."

Marlow does not deny the conventional perspective of the narrator or the reader; he places it within a larger perspective, a perspective so huge that it reduces the conventional sense of history from blaze to flicker. The narrator feels the weighty English history of four hundred years. For Marlow the coming of the civilized Romans to savage England two millenia earlier happened only yesterday. And suddenly England itself, hoary with age and civilization, appears as a wretched frontier of swamps, blue-painted tribespeople, and untold human misery. Everything that Marlow learned on his trip up the Congo is present in this brief, imaginative re-creation of pre-Roman Britain: the greed, the folly, the violence, the shock to a Kurtz-like young Roman who came out to the edge of empire to redeem his personal fortune. The ugliness and evil that attend the "conquest of the earth," or, as Marlow puts it, "the taking it away from those who have a different complexion or slightly flatter noses than ourselves"—all this Marlow sees in his mind's eye.

Although he condemns the conquest morally, he does not simply dismiss it as unfortunate. "What redeems it is the idea only. An idea at the back of it; not a sentimental pretense but an idea; and an unselfish belief in the idea—something you can set up, and bow down before, and offer a sacrifice to . . ." Here Marlow breaks off; he does not tell his friends or us what he means by the idea or how it differs from a sentimental pretense. But that, in fact, is to be the burden of his whole story. To see that idea in all its awful truth, to believe in it unselfishly, to set it up, to bow down before it, to offer a sacrifice to it—that is what Conrad saw in the Congo and what, through Marlow, he hopes to make clear to the man who can look on without a wink.

From the opening pages of the story it is clear that Marlow is far more complex than he himself gives out. On the surface he is a garrulous old sailor given to telling pointless stories, and this story is simply the account of a deep-sea sailor who got out of his depth by going up the snag-filled Congo. But Marlow not only tells what happened to him; he constantly interprets its meaning through his mode of narration. His journey is described through a series of images that give it a depth and significance far beyond the literal scope of the events.

Let me suggest a few of the devices by which Marlow gives significance to his tale. His story is of a journey from the center of European civilization down the coast of Africa and up the Congo to the heart of the "dark continent," to the worst scene of European colonization and exploitation. Marlow starts this journey as an interested traveler, a sightseer who impulsively and innocently wants to know what is in one of the blank spaces on the map. Unfortunately, as he is aware from the beginning, to reach the center of that blank space he must go up a river, a river "resembling an immense snake uncoiled, with its head in the sea, its body at rest curving afar over a vast country, and its tail lost in the depths of the land. And as I looked at the map of it in a shop-window, it fascinated me as a snake would a bird—a silly little bird."

Marlow knows that he has not merely chosen to go; he is also being drawn hypnotically by something bigger and more powerful than himself, something that does not have his best interests at heart. In a sense, the whole story is an account of Marlow's transformation from a silly little bird to the Buddha-like sage who sits on the deck of the *Nellie* and reveals the enlightening and saving truth to those who will listen.

When he enters the office of the trading company in Brussels (called just a sepulchre city in the book), the anteroom is dark, inhabited by two old women dressed in black, knitting. One stands up and, without looking at him, escorts him in. There is a deal table in the center of the room and, on the wall, a map of the world with colonial possessions marked in red, blue, purple, and, in the center, yellow. The scene alludes to a number of myths. The old women could be the Fates. Marlow is also reminded of the gladiators' greeting, "We who are about to die salute you."

Most directly the scene calls up the entrance to Hell. The woman who, he says, "pilots" visitors back and forth is Charon, the boatman on the river Styx, and the other woman is Cerberus, the three-headed dog who guards the gates of darkness. In going to the yellow at the center of the map, Marlow feels that he is going to the center of the earth, the traditional pagan and Christian setting for hell. Thus, through this visit to the company office, the first mythical dimension is added to the story. In going up the Congo, Marlow is undertaking a journey to hell. This theme is picked up and reinforced throughout the story as Marlow more and more slowly approaches his ultimate destiny—the confrontation with Kurtz.

On the ocean voyage from Europe, Marlow is struck by the increasing unreality of the situation: the silly little battleship bombarding a continent with men dying of plague on board, the impenetrable coastline, and so on. He says, "It was like a weary pilgrimage amongst hints for nightmares." The image of the nightmare, like that of the journey to hell, recurs and becomes increasingly insistent as he proceeds. For a long time Marlow struggles to retain his sense of being awake, of seeing things clearly and honestly for what they are. At the end, he is overwhelmed and admits that his only choice is between two nightmares—that offered by the company manager or that offered by Kurtz.

Insofar as the journey is dreamlike, a nightmare, it is an interior journey, a voyage into the depths of the human soul. This is a second dimension to the tale. Notice that the journey to hell and the journey into the human soul are different ways of describing the same event—that visiting hell is identical to visiting the soul!

When the river steamer leaves the Central Station and heads upriver, it is, Marlow says, "like traveling back to the earliest beginnings of the world." The journey is also a trip back in time, to the beginning of human time. Finally, as the steamer sails nearer to the inner station, Marlow says that "the approach to Kurtz grubbing for ivory in the wretched bush was beset by as many dangers as though he had been an enchanted princess sleeping in a fabulous castle." Now the story becomes a fairy tale, with Kurtz as Sleeping Beauty waiting to be awakened by a kiss from her Prince Charming, Marlow, who is gallantly inching his way upstream in a miserable old tub that threatens to blow its boilers any minute. Nightmarish joke it may be, but the analogy holds true: Marlow does rescue Kurtz, he does save his soul, and a feeling perilously close to love lies between them.

All these dimensions are accompanied by a pattern of light and dark imagery, making Marlow's journey a trip into both light and dark. Consider, for example, the passage in which Marlow is talking to the papier-mâché Mephistopheles at the Central Station after one of the buildings has burned down: "He blew the candle out suddenly, and we went outside. The moon had risen. Black figures strolled about listlessly, pouring water on the glow, whence proceeded a sound of hissing; steam ascended in the moonlight; the beaten nigger groaned somewhere." From the light of the candle to the dark of the room, to the light of the moon, to the black figures, to the light of the glowing embers, to the light of the steam rising and the groaning of the invisible black man somewhere in the night, the images of light and dark succeed each other with bewildering speed and profusion.

The climax of darkness, ironically enough, comes in the full light of day. Standing on the steamer at the inner station talking with the Russian harlequin while the pilgrims are on shore looking for Kurtz, Marlow says: "I looked around, and I don't know why, but I assure you that never, never before, did this land, this river, this jungle, the very arch of the this blazing sky, appear to me so hopeless and so dark, so impenetrable to human thought, so pitiless to human weakness."

The imagery of light and dark, with its ironic inversions and confusions, suggests what is probably the basic mythical dimension of the story, the journey from ignorance to knowledge. Traditionally, as in the parable of the cave in Plato's *Republic,* that journey is from darkness to light. Here, light and dark interpenetrate. What we are trying to see is a darkness, and the extraordinary difficulty of seeing it is what makes Marlow's narrative task so complicated. The function of the many interlocking mythical dimensions is to indicate just how complex Marlow's tale is.

The multiple dimensions of Marlow's narrative spring from more than the complications of his story. They also signal the complexity of Marlow's character. I have already suggested that the true center of the story is Marlow, not Kurtz, and that Marlow changes from an acute observer to a participating agent during the course of his adventure. It is not that Marlow stops observing and begins acting, however. Rather, as he gradually and unwittingly takes on the role of an actor he has difficulty observing himself and his own responses.

Part of the difficulty lies in the complexity of Marlow's responses. He is always judging people and events from several points of view simultaneously. During the early stages of his journey he is able to keep these diverse viewpoints relatively clear and distinct. But as he becomes involved in Kurtz's fate, they merge and conflict with each other.

As I see it, Marlow judges people and events according to at least four principles. First is morality. Marlow is an upright man who respects the common decencies. There is nothing radical about his moral views. He admires truthfulness and detests falsehood, he is in favor of justice and against bullies, and he believes that human life, all human life, is sacred. Throughout the story, for example, Marlow presents women as by and large good. They have other failings, so he believes that they are "out of it," but there is never any question of their fundamental morality and decency. In contrast to the women, the pilgrims searching for ivory and, most of all, those on the Eldorado Exploring Expedition are evil. Marlow is never uncertain or hesitant about calling the colonials evil; they are at the bottom of the scale. It would be possible to rank everybody else in the story somewhere between the women and the Eldorado Exploring Expedition. The only possible exception is Kurtz, who perhaps would have to be placed simultaneously at both ends of the scale. But we will come to him shortly.

Marlow's fundamental and essentially conventional moral sense does not account for all the judgments that he makes. In addition to the scale of good and evil, there is also a scale of intelligence and stupidity. Here intelligence can be equated with insight, with the ability to look at things and see them for what they are, and stupidity amounts to the corresponding inability to do so. The most intelligent person in the story is Kurtz. He is never deceived. The stupidest is the Russian harlequin, who can prattle on about Kurtz's mind and his discourses on love while Kurtz is trying to kill him.

Strangely enough, the women seem, as a group, to be stupid in the same way as the pilgrims are; so on this scale, the extremes of good and evil are equally stupid. In one scene Marlow, resting on the damaged steamer, overhears the company manager and his uncle talking of Kurtz. The uncle gestures toward the jungle and says, "Ah, my boy, trust to this," shocking Marlow not so much for its immorality as for its incredible stupidity—how could anyone living in the heart of the Congo possibly think of the jungle as an instrument for achieving his own petty, selfish ends?

Closely akin to the scale of intelligence and stupidity is the spectrum of appearance and reality. Reality is always hidden beneath a veneer. The women filled with schemes for moral uplift, the accountant talking of the heat and the difficulty of training native women to starch his collars while a man lies dying on the floor, the battleship bombarding a continent—these are cases of appearance being taken for reality. Human lusts, seen by Kurtz; one's self doing pointless work, described by Marlow; despair, seen by the natives and particularly by the magnificent native woman when the god-king Kurtz leaves—Marlow tells about each of these truths as he sees it. Whatever the moral content of the reality, he clearly respects its truth, as opposed to the deception of appearance.

Beyond all these and different from them is Marlow's concern with restraint and its lack. Marlow has considerable respect for restraint in the face of temptation, perhaps more respect for that than for anything else. It is no accident that the outstanding example of restraint in the story is the behavior of the cannibals on the steamboat. In the face of agonizing, slow starvation, after their rotting hippo meat is thrown overboard, they do not take advantage of their superior numbers to slaughter the whites. Marlow confesses to complete bewilderment as to why they should have restrained themselves. The bookkeeper who, despite the heat and decay about him, manages to wear clean cuffs and to keep his books in order is another case. Marlow himself, in refusing to go ashore and dance with the native Africans, is another. He gives as his excuse that he had to keep the ship going, but in truth, he restrained himself. In all such cases, there does not seem to be any particular reason for restraint beyond the flat refusal to give in.

The women and the Russian are so stupid or so blind to reality that restraint is nonexistent. The wretched pilgrims see just enough to realize that they are free of the external restraints of having an address in a civilized place with a butcher around one corner and a policeman around the next. Consequently they become those flabby, rapacious, unconstrained devils whom Marlow detests so much. The great example of lack of restraint is Kurtz, who, alone in the middle of the jungle, feels utterly free and thus able to do anything he wishes.

These several principles of judgment employed by Marlow—goodness, intelligence, reality, and restraint—are not commensurate with each other. People who rank high on one scale may rank low on another. The women are admired for their decency but brushed aside for their hopeless inability to come to grips with the simplest facts of the real world. The bookkeeper is admired for his restraint and fundamental decency and tacitly condemned as a fool.

So long as Marlow is a sightseer, a neutral observer of the general disorder and insanity in the Congo, these discrepancies pose no particular problem. But when circumstances and his own character force him to play a part in Kurtz's life, he is in trouble. No matter what he does, he must inevitably do something bad. He wants desperately to meet and talk to Kurtz. But, as he says in speaking of the native helmsman killed on the way upriver, "I am not prepared to affirm the fellow [Kurtz] was exactly worth the life we lost in getting to him. I missed my late helmsman awfully . . . don't you see, he had done something, he had steered."

For Marlow personally, the climax comes in the final scene when, in his interview with Kurtz's intended, he lays the ghosts of Kurtz's gifts by telling a seemingly harmless lie to protect her illusions. But in trying to preserve her light, Marlow feels as if the skies almost collapse about his head. He tells the lie because he must, because it would have been "too dark altogether" if he had told the truth. But in deceiving her he does a fundamental injustice to Kurtz and advances the cause of darkness. The dispassionate onlooker, the devotee of morality and work, the apostle of restraint, the modest bearer of the torch, ends his story by admitting his failure, by confessing his duplicity, by revealing his own moral and intellectual inadequacy.

The cause of his failure is Kurtz, at the center of Marlow's encounter with darkness. Kurtz first appears indirectly in the anonymous young Roman who came to Britain to mend his fortunes, but that is only the faintest hint of what is to come. Kurtz explicitly enters the story on the lips of the accountant at the Company Station, who tells Marlow that Kurtz is a remarkable man, a superb ivory trader, a man with a future. Kurtz is next mentioned by the manager of the Central Station in his first interview with Marlow. The manager tells Marlow that one of the important stations upriver is in danger, that its chief, Mr. Kurtz, is ill. Marlow, tired from the long overland trip and uneasy in the manager's presence, is annoyed: "Hang Kurtz, I thought. I interrupted him by saying I had heard of Mr. Kurtz on the coast. 'Ah! So they talk of him down there,' he murmured to himself."

The night of the fire Marlow hears the name Kurtz mentioned in the crowd and the phrase "take advantage of this unfortunate accident." Later that evening in his conversation with the papier-mâché Mephistopheles he sees Kurtz's symbolic painting of a blindfold Justice carrying a lighted torch. Marlow asks about Kurtz and is told that "he is a prodigy . . . an emissary of pity, and science, and progress." Then he discovers that through his dear aunt's efforts he has already been identified with Kurtz's party; so he playfully teases the bearded agent by acting as if he really were allied with Kurtz.

By such trivial beginnings are men's fates decided. From that point on, Kurtz looms larger and larger in Marlow's consciousness and in the reader's. The trip upriver becomes a trip to meet Kurtz. With every bit of additional information, Kurtz's dimensions grow until he becomes a universal genius, the enemy of everything evil and ugly that Marlow has so far met in the Congo, a mysterious figure who becomes more enigmatic as knowledge about him increases. But most of all, he becomes a voice, something to listen to. In this as well as in his other features, we can see that Marlow's aunt and the pilgrims were right: Marlow and Kurtz have a remarkable resemblance and affinity. Marlow tries hard to deny it, he fights to maintain his separate identity, but like Kurtz, he has a destiny, and for better or worse, that destiny involves his kinship with Kurtz.

Kurtz was educated partly in England. His mother was half-English, his father was half-French, but all Europe contributed to the making of him. Remarkably, all Europe is also involved in his downfall: there are the English captain Marlow, who replaces the Danish captain Fresleven; the Belgian French-speaking pilgrims; the Russian harlequin who wants to work for a Dutch trading house; and Kurtz himself, with his German name. Kurtz is sponsored by the International Society for the Suppression of Savage Customs. His brilliant, altruistic seventeen-page report with its one-sentence postscript of practical advice gives some idea of the complexity of his background and his character.

If Kurtz embodies Europe and is, in his own person, the highest creation of European civilization—the human product of nineteen hundred years of Christian civilization, the sad truth is that he is only a voice; he is hollow inside. Marlow, with his usual tact, does not bother to detail Kurtz's unspeakable degradation; it is enough to know that Kurtz allowed himself to become a god-king to the savages, that he tried to kill his one friend, that he surrounded his house with a decorative fence of shrunken heads facing inward, and that in his absolute freedom he became completely enslaved to the darkness of his own lusts.

When Kurtz tries to escape from the boat and return to the natives, Marlow describes the impossibility of making human contact with him. "He had kicked himself loose of the earth. Soul! If anybody had ever struggled with a soul, I am the man. And I wasn't arguing with a lunatic either. Believe me or not, his intelligence was perfectly clear. . . . But his soul was mad. . . . He struggled with himself too. . . . I saw the inconceivable mystery of a soul that knew no restraint, no faith and no fear, yet struggling, blindly with itself."

Marlow is a modest man, and he says little of his own role in that struggle with Kurtz. Yet it seems obvious that Marlow was the one who tipped the balance. Kurtz may have kicked himself free of the earth, but in that incredible scene in which the two men face each other, barely thirty yards from the nearest fire of the natives, with the beating of the drum matching the beating of their hearts, somehow Marlow reestablishes human contact with Kurtz so that Kurtz can win that inner struggle. In the days that follow, as they return downstream, Kurtz and Marlow talk and Marlow feels the power of Kurtz's voice as Kurtz's life ebbs. Then one night when Marlow comes in, Kurtz says, " 'I am lying here in the dark waiting for death.' Anything approaching the change that came over his features I have never seen before and hope never to see again. O! I wasn't touched. I was fascinated. It was as though a veil had been rent. I saw on that ivory face the expression of sombre pride, of ruthless power, of craven terror—of an intense and hopeless despair. Did he live his life again in every detail of desire, temptation, and surrender during that supreme moment of complete knowledge? He cried in a whisper at some image, at some vision— he cried out twice, a cry that was no more than a breath;—'The horror! The horror!'"

After a bout of sickness during which Marlow himself approaches the edge without seeing anything but grayness, he asserts, "This is the reason why I affirm that Kurtz was a remarkable man. He had something to say. He said it." Beyond that, Marlow insists that Kurtz's last cry "was an affirmation, a moral victory paid for by innumerable defeats, by abominable terrors, by abominable satisfactions. But it was a victory. That is why I have remained loyal to Kurtz to the last."

So much for Kurtz. He appears as a remarkable man after all, a man of genuine talent who, when external restraints were removed, was found lacking in some inner stuff. So he was destroyed, although he gained a moral victory at the end. This, at any rate, is the way the story looks on the surface. All that remains is for Marlow to distribute Kurtz's belongings to various people who knew him. These final scenes in Brussels are rather strange, and apart from their irony, they seem redundant.

Marlow visits the company, where he hands in Kurtz's report on the suppression of savage customs with the postscript torn off. The company official is furious with the report because, he says, "this is not what we had a right to expect." What he wants is information of practical value for collecting ivory.

Next Marlow sees Kurtz's cousin, who tells him that Kurtz's proper sphere was politics "on the popular side." When Marlow asks of what party, the answer is, "Any party. . . . He was an—an extremist." Finally there is the interview with the fiancée, who tells Marlow that to know Kurtz was to love him and that Kurtz "died as he lived." Marlow is sufficiently upset by the interview to admit inadvertently that he was present when Kurtz died, and so he is forced to lie about Kurtz's last words. Why are these scenes there? What is their point?

The answer is hard to put fairly for Marlow and Conrad have concealed a great deal more than they have revealed. Marlow and his auditors learn that their judgment of Kurtz up to that point has been wrong.

The company is disappointed because Kurtz, their best ivory collector, did not leave any information about his marvelous methods. They are wrong, of course. He did leave information, deliberately and knowingly suppressed by Marlow—that postscript: "Exterminate the brutes." That is the entire secret of Kurtz's fabulous commercial success.

Kurtz's cousin says that he could have been a great musician; Marlow, until then, had thought of him as potentially a great painter. But both are wrong. Kurtz's musical talents seem to have been fully exercised in those beating drums, and no painting, however superb, ever expressed with equivalent power the symbolic content of those shrunken heads on the posts around his house.

The journalist friend says that Kurtz missed his calling as the leader of a popular party. But Kurtz did not miss this calling, either. What popular leader has ever succeeded in becoming a literal god to his people?

The intended says that to know him was to love him, and there is at least one magnificent woman in Africa, remarkably like the European fiancée, who can testify to that.

No, Kurtz was not a man who went wrong, a man who lacked the inner stuff to realize his great potentialities. On the contrary, as Marlow learns in Brussels, in Africa Kurtz realized all his potentialities to the full. For him the darkness, the lack of restraint, was the stimulus to total realization. The wilderness, Marlow says, "had taken him, loved him, embraced him, got into his veins. . . . He was its spoiled and pampered favorite." The story of Kurtz's life is neither pathetic nor tragic. It is, instead, truly horrible—for it is a story of undreamed-of success.

This is what Marlow learns in Brussels and what Kurtz realized in his last moment when he pronounces his judgment—not on his last years in Africa but, as Marlow rightly guesses, on his whole life. That judgment is all the more remarkable for its terrible honesty. It represents a moral victory, a genuine redemption. Is it any wonder that Marlow, having learned the horrifying truth, feels the need to expiate his sin of deceit?

In lying to the fiancée Marlow goes against his innate respect for the truth. Worse, Kurtz's life, as he summed it up himself in his last words, was a sacrifice to the truth, and such a remarkable achievement deserves to be known. Simple justice requires that as the executor of his will, so to speak, Marlow must give Kurtz his due. This requires that the full truth about him be told. Telling his true story is what Marlow does on the yawl *Nellie,* where the story of Marlow's trip up the Congo finally ends.

Marlow succeeds in telling the truth about Kurtz, despite his concealments, because he has picked the right audience, a group of men who can grasp what he has said. This is evident in the last paragraph, where the narrator's point of view has changed completely from what it was in the opening passage. No longer spouting pretentious clichés about the light, the seeds of empire, the bearers of the torch, the narrator is man enough to face the truth when it appears before him. After hearing Marlow's story he can see that "a black bank of clouds, and the tranquil waterway leading to the uttermost ends of the earth flowed sombre under an overcast sky—seemed to lead into the heart of an immense darkness."

Heart of Darkness, then, despite its brevity, is a large work. It is not hard to see why the man who underwent the experience should say that before his journey he was just a mere animal. Nor is it hard to see how such an experience could confirm his recent impulse to write, thus converting him from a sailor into an artist. The vision of humankind expressed in the story is horrifying, but it does conform to history in the twentieth century. I am not prepared to say that the story tells the truth. But for good or evil, Conrad's is a voice that cannot be silenced; it must be attended to. Remarkably, it is not a cynical voice or a despairing one. Conrad is deeply concerned with good and evil. He cares greatly about the truth as he sees it. Since he has no optimistic illusions that the truth itself is necessarily good, he conceals it from fools at the same time that he reveals it to those who can face it.

What I find most terrifying in his vision is the idea that goodness, morality, decency, whatever one wants to call it, has no foundation in reality. Reality is the darkness, a howling nightmare, the insane desires of the primeval human soul. Civilization, morality, and restraint are fragile constructs. They are the idea at the back of it; not a sentimental pretense but an idea; and an unselfish belief in the idea   something you can set up, and bow down before, and offer a sacrifice to . . .

The notion that our only redemption from the darkness in ourselves, as in the world, is to be found in such constructs is not easy to live with. It requires that we be clear-eyed realists who refuse to give in to reality. Conrad's unflinching vision of the world we live in and the demands it makes on us is, I think, both the source and the substance of his artistry.

10 Shelley's *Frankenstein*
Reflections on the Monster

It would be hard to find another work that stands in sharper contrast to Mary Shelley's *Frankenstein* than Plato's *Phaedrus*. In the *Phaedrus,* that altogether beautiful, charming, even enchanting drama set on the banks of the Ilissos, Socrates and Phaedrus while away a few intimate hours engaged in a conversation that celebrates the joys, possibilities, and demands of human love and human rhetoric. Perhaps the contrast is most sharply etched by recalling to mind the opening and closing words that the two pairs of lovers address to each other, the words that mark the beginning and the end of their relationships.

At the beginning of the *Phaedrus,* Socrates encounters Phaedrus by chance on the streets of Athens and asks, "Dear Phaedrus, where are you going and where have you been?" (227a). Even before asking the question Socrates tells Phaedrus that he is "dear" to him, that Socrates cares. Was there ever a more inviting way to begin a relationship? In effect, Socrates says, "Tell me about yourself, Phaedrus. I'm interested in everything about you." Because he asks first about where Phaedrus is going and only afterward about where he has been, Socrates seems, in his subtle, insinuating way, to be suggesting that the future, the part of Phaedrus' life which he might share with Socrates, is of greater interest to him. Is it any wonder, with such a beginning, that the ensuing conversation and the later relationship are open, free, intimate, and marvelously satisfying?

By contrast, think of the way Frankenstein and his monster encounter each other. The first two times they meet, no words are exchanged. Chapter 5, the chapter with which Mary Shelley began writing the novel, opens with these words: "It was a dreary night of November that I beheld the accomplishment of my toils" (p. 56). Frankenstein describes the scene to Walton:

> Unable to endure the aspect of the being I had created, I rushed out of the room, and continued a long time traversing my bedchamber, unable to compose my mind to sleep. At length lassitude succeeded to the tumult I had before endured; and I threw myself on the bed in my clothes, endeavoring to seek a few moments of forgetfulness. But it was in vain; I slept, indeed, but I was disturbed by the wildest dreams. I thought I saw Elizabeth, in the bloom of health, walking in the streets of Ingolstadt. Delighted and surprised, I embraced her; but as I imprinted the first kiss on her lips they became livid with the hue of death; her features appeared to be changed, and I thought I saw the corpse of my dead mother in my arms; a shroud enveloped her form, and I saw the graveworms crawling in the folds of the flannel. I started from my sleep with horror; a cold dew covered my forehead, my teeth chattered, and every limb became convulsed: when by the dim and yellow light of the moon, as it forded its way through the window shutters, I beheld the wretch—the miserable monster whom I had created. He held the curtain of the bed; and his eyes, if eyes they may be called, were fixed on me. His jaws opened and he muttered some inarticulate sounds, while a grin wrinkled his cheeks. He might have spoken, but I did not hear; one hand was stretched out, seemingly to detain me, but I escaped, and rushed down the stairs. I took refuge in the courtyard belonging to the house which I inhabited; where I remained during the rest of the night, walking up and down in the greatest agitation, listening attentively, catching and fearing each sound as if it were to announce the approach of the demoniacal corpse to which I had so miserably given life.
>
> (pp. 56–57)

Later, when the monster tells his story to Frankenstein, he does not mention this scene but begins his narrative with an account of how he came to full consciousness as he was wandering in the countryside near Ingolstadt. Apparently, the incident that so impressed Frankenstein was not even remembered by his creature.

The second encounter between the two, also wordless, is even briefer. It occurs two years after the first, when Frankenstein returns to Geneva in response to his father's letter telling him that his younger brother, William, has been murdered. A storm breaks out as he goes toward the spot. He reports to Walton,

I perceived in the gloom a figure which stole from behind a clump of trees near me; I stood fixed, gazing intently; I could not be mistaken. A flash of lightening illuminated the object and discovered its shape plainly to me; its gigantic stature, and the deformity of its aspect, more hideous than belongs to humanity, instantly informed me that it was the wretch, the filthy demon, to whom I had given life. What did he there? Could he be (I shuddered at the conception) the murderer of my brother? No sooner did that idea cross my imagination than I became convinced of its truth; my teeth chattered, and I was forced to lean against a tree for support.

(p. 73)

Finally, after the pathetic and innocent Justine has been accused, tried, convicted, and executed for the murder of young William, Frankenstein goes on a trip to the high Alps. On a glacier the monster pursues him.

He approached; his countenance bespoke bitter anguish, combined with disdain and malignity, while its unearthly ugliness rendered it almost too horrible for eyes. But I scarcely observed this; rage and hatred had at first deprived me of utterance, and I recovered only to overwhelm him with words expressive of furious detestation and contempt.

"Devil," I exclaimed, "do you dare approach me? and do not you fear the fierce vengeance of my arm wreaked upon your miserable head? Begone, vile insect! or rather, stay, that I may trample you to dust! and oh! That I could, with the extinction of your miserable existence, restore those victims whom you have so diabolically murdered!"

"I expected this reception," said the daemon.

(p. 94–95)

And so, at last, Frankenstein and his monster embark on their first conversation.

These are the beginnings. Let us now look at the ends. In *Phaedrus,* having completed a discussion of love and rhetoric, Socrates and Phaedrus have the following exchange.

Socrates: Is it not well to pray to the deities here before we go?
Phaedrus: Of course.
Socrates: O beloved Pan and all ye other gods of this place, grant to me that I be made beautiful in my soul within and that all external possessions be in harmony with my inner

man. Do we need anything more, Phaedrus? For me that prayer is enough.

Phaedrus: Let me also share in this prayer; for friends have all things in common.

Socrates: Let us go.

(279b–c)

In Mary Shelley's novel, Walton, in fascinated horror, finds the monster in his cabin standing over the corpse of his creator. The monster's last words to the unhearing Frankenstein are:

"Farewell, Frankenstein! If thou wert yet alive, and yet cherished a desire of revenge against me, it would be better satiated in my life than in my destruction. But it was not so; thou didst seek my extinction that I might not cause greater wretchedness; and if yet, in some mode unknown to me, thou hast not ceased to think and feel, thou wouldst not desire against me a vengeance greater than that which I feel. Blasted as thou wert, my agony was still superior to thine; for the bitter sting of remorse will not cease to rankle my wounds until death shall close them forever.

"But soon," he cried, with sad and solemn enthusiasm, "I shall die, and what I now feel be no longer felt. Soon these burning miseries will be extinct. I shall ascend my funeral pile triumphantly, and exult in the agony of the torturing flames. The light of that conflagration will fade away; my ashes will be swept into the sea by the winds. My spirit will sleep in peace; or if it thinks, it will not surely think thus. Farewell."

He sprang from the cabin-window, and as he said this, upon the ice-raft which lay close to the vessel. He was soon borne away by the waves and lost in darkness and distance.

(p. 211)

Rage, misery, pain, frustration, mutual isolation, melodrama—how strongly these contrast with the calm, warm, sustaining friendship of the end of the *Phaedrus*. Could any two relationships be more different?

Yet it is not so simple. For a moment in the *Phaedrus,* Socrates and Phaedrus touch on a theme that runs like a hidden golden thread through the dialogue, a theme that is also at the center of Mary Shelley's novel. The theme surfaces in the *Phaedrus* very near the beginning of the dialogue, when Socrates and Phaedrus are making their way cross-country from the road to the plane tree by the banks of the Ilissos where they will sit in the shade and talk. Phaedrus asks Socrates if they might not be on the very spot where the god of the north wind, Boreas, carried off Oreithyia, the daughter of the king of Athens, and whether Socrates believes in the truth of such stories.

Socrates' reply is long and complex. He says that it would hardly be extraordinary if, like the wise, he disbelieved the story. He could give a rational, naturalistic explanation of the story by saying that the girl was blown off the rocks by the north wind and fell to her death. The story, he could argue, was invented to explain what happened. The trouble with such explanations, he says, is that once you are launched into giving them, the task is endless, and every wild, crazy myth requires a similar account. Unfortunately, these accounts take a great deal of time to invent. He himself has no time for such business because he is fully occupied with carrying out the injunction of Apollo inscribed over the door of his temple at Delphi: "Know thyself." Until I know myself, he asserts, I have no time for frivolous stories about Gorgons and Chimeras and centaurs. I investigate, "not these things, but myself, to know whether I am a monster more complicated and furious with passion than Typhon or a gentler and simpler creature, to whom a divine and quiet lot is given by nature" (230a). Typhon, from whom the violent tropical storms known as typhoons take their name, was a gigantic mythical snake that encircled the earth and whose breath created storms.

In the reply to Phaedrus about the myth of Boreas and Oreithyia, Socrates neither accepts nor rejects myths. He remains open to but dubious about myths as literally true. But he does reject the rationalizing interpretation of myths that reduces them from astonishing accounts of extraordinary events about the interaction of divine and human beings to fanciful explanations of otherwise ordinary events. The authentic question for him, however, is not whether the myths are true but how we should spend our time.

He flatly rejects as ridiculous any expenditure of time and energy on attempts to develop a crude natural philosophy as long as we remain ignorant of the single overwhelming question that confronts each of us: "Who and what am I?" But surprisingly, when he comes to explain what he means by this question to Phaedrus, he articulates it in mythical terms: Is he himself a monster like Typhon or a gentler and simpler creature? In casting the question in these terms Socrates is suggesting that the telling of myths and their investigation may be a crucial element in the search for an answer to Apollo's injunction to know thyself. Indeed, this suggestion of Socrates is implicitly but fully developed in his great speech on love later in the *Phaedrus,* in which he presents a comprehensive account of love in purely mythical terms.

Another aspect of his explanation to Phaedrus is more immediately germane to our concerns. When Socrates poses possible answers to the question of who and what he is, he asks whether he himself might not be a gigantic, terrifying, passionate, irrational, and destructive monster. At this point the kinship between *Frankenstein* and the *Phaedrus* emerges: both Plato's dialogue and Mary Shelley's novel are centrally concerned with monsters. In the *Phaedrus,* Socrates never again explicitly raises the theme of the relationship between the human and the monstrous. But if we reflect on the myth in his great speech, we see that his answer to the question of human nature is even more monstrous than his earlier remark on Typhon would imply.

In that earlier remark he suggested that he is either a monster like Typhon or a simpler, gentler creature. In the great speech he likens the human soul to the union of powers: a chariot, a charioteer, and two winged horses, one white, noble, and tractable and the other dark, ugly, ill-tempered, savage, and almost uncontrollable. This image suggests that the human soul is both like Typhon and like a gentler creature and that it is also human. The three mismatched parts are functionally linked to control and drive a fantastic contrivance—a chariot that can fly. Are we like that? We do not look like that, and, we would like to believe, we do not act the way such a monster would act—or do we?

What makes a monster monstrous? Monsters are bigger or uglier or more powerful than we are. They frighten us. We do not like them. And yet some monster or other is constantly frightening us in some elemental way. In childhood we encounter them again and again—in fairy tales, in ghost stories, in dark closets, attics, and basements, and in the shadowy places under our beds when we are home alone at night. Worst of all, in childhood we meet monsters night after night in our nightmares—those terrifying horses of the dark hours.

Once we are grown up, we know that those stories and dreams were childish fantasies. Such things don't exist except in our imagination. Yet we still dream, and we occasionally have terrifying nightmares. As adults, we are even haunted by real monsters: the Hitlers, the Stalins, the Saddam Husseins. Beyond them loom even worse monsters, such creations as the hydrogen bomb, symbolically rendered in Herblock's cartoons as a big, tough, stupid bully who keeps intruding in our lives, reminding us of his presence. Ranged alongside the hydrogen bomb are the horrors of ecological disaster, recombinant DNA, the population explosion—you name it, the monster is there waiting for us, like that vague, shapeless thing that used to lurk in the far corner of the basement.

Monsters frighten us because they are different and because they don't seem controllable. Yet they live in the same world that we do, and willy-nilly we have to deal with them. Sometimes they even seem to talk our language, yet they resist our best efforts to make sense of them, to reduce them to manageable proportions, to fit them into that reasonable, orderly, safe, and humane world in which we would like to live. The Loch Ness monster is more a source of amusement than fear to most of us, but it is still a monster. If, however, those monster-hunting zealots with their radars, sonars, and automatic cameras should ever prove conclusively that it is indeed a living animal, a survivor from the days of the dinosaurs, then it would promptly cease to be a monster and become a scientific curiosity—a freak, to be sure, but a freak of nature.

Monsters are not only different and frightening; they are also unnatural. To most of us, nature is an ordered, rational whole in which things run to type. Monsters tend to be one of a kind, unique. To encounter a monster is to meet a creature that challenges, by its very existence, our whole sense of nature. If even one thing in the world doesn't fit into the universal scheme of things, we must consider that maybe the fault lies not with the monster but with our understanding of nature. That is, maybe nature is not an ordered, rational whole; maybe the world is a chaos. If the world, nature, is not natural, perhaps our profoundly held adult conception of an ordered, rational nature is a pipe dream, a childish security blanket that we clutch frantically in hopes that it will protect us in the presence of monsters.

If monsters are unnatural, we may ask, where do they come from? If they are different, unnatural, why do they somehow look familiar? Here we touch on a strange and puzzling aspect of monsters, perhaps the most frightening of all, that will bring us back to the *Phaedrus* and *Frankenstein*. If we control our fear and disgust long enough to scrutinize the monster, we discover that not its whole self but its parts are familiar. Monsters tend to be compound beings, composed of parts each of which is natural and familiar in its proper setting but which, in the new combination, become monstrous. The centaur is half man, half horse. Neither men nor horses are monstrous, but their combination is. What is monstrous is the whole, the new, unnatural combination of familiar parts.

This strange phenomenon, that what is monstrous about a monster is the combination of old elements into a new form, has long been known. The wise, as Socrates calls them—the rational, scientific investigators of nature—have tended to interpret this fact as evidence that monsters are merely creations of our imagination. Thus, they debunk monsters, resolve them into their constituent parts, thereby destroying their monstrous character and restoring the rational, natural order of the world. The monster-debunking tradition is a venerable one, stretching from Protagoras and his fellow sophists to Marx, Bertrand Russell, and Carl Sagan in the modern world.

From this skeptical perspective, the monster belongs to the childhood of *Homo sapiens,* considered individually and historically. The monstrous represents the childish, irrational fears and anxieties that we outgrow as we achieve adulthood, both as individuals and as a race. There is much to be said for this point of view—we would all like to be adults, and we all recognize the deep childishness pervading our experience of the monster. Yet this view of the monster seems flawed, inadequate, for if the monster is to be outgrown, put behind us, why is the world still so full of monsters? Something about the monster is tenacious and does not yield to the enlightened views of those wise men. We must probe deeper.

A modern variant of the enlightened, debunking view of monsters as childish projections may be helpful here. This view, associated with psychoanalysis, has been articulated in the work of Bruno Bettelheim on fairy tales. Bettelheim, following Freud, argues that monsters are indeed projections of our childish fantasies. But, unlike the more simplistic views of the sophistic enlightenment, Bettelheim's argument is that the childish projections represented by monsters are not simply to be outgrown; rather, they are an important part of a necessary and healthy stage in our development from impotent children into coping, realistic adults.

As I understand his position, the monster is a projection of our deep, unconscious fears of our own hostile, destructive impulses. By projecting these impulses onto the constructed figure of the monster, children give concrete expression to those destructive, hostile impulses, acknowledge them, explore them, learn to cope with them, and finally, learn to integrate them into themselves in ways that are neither hostile nor destructive. This view explains the perennial appeal of the monster, and its familiarity. After all, if Bettelheim is right, in encountering a monster we are encountering aspects of ourselves, aspects that are difficult to accept without such marvelous devices as the fairy tale.

Yet Bettelheim's concept leaves me dissatisfied. For all his sophistication, he, too, believes that fairy tales and monsters belong to the realm of childhood and that for adults they are, at most, an experience for parents to share with their children. Parents may enjoy watching and helping their children on the perilous journey from childhood to adulthood if they have already completed the journey themselves. If Bettelheim is right, only children and adults who have not grown up would find monsters interesting. This brings me back to Mary Shelley's *Frankenstein*.

Is *Frankenstein* for children and childish adults? Possibly. The many cinematic versions of the novel so appealing to children and adolescents would strongly support such a view. Indeed, many things about the novel and its author also point in that direction.

Mary Shelley wrote *Frankenstein* when she was nineteen; it was her first serious attempt at writing. As the man said about the talking dog, the wonder is not that it talks badly but that it talks at all. *Frankenstein*, to be candid, is not a very good novel. It is atrociously overwritten; the style is pretentious, and the prose purple. The narrative technique is clumsy, even primitive; the novel is full of awkward flashbacks, unnecessary information, dull, pointless descriptions. The characterizations are flat, shallow, and conventional, even if we make allowances for the fact that they are part of the first-person narratives of Walton, Frankenstein, or the monster, none of whom is an acute observer of humankind. The plot, the construction of the story, is amateurish. Everything that occurs is so filled with chance, coincidence, improbability, that the story can hardly be taken seriously. All this needs to be said straight out; we must not forget that *Frankenstein* is a first novel by a teenage girl.

My usual practice in discussing a book is to give the author every benefit of the doubt, to assume that the writer knew what he or she was doing. The duty of the reader hoping to grasp the full intention of the author is to pay attention to everything in the work as if it were purposeful. With *Frankenstein* this approach is impossible. I do not think that Mary Shelley knew what she was doing or, more important, what she achieved. Like a dream reported by a child, *Frankenstein* says a great deal more than was either consciously intended or plainly understood by its author.

The book began as a frightening reverie, and Shelley has managed to render exactly that quality in her novel. Her success is not the result of artistic skill; all her attempts at artistry are obvious, clumsy, and relatively ineffective. The success of the novel, and successful it is, lies rather in her honesty in following her own imagination. Was Shelley aware of the shallowness, the absurdity, the hypocrisy, of Walton's and Frankenstein's claims to be the benefactors of humanity? They certainly are not aware of those qualities in themselves, nor, evidently, was she. I have no quarrel with Walton's desire to be the first man to reach the North Pole. It seems like an innocent enough ambition. But to describe the achievement as conferring an "inestimable benefit . . . on all mankind to the last generation" (p. 16) is nonsense. Walton is after fame, honor, glory—not the benefit of mankind. I wish only that he had been more honest and his creator more aware.

What is true of Walton is far truer of Frankenstein. His ambition far transcends Walton's. When God banishes Adam and Eve from the Garden of Eden, the last thing he says is, "See, the man has become like one of us, knowing what is good and what is bad. Therefore he must not be allowed to put out his hand to take fruit from the tree of life also, and thus eat of it and live forever" (Genesis 3:22). But is that not exactly what Frankenstein aims at—to be the sole creator of a new race of men and live forever? Frankenstein's ambition, to achieve full godhead, is not quite so innocent as Walton's.

But like Walton, Frankenstein seems to be unaware of his full purpose, although in this case Mary Shelley is not herself unaware. She knows what he is trying to do, even though she has not thought through the implications of that purpose nor the means by which Frankenstein sought to realize it, nor, finally, why his achievement of his goal went wrong. Mary Shelley dreamed and then wrote the story of a man who aspired to the condition of godhead, but she never quite understood it. Nevertheless, the story is there for us to read, to reflect on, and, perhaps with the help of the *Phaedrus,* to understand, at least in part.

Before exploring Shelley's achievement, I would like to indulge myself in a rather Freudian speculation on why she had difficulty grasping and expressing the meaning of her own creation. Frankenstein views himself as the creator and father of his monstrous creation, and the monster accepts that view. Frankenstein is the father, and the monster, his child. Mary Shelley insists with pride in her introduction of 1831 that she alone is the creator of her novel, apart from the preface written by her husband. In this relationship, Mary Shelley is the father, and the novel is the child. She dedicated the novel to her father, William Godwin. What Frankenstein did for his monster, Mary Shelley did for her book, and her father did for her.

If we play with the usual Freudian transformations implicit in these parallel formulas, we see that Mary Shelley is thoroughly identified with both Frankenstein and his monster and that, just as Frankenstein and his monster are in a fateful and tragically irreconcilable conflict, so, too, is she with herself about her creation. Further, just as neither Frankenstein nor his monster understand each other, so, too, I would speculate, did Shelley fail to understand the tremendous internal conflict that both generated the book and is expressed in it.

What is the nature of the conflict? The key lies in the relationship between Frankenstein and his monster. Emotionally, they have intense mutual love-hate feelings. Each views himself as morally decent and innocent and as the passive victim of the other—and with considerable justification. Thus each sees the other as the sole cause of his misery and pain.

Yet for each of them, the other also, for a time, represents everything that he hopes for. Frankenstein originally sees the monster as a means to the realization of his inordinate ambitions, whereas the monster sees Frankenstein as the only possible means to escape the unbearable loneliness of his existence—the doctor could make him a mate. Each of them, when his hopes are blasted, becomes the other's implacable foe.

In a strange sense, however, each of them already has what the other wants. The monster wants love, companionship, and an end to his isolation. Frankenstein has all these things in his family, his friends, his community. On the other hand, Frankenstein wants unlimited power, strength, the ability to work his will—all of which the monster with his great size, strength, endurance, and unrelenting pursuit of his desires already possesses. Each is the complement and alter ego of the other. Inside the monster's ugly carcass there beats a simple heart of gold. His mind was educated by Plutarch, Goethe, and Milton to embrace high and noble thoughts and turns vicious and vengeful only when frustrated. Behind the soaring ambition and drive of Frankenstein there beats the heart of a banal, conventional, rather dull and decent Swiss burgher, one who can be obtuse, uncaring, unimaginative, and vicious when faced with the unexpected and ugly consequences of his own actions.

Frankenstein and his monster are like the white and dark horses of Socrates' myth of the soul in the *Phaedrus*. If properly directed and controlled, they make an excellent pair; left to their own limited devices without the presence of that human charioteer, they fall into mutually destructive conflict. What they need and lack is reason and, with reason, the possibility of moderation, that most humble and yet most divine of the virtues. Moderation, a strange and necessary excellence, enables us to live with our otherwise uncontrollable and destructive drives and impulses. Mary Shelley was frightened by the reverie in which she conceived the story, and she wrote the novel to frighten us as she had been frightened. Although she probably never understood why the story is so frightening, she may have succeeded better than she dreamed possible.

This brings me to my last point. The monster is Frankenstein's creation or, more properly, the product of his art. The monster is a made thing; it comes into being as a result of what Aristotle calls the intellectual virtue of art, the rational capacity to make things. The word in Greek is *techne,* from which our words *technique* and *technical* are derived. Because the monster is made in the likeness of a man, it is also an imitation, a work of art.

All monsters, I suggested earlier, are compound beings, made things composed of already existing elements but new in how those elements are assembled. The elements and, more important, the impctus to put them together arise from our human needs and impulses. All the things that we make are, in fact, nothing more than some aspect of our inner selves projected into the world. The childish monster of the fairy tale, as Bettelheim suggests, is essentially a projection of the child's dark, destructive, frightening impulses, impulses that the child cannot yet acknowledge directly. Bettelheim may be right about children, but if he is, there is a further implication to his account that needs to be considered.

The imaginative processes by which children form and project fairy-tale monsters, the processes of techne and mimesis, of art and poetry, are the same processes by which adults make the instruments and implements, the discoveries and inventions, the fabrications, by which the realm of raw nature is converted into the civilized human world. The world in which we live is a world of made things—of artifacts, of social, political, and economic institutions, of art, of science, of culture. We reshape the world of nature to accord with our perceived needs, wishes, desires, and impulses. We remake it to reflect ourselves. The human world, the world of *Homo faber,* "man the maker," is made by giving outward reality to our inner fantasies.

For all the familiarity and ordinariness of the fabricated world that we have made from our own projections, if we step back for a moment and reflect on it, does it not seem strange and a little uncanny? Does it not have more than just a whiff of the monstrous about it? If we turn our reflections back on the makers of that world, on ourselves, are we not the strangest of the strange beings in the world, the only ones whose nature impels them to remake the world in their own image, the only beings for whom nature is not a home but an alien, frightening place that needs reshaping and re-creating in order that humans may fully realize themselves? We are Frankenstein, and the fabricated human world in which we live is our monster. In reading and reflecting on Mary Shelley's youthful, marred novel, we may catch a glimpse of ourselves if, as we read, we try to fulfill, as Socrates did, the injunction over the door of Apollo's temple at Delphi.

11 The *Analects*
Confucius' Claim to Philosophical Greatness

Some time ago, while talking with a philosopher friend, I mentioned that it has now been several centuries since the thought of the great early Chinese thinkers has been available to Western readers and students of philosophy. Although many of us still read and study Plato and Aristotle, the Confucian and Daoist classics are, however, still largely unknown to even the most sophisticated and well-read Westerners. My friend's response was shocking. "Of course philosophy students read Plato and Aristotle rather than Confucius. Plato and Aristotle are much better philosophers." When I got over my indignation at this example of Western arrogance, I realized that my friend had a point. After all, what had he ever heard about Confucius that might have led him to read Confucius with the same seriousness with which he approached the writings of Plato and Aristotle? The answer, I am afraid, is very little.

Part of the difficulty lies in the deceptive simplicity of Confucius' thought. The experience of James Legge, who lived in China for many years as a Christian missionary and later taught Chinese subjects at Oxford, is instructive. Legge translated the *Analects,* and his rendering of that classic, published in 1861 after years of careful study and research, remains one of the best available in English. At the end of his long introduction he takes up Confucius' influence, concluding with the following remarks.

> But I must now leave the sage. I hope I have not done him injustice;
> but after long study of his character and opinions, I am unable to re-
> gard him as a great man. He was not before his age, though he was

above the mass of officers and scholars of his time. He threw no new light on any of the questions which have a world wide interest. He gave no impulse to religion. He had no sympathy with progress. His influence has been wonderful, but it will henceforth wane. My opinion is that the faith of the nation in him will speedily and extensively pass away.

(p. 113)

When he returned to England, he taught for many years at Oxford. In 1893, some thirty years after he published his translation of the *Lun yü,* or *Analects,* a second edition was issued. This edition is substantially identical with the first, with one significant change: Legge rewrote this concluding paragraph.

But I must now leave the sage. I hope I have not done him injustice; the more I have studied his character and opinions, the more highly I have come to regard him. He was a very great man, and his influence has been on the whole a great benefit to the Chinese, while his teachings suggest important lessons to ourselves who profess to belong to the school of Christ.

(p. 111)

Pondering and teaching the *Lun yü* for thirty years after he had translated it with scrupulous accuracy, Legge reversed his judgment of Confucius. It is possible to read through a translation of the *Lun yü* in a few hours. But Legge's experience may be taken as a warning: Confucius is not to be grasped or appreciated quite so quickly.

Beyond the inherent difficulties in reading Confucius, which I shall return to shortly, there is the problem of Western parochialism—the belief, usually not conscious, that the Western tradition, culture, way of life, is superior to all others. Beyond this parochialism are other, more subtle reasons why we still read Plato and Aristotle and ignore Confucius. Plato and Aristotle, everybody knows, were great philosophers, and therefore, even if we no longer agree with them, they are worth studying; even their mistakes are illuminating and instructive. Confucius, on the other hand, has had a shifting reputation over the past century. In traditional China, up to the Revolution of 1912, he was revered as a great sage. After 1912, when the Chinese republic was established, many of the reformers rejected Confucius as authoritarian and antidemocratic, and when the communists triumphed in 1949 he was rejected again, this time in favor of Marxism. In recent years with the rapid economic development throughout East Asia, where Confucian ideas have been influential, he has had a kind of revival. Despite these ups and downs, he has generally been regarded in the

West as a great man in the sense that he has had a tremendous influence on China and other East Asian cultures—to the point where they are sometimes, and with justice, called Confucian.

But although historicism has sunk deep into the Western soul, it has not sunk so deep that Western intellectuals automatically concede intellectual greatness to a thinker merely because that thinker's ideas have profoundly influenced history. Thus, Max Weber seems to regard Confucius primarily as the codifier of a system of ethics for civil servants, whereas to many others he is a quaint old Chinese gentleman given to uttering sententious remarks. I am convinced that these views are wrong. I think that Confucius was a great thinker and deserves serious philosophical attention.

In China, as I said, Confucius' greatness was almost axiomatic for more than two thousand years. There were exceptions, naturally; the Daoists have always been skeptical of Confucianism, and the *Zhuangzi,* one of the earliest Daoist texts, is full of amusing apocryphal stories about Confucius' pedantic stupidity and ignorance. Yet on the whole, Confucius has been treated with the respect, veneration, and awe reserved for the greatest of sages. It is this image of Confucius with which the West is largely familiar and which is so unimpressive philosophically to Westerners.

I am not saying that Confucius needs to be rescued more from the embraces of his friends than from the attacks of his enemies. But I do suggest that the traditional Chinese picture of him is distorted in at least two ways. It involves a good deal of later accretion and embellishment, and it is highly anachronistic. Confucius, so far as anyone can tell, was an extremely obscure and highly insignificant man during his lifetime. We know very little about his life. When, in the centuries after his death, he became a figure to be reckoned with in China, the obscurity of his life became both an embarrassment and an opportunity. His later followers were embarrassed that a man of such obvious wisdom and talent should have been so insignificant while he was alive. At the same time, the absence of much hard information made it possible to fill in the gaps with details appropriate to his stature.

Although Confucius probably never held an administrative or political position of importance, in time it came to be accepted that he had served in a number of quite important posts. Similarly, Confucius probably never wrote anything; if he did, none of it has survived. Here, again, the tradition filled the hiatus by crediting Confucius with the authorship or editorship of several anonymous works. This sort of pious fraud is bad enough for the accurate perception of Confucius, but the problem is compounded by the anachronisms inevitably involved in such a process. For example, when Confucius was known simply as an obscure, private person with a few disciples or students, it was natural that on occasion he should give evidence of a sense of humor. But when he was elevated to the status of sage, levity became improper and needed to be explained away. Not only was Confucius supplied with a career and a noble background commensurate with his position, but his character, personality, and thought were largely re-created to accord with later generations' sense of propriety.

Modern critical scholarship has cut through the accumulated embellishment and anachronism surrounding and veiling Confucius' life and thought. What has emerged is in many respects much less satisfying than the traditional picture of Confucius, but it is also more interesting and suggestive. We now know that we know very little about Confucius; we know that he was an obscure man with only a small circle of students, that he had little, if any, personal impact on the China of his day, and that he has left no written record of his ideas.

Along with this negative knowledge, and to some extent counterbalancing it, there is considerable evidence that Confucius was a far more original thinker than the traditional picture implied. According to the tradition, Confucius was merely one, and one of the last, of a long line of sages stretching back into antiquity. Much of what was original to Confucius was piously attributed to earlier figures, thus inadvertently diminishing his remarkable contribution to Chinese thought and culture. We now know that the only literary work with any claim to being an authentic record of Confucius' thought is the small work known to us as the *Analects*. Even it contains a certain number of spurious interpolations, late redactions of original remarks, and so forth. Unfortunately, but not surprisingly, it is often these less authentic portions of the *Analects* that the tradition has fastened on and made central to its picture of Confucius. Yet if we make allowances for accretion and concentrate on the *Analects,* a fresh and positive picture of Confucius emerges dimly, a picture of a man far more complex, subtle, original, and interesting than the traditional account suggested.

The *Analects* consists of about four hundred separate passages divided into twenty chapters. The passages range from a few words to fairly ample discussions. They purport to be remarks of Confucius to his disciples, conversations with various political figures, anecdotes, and so forth. They are not arranged in any discernible order either within the chapters or from chapter to chapter. There is no particular reason to believe that they are arranged in the chronological order in which Confucius or his disciples uttered them. In short, the *Analects* has no author or any recognizable organization. It is a collection of fragments. Apparently, in the generations following his death, many of Confucius' remarks were handed down orally by his disciples to their own disciples, and at some point this oral tradition was collected from various sources and set down in writing. The result is that we must approach Confucius' thought not through his own words put down in a form and order chosen by himself but through the diffracting lens of several generations of disciples.

If this situation makes it difficult, if not impossible, to get back to the original thought of Confucius, let me remind you that we have one highly analogous situation in the Western tradition. Socrates, like Confucius, never wrote anything, and our only knowledge of his thought comes to us through the writings of several friends and, possibly—in the case of Aristophanes—an enemy or a friendly critic. The parallel with Socrates is instructive in other ways as well. In addition to the fact that he never wrote, he, too, was a rather obscure individual who made little, if any, significant impact on his community beyond a small circle of friends and disciples. Yet whatever difficulties there may be in determining the substance of Socrates' thought, everyone agrees that he revolutionized Greek and ultimately Western thought. The uncertainty and mystery that surround Socrates should never be allowed to shroud this critical consequence of his having lived. The same is true of Confucius.

The parallel between Socrates and Confucius breaks down when we compare the nature of the literary sources about them. For Confucius we have the *Analects;* for Socrates, the works of Plato, Xenophon, and Aristophanes and fragments of others. The problem of arriving at a clear picture of Socrates stems not only from the diversity of these sources but also from their literary brilliance and originality. We can never be sure in reading Plato and Xenophon whether we are seeing an accurate representation of Socrates or whether these two men are not using the figure of Socrates for their own purposes and putting words in his mouth.

With Confucius the difficulty is exactly the opposite. Not only did he not have any disciples or opponents of the caliber of Plato, Xenophon, or Aristophanes, but there is a serious question about whether any of his disciples understood him well. I used to think that the tragedy of Confucius was that he never had as talented a disciple as Socrates had in Plato. Now I am not so sure. Maybe the *Analects,* for all its apparent defects, is a better source for the thought of Confucius than the multiplicity of brilliant Greek works are for Socrates. The *Analects* is at least a straightforward, if fragmentary, collection of what Confucius' admirers thought that he actually said. Even when they did not understand him, they had sufficient respect for him to try to preserve accurately the substance of his remarks.

Assuming, then, that the *Analects* more or less accurately represents Confucius' thought, what can we say about him as a thinker? Honesty compels me to admit that the first, and even second, impression of a reasonably intelligent and sophisticated Westerner who sits down with a recommended translation is one of boredom and bewilderment. The *Analects* seems to be filled with inconclusive and obscure discussions and remarks about unknown persons and events, including a good deal of talk about filial piety, perfect virtue, being a good minister of state, and so forth. There is almost nothing that could be labeled philosophy in the ordinary sense of the word, and precious little of the aphoristic brilliance that we have come to expect from reputed sages. Our boredom comes from the apparent triviality of much that is said in the *Analects,* and our bewilderment arises from our inability to understand how the speaker could have put his mark on an entire civilization. This common response of Westerners to the *Analects* is usually based on a failure to understand the historical context in which Confucius lived and to appreciate what he was trying to do within that context.

China in Confucius' day was essentially a feudal society. An emperor supposedly ruled over what was then China, and the feudal nobles ostensibly owed him allegiance and support. In fact, the emperor had long since been reduced to a figurehead, and the various feudal domains were independent states. The fragmentation of the empire did not stop at this point, however, for within the feudal states, actual power was frequently wielded not by the nominal duke or lord but by one or more of his feudatories. As might be expected, warfare and revolt were endemic, and the old, established ways were breaking down. In time, the feudal structure of China was replaced when more or less centrally organized states emerged. They fought among themselves for control of all China until finally, in 221 B.C., the state of Qin conquered its last opponent and produced the first centrally organized, bureaucratic empire in Chinese history.

Confucius lived near the beginning of this period of change; the old ways still existed, although they had begun to be seriously eroded. Considerably more perceptive and humanly sensitive than his contemporaries, he was deeply concerned about the critical condition of the empire. He even tried to do something about it. In short, he was a reformer. He apparently talked with acquaintances about his ideas for reform, and gradually there grew up around him a small group of like-minded people. After trying and failing to secure a position in his home state in order to put his ideas into practice, he traveled about China with his disciples for some years, going from court to court to persuade the ruling nobles of the validity of his ideas and of his ability to put them into effect. Here again he failed. In his last years he seems to have devoted himself almost entirely to his students and disciples in the hope that they might accomplish what he could not.

This history explains much of the disappointment felt by his readers. Confucius' statements were not meant to be read centuries after his death by people seeking to understand the wisdom of a great sage. The statements, all of them, were uttered by Confucius to a particular person—disciple or noble lord—in a particular context. In many cases both the person and the context have been lost, so we are left with what look like flat generalizations. But there are enough examples in the *Analects* of how Confucius adjusted his remarks to specific situations to make me at least suspicious of the generality of those passages that lack a context. Here is an example.

> Zilu, a disciple, once asked whether he should immediately carry into practice what he heard. The Master said, "Your father and elder brother are still alive; how can you immediately put into practice what you have heard?" Ran You, another disciple, then asked whether he should immediately carry into practice what he heard. The Master said, "When one hears it, one should immediately put it into practice." Gongxi Hua then said, "When Zilu asked about immediately putting into practice what he heard you said his father and elder brother were still alive, but when Ran You asked the same thing you said he should immediately put it into practice. Now I am confused by this and should like to ask what you meant." The Master replied, "Ran You is retiring and therefore I urged him forward, but Zilu has more than his share of energy, so I held him back."
> (BOOK XI, CHAP. 21)

This passage is simple and obvious. We can see how easily the whole sense of the passage could be changed, however, if only part of Confucius' remarks had been preserved—say, his advice to either one of the disciples—and the rest of the conversation lost.

The discretionary and contextual character of Confucius' remarks is even more marked in his reported conversations with the nobles, the men who exercised political authority. When I say "discretionary," I do not mean that he was particularly cautious and tactful. On the contrary, he tended to be blunt and even tactless—and this may in part explain why he was not successful in persuading the authorities to give him an important position. By "discretion" I mean rather that Confucius framed his remarks to remind the ruler that his decisions about what was right and wrong or about what policy to follow carried implications for all under his sway.

When Duke Ding asked Confucius how a ruler should employ his ministers and how a minister should serve his ruler, Confucius replied, "A ruler should employ his ministers according to Li [the accepted forms of propriety] and the minister should serve his ruler with integrity" (book III, chap. 19). Confucius' reply has the appearance of a pious little formula, but notice how neatly it puts Duke Ding in his place. The ruler, the superior, must restrain himself and act toward his inferiors with the strictest sense of propriety, whereas the minister, who supposedly serves his ruler and carries out his commands, must follow the dictates of his conscience. The remark strongly suggests that in choosing his ministers Duke Ding ought to look for men of personal integrity rather than lackeys who obey his every command. As I ponder the passage I wonder who is doing the employing and who the serving. That is exactly the uneasy feeling that Confucius hoped to engender in the duke.

In another famous conversation, this time with the Duke of She, the duke said to Confucius, "'Among us here there are those who may be styled upright in their conduct. If their father has stolen a sheep, they will bear witness to the fact.' Confucius replied, 'Among us, in our part of the country, those who are upright are different from this. The father conceals the misconduct of the son and the son conceals the misconduct of the father. Uprightness is to be found in this'" (book XIII, chap. 18). The passage, which has been important in traditional Confucianism, is often interpreted to mean that Confucius puts the claims of family loyalty above the claims of the state to the loyalty of its subjects. Such a passage was apparently in Max Weber's mind when he described Confucius as an ethical particularist. By this he means that Confucius conceived of the individual's moral obligations as varying in relationships with different people. James Legge, the great nineteenth-century translator of Confucius, remarks dryly, "Anybody but a Chinese will say that both the duke's view of the subject and the sage's were incomplete" (p. 270).

Both Weber and Legge have missed the point of this passage—Weber because he has drawn from it a general, abstract conception of the ethical particularism of Confucius and Legge because he assumes that Confucius intended it as a complete and final statement on the conflicting claims of the state and the family. Confucius is doing neither of these things; he is responding to a ducal remark apparently intended to provoke discussion. By the abrupt manner of his response he seems to be reminding the duke that in addition to the codified legal morality of the state there are other, equally binding claims on the individual.

What I am suggesting is that the import of Confucius' remark cannot be understood without reference to the situation in which it is uttered. Viewed in this light, Confucius' statement does not so much constitute the solution to a moral-political problem as define that problem for a man who, as ruler, is vitally concerned with the issue involved.

When we read and ponder the *Analects* in this contextual fashion, we stop trying to extract universally valid principles from Confucius' remarks. Instead, we try to grasp the heuristic or rhetorical points that Confucius is making. Read this way, the *Analects* ceases to be a trivial collection of fragments, and we can begin to see the basis of Confucius' reputation.

With the contextual character of Confucius' utterances firmly in mind, we can now turn to the substance of his thought. I have said that he was primarily a reformer and secondarily a teacher. What, then, was his program of reform, and to what end did he train his pitifully few students and disciples? The tradi-

tional answer, still given in the majority of modern accounts of Confucius'
thought, is that he wished to root out the corrupt modern practices of his day
and return to the ways of antiquity.

At one point, Confucius does speak of himself as "a transmitter rather than
an originator, a true lover of antiquity" (book VII, chap. 1). In fact, throughout
the *Analects* Confucius appears as a conservative man who deplores the corrupt
and unjust behavior of contemporary society. But to say this is very different
from asserting that Confucius wished to effect a return to the traditional ways
of remote antiquity. There is remarkably little in the *Analects* itself about remote antiquity and the sage-kings who ruled then, in part because those sage-
kings and the golden age of their reigns seem to be largely the creation of Con-
fucians living in the generations after Confucius—as is the Confucius who
wanted to return to that mythical world. You will not find him in the *Analects*.

Another representation of Confucius as a conservative makes him a
defender of feudalism, and his reforms, an attempt to restore the feudal institutions established five hundred years earlier at the founding of the Zhou dynasty. This version of his conservatism is particularly attractive to modern
intellectual historians, who are always trying to see individuals in relation to
their age. Yet there is remarkably little in the *Analects* about feudalism and its
institutions, either pro or con. The truth seems to be that Confucius mostly
ignored political institutions.

What, then, was Confucius' program for reform, and in what sense was it
conservative? Here, again, the parallel with Socrates is instructive. Socrates, or,
at any rate, the Platonic Socrates, seems to have been politically conservative
and to have been opposed to many of the characteristically modern developments of his day. Some readers have even seen his description of the just city in
the *Republic* as essentially an elaborate rationalization of the Archaic city and a
plea for a return to an earlier way of life.

Although one cannot reasonably deny the strong archaic elements in the
Republic, it is a travesty of Plato's intention to see them as dominating the work.
On the contrary, the *Republic* is probably one of the most radical works ever
written, and the archaic elements of the just city are defended not on the
grounds that they are traditional but on the grounds that they are just and reasonable. Socrates thus subordinates tradition to reason; and in political matters, that is nothing less than revolutionary.

What Confucius did is analogous and equally revolutionary. Rather than
reason or justice or any other formal principle, Confucius subordinates tradition—and indeed everything else in political life—to the trained, realistic
judgment of morally upright and politically dedicated men. This is the sum and
substance of Confucius' program for reform. It sounds obvious and even su-

perficial, but it is truly radical and at the same time helps explain Confucius' rooted conservatism.

To say that real reform, reform that is effective and not merely on paper, depends on the education of the people involved is a cliché. Genuine racial integration will occur in the United States when its citizens, both white and black, cease regarding skin color as a primary factor in human relationships. Similarly, courts will cease to be corrupt when citizens, be they judges, lawyers, litigants, police officers, or bailiffs, no longer want or tolerate a corrupt judicial system. This point is made in every extended discussion of some social or political problem. Yet when we come to talk seriously about reform, we almost always think in terms of the protesting petition that citizens will circulate, the legislation that citizens want passed, or the administrative ruling that citizens hope to force from some unwilling bureaucrat. If by chance we do take seriously the notion that only through education will reform be accomplished and a more just society achieved, we rarely ask what kind of education we want or need.

By now Americans should realize that the answer to racial discrimination does not lie in arguing that there is no essential difference between the races. Better training in civics, constitutional law, and court procedure, no matter how desirable, is not going to effect many changes in the way justice is served. We tend, in our tradition, to think of political-social problems in abstract terms and to formulate solutions for them in the same way, even when the solution is to be achieved through education. On the higher levels of thought, in political philosophy, the same tendency exists. Western philosophers traditionally ask, "What is the best constitution or form of government for the community?" Our tradition of political thought consists largely of long, detailed discussions of this question and the various distinctions and subordinate questions that it entails.

We do not find any such discussions in the *Analects*. Whether Confucius deliberately rejected this general approach to politics is not known, although I suspect that he was a good deal more aware of what he was doing than most modern commentators give him credit for. Starting in medias res, Confucius does not ask about the essential structure of politics, its nature, or its causes; he asks rather what should be done by certain people in certain situations. Instead of exploring the best regime both ideally and in practice, he explores with his students and the ruling nobles who talk to him the best actions that they can take as individuals. He never questions, so far as I can see, the existing feudal order or examines alternatives to it; he accepts it as given and asks what kinds of men are needed to make that order work effectively and justly so that the common good can be achieved.

The answer that emerges is not restricted in application to the feudal society in which Confucius lived. In ignoring all questions about the formal theoretical structure and operation of the community and concentrating instead on the men who run it, Confucius undercuts the significance of those abstract questions. He examines the human rather than the theoretical roots of politics.

Every human community has a particular structure putting some men and women in positions of power and authority. What matters ultimately is not the formally defined character and limit of that power and authority or its support by written or traditional, religious or secular law. What matters is how that authority is used and to what end. Venal and selfish people will always find ways to pervert the law or get around it for their own purposes. No legal structure will ever be devised that can thwart them by itself. Furthermore, the law is general by nature, and its sanctions are normally punitive. That is to say, the law can at best achieve only minimal compliance from those to whom it applies, and, as we all know, "It is impossible to legislate morality."

Confucius goes further. He says, "If one tries to guide the people by means of laws, and keep order by means of punishments, the people will merely seek to avoid the penalties without having any sense of shame or moral obligation; but if one leads them with virtue and depends upon Li to maintain order, the people will then feel their moral obligation and correct themselves" (book II, chap. 3). In this remark Confucius not only states the limitations of a reliance on law but sees such reliance as having a bad effect on the community because it tends to reduce morality to the external observance of formal rules. A sense of shame or moral obligation cannot be produced by threats or coercion; it can be evoked in members of a community only by the moral example and understanding of those in authority.

If even well-intentioned and well-administered laws can have an unfortunate effect, it follows that the community can be completely demoralized by the spectacle of corrupt authorities using the law for their own advantage. The measure of the worth of a community is not the law but the men who devise, administer, apply, and interpret it. In short, Confucius advocates a government by men rather than a government by law.

Some time ago, when I became aware of this reading of the *Analects,* I decided to acquaint myself more fully with the controversy between government by law and government by men in the Western tradition. Sure enough, in Mortimer Adler's *Syntopicon,* under the heading of Law, I found a discussion of that very topic. When I checked the references, starting with Herodotus and coming down to the present, I was surprised, however, to discover that only two of all the great books recognized by Adler favored government by men: Plato's *Republic* and Aristotle's *Politics.* But the government by philosopher-king advanced in the *Republic* is generally understood to be either impossibly utopian or simply impossible. Aristotle, too, is very careful in his *Politics* to make it clear that although a government by the very best men would be superior to any government by law, such a state of affairs is unlikely to come about and, therefore, is not a practical alternative.

With the exception of these two highly qualified versions of it, the notion of government by men is never considered a serious alternative in the Western tradition of political thought. It is a pejorative notion in contrast to which each political philosopher develops his own notion of the best form of government by law. Confucius is the only political thinker that I know of who seriously advocates government by men as a practical, realistic, and intrinsically superior form of political life. Is it any wonder that Confucius' political ideas have not been highly appreciated by Westerners? They run counter to the overwhelming consensus of all the political thinkers with whom we are familiar.

In the Western tradition, government by law does not mean any or every law, but the right law. Similarly, for Confucius government by men requires the right kind of men. This is the point at which Confucius' discussions with rulers and his education of his disciples become politically as well as methodologically relevant. Given the China of his day, where ruthless power politics were played out beneath a veneer of respect for the old feudal forms, Confucius' main concern was to convince the feudal nobles that morality, dignity, respect for the people, and a dedication to the common good were not foolish or impractical, nor were they an open invitation to disaster. The nobles were concerned for their personal security and the security of their states and frequently ambitious to expand their power, so it is not surprising that many were dyed-in-the-wool cynics.

Confucius constantly tries to show them that morality is more realistic politically than cynicism, that the security of the ruler and his state depends on the happiness and loyalty of his subjects. When the Duke of She asks about government, Confucius replies: "[Good] government obtains when those who are near [that is, people living in the state] are happy, and when those who are far off [in other states] come [to live under your rule]" (book XIII, chap. 6). When Duke Ding asks whether there is a single sentence that can make a country prosperous, Confucius replies, "No single sentence could do that. But there is a saying that comes near to it: 'To be a ruler is hard, and to be a minister is not easy.' If a ruler really understood the difficulty of being a ruler, wouldn't that almost be a single sentence that could make a country prosperous?" When the duke asks whether there is a single sentence that can ruin a country, Confucius replies, "No single sentence can do that. But again there is an old saying that comes close to it: 'I take no pleasure in being a ruler except that no one dares to disagree with what I say.' If the ruler's words are good, isn't it also good that no one disagrees with him, but if they are not good and no one disagrees with them, won't this come very near to being a single sentence that can ruin a country?" (book XIII, chap. 15).

Another time Ji Kang Zi, the de facto ruler in Confucius' home state of Lu, facetiously asks Confucius, "What would you say if I were to kill everyone who did not follow the right way in order to help those who did?" Confucius replies, "You are there to rule, why should you kill at all? If you really desired what was good, the people would be good. The superior man's nature is like the wind and the small people's like the grass; when the wind blows the grass must bend" (book XII, chap. 19).

In all these examples, and there are many more like them in the *Analects,* Confucius seeks to shift the focus of discussion from the ruler's concern with the technical, administrative problems of government to the primary moral responsibility of the ruler and to show that the ruler's success depends on his own sense of responsibility.

Confucius does not seem to have attempted much more in his discussions with rulers. The reason is not hard to see. Political power in the China of Confucius' day was almost purely hereditary, and it would not have been very realistic to expect hereditary rulers to be men of perception and intelligence. It was enough to persuade a ruler, if one could do so, that honesty is the best policy and that it was to his advantage to select ministers who were trained and capable and whose primary allegiance was not to him personally but to the principles of effective and just government. Thus, Confucius' most interesting and illuminating discussions of politics were not with the feudal nobles but with his own disciples, men whom he trained to be the kind of minister that a true government by men requires.

The kind of government that Confucius envisioned and worked toward was one in which the hereditary rulers would continue to occupy their positions but would, for the most part, turn over effective control of their states to their ministers. Naturally, a man as discreet as Confucius would never say openly to a ruler that he should reign but not rule, but many of his remarks to rulers bear that implication. In his discussions with disciples it is clear that they were not being trained to be technically proficient civil servants who could carry out limited administrative tasks assigned to them by their superiors but were being educated to carry out the actual, if not the nominal, role of a ruler. They, and not the hereditary nobles, could be trusted to refuse the temptations of their position of power and authority and to devote themselves to the good of the community.

"Power corrupts," said Lord Acton, "and absolute power corrupts absolutely." This statement, borne out time and again over the centuries, was, appropriately, uttered by a historian, a man who spent his life studying what men have actually done. Confucius, as I have showed, was no stranger to the corrupting effects of power; he knew them all too well. Yet his whole effort in the training of his students was, in essence, to put the lie to the despair embedded in Acton's remark.

Confucius' career as a teacher apparently started informally, presumably when he was a member of a discussion group consisting of politically interested individuals. Some members of this early group were not much younger than Confucius. Not until his later years does he seem to have taken on students for the explicit purpose of educating them. For those who make much of Confucius' supposed adherence to the traditional feudal order, it is interesting to note that he once said, "In teaching there is no distinction of classes" (book XV, chap. 39).

At another time he remarked, "From the very poorest upwards—beginning even with the man who could bring me no better present than a bundle of dried flesh—none has ever come to me without receiving instruction" (book VII, chap. 7). But he apparently placed some restrictions on whom he would accept as a student, for he also said, "Only one who bursts with eagerness do I instruct; only one who bubbles with excitement do I enlighten. If I hold up one corner and a man cannot come back to me with the other three, I do not continue the lesson" (book VII, chap. 8). In education Confucius was elitist, but the only merits he recognized were talent and virtue. Considering the political significance of the training that he gave his students, I believe that he was after much more important things than buttressing a decaying feudal society.

Precisely how Confucius taught his students is unknown. Apparently they studied history, music, and diplomatic practices. But from the fragments in the *Analects* the strongest impression I have is that Confucius talked with them—about government, virtue, the way a minister should serve his ruler, and so forth. The talk seems to have been free and informal, and the disciples did not hesitate to take issue with Confucius or to correct him when they thought he was wrong or inconsistent.

> Once Zilu, Zeng Xi, Ran You, and Gongxi Hua were sitting by Confucius. He said to them, "Though I am a day or so older than you, do not think of that. At present you are out of office and always saying that you are not known. If some ruler were to know you, what would you like to do?"
>
> Zilu quickly and confidently replied, "Suppose the case of a state of 10,000 chariots; let it be suffering from invading armies; and to this let there be added a famine in corn and in all vegetables. If I were entrusted with the government of it, in three years' time I could make the people courageous and teach them in what direction right conduct lies."

The Master smiled at him. Turning to Ran You he said, "And what are your wishes?" You replied, "Suppose a state of 20 or 30 square miles, or 15 or 18, and let me have the government. In three years' time I could make plenty abound among the people. As to teaching them propriety and music, I should leave those things to a truly superior man."

"And what about you?" he asked Gongxi Hua. He replied, "I do not say that I could do this, but I should like to study it. At the ceremonies in the ancestral temple and at the gatherings of the princes I should like, clad in the straight gown and emblematic cap, to play the part of a small assistant."

Finally he turned to Zeng Xi and asked, "And you?" Zeng Xi, pausing as he was playing the lute, while it was yet twanging, laid aside the instrument and rose. "My wishes are different from the cherished purposes of these three gentlemen." "What harm is there in that?" said Confucius. "You also, like them, should tell us your desire." Zeng Xi said, "At the end of spring, when the making of the spring clothes has been completed, to go with five or six newly capped young men and six or seven boys, to perform the lustration in the river, enjoy the breeze among the rain altars, and return home singing." Confucius sighed, "I am with you."

When the three others went away, Zeng Xi remained behind and said, "What do you think of the words of these three friends?" Confucius said, "Each one simply told his wishes." Xi pursued, "But why did you smile at Zilu?" "Because the governing of a state requires Li, and his words were not humble, therefore I smiled at him." "I suppose you were contrasting him with Ran You, who did not mean a real state?" "Did you ever see a territory of 20 or 30 square miles, or even 15 or 18, which was not a state?" "But certainly Gongxi Hua did not ask for a state?" "The business of the ancestral temple and such things as a gathering of the princes, if the feudal lords aren't concerned with these, then who is? If Gongxi Hua were to play a small role, who would be able to play a large one?"

(BOOK XI, CHAP. 25)

It is unfortunate that there are so few passages in the *Analects* as extended and full as this one, but I think this one gives us a sense of the kind of conversation through which the disciples came to know their own characters and develop the disciplined self-restraint required for the responsible exercise of power.

Bi Xi having invited him to visit, Confucius was inclined to go. His disciple Zilu said, "I once heard you yourself say, 'When a man in his own person is guilty of doing evil, a superior man will not associate with him.' Now Bi Xi is holding the town of Zhong Mou in revolt, so how can you possibly consider going to him?" Confucius replied, "Yes, I said those words. But is it not also said that if something is really hard it can be ground without being made thin? Is it not said that if something is really white it may be steeped in a dark fluid without being made black? Am I a bitter gourd fit only to hang up out of the way, not good enough to eat?"

(BOOK XVII, CHAP. 7)

Apart from the pathos of this passage, we can feel the toughness of spirit and the utter political realism that Confucius attempted to inculcate in his disciples along with moral integrity and dedicated idealism.

This, then, was the goal Confucius set for himself, his disciples, and, although he didn't know it, Chinese civilization for the next two thousand years. He urged the development not of an ideal community organized according to a specific formal pattern but of a kind of man who was personally able and moral, who sought a career in politics if at all possible, who was dedicated to the good of his community. This kind of man could resist the temptations of power and was sufficiently realistic to know that there were others like himself, but not many. To work toward his aims such a man would have to accept this imperfect world and make the best of it that he could.

In one sense, this image of the virtuous politician is as impossibly utopian as Socrates' description of the best regime in the *Republic*. Confucius presents an ideal goal, a conception of the good man against which individuals can measure themselves, just as Socrates measures all existing cities in terms of his perfectly just city. But in another and stronger sense, Confucius' goal is intensely practical in a way that the city of the philosopher-king is not and cannot be. There is no practical way of working toward or even approximating the city of the *Republic;* its peculiar institutions are too far removed from the realities of political life for that.

But Confucius' image of the superior man or the true knight can be approximated. An individual can act as such a man would act. It is possible, through the force of personal example, to evoke a sense of moral responsibility in members of one's community. A single person can, with courage, resist the corrupting effects of power, and so on. This is what Confucius tried, with varying success, to teach his disciples.

This conception of reform does not necessarily require reform of institutions, social structure, or political procedures. A community can be completely revitalized from a Confucian point of view without effecting any formal changes that would be visible to a sociologist or cultural anthropologist. This acceptance of existing institutions is one aspect of Confucius' conservatism, but another is more critical.

In Confucius' program for reform through the education of gifted individuals the inculcation of morality in the sense of good intentions is not sufficient—that seems clear enough. To be effective in politics in the way Confucius trained his disciples to be, a man must not only be determined to be just; he must know what justice is and how to go about achieving it. It is not enough for him to favor participation in politics; he must know when and under what conditions participation is possible and effective and when it is not. It is not enough to urge cooperation with all men who share the same goals; it is also necessary to know what those goals are so that he can recognize his true friends and enemies. In short, he must have principles that are both habitual and accessible to intelligence.

Clearly, Confucius had such principles, which he was only too happy to articulate whenever the opportunity arose. Yet as soon as we ask what those principles are, a difficulty presents itself: pinning Confucius down. The disciples themselves admit to this difficulty, and most Chinese and Western students of the *Analects* have felt it. Behind the pieced-together, unordered remarks in the *Analects,* even behind what I have called Confucius' program for reform, one senses the presence of a coherent, consistent body of principles on which all the disparate remarks and ideas are based.

Confucius himself once said to his disciple Xigong, "You think of me, don't you, as someone who simply studies and remembers many things?" "Yes," Xigong answered, "isn't that so?" "No," said Confucius, "I have one thing which I use as a thread upon which to string them all" (book XV, chap. 2). And another time Confucius said to another disciple, Zeng Zi, "The way that I follow has one thing upon which everything is strung, doesn't it?" Zeng Zi said, "Yes," and after Confucius had left, the other disciples asked Zeng Zi what Confucius had meant. He said, "Our Master's Way is simply this: Integrity toward ourselves and reciprocity in our relations with others" (book IV, chap. 15).

Here it is not Confucius but one of his disciples who explains in Confucius' absence what runs through and unifies Confucius' thought. I think Zeng Zi's answer is a good one, but it is not Confucius' own answer, and it must therefore be taken with a grain of salt. Sadly, Confucius himself, so far as we know, never labeled that thread, articulated that one principle. I think that this absence of an explicit principle is not the fault of the fragmentary character of the *Analects*. The way the other disciples question Zeng Zi implies that Confucius never articulated it at all.

Confucius' silence on this matter is no minor thing, particularly to a Westerner, for this principle plays a role in his thought analogous to the role of political philosophy in the thought of a Westerner. That is to say, the very subject about which Western thinkers write their soberest books is the subject that Confucius apparently never discussed. I would like to conclude with an admittedly speculative attempt to describe that subject, thread, principle, and to explain why Confucius never talked about it directly. His claim to intellectual greatness depends on a satisfactory answer to this question.

Mushin Mahdi has defined political philosophy as the "love or quest of wisdom about the nature or principles of all human or political things." The definition is a good one, first, because it accurately describes the tradition of medieval Islamic political philosophy that he is discussing and, second, because philosophically it makes sense. We find it hard even to conceive of political philosophy except in the terms that Mahdi uses or some variant of them.

Yet this conception of political philosophy is deeply paradoxical. Politics, as described by Mahdi, comprehends the whole of a person's active life. Philosophy, on the other hand, is not normally thought of as an activity except in a metaphorical or analogical sense. Philosophy is essentially a matter of thinking, of knowing, not of acting. Political philosophy is that particular branch of philosophy which concerns thinking about and seeking knowledge of human action.

Yet politics itself does not seek knowledge; it aims at effective action. Thus political philosophy, as conceived in our tradition, is by its very nature different from and even opposed to the subject matter into which its practitioners inquire. The thinkers in our philosophical tradition are almost unanimous in their agreement that philosophy or thinking is intrinsically superior to politics and acting. In *The Human Condition,* Hannah Arendt begins her inquiry from this point. She says of the relation between thought and action that "the enormous superiority of contemplation over activity of any kind, action not excluded, is not Christian in origin. We find it in Plato's political philosophy, where the whole utopian reorganization of *polis* life is not only directed by the superior insight of the philosopher, but has no aim other than to make possible the philosopher's way of life" (p. 15).

In speaking of the distinction of the active from the philosophical life she says "the term *vita activa* is loaded and overloaded with tradition. It is as old as (but not older than) our tradition of political thought. And this tradition, far from comprehending and conceptualizing all the political experiences of Western mankind, grew out of a specific historical constellation: the trial of Socrates and the conflict between the philosopher and the *polis*" (p. 13). She concludes her discussion by saying,

> If, therefore, the use of the term *vita activa,* as I propose it here, is in
> manifest contradiction to the tradition, it is because I doubt, not the
> validity of the experience underlying the distinction [between the

active and the contemplative lives], but rather the hierarchical order inherent in it from its inception. . . . My contention is simply that the enormous weight of contemplation in the traditional hierarchy has blurred the distinctions and articulations within the *vita activa* itself and that, appearances notwithstanding, this condition has not been changed essentially by the modern break with the tradition and the eventual reversal of its hierarchical order in Marx and Nietzsche.

(p. 17)

Whether Arendt has succeeded in doing justice to the active life by denying the traditional hierarchical subordination of that life to the life of the philosopher remains an open question. The very attempt involves a radical break with the dominant Western tradition of political philosophy. Yet Arendt is still enmeshed in the paradox of investigating the active life philosophically: she, like all Western philosophers, is examining politics from the outside, so to speak. She has rejected part of the tradition, but the essential element remains.

I would suggest that to see politics and the active life from the inside, on its own terms, requires studying the *Analects*. Arendt and the other Western philosophers who have rejected the traditional view that philosophy is superior to politics, that knowledge is intrinsically higher than action, still offer us *theories* of politics. They think about politics; they do not yet think politically. That, I suggest, is precisely what Confucius did, and his genius lies in the profundity with which he did it.

I have said that Confucius' utterances as recorded in the *Analects* are based on a coherent body of unexpressed principles. Most students of the *Analects* would agree. However, the assumption that these scholars usually make, which I am denying, is that the principles constitute a theory. The scholars try to make up for Confucius' reticence in this area by stating his general theoretical position. Unfortunately their attempts always leave something to be desired. The peculiar quality of tough-minded realism combined with personal integrity and dedication to the good of the community that marks his thought is somehow blunted and lost when his views are restated in a well-organized theoretical form. This could be avoided if the *Analects* is seen not as theoretical thought about political issues in the manner of Western political philosophy but as political thought about political issues in a manner perhaps unique to Confucius.

Many of the peculiarities that Western readers find in the *Analects* disappear if they read from this point of view. Confucius is concerned with a fundamental reform of political life but does not consider the various forms of political institutions. His lack of interest in metaphysics, in epistemology, in theoretical psychology, in the nature of human beings and society—all this is not an oversight on his part or a severe limitation in his thinking. These problems are functions of a theoretical point of view, and Confucius' point of view is not theoretical.

It is not what Confucius doesn't do that I find most interesting; it is what he does do. The active life seen from within looks very different than it does from the contemplative viewpoint. The questions asked, the terms employed, the knowledge sought, the goals to be achieved, the meaning of success and failure, even the virtues, are different. I cannot possibly do justice to the extraordinary reevaluation of all values that occurs when, rather than forcing inherited categories of Western thought on the *Analects,* a reader comes to grips with Confucius' thought in Confucius' terms. Let me give a few examples.

If I had to pick a single key term in the *Analects,* I would probably pick *Dao.* The character originally meant a "road" or "path" or "way." From that, its meaning was extended to include a way of action or way of doing things. Confucius uses the term in these limited senses, but he also and primarily uses it in a new sense, to signify The Way. In this emphatic sense, which may have been original with Confucius, Dao indicates the right course of action for an individual or a state. The Dao embodies all the particular values, principles, virtues, and policies that Confucius advocated. It is, in this sense, analogous to the idea of the Good set forth by Socrates in the *Republic.*

But the Dao, unlike the idea of the Good, is not an object of knowledge; it is not known—it is followed. Confucius doesn't expound the Dao to his disciples; rather, he helps them acquire the moral and intellectual abilities required to follow it. The Dao is, I think, that one thing upon which everything is strung, the one principle that Confucius uses to string together all the particular things he knows and says. In following the Dao a person's life takes on meaning and value. "If one hears the Dao in the morning," he said, "he may die in the evening without regret" (book IV, chap. 8). It is the inner satisfaction that comes from such a life that compensates a person for whatever material difficulties he has. "A gentleman," he said, "who has ambitions toward the Dao and yet is ashamed of poor clothing and bad food is not yet fit to be talked to" (book IV, chap. 9).

Beyond that, the Dao gives a sense of common purpose and community to its followers. One of the most famous and beautiful passages in the *Analects* records a conversation between two disciples. Confucius was not there, although he makes his presence felt. "Sima Niu, full of anxiety, said, 'Other men all have their brothers, I alone do not.' Zixia said to him, 'I have heard this saying, "Death and life are fated; riches and honors depend upon heaven." Let the superior man never fail reverentially to order his own conduct and let him be respectful to others and observant of propriety—then all within the four seas will be his brothers. Why should the superior man be anxious that he has no brothers?'" (book XII, chap. 5).

Despite the obvious centrality of the Dao in his thought, Confucius does not think of it as fixed or constant. It is the possession of the people and communities that follow it, and they are responsible for it. In a brief passage which Legge says is "quite mystical in its sententiousness" but which I think is central to an understanding of Confucius' thought, he says, "Men are able to enlarge the Dao, but the Dao of itself does not enlarge men" (book XV, chap. 28). The Dao is what the men who follow it make it. The Dao has no meaning or reality apart from their actions, and it is inherent in everything they do. In a sense, then, we could say that far from being reticent about the Dao, Confucius is always talking about it when he gives advice to princes and disciples, when he discusses the virtues, when he speaks at all.

Of the various terms that are somewhat misleadingly considered to name Confucian virtues, there are two that I would like to discuss because they are so different from the standard virtues that Western political philosophers discuss. *Li,* which I defined earlier as "the accepted forms of propriety," is perhaps the most interesting. The character for *Li* originally represented a sacrificial vessel, and the original meaning of the word was "to sacrifice." *Li* retains that meaning but now takes in all forms of social intercourse from formal ritual practice and diplomatic protocol down to what we would call etiquette and informal interpersonal relations.

The term as used in the *Analects* is sometimes translated as "ritual," sometimes as "propriety." Yet such translations fail to do justice to Confucius' use of the term; worse, they pervert his intention. For Li involves not merely the outward forms of behavior and expression but also, and essentially, the inner feeling or spirit that animates those forms. To mask true feelings behind a facade of formal politeness, to participate in rituals that are personally meaningless— these are the opposite of Li. "It is *Li,* they say! It is *Li,* they say! Is *Li* no more than jade and silks?" asked Confucius (book XVII, chap. 11). At another time he said, "The linen cap is that prescribed by *Li,* but nowadays a silk one is worn. It is economical, and I follow the common practice. Bowing at the foot of the dais when approaching a lord is prescribed by *Li.* Nowadays people bow after they have ascended the dais. That is arrogant, and, even if it means that I oppose the common practice, I will continue to bow down below" (book IX, chap. 3).

To have or to be Li means, for Confucius, to have internalized the forms of behavior so that they are genuinely expressive. In the passage just quoted, Confucius is aware of the purely conventional character of much that is prescribed by Li. He is also aware that behind the conventions there is a human reality. He does not, however, pay his respects to the surface convention and then consider the inner reality—that is what philosophers interested in theory, in uncovering the reality behind the appearances, usually do. Whatever the ontological status of the forms of social intercourse, Confucius saw that they were essential to political life. Whether the rules are according to nature or according to custom makes little or no difference. What matters is that without these rules, political life, and that means civilized life, is impossible; without these rules human beings are barbarians. To be Li does not mean observing slavishly all the prescribed ritual and conventional minutiae, but it does entail understanding that breaking the rules loosens the bonds of political life.

Confucius is not opposed to justified change. But he would not accept clever and possibly superficial arguments based on abstract formal reasoning as an adequate justification for change. Civilized life is too precious a possession to be subject to irresponsible experimentation. This is another and deeper aspect of his conservatism, which we can understand through a consideration of his sense of Li. There is a great deal more to be said about Li, but I have said enough to indicate that Confucius' use of this term contains an entire dimension of political life that the dominant tradition of Western political thought—with the exception of a few thinkers such as Edmund Burke—has left largely unexplored.

Because nothing in Western philosophy is quite equivalent to Li, I thought that for my second and final example of how the virtues take on a wholly different character in the context of Confucius' thought, I would examine a concept with which we are all familiar. "Knowledge" or "wisdom" has from the beginning played an important role in Western political thought, and Confucius is concerned with it as well. But how differently he conceives it. He once said to his disciple Zilu, "Shall I teach you what wisdom is? When you know a thing, to recognize that you know it, and when you do not know a thing, to recognize that you do not know it. That is knowledge" (book II, chap. 17). Lest the apparent simplicity of his formula put you off, let me remind you that the equivalent remark of Socrates, "I know that I know nothing," has long perplexed Western philosophers. Confucius, like Socrates, insists that an awareness of one's own ignorance is an essential part of wisdom or knowledge, but unlike Socrates, Confucius also insists that knowledge requires an awareness of what we do know.

The Socratic formula is the deeply ironic starting point of theoretical thought; the Confucian formula is also, in its own way, ironic, but it is profoundly sober. The Socratic irony has a paralyzing effect; it pulls us up sharply and turns us away from the myriad commitments of our everyday life to a consideration of our nature. The Confucian irony, by contrast, reminds us of our limitations and circumstances.

Thus for Confucius, knowledge or wisdom—*Zhi*—is primarily prudential and humanistic. "There may be those," he said, "who can act without knowledge, but I am not one of them. To hear much, select what is good, and follow it; to see much and remember it—these are the steps by which knowledge is attained" (book VII, chap. 27). When Zilu asked about serving the spirits, Confucius replied, "You aren't yet able to serve men; how can you serve the spirits?" Zilu then asked about death, and Confucius said, "You do not yet know about life; how can you know about death?" (book XI, chap. 11).

On another occasion the disciple Fan Chi asked about *Ren,* another so-called virtue discussed in the *Analects,* sometimes translated as "goodness" or "benevolence" or "perfect virtue." In any event, Confucius replied, "It is to love men." Fan Chi then asked about knowledge, and Confucius said, "It is to know men." When Fan Chi admitted that he still didn't quite understand, Confucius elaborated. "Raise the morally upright and put aside all who are crooked, and in this way you can make the crooked upright" (book XII, chap. 22). In addition to the prudential, humanistic conception of knowledge implied in this answer, Ren and Zhi, goodness and knowledge, are given an explicitly political meaning.

As Confucius elaborates their meaning for Fan Chi, both virtues are realized together in the same political act; that is, to know men and to love men are indistinguishable in practice. For Confucius the virtues are not the formally distinct perfections of separate human abilities but aspects of action. They have no meaning apart from action or from each other. This is why, despite the best efforts of later commentators, it is impossible to define the separate virtues or even to arrive at a final list of them. Knowledge is not, therefore, a virtue in the sense that the term is commonly understood, and neither is Li; they are both parts or aspects of virtuous activity.

Socrates, the figure in Western tradition most comparable to Confucius in traditional Chinese culture, was also interested in knowledge. The Socratic technique of abstract, rational cross-examination has remained to this day a model of the way wisdom, as Socrates understood it, can be approached, even if never attained. Confucius died about ten years before Socrates was born. In the fifth-century B.C. China was very different from its contemporary, classical Greece, and Confucius' relation to the China of his day was very different from Socrates' relation to Athens. Yet Confucius' life defined China's core intellectual tradition, as Socrates' life and death defined the Western intellectual tradition. Confucius devised no new techniques of discourse or rational investigation, but he, no less than Socrates, was interested in wisdom.

Whatever degree of wisdom he was able to attain was passed down through generations of followers, contributing greatly to the remarkable staying power of traditional Chinese institutions and culture. This is no small achievement. If the Socratic tradition is still alive, if we are interested in wisdom and not just in the appearance of wisdom, and if we acknowledge our own ignorance and don't just pretend to do so, then at the very least we must admit that the thought of Confucius stands as a challenge to the basic assumptions of the Western tradition. It invites us to reconsider the very notion of philosophy as it has come down to us from Socrates.

1 2 Chinese and English Lyric Poetry
Art and the Comparison of Cultures

Is it possible to grasp the quality of a culture through its literature and, further, to compare cultures by comparing their literatures? Some have argued that this approach is valid. I myself am skeptical of the notion of literary anthropology and cross-cultural literary comparison unless the methodology is very carefully qualified. What the qualifications might be, I am not sure. I propose, therefore, to explore the notion of the comparison of cultures through the comparison of literatures without coming to any definite conclusions. I do reach some tentative conclusions, but they are clichés. To avoid devoting too much attention to a fruitless discussion of these clichés, I will direct most of my remarks to two Chinese and two English poems.

Before I remark on the poems, let me set forth my clichés. In the jargon of the trade, this means beginning with a statement of the formal, methodological, and theoretical assumptions underlying my comparison of the four poems. The first of these assumptions, or clichés, as I prefer to call them, was given its classic and most precise formulation by that great master of the cliché Aristotle. He starts the second chapter of his *Poetics* with the sentence "The objects the imitator represents are actions with agents who are necessarily either good men or bad—the diversities of human character being nearly always derivative from this primary distinction, since the line between virtue and vice is one dividing the whole of mankind" (1448a1–3). Now, whenever I have had occasion to teach the *Poetics,* students who have studied the social sciences or who have taken a course in anthropology greet this sentence with a chorus of hoots. Then one of the more articulate members of the class explains to me that while the line between virtue and vice does divide mankind, different cultures conceive of virtue and vice differently. As a consequence, although Aristotle's statement remains formally correct, it takes on substantive meaning only within the context of a particular culture, for what is good in one culture may be bad in another, and vice versa. I am told, for example, that if the Dobuans wrote tragedies, the noble, long-suffering hero might look to us like a thoroughly despicable man who got exactly what he deserved.

However, no one has yet been able to show me an actual work of art that corresponds to that hypothetical Dobuan tragedy. Despite the obvious truth of cultural relativity, I have never had much trouble telling a hero from a villain, whether he or she be Chinese, Japanese, or Indian, and I doubt very much that many others have, either. There are, of course, difficult cases, but they always seem to be the exceptions that prove Aristotle's rule. It is, for example, extraordinarily difficult to decide whether Captain Ahab in *Moby Dick* is a good man or a bad man, but not because we and Melville inhabit different cultural universes. It is because Melville has deliberately fudged the moral dimensions of Ahab's character. That is to say, Melville has understood the truth of Aristotle's remark and has consciously produced a character who puzzles us.

For me, the truth expressed in Aristotle's remark is what makes the cross-cultural comparison of literature possible. If we were all fully culture-bound, non-Japanese could not understand the human content of a Japanese novel or non-Indians an Indian epic. We could not even undertake to compare works of art from different cultures except possibly in purely formal terms. That we can appreciate and understand literary works from different cultures implies that in some not insignificant sense literature and art appeal to us not as Chinese or Westerners or Muslims but as humans.

The second cliché upon which my comparison of the four poems depends is in certain respects the exact opposite of the first. It can be understood best through a visual example. Both the Fan Kuan and El Greco landscapes illustrated here are masterpieces, although someone who has not seen the original Fan Kuan will have difficulty feeling its immense power. Try to imagine it not as a small print that you can hold in your lap but as a large scroll almost seven feet high. The towering mountain that dominates the scene also dominates and literally towers over the spectator. Those who have seen the Sistine ceiling will know what I mean when I speak of the inability of the reproduction to convey the power of the original.

The point I want to make is that the Fan Kuan is a Chinese painting, and the El Greco a European or Western one. The fact that the El Greco is an oil painting and the Fan Kuan an ink painting, and the fact that there are no mountains in Europe resembling the one Fan Kuan has painted and no cities in China like Toledo—these and many other differences are beside the point. What I am concerned with is the feeling, the mood, the emotional quality of the two

Fan Kuan, *Travelers amid Mountains and Streams*. 8 1 ¹/₄ ×
40 ³/₄ in. National Palace Museum, Taibei, Taiwan, Republic of China.

works, which seems to me to be characteristically Chinese in the one and characteristically Western in the other. The El Greco is intensely dramatic and dynamic. Everything on the earth seems to be in motion, with wandering hills,
streams, and roads and tangled buildings. Above the earth, almost pressing
down upon it, are the massed, threatening clouds of the imminent storm.

I don't know whether El Greco "meant" anything by this painting, whether
symbolism or compositional requirements dictate that the storm seem most

El Greco, *View of Toledo*. 47¾ × 42¾ in. Metropolitan Museum of Art. (Bequest of Mrs. H. O. Havemeyer, 1929. The H. O. Havemeyer Collection. [29.100.6].)

ominous and threatening just where the cathedral and the castle of the city jut up against the sky. We could argue about which adjective or phrase best describes the sky—*ominous* or *foreboding* or *angry*—but all the choices are within the range of humanly meaningful emotional experience.

With the Fan Kuan we are faced with a scene that has none of the tension, drama, or dynamism of the El Greco. There is motion: at the lower right, two men are driving some pack donkeys; in the center, to the left of a small waterfall, a monk is coming around the side of a hill; and a fine high waterfall drops down the mountain just above the travelers and the temple whose roof is visible on the hill to the right. Yet these details are insignificant compared with the overwhelming and mysterious contrast of foreground to background. The foreground is prosaic enough with the lonely road, the scattered travelers, the isolated temple. All this we can understand. But what are we to make of that towering mountain? Just how far away is it? Does it rise out of the mist right behind the low hill, or is it miles away? Is the small waterfall in the center of the picture the continuation of the long, thin waterfall on the mountain? Do the travelers see the mountain that dominates the scene, or is their view cut off by the hills and the mist behind them?

These questions are unanswerable. We are left with the brute fact of the mountain, overpowering in its presence, toward which we feel a kind of awe but which cannot itself be described in any specifically human terms. It does not menace or threaten, it is neither ominous nor comforting; it is simply there, and it is nonhuman with all the mystery that implies. Being Western rather than Chinese does not seriously inhibit a response to the picture or distort the viewer's sense of it. But no Westerner has ever painted a picture quite like Fan Kuan's—only Chinese, and precious few of them at that.

These, then, are the two principles underlying my comparison of the four poems. First, we are all human and, as such, can perceive, appreciate, and share one another's experiences; and second, despite our common human nature, whether we are Chinese, Western, Muslim, or whatever does make a difference.

Let me turn now to the first pair of poems, "The Sick Rose," by William Blake, and "Night Thoughts," by Li Bai. Both are short and thus illustrate in miniature the techniques, possibilities, and dominant characteristics of Chinese and English poetry as employed by two master poets.

THE SICK ROSE
William Blake

O Rose, thou art sick!
The invisible worm,
That flies in the night,
In the howling storm,

Has found out thy bed
Of crimson joy,
And his dark, secret love
Does thy life destroy.

"The Sick Rose" comprises only two complete sentences; it has two stanzas of four lines each, and each line is about as short as a line of English poetry can be, consisting of two metrical feet. Strikingly, the poem is a description of neither the rose nor the feelings of the speaker about the rose; it is a direct address by the speaker to the rose. Yet if we ask, Who is speaking? What is the speaker's relationship to the rose? What is actually happening? no clear or satisfactory answers are forthcoming. About the best I can do is imagine a gardener puttering in his garden, coming upon a favorite rosebush, and saying, half to himself, "This rose is diseased. The petals were eaten last night by some sort of flying insect that is killing it." But this is not a prose restatement of the poem:

it is the destruction of the poetry in it. Yet the restatement is instructive, for it shows what Blake has accomplished.

The poem, though built around a number of direct, commonplace images, such as roses, worms, night, storms, points away from those images in their natural setting to another realm. Nature is not scenery to look at; it is a realm charged with human emotion and meaning. The speaker is not a gardener distressed that one of his rosebushes is being eaten by bugs; he is a human anguished at the vision of a tragic love affair in which beauty, innocence, and joy are being deliberately destroyed by something radically evil. In effect, the poem is not a fancy description of a simple, natural event; it is a symbolic drama about the nature of the world. A look at the details of the piece will give an idea of how Blake achieves this in such a small compass.

The poem is built around a complex series of contrasts between the rose and the worm. Here Blake can rely, to start with at least, on our conventional sense of these two images. Roses are among the most beautiful of flowers, whereas worms are wriggling, slimy, dirty creatures used for fish bait. There are also many highly suggestive associations to be made. The rose and the worm are old Christian symbols. The rose, associated with the Virgin Mary, is a sign of purity. In the chivalric language of flowers the red rose stands for true love. The worm, by contrast, is the medieval name for the serpent in the Garden of Eden, the agent of evil that tempted Eve and caused the expulsion from the earthly paradise. It is also conventionally used as a metaphor for a human being, who, in contrast to the majesty of God, is a miserable worm crawling on the face of the earth.

If these are the conventional associations that Blake can assume are more or less present in the minds of his readers, what is poetically interesting is the way he shapes, specifies, and concretizes them within the context of the poem. The rose has both vivid color and form; the worm is "invisible," and its shape vague. The rose is passive and motionless, its only activity being to come into full bloom; the worm is active and in motion—it seeks out the rose. The worm is explicitly male, and the rose is female by implication. The rose lives in the sunny day; the worm, in the night, in the howling storm. But the night here is not a specific period of time. It has the sense, rather, of a region, a place characterized by the howling storm.

These two images are not simply contrasted with one another. They are in violent and tragic interaction. The rose, by virtue of its beauty, its joy, its enormous erotic appeal, invites the worm to seek it out and destroy it. It is as if beauty, joy, and innocence bring about their own destruction by the forces of evil. So much for the structure of the poem and its imagery and symbols.

Blake has still other devices with which he can reinforce and heighten the impact of the poem. Notice the grammar. After the initial statement to the rose, the single sentence that constitutes the rest of the poem has as its subject the worm that is the cause of the present sickness of the rose. The worm "that flies in the night . . . has found out thy bed of crimson joy." Its discovery of the rose has already occurred. Only with the very last word of the poem are we told what the worm is doing right now.

The present tense of the opening line creates a grammatical tension and anticipation that is not resolved until the end of the poem. In terms of grammatical structure, the poem could read, "O Rose, thou art sick! / The invisible worm / Does thy life destroy." Everything in-between is grammatically unnecessary. Yet the forceful separation of subject and verb serves both to increase the tension of the poem and to integrate the subordinate phrases into the sense of the whole.

Finally, it is worth looking at the metrical pattern. The meter of the first line is unclear, consisting as it does of five stressed syllables. But from that point on, something remarkable happens. The lines and images referring to the worm tend to be in anapestic meter, two unstressed syllables followed by a stress beat—"The invisible worm, / That flies in the night"—and so on, while those referring to the rose follow an iambic beat—"Has found out thy bed, / Of crimson joy;" This continues until the last line, where suddenly the pattern is reversed. The first foot of the line "Does thy life" refers to the rose but is an anapest, while the second foot, "destroy," refers to the worm but is an iamb. The sudden shift in metrical pattern reflects the tragic fate that unites the rose and the worm.

Let us turn now to the Li Bai poem, shown here in Chinese characters with

低 dī lower	舉 jǔ raise	疑 yí suspect	床 chuáng couch	
頭 tóu head	頭 tóu head	是 shì is	前 qián before	夜 Yè Night
思 sī think	望 wàng gaze	地 dì ground	明 míng bright	思 Sī Thoughts
故 gù former	明 míng bright	上 shàng on	月 yuè moon	李 Lǐ
鄉 xiāng village	月 yuè moon	霜 shuāng frost	光 guāng glow	白 Bái

the romanized pronunciation and a literal rendition in English beneath each character. The poem should be read Chinese style, from top to bottom starting at the right. Provided for comparison are two published English translations.

IN THE QUIET NIGHT
   Li Bai

So bright a gleam on the foot of my bed—
Could there have been a frost already?
Lifting myself to look, I found that it was moonlight.
Sinking back again, I thought suddenly of home.
TRANSLATED BY WITTER BYNNER

THOUGHTS IN A TRANQUIL NIGHT
   Li Po

   Athwart the bed
I watch the moonbeams cast a trail
   So bright, so cold, so frail.
      That for a space it gleams
Like hoar-frost on the margin of my dreams.
      I raise my head,—
   The splendid moon I see:
      Then droop my head,
And sink to dreams of thee—
      My Fatherland, of thee!

TRANSLATED BY L. CRANMER-BYNG

   This poem is even shorter than Blake's. It consists of four lines of five words each—a grand total of twenty words, only three more than a Japanese haiku, which may be the absolute minimal size of a complete poetic form. Unlike Blake's "The Sick Rose," Li Bai's "Night Thoughts" is written in a conventional form, called a *jue-ju*, or "cut-short verse." A jue-ju is a four-line poem, each line having five or seven characters. The characters in each line must be arranged according to pronunciation, or, more precisely, according to a fixed tonal pattern—there is some resemblance here to the metrical requirements of English poetry. The lines must also follow each other in a certain order.

   To get some idea of what Li Bai has accomplished in his twenty words, let us look at the two published English translations. In the second one, by Cranmer-Byng, the four lines and twenty words of the original have become ten lines and fifty-four words. Cranmer-Byng tried to put into his English version everything he saw or felt in the Chinese original. The result is a parody. Everything that is light, suggested, and dramatic in the original has become heavy, explicit, and almost frivolous in English. What is perhaps barely excusable in an analysis of a poem is beyond justification in translation.

Bynner and Kiang have done better. They keep the four lines of the original and thus something of the poem's development. But they, too, have introduced new elements and changed much of the original quality of the poem.

In the original Chinese, the poem is simple and straightforward. There are no complex images or associative patterns. The dramatic situation begins in medias res: a man lying in bed at night sees the peculiarly brilliant glow of the moonlight at the foot of his bed. We don't know that he has been asleep. All we are told is that the moon is casting a bright light on his bed. The emphasis is not on the man or what he is doing but on the presence of moonlight.

Not until the second line, with the two characters *yi shi,* does the focus shift from the scene to the man. He suspects that it is not moonlight he sees but frost on the ground. Thus a tension is created between the first two lines, between the actual situation and how it appears to the speaker.

In what situation might a man mistake the light of the moon for the glow of frost? Although Li Bai does not tell us explicitly, the circumstances seem unambiguous to me. The man has been asleep; he wakes up and opens his eyes. In that fleeting moment between sleeping and waking, he imagines that he is in a familiar place, perhaps his home, where he is used to waking up and seeing the glow of the frost on the ground—only this time he is wrong. He is not at home in the north, where that bright nighttime light means that the first frost has come. He is away, maybe in the south, where the brilliance of the tropical moonlight has deceived him. But I am getting ahead of myself. At the end of the second line all that has been established is a tension between the presence of moonlight and the man's feeling that there has been a frost.

In the third line the movement begun in the second is continued. Still half asleep, still in that moment between sleeping and waking, and thus still believing that frost has caused the brightness on his bed, he raises his head and looks at the moon. The phrase *ju tou,* "I raise my head," has an idiomatic and metaphorical sense beyond the literal sense. "To raise one's head" means "to push oneself forward, to come to the front, to exert oneself." The verb that follows, *wang,* which means "to gaze at something in the distance," connotes hope and expectation in the sense that one looks hopefully or expectantly into the distance. Taken together, the three characters *ju tou wang* not only describe literally what the man is doing but also imply an energetic, hopeful expectancy. Yet what he sees is not the frost but the bright moon.

In the last line he lowers his head and thinks of his old village home. Here, again, a few purely conventional Chinese images need to be made explicit. In China the moon is a traditional symbol of homesickness. The autumn harvest festival is somewhat analogous to the de-Christianized Christmas, when everyone goes home to visit family. The moon at that time of year is at its biggest and most beautiful. To look at the moon in the autumn when one is away from home is to be reminded of home. The moon that shines on the traveler is the same moon that shines on family and friends gathered at home. So the moon functions in this poem in much the same way that the conventional European associations with roses and worms function in Blake's poem. Seeing the moon, the man lowers his head and thinks of home. That response is purely conventional.

But the phrase *di tou,* "to lower the head," while it describes an action that is the opposite of *ju tou,* also carries a metaphorical sense that contrasts with the metaphorical sense of *ju tou.* If raising one's head expresses a certain aggressiveness, lowering the head expresses resignation, defeat, submissiveness, passive acceptance. The same contrast between opposing actions holds for the next character, *si,* "to think," which corresponds to *wang,* "to gaze," in the preceding line. *Wang* means "to gaze hopefully into the distance or the future," whereas *si* means "to think" in the sense of reflecting on, or recalling, the past.

Here the poem ends. The moment between sleeping and waking is over. The man has awakened, been deceived by the moonlight, looked up hopefully to see not the frost but the moon, and sunk back to think of home. The four lines and twenty words of the poem re-create an experience that has about the same duration as the experience of reading the poem itself.

Both the poem and the experience that it renders are almost instantaneous, although in another sense both poem and experience go on reverberating in the speaker and the reader. What Li Bai has done is to grasp and articulate poetically what it means to wake up at night far from home. He has had the extraordinary tact, characteristic of only the greatest artists, to say just enough to evoke the experience without supplying information that would make it someone else's experience rather than the reader's own. The personal details that make waking up in a strange place a unique experience for each individual are supplied by each reader. Li Bai articulates that evanescent moment we have all known. He does it so simply and matter-of-factly that his artfulness is difficult to see.

I have already mentioned the tension created in the first two lines and some of the associative patterns evoked by the words in the last two lines. These last two lines constitute what is known in Chinese poetry as a parallel couplet. Grammatically, the lines are perfectly parallel, and they match each other word for word. Beyond that, they are in perfect contrast, so that each word, phrase, action, and object in the third line is matched by and contrasted with a word, phrase, action, and object in the fourth. As a result, the tension in the first two lines between the facts of the situation and the man's response to it is sharpened and at the same time completed by the contrasting parallelism of the last two lines. The vague, inchoate feelings of the first two lines are articulated and shaped in the concluding two.

When the feeling is articulated, the poem stops. There is nothing more to say, even though the feeling itself goes on. The poem ends just where the momentary experience culminates in a definite mood. The poem creates and establishes the mood by evoking it, not by describing it directly. Parallel lines are not very hard to write in Chinese, no more difficult than writing a line of English in iambic meter. But just as it takes the genius of Blake to realize the poetic potentialities of conventional meter, so it takes a Li Bai to employ so conventional a technique as a parallel couplet to give meaning, articulation, and finish to a genuine poetic experience.

With the Blake and Li Bai poems, we have been dealing with poetry at its most minute. With the next pair I shall be comparing examples of longer, highly conventional poetic forms: a *lu shi,* or "regulated verse," by Du Fu, and a sonnet by Gerard Manley Hopkins. Even the loosest of Chinese forms seems tight in comparison to the the sonnet, which is about the most rigid conventional form employed in English. To write his Italian sonnet all Hopkins had to do was compose fourteen iambic pentameter lines divided into an octave of eight lines and a sestet of six. In sonnets the octave normally consists of two quatrains having the same rhyme scheme, but the formal relation between the octave and the sestet is very free. The verse form employed by Du Fu is much more exacting in its formal requirements. That is perhaps why it has been employed successfully by only a relatively few Chinese poets. Since the ninth century, when it was first developed, a great many lu shi have been written, but few, I am told, worth reading.

Hopkins is one of the most technically proficient poets who have ever written in English. His control of meter, rhythm, and images is breathtaking. He can compress more poetic meaning into fewer words than almost any other lyric poet. "God's Grandeur," discussed here, is a relatively simple example of his work; to see what he can do at full stretch, read "The Windhover."

GOD'S GRANDEUR
Gerard Manley Hopkins

The world is charged with the grandeur of God.
    It will flame out, like shining from shook foil;
    It gathers to a greatness, like the ooze of oil
Crushed. Why do men then now not reck his rod?
Generations have trod, have trod, have trod;
    And all is seared with trade; bleared, smeared with toil;
    And wears man's smudge and shares man's smell: the soil
Is bare now, nor can foot feel, being shod.

And for all this, nature is never spent:
    There lives the dearest freshness deep down things;
And though the last lights off the black West went
    Oh, morning, at the brown brink eastward, springs—
Because the Holy Ghost over the bent
    World broods with warm breast and with ah! bright wings.

The general sense of the poem is clear: it celebrates and glorifies the grandeur of God. Yet glorification is achieved not through a straightforward description but through a dramatic series of tensions and discoveries. Hopkins begins powerfully: "The world is charged with the grandeur of God." The reader needs a moment of reflection to feel the pun in the crucial word "charged." Does the line mean that the world is charged with God's grandeur the way a battery is charged with electricity, so that it exists as a potential force ready to burst out whenever the terminals are touched, so to speak? Or does "charged" have the sense of moral responsibility, so that the world has the responsibility to express and care for the grandeur of God?

In the second line Hopkins seems to opt for the first alternative. In the image "It will flame out, like shining from shook foil," he recalls the flashes created by light playing upon the surface of shaken tinsel. One has only to touch the world for God's grandeur to flash and shimmer over its whole surface. The third line, however, suggests that the other reading of "charged" is not to be ignored. There Hopkins is thinking of the slow extraction of olive oil in a press. Here God's grandeur is the accumulation of the precious essence of things extracted through suffering. In typical Hopkinsesque fashion the two images are not presented as alternatives. Hopkins affirms both images: "It will flame out" and "It gathers to a greatness." Thus he insists on both possible meanings of "charged."

Playing with puns and images, though necessary to gather the full sense of the poem, is misleading if it is overemphasized, for this can lead a reader to ignore the dramatic movement of the piece. The fourth line, in fact, clarifies the dramatic situation, and we see that the first three lines represent the speaker's sense of God's grandeur in the world. The poet feels and sees it all around him, so why don't others?

"Why do men then now not reck his rod?" The skill with which Hopkins has linked those nine words by internal rhyme, consonance, and assonance is astonishing, but his achievement is more than technical. The same marvelous functional ambiguity exhibited in "charged" is present here—in the word "then." It can mean "then" in the logical sense of "therefore," so that the question emphasizes the blindness of men in failing to see God's greatness. But because of its odd placement in the sentence, just before "now," it also carries the sense of time past. In this reading, the question emphasizes the continual blindness of men, in the past and in the present. Similarly, "reck his rod" is ambiguous in that "rod" could refer to God's scepter, the symbol of his kingship, but might also refer to a stick used for punishing his recalcitrant children.

At this point, at the end of the first quatrain, the focus of the speaker's attention has shifted from a direct concern with God's grandeur to the strange, frustrating fact of men's disregard of it. When the second quatrain begins, the emphasis is not on the blindness of man, however, but on his miserable worldly condition and what he does to God's world. The repetitive rhythm of "Generations have trod, have trod, have trod" suggests the hopeless, meaningless activity of a squirrel in a revolving cage. But man's endless treading is more awful than the squirrel's, for man not only gets nowhere but manages to befoul the world in the process. We need not examine the disgust, anger, anguish, and horror expressed in "all is seared with trade; bleared, smeared with toil; / And wears man's smudge and shares man's smell." But then a strange thing happens: out of this terrible vision of human life comes an explanation for what has happened and why it continues—"the soil / Is bare now, nor can foot feel, being shod." That is, man has not only destroyed the world that was charged with God's grandeur but insulated himself from feeling any residual effects of its original glory.

The octave ends on this note of despair. Yet already some of the anger toward man expressed at the end of the first quatrain has been dissipated and replaced with compassion. Man's disregard for and destruction of God's world may be terrible, but the hopelessness of his condition begins to invite pity. In a not-too-literal way, the speaker's vision of an awesome, terrible God in the first quatrain is characteristic of the Old Testament, and in the second quatrain the speaker is moving toward a vision of the infinitely loving God of the New Testament.

With the start of the concluding sestet, the speaker's attention shifts again—this time to the world's mysterious beauty and power of regeneration, retained despite man's depredations. In the line "There lives the dearest freshness deep down things," I don't know whether Hopkins means that there is a freshness deep down in all things or whether he means that there is a freshness in deep-down things, but I suspect that he means both. At this moment the speaker has begun to see a new possibility—the possibility of regeneration through the grace of God.

To get the sense of this culminating vision, let us look at Hopkins' image in the final four lines. At the last and darkest moment of the night, when despair is greatest, even the stars, the only lights left, go out in the west. But turning around and facing east, one can see that the disappearance of the stars does not mean the coming of utter darkness. It marks the beginning of morning, when the sun rises above the brown and barren horizon. Morning comes, not because the earth rotates on its axis once every twenty-four hours, but because the Holy Ghost broods over the bent world. The rising of the sun every morning is a miracle, an act of grace.

But it is even more, for if we look again at the last two lines, we see that the Holy Ghost, conventionally symbolized as a bird of flame, is here represented as the rising sun. The final image is of a sunrise. At first, the sun is partly above the horizon—that is the "warm breast" of the Holy Ghost. As the sun comes up, the light spreads outward from it like a pair of "bright wings" to encompass and regenerate the world.

The difference between my prose restatement and Hopkins' original is that Hopkins does not liken the rising of the sun to the coming of the Holy Ghost. He does not present us with an extended simile; rather, the rising sun and its light are the Holy Ghost. Is the theology of this sonnet orthodox? I suspect that it comes perilously close to the heresy of pantheism. But the sonnet is astoundingly good poetry. To render the full development of an authentic religious experience—in this case, a vision of divine grace—in the fourteen lines of a conventionally determined sonnet form is no mean feat.

The last poem that we will look at, Du Fu's "Night in the Watchtower," is presented here in Chinese and in three English translations. As with the Li Bai poem, the Chinese version should be read column by column starting at the right. The romanized pronunciation and a literal translation are under each character. I have amplified the literal translation into my own version of the poem, which precedes the two published translations.

NIGHT IN THE WATCHTOWER
Du Fu

At the year's end the yin and the yang hasten on the short daylight.
At the limit of the sky the frost and snow brighten the cold night.
In the fifth watch the drum and bugle sounds are sad and brave,
On the three gorges the star river shadows shake and waver.
Cries in the countryside; how many homes hear fighting and attacking?
Songs of the native Yi; in many places the fishermen and woodcutters are rising.
Sleeping dragon and leaping horse ended in the yellow earth,
Human affairs, letters, and messages are inundated in silence and loneliness.
TRANSLATED BY HERMAN SINAIKO

A NIGHT AT THE APARTMENT
Tu Fu

Light and dark compete to shorten the day toward the close of the year. Snow has stopped, and we have a clear cold night in this remote corner of the world.

杜 *Dù*

甫 *Fǔ*

人 *rén* human	臥 *wò* sleeping	夷 *yí* people (peaceful)	野 *yě* countryside (wide)	三 *sān* three	五 *wǔ* fifth	天 *tiān* heaven's	歲 *suì* year's	閣 *Gé* Watchtower
事 *shì* affairs	龍 *lóng* dragon	歌 *gē* songs	哭 *kū* cries	峽 *xiá* gorges	更 *gēng* watch	涯 *yá* uttermost limits	暮 *mù* end	夜 *Yè* Night
音 *yīn* letters	躍 *yuè* leaping	數 *shù* several	幾 *jǐ* how many	星 *xīng* star	鼓 *gǔ* drums	霜 *shuāng* frost	陰 *yīn* dark	
書 *shū* messages	馬 *mǎ* horse	處 *chù* places	家 *jiā* homes	河 *hé* river	角 *jué* bugles	雪 *xuě* snow	陽 *yáng* light	
漫 *màn* overflow	終 *zhōng* end	起 *qǐ* rise	聞 *wén* hear	影 *yǐng* shadows	聲 *shēng* sounds	霽 *jì* clear (brighten)	催 *cuī* urge on (hasten)	
寂 *jì* silent	黃 *huáng* yellow	漁 *yú* fisherman	戰 *zhàn* fighting	動 *dòng* shake	悲 *bēi* sad	寒 *hán* cold	短 *duǎn* short	
寥 *liáo* solitary	土 *tǔ* earth	樵 *qiáo* wood-cutter	伐 *pá* attacking	搖 *yáo* waver	狀 *zhuàng* brave	宵 *xiāo* night	景 *jǐng* daylight	

The drums and bugles of the fifth watch before dawn sound especially impassioned, while the stars in the Heavenly River above the Three Gorges are twinkling.

Some people are crying for the war-dead—I wonder in how many homes? I hear too the native songs of the early rising fishermen and woodcutters. Both the loyal Chu-ko Liang and the unsubmissive White Emperor ended in graves under the yellow earth. It does not matter that I am lonely—that even letters have ceased to come.

TRANSLATED BY WILLIAM HUNG

192   *The Human Condition*

   Du Fu

While winter daylight shortens in the elemental scale
And snow and frost whiten the cold-circling night,
Stark sounds the fifth-watch with a challenge of drum and bugle,
. . . The stars and the River of Heaven pulse over the three mountains;
I hear women in the distance, wailing after the battle;
I see barbarian fishermen and woodcutters in the dawn.
. . . Sleeping-Dragon, Plunging-Horse, are no generals now, they are dust.
Hush for a moment, O tumult of the world.

TRANSLATED BY WITTER BYNNER

Du Fu's poem achieves the same fusion of intense personal experience and conventional poetic form as Hopkins' "God's Grandeur," although both the poetic form and the experience are characteristically Chinese. The poem was written, according to William Hung, in the late autumn of A.D. 766, when Du was staying in Kuizhou, a southwestern city on the Yangzi River. This poem is so rich and complex that we must work through it line by line, image by image, to gain some idea of Du's achievement.

The poem begins by locating the speaker in time. *Sui mu*, which I have rendered as "year's end," is more suggestive than the English indicates. *Sui* means "year," but it also means "harvest," and *mu* means "end" in the specific sense of sunset or evening. Thus the time is not merely the end of the year but the year's sunset. The suggestion is inescapable that the speaker is in that watchtower at the sunset of the day, as well as at the end of the harvest and the year.

Yin and *yang* are the two elemental cosmic forces. They are complementary; as one waxes, the other wanes. In their interaction they are the primary forces behind all motion in the universe. In the poem the speaker is saying that yin and yang are urging on the short daylight. *Cui*, "urge on" or "hasten," carries a sense of pushing, hurrying, accelerating.

Duan jing, "short daylight" or "shortening daylight," carries another sense that picks up the ambiguity in the character *mu*, "end" or "sunset," at the beginning of the line. Thus *jing* means "day" or "daylight," but it also means "a view, scenery, a prospect," and from that, it comes to mean what one can see ahead— not in space but in time. Hence we can speak of a man's *jing,* or "prospects."

In the context of the first line all of these meanings work. Literally, the yin and the yang are urging on the shortening days; that is, the days are getting shorter and shorter toward the end of the year. Because *mu* suggests that the time is evening, one gets the sense that the yin and the yang are squeezing out the daylight, and night is coming on rapidly. There is the merest suggestion through the character *jing*, "daylight" or "prospects," that the yin and the yang are cutting short the prospects of the speaker himself, that he is in the sunset of his life.

Through direct image, puns, and overtones, then, the first line anchors the poem in time: it is nearing the end of the year, the end of the day, and the end of the speaker's life. Since the dominant image is of year's end, and the forces spoken of are the great powers of yin and yang, the sense of time is great. Time is conceived primarily in cosmic terms, and the personal dimensions of the day and the speaker's own life are microcosmic reflections of the moment in cosmic time.

The second line, which completes the first couplet, parallels the first perfectly. It completes the setting of the poem, only now the setting is defined spatially rather than temporally. *Tian ya,* literally, "shore" or "limit" of "heaven" or "the sky," is ambiguous. Hung has translated the characters to mean "this remote corner of the world," making them refer to the speaker's geographical location near the limits of the Chinese world. Bynner and Kiang have translated the characters to mean "cold-circling night," making them refer to the visible edge of the heavens: the line of the horizon. I think that Du Fu intends both senses. He is spatially located near the limits of the civilized world (near the border of Sichuan province), and he is also located in a watchtower looking out toward the encircling horizon. Not only does the ambiguity work in the context of the line, but it beautifully matches the ambiguity in the corresponding two characters of the first line. There the characters *sui mu* suggest both the moment of the year, late fall, and the moment of the day, sunset. Here *tian ya* suggest both the speaker's location in the world and the particular space, bounded by the horizon, in which he finds himself. The parallelism of *sui mu* and *tian ya,* which is completely lost in both published translations, indicates the complexity that Du Fu's poetry achieves.

The parallelism continues. The frost and the snow serve as the spatial equivalents of the yin and the yang. But where the yin and the yang constricted time, the frost and the snow brighten and clarify the cold night. Space is not constricted—frost and snow expand space enormously with their brightness. Yet the sense of diminishing time and expanded space do not negate each other; they complement one another emotionally.

At the end of the first couplet, which is called the rising or introductory couplet, the speaker is precisely located in space and time conceived on a cosmic scale. There has been no explicit mention of anything human. We have merely been presented with an objective description of where the speaker is. Yet how easy it is, once we have considered these two lines, to know exactly what the speaker feels. No one can imagine being in that enormous setting without feeling very, very small, lonely, and impotent. The formal parallelism of the urgent motion of time with the still immensity of space heightens and gives precision to that feeling in a way that is completely lost if the meaning of the two lines is abstracted from their formal parallel structure.

The next two lines of the lu shi verse form constitute the second or "receiving" couplet. They are supposed to develop the theme and image expressed in the opening couplet. The formal character of the third and fourth lines thus presents a double problem to the poet, who must construct another parallel couplet at least as powerful as the first, and that couplet as a whole must parallel the first couplet as a whole. Du Fu was equal to the task: the third and fourth lines are generally considered to be among the most beautiful in all of Chinese poetry: "In the fifth watch the drum and bugle sounds are sad and brave, / On the three gorges the star river shadows shake and waver."

The fifth watch is the last of the five night watches; it extends from three to five in the morning. Within the course of the night it is exactly parallel to the end of the year and the limits of the heavens. Drums and bugles are military instruments, reminding us that we are on the edge of the empire. The sounds that are both sad and brave are the signals of the watchmen that a new day is beginning. It is clear in this third line that time is passing, the night is now moving toward its close. More than that, the time of night has now been specified and associated with sound. The military character of the sounds and the combination of adjectives—"sad and brave"—carry a strong suggestion of coming sorrow.

The fourth line parallels the third directly. Where the third locates the speaker in time, the fourth locates him at the three gorges, the great cliffs and rapids, of the upper Yangzi that mark the border between China proper and the province of Sichuan, which was then only partially sinified. The sounds of the drums and bugles are matched by the twinkling of the stars in the star river, the Milky Way. It is unclear in the fourth line whether we are meant to visualize the twinkling star river stretched above the Yangzi River or the Milky Way reflected in the waters of the Yangzi, as ying, "shadows," suggests. Although "shakes and wavers" could refer to the twinkling of the stars or to their wavering reflections in the river, the phrase also carries an ominous tone, paralleling the sad, brave tone of the drums and bugles. It is a commonplace in China that when the stars shake in the heavens, affairs on earth are unstable. Trembling stars are a portent of evil, as are the sounds of the fifth watch.

Considered as a whole, the couplet preserves and continues the time and space parallelism of the first couplet, but it also introduces a number of dimensions. To begin with, as the night has moved on, the scope of the imagery has been considerably reduced, and for the first time, human elements and qualities appear. Time and space are specified in human rather than cosmic terms, and there are now tangible noises and objects to hear and to see. The setting described in the opening couplet was terrifyingly empty. In this second couplet, although the emptiness is gone and human elements are present, the vision of the world is no more pleasant. Everything seen and heard is sufficiently portentous to reinforce rather than diminish the loneliness and impotence evoked in the first couplet. Moreover, Du Fu has rung at least one little variation on the pattern established in the first couplet. There it was the temporal image of the first line that contained movement and the spatial image of the second line that was motionless. Here in the third and fourth lines it is the temporal image of the sounds that seems motionless and the spatial image of the river and sky that contains movement.

The fifth and sixth lines are conventionally designated the turning couplet. Here, at the midpoint in the poem, the poet is expected to shift the focus. Du Fu drops the space and time contrast that dominates the first two couplets and emphasizes the sound and sight contrast, employed only as a subordinate element in the second couplet.

Again, the first two characters of each line are ambiguous. *Ye ku* could simply mean the "cries and wails arising from the countryside," in which case it would refer to the weeping of Chinese peasant women for their sons and husbands who have died or will die in the fighting. In the parallel reading, *Yi ge* would then refer to the songs of the Yi people, the non-Chinese aboriginal inhabitants of the region. But *ye* also means "to be rude, uncultivated, wild." And *Yi* also means "to be peaceful and tranquil." Thus there is a double contrast here, between the character of the noises—wild (*ye*) and peaceful (*yi*)—and between the identity of those making them, the Chinese peasants (*ye*) and the semi-sinified Yi people.

The ironic parallel is continued in the next characters of each line. Although *ji* in line five and *shu* in line six both indicate quantity, *ji* suggests a larger number than *shu* does. It is the Chinese, naturally, who inhabit many *jia,* "homes," and the Yi people who live in several *chu,* "places." Yet what is heard in the civilized Chinese homes is the sound of violent human struggle, while in the "barbarian" Yi dwellings the fishermen and woodcutters stir, preparing to take up their peaceful pursuits.

Although the two lines are parallel, there is a sound and a sight in each line rather than a sight in one and a sound in the other. Nor is this couplet as tightly parallel as the previous two. In Li Bai's poem the parallelism does not emerge until the last two lines, and there it gives definition and closure to the experience described. Here the opposite happens. The poem begins with a sharply defined parallel couplet in order to give form to the experience. But toward the end, that rigid discipline is no longer appropriate, and the parallelism grows a little uncertain. By the end of the third couplet day has come, night is over, and the meaning of the night spent in the watchtower needs to be summed up. This is the function of the fourth and final couplet.

The couplet begins with *wo long* and *yue ma,* "sleeping dragon" and "leaping horse," ending, or dying, in the yellow earth. *Huang tu,* "yellow earth," is the Chinese term for loess, the wind-deposited soil that covers much of north China. It so happens that Wo Long and Yue Ma are the nicknames given to two famous figures in Chinese history who were closely associated with this particular region of the upper Yangzi. Zhuge Liang, one of the heroes of Chinese history, was given the name Sleeping Dragon by his friends, so the story goes, because he was a great man, though unknown to the world at large. During the Three Kingdoms period (A.D. 220–265), Liu Bei, the ruler of one of the kingdoms, visited Zhuge Liang and persuaded the great man to come out of obscurity. Zhuge became a general for Liu Bei and fought several battles near Kuizhou. In Du Fu's time there was a temple in his honor in the city. Yue Ma is the epithet given to Gongsun Shu, prince of the region centuries earlier, during the Han period (206 B.C.–A.D. 220). He reportedly received the name Leaping Horse when he leaped on a horse and declared himself emperor. In contrast to Zhuge Liang, Gongsun Shu was a villain and a traitor.

What is interesting to me is the way these men are referred to. A dragon and a horse are both powerful, vital animals, and whether or not the reader knows that they are the epithets of the two men, one a traitor and one a hero, the point is that dragon and horse and men end in the yellow dust.

The contrast of the men with each other and with the large numbers of unnamed common people referred to in the preceding couplet reinforces the despair and desolation that has been taking shape in the poem. This feeling reaches its climax in the final line, whose meaning is clear even though the syntax of the line is hopelessly obscure to me: "Human affairs, letters, and messages are inundated in silence and loneliness." I take comfort from the similar bafflement of Hung and Bynner and Kiang, apparent in their translations. The first four characters, *ren shi yin shu,* clearly refer to the whole world of human affairs, with its letters and messages (literally, "sounds" and "writings") that connect people to one another. The last three characters, *man ji liao,* imply that that world is inundated in silence and solitude. That Du Fu should choose to end his poem with a line whose meaning is clear but whose grammar is practically nonexistent seems to me no accident. It is as if the enormously disciplined structure of the first six lines had served its purpose and was of no further use —so he dispensed with it.

What matters is that Du Fu's sense of the night spent in the tower is evident to the reader at the end. It may even be that he wants the reader to see the artificiality of the early structure, the discipline employed in creating those first couplets, as artificial, as intrinsically false to the inchoate despair of the final line. The integrity of the poem may itself require that formal structure be dispensed with.

The first of the two clichés or principles with which I started, the common humanity implicit in Aristotle's remark about what poets imitate, seems to me to be substantiated by my reading of these four poems. If anything, the experiences expressed in Blake's and Hopkins' poems are stranger and more foreign to me than those rendered in the poems by Li Bai and Du Fu. Once past the cultural barriers of language, historical allusion, and conventional imagery, the poems of the two Chinese speak to me, at least, with a directness that is refreshing and unusual in much of English poetry.

At the same time, the more I read and ponder these Chinese and English poems, the more characteristically Chinese and English they seem. This sounds paradoxical. But it strikes me that lyric poets usually express themselves through the medium of conventionally determined poetic forms. The object of poetry, after all, is not to force one's true feelings into an artificial form but to fuse the conventional form and the authentic feelings into an expressive whole. This means that to be successful, poets must come to terms with their culture as it is expressed in its conventional forms. They need to be extraordinarily sensitive to the possibilities of their language—its rhythms, ambiguities, strengths and weaknesses—as a vehicle for expression. Poets need to be familiar with the conventional images and associations of their culture in order to adapt them to their personal feelings and ideas. They need to be aware of the characteristic feelings and ideas of their culture in order to make contact with readers. If all these things are so, poetry—particularly the best poetry—may well serve as the basis for a significant comparison of cultures.

13 Tragedy and Psychoanalysis
Tragedy in Poetry and in Life

Tragedy and psychoanalysis: at first glance they form a strange pair. An ancient art form and a recently developed branch of modern medicine—what do they have in common? Can something serious be learned from the encounter between two such dissimilar entities? Psychoanalysis is a recognized medical specialty and, at least in principle, a comprehensive theory of human psychology. Tragedy, by contrast, is the generic name given to a large number of works of art with certain basic features in common. To confront psychoanalysis with tragedy, we need a systematic, if rudimentary, account of those features.

Unfortunately, there is no general agreement on what features are common to all tragedies, although there is a rough consensus about which works of art are tragedies. In fact, one of the central issues of the entire tradition of Western aesthetics, from Plato to the present day, is precisely what constitutes the tragic. To make my account less controversial, I shall follow the lines laid down by Aristotle in the *Poetics,* which has set the tone and established the terms for much of the Western discussion about art and tragedy since antiquity. Although arguing with philosophers is always legitimate, Aristotle is about as authoritative in these matters as it is possible to be.

Aristotle understands tragedy as one of several species of fine art, along with other such forms as comedy, lyric poetry, music, painting, and dance. Art, for Aristotle, has the primary sense of "craft" or "skill." It refers to the human capacity to make or fabricate things. As such, art is one of three fundamental human capacities, along with knowing and doing. The three are intimately related to one another, and all are involved in every human act. Nevertheless, they are distinguishable by simple but fundamental differences in their ends or purposes. The aim of knowing is to grasp a truth, to see with the mind the nature of the thing being sought. The aim of doing is to realize an intention, to achieve a purpose. The aim of art is, by contrast, neither knowledge nor the realization of a purpose but production.

Using this tripartite distinction, Aristotle differentiates the fundamental forms of human activity. Thus science is the methodical, disciplined process by which we come to know the nature of things, and its realm is the realm of the theoretical. The domain in which achieving a purpose is paramount is the realm of the practical, the realm of action, the realm of the ethical and the political. Art, in the most general sense of craft or skill, always culminates in the creation of a product, which frequently but not always persists after the making is completed. Art, then, is the realm of productive activity, of made things.

There are many kinds of made things in the world: shoes and ships and sealing wax, laws and poems. Each kind of made thing is the product of a distinct art or craft. All the arts have four characteristics in common. Taken as a whole, these characteristics clarify the complex set of relations that define a work of art, according to Aristotle.

First, each art or craft is distinguished by its product, the thing or kind of thing produced. Thus medicine produces health when the physician exercises skill in healing. Shipbuilding produces ships, legislation laws, shoemaking shoes. Ultimately, everything else concerned with the art is understood in terms of its product.

Second, the products of every art are produced by an artist, a maker—that is, by somebody who controls a specific skill that allows him or her to fabricate the product. Not everyone can remove a ruptured appendix, only a person with the learned skill of a surgeon. The same holds for making shoes or writing tragedies.

Third, every art has a function or purpose to fulfill, and the quality of its products are judged primarily by how well they serve that function. The art of shipbuilding exists because nature has not provided human beings with other means to cross large bodies of water; medicine has been developed to overcome the tendency of human bodies to get injured or to malfunction.

Finally and most important, the products of each art bear a special relation to nature, a relation that Aristotle calls *mimesis*. A fairly accurate translation is "imitation," although Aristotle's understanding of the term extends far beyond the commonplace notion that an imitation is a mere copy of something else. For Aristotle, all artificial things are imitations of nature. A craftworker who fabricates a product makes something that serves a purpose. A tailor sews together a number of pieces of fur to make a coat. The coat keeps someone warm in cold weather. That seems obvious enough. But the need for the coat and thus the need for the skills of the tailor who can fabricate the coat depend on the failure of nature to provide humans with an inherent means of keeping warm in cold weather. In effect, we humans have had to imitate the fur-bearing animals and provide ourselves artificially with what nature provides bears and wolves naturally.

Here is another example. Presumably humans took shelter in natural caves when they could find them. But caves are often dark, damp, and inconveniently located. So, at some point, humans began to fabricate shelters that served the purpose of a cave, although they gradually improved on what nature had inadvertently provided. We know that caves were not made by nature for human use but were adapted to human purposes. The art or craft of architecture is the logical extension and development of that original adaptation. It is a long way from a stone cavity that provides shelter in a storm to Water Tower Place in Chicago. The distance marks how far the art of architecture has developed.

Fabrication, then, consists of shaping material to fulfill a desired function. The form given to the material is taken from nature, and it is in this precise sense that all artificial things imitate nature. All things, according to Aristotle, are composed of form and matter, and in natural things the form and the matter are fitted to each other in such a way that they can be distinguished only in principle. But in artificial things, the form and the matter do not naturally go together, so the form, which is abstracted from nature by the craftworker, is imposed on the matter. That is to say, the matter is shaped by the craftworker to have the form the craftworker wishes it to have.

As we look around at the world of fabricated things, we see that most such things serve specific, practical purposes of one sort or another. Shoes protect our feet or keep them dry or make them attractive; fur coats keep us warm in the winter or display their owners' wealth; buildings provide spaces in which to live and work. Shoes and coats and buildings serve their specific functions well or badly depending on how well the product was conceived and how well it was made. If the product fails to fulfill its function or fulfills it badly, we consider it a failure and may attempt to improve or replace it. In these useful or practical arts, the function of the product is usually obvious.

But what is the function of a work of art? What is the purpose of fine art— of tragedies, paintings, symphonies? To answer this question we need to consider imitation as a fundamental human activity in its own right.

Imitation, as Aristotle conceives it, is the process by which we grasp the form or shape of something and then reembody that shape in something else. The nursery school child who bends over, extends her arm in front of her nose, and waves it back and forth has grasped something about the way an elephant looks, and has managed to find in the movement of her own body a way to render that look. She has made an imitation. At the far end of the scale from such a small, simple, improvised imitation is a work like Homer's *Iliad,* a monumental product of unparalleled human skill. Insofar as it portrays the anger of Achilles from its accidental and trivial beginning through its heroic climax to its final, tragic purging, the *Iliad,* too, is an imitation.

Aristotle argues that two crucial facts about imitation are necessary to understand fine art. First, all humans imitate by nature; in fact, our superiority over the other animals is based on this ability, because all human learning begins with imitation. The second fact is related to the first but is a little different in its emphasis. Not only do we imitate by nature, but we also naturally take pleasure in looking at or listening to imitations. This second fact is the key to understanding the nature and function of art. Aristotle accounts for the pleasure we take in imitations by arguing that it is a special form of the pleasure all humans take in learning something. He points out that when we look at an imitation and recognize it for what it is—that is, recognize what is being imitated—we are learning something, we are grasping the nature of the object that we are experiencing. The fact that we like to look at pictures and hear stories is what allows teachers to employ imitations, such as pictures, stories, and role-playing, in teaching children. Similarly, Jesus told parables to instruct his followers. And generals play computer-simulated war games to learn nuclear strategy.

But the pleasure humans take in looking at imitations can be used for purposes other than learning or instruction. Our pleasure can also be used rhetorically to persuade us of practically anything. Think of what Joe Camel did for Camel cigarettes. Imitations can also be used to sell political candidates for election or to attack their opponents. Think, for example, of the picture of Willie Horton used in the 1988 presidential election to suggest that the Democratic candidate Michael Dukakis was "soft on crime."

Aristotle was explicitly aware of the wide range of instructional and rhetorical uses to which imitations could be put. He had no quarrel with such uses but thought they were not art in the full and proper sense of the term. When used for instruction or persuasion, imitation is essentially a tool used to bring about some extrinsic end or fulfill some purpose. Its value, like that of any other tool, is determined by how well it does so. But just because imitations can be used to serve nonartistic purposes, that does not mean they have no other use.

What if an imitation is constructed to serve no other purpose than to provide that special pleasure we get from imitations? That is, what if it is constructed, not to teach or to persuade, but to be as good an imitation as possible? In a nutshell, that is Aristotle's conception of fine art.

Lest there be any confusion about this conception of fine art as imitation, let me clear up a common misunderstanding of Aristotle's view. Imitation is frequently understood as the complete and purely mechanical reproduction of something. Thus a camera can, from this point of view, imitate a face more accurately than any portrait painter can possibly hope to do. A tape recorder can produce an imitation of human conversation far more accurate and precise than any playwright or novelist. So it is often said that, unlike the artists of earlier times, modern artists no longer need to attempt to reproduce the appearance of things. The assumption here is that before the invention of cameras, painters were attempting to produce exact visual representations of things and that before the invention of tape recorders, playwrights were attempting to copy human dialogue. The assumption is dubious in the extreme. In any event, I want to argue that an imitation in Aristotle's sense is not a copy of something the way a photograph or an audiotape is.

A camera records on light-sensitive film whatever happens to be in front of the lens when the aperture is opened, and a tape recorder indiscriminately records whatever noise is within range of the microphone. But imitation for Aristotle is the process by which humans grasp the perceptible form of something and embody that form in another matter. Thus a skilled portrait painter is not simply recording whatever is in front of his eye but is attempting to grasp the visible form of the person before him, and he sees that person's face as expressing the character of the person to whom it belongs. That is, the portrait painter is attempting to grasp and to render the full human character of his subject, and no mere camera can ever see that; only another human being can.

Aristotle knew nothing about cameras but I think he would have been delighted with them. Apart from their impressive use as scientific instruments, he would have seen photography as potentially a kind of painting. That is, rather than seeing the painter as at best a second-rate photographer, Aristotle would have seen the photographer as able to aspire to the condition of a painter.

Camera and tape recorder can capture only a very small portion of the world that is available to artists when they set out to imitate. No camera will ever take a picture of a unicorn or of God, although painters have been depicting both for thousands of years. The point is that the world imitated as a matter of course by artists is bigger, richer, more complex, and infinitely more interesting than the world the camera can see. Artists imitate not only what is but what can be, what might be, what we would like to be, what we might fear to be, and so forth. Anyone who has listened to Beethoven's *Ninth Symphony* knows that if joy had a sound, it would sound like that symphony.

Artists are not limited to palpable, physical objects. Are not emotions just as real, even realer perhaps, than rocks? Are not human actions, no matter how evanescent and hard to perceive, just as actual as trees? Must we assume that Michelangelo, when he painted the Sistine Chapel, thought that God was an old man with a long white beard? Must we be fundamentalists to enjoy the painting? Regardless of Michelangelo's theology—and ours, too, for that matter—

he has rendered God so powerfully that we recognize the figure immediately and are deeply moved by it—even if we don't believe in the existence of God.

Far from being a mechanical process of copying, then, imitation is a profoundly human activity that calls into play the whole range of human capacities: thought, imagination, reason, perception, memory, passion, and sensation. Artists use all these in making their imitations, and we must use all of them in perceiving what they have made.

But that means that the things artists imitate always have a full and concrete human meaning. Scientists must abstract rigorously from the affective and personal in order to grasp the truth of things as they really are. But artists are not scientists. They do not seek knowledge of things as they are; they seek to represent things as human beings experience them, and in their renderings they cannot abstract all humanity from their own person.

This is not to say that successful imitation is or can be private and idiosyncratic; it cannot. An effective imitation must be objective and in principle accessible to anyone. But the objectivity of the artist includes the artist's humanity; it does not abstract from it. The artist's subjects are always humanly meaningful, and therefore when we recognize them, we recognize them as meaningful. The pleasure of imitation—what Aristotle calls "the proper pleasure of poetry"—is a pleasure we enjoy by exercising the whole range of our human powers to perceive the human meaning of a well-constructed imitation. The job of a poet is to imitate well, not to teach anything, not to persuade an audience to do or to believe, not even to be concerned with what will please or displease an audience. If the poet imitates well, the poet will make a work that is intrinsically pleasurable to us in the way that only a work of art can be.

Much more could be said about Aristotle's general understanding of art, but this will suffice for my purpose. Let me turn now to his account of particular works of art: tragedies. Tragedy has exercised an extraordinary fascination for artists, philosophers, and lovers of art for at least three thousand years. Homer's *Iliad,* probably the oldest literary work in the Western tradition, is also the first tragedy. Aristotle's *Poetics,* the oldest systematic analysis of art in the Western tradition, is mainly devoted to a discussion of tragedy. Almost every major artist in the tradition has at one time or another tried writing tragedy. Yet, strangely enough, surprisingly few artists have managed to produce a successful tragedy. In antiquity there are the three great Greek tragedians besides Homer: Aeschylus, Sophocles, and Euripides. In the Renaissance there are Shakespeare, Corneille, and Racine. Among moderns only Tolstoy and Dostoyevsky undoubtedly deserve to be listed. Each of us could add a favorite or two, but the consensus list is quite short. That so few artists, and only the very greatest, have written successful tragedies suggests that something about the form is difficult to bring off. By contrast, comedy seems much easier to realize.

Let me begin my account of Aristotle's understanding of tragedy by presenting one of his arguments. Early in the *Poetics,* when he is attempting to prove that we all take pleasure in works of imitation, he says: Experience shows that although there are many things in the world that we do not want to look at— dead bodies and vermin, for example—we enjoy looking at even the most realistic representations of them in art. Aristotle's point here is that the pleasure of art stems not from the subject matter but from the fact that something has been rendered. To enjoy a painting of a panoramic landscape would hardly demonstrate that we enjoy art. We might take just as much pleasure in standing where the painter stood and looking at the real landscape. Therefore, Aristotle argues, only if we enjoy looking at a work of art where we would *not* enjoy looking at the original subject can he establish that the pleasure is in the work of art and not merely in the thing represented.

Aristotle's example of the dead body is well chosen. I imagine that most of us would not only not enjoy seeing someone crucified but would be genuinely horrified. Yet most of us have gazed with rapt attention and deep pleasure at paintings and sculptures of the Crucifixion and the Pietà. Although Aristotle is talking here about art in general, his example points directly to an extraordinary feature of tragedies.

Tragedies—think of *Oedipus Rex, Hamlet, Othello,* or *King Lear*—depict the most serious and painful of human events. In fact, they focus sharply on the most pitiful and fearful aspects of those stories. Imagine the events of *Othello,* not as they occur in the play but as if they were happening to a very good friend of yours who happened to live next door. Happily married and deeply in love with his wife, he suddenly begins to entertain terrible suspicions about her fidelity and then, after going through all the agonies of jealousy, rage, betrayal, and breakdown with him, you look out your window one evening and witness him strangling his innocent wife. The example is ludicrous, but it makes my point. Every one of us has suffered a great loss or a deep, irrevocable failure— or we are close to someone who has. It is the stories of losses and failures that we watch in tragedy and find a source of extraordinary pleasure. Tragedy, I want to argue, is the quintessential art form because the things that it imitates are extremely painful to see. It is the only kind of art in which the pleasure we derive must be due entirely to its artful, poetic qualities. It is through an exploration of the relation between the painful events of tragedy and the artful way these events are rendered that I hope to generate some questions for psychoanalysis.

Tragedies deal with extreme and painful events. Murder, incest, and parricide are their stock-in-trade. These events in and of themselves produce powerful, overwhelming emotions of horror, revulsion, distaste. They are, in the root meaning of the term, obscene: they do not deserve to be seen. Yet tragedy brings them onto center stage and makes them the focus of attention. This poses a difficult problem for the tragedian; the emotional materials out of which the work is shaped always threaten to overwhelm it.

Tragedy may well entail moments of horror, but horror in and of itself is not tragic. Tragedy may push right up to the very edge of bad taste, but it crosses that line at the price of becoming offensive and, further, ceasing to be tragic. The events depicted in the film *The Texas Chainsaw Massacre* are shocking and horrible, but not tragic. On the other hand, if the effect of the events is attenuated so that they cease to be felt as terrible, they become melodramatic at best and ludicrous at worst. Television soap operas are no more tragic than *The Perils of Pauline*. The tragedian needs to find a way to express, even to heighten, the painful aspects of the story while, at the same time, containing them so they do not overwhelm and destroy the telling of the story. In short, the tragedian needs to find a way to transmute the obscene into art.

The primary device by which tragedians effect this change is with what Aristotle calls a plot. In its simplest sense, the plot of a tragedy is the story, the sequence of events that make up what happens. At a slightly deeper level, the story or plot can be seen as the "principle of relevance" that the artist uses in constructing the work. If an incident is not part of the story being told by the storyteller, then no matter how interesting or powerful it is, it must be left out. If the incident is a part of the story, then no matter what difficulty it poses, it must be included.

Every work of art requires such an organizing principle in terms of which the artist decides what to include and what to exclude, what to emphasize and what to downplay, what to put first and what last. Without such a principle, an artwork would disintegrate into incoherence and dissipate its poetic effect. Thus, the artistic power, the poetic effect, of a work of art depends on the degree to which the audience understands and experiences that organizing principle both intellectually and emotionally.

The rigor with which the organizing principle orders and dominates a work of art depends in large part on what kind of work it is. In a comedy, for example, there is no reason the poet should not throw in a funny incident or two, a couple of jokes, some pratfalls. Too many irrelevant or unnecessary jokes will turn a comedy into a string of one-liners. The best comedies are those in which all the jokes and pratfalls are effectively integrated into the work as a whole. Compare the great movies of Charlie Chaplin to the funny but disjointed early movies of Woody Allen to see the difference.

In tragedy, where the events represented are meant to evoke, not laughter, but tears, the discipline governing the poet is much more rigorous. A comic artist can throw in a joke or two without damaging the work as a whole. But tragedians who throws in gratuitous murders do not heighten the tragic effect; they blunt and dissipate it. The reason is not hard to see. We will tolerate the inclusion of painful and terrible events in a work of art if and only if we feel that their presence is unavoidable. Ophelia's death in *Hamlet* is exceptionally painful not only for the other characters in the play but for us, the audience, as well. The characters accept her death because it is, for them, an event in the real world in which they live. For us, Ophelia's death is not a part of the real world; it is a fictional event. We accept it only because we can see how a woman like Ophelia could despair to the point of suicide. We know that she is torn by the intolerable conflict she feels at the fact that the man she loves, but whom she has betrayed, has killed her father, whom she also loves, but who had used and misused her. Given the situation and the previous sequence of events, we perceive the death of Ophelia as intellectually and emotionally unavoidable.

The organizing principle, the plot, of a tragedy, therefore, is more than just a story, a sequence of events. It is a story whose incidents are linked by bonds of necessity; each event emerges naturally from the preceding one. At the same time, each event, no matter how inevitable, is unexpected, its necessity evident only after it has occurred. I am not talking here of the capacity of the story-teller to hold us in suspense, to maintain our interest by teasing us with delays and uncertainties about the outcome of events. Detective stories and adventure stories employ these devices, which are probably as old as the art of story-telling. But tragedy relies on these devices very little, if at all. Unlike the suspense story, which loses much of its punch once we know how it comes out, tragedies retain their power to grip us even though we know the story well and have read, or seen the work performed, many times before. The suspense of a tragedy is not merely a consequence of the narrative devices employed by the artist; it is a function of the story itself.

Tragic plots are intrinsically astounding and surprising. The process by which Oedipus discovers who he is and what he has done is as amazing to watch the tenth time as the first. But if the events that constitute a tragic plot are linked by a chain of necessity, the logic that governs the developing story from beginning to end is deeper than the causal chain whereby each event is the immediate cause of the following event, which in its turn becomes the cause of the next event, and so on. That kind of mechanical linkage does occur, but only on the surface. In tragedy, as in real life, genuinely significant events emerge primarily from the personalities of the people who enact them. It is not simply the state of affairs in Denmark that triggers the events of *Hamlet* but the way the characters in the play respond to those events and to each other. To grasp what is happening, we have to understand each of the characters whose interactions constitute the story. The poet has done his job well, so the story unfolds naturally out of the given situation and the interaction of the characters.

But the personalities of the characters are not stated in so many terms; we have to infer the kind of people Hamlet, Ophelia, Gertrude, and Claudius are by paying close attention to what they think and feel, how they respond to what happens, and so forth. If the action of the play emerges naturally from the interaction of the characters, then, at a lower level, the personality of each character emerges naturally from everything he or she thinks and feels. What they think and feel emerges in turn from everything they say, from the sentences they utter, from the very words they use.

When we reach the level of language, we have reached the base level of tragedy, because, after all, a work is made up of words chosen and arranged by the poet. To reverse the order of my argument, I could say that a tragedy is entirely composed of words arranged to make intelligible sentences and utterances. In turn, the sentences and utterances are arranged to express particular thoughts and feelings. These thoughts and feelings articulate individual personalities. These individuals jointly act and interact to create the events that constitute the plot of the tragedy.

From this point of view, the plot of the work is the organizing principle of everything in the work down to and including the words of the text. The plot is, in Aristotle's words, "the soul of the tragedy," the animating principle that informs and energizes everything in the work. Nothing in a well-constructed tragedy is accidental, irrelevant, or trivial. Everything down to the individual words is necessary and functional. If we do not grasp that necessity and perceive how the parts function within the economy of the whole, we may have failed to appreciate the full success of the artist's work. Aristotle describes the high level of skill required of a successful tragedian; he also assumes an equally demanding acuteness of perception from the audience of a tragedy.

What is it, then, that the audience sees when they watch a tragedy? Can we describe it more concretely? As I have argued, when we watch a tragedy, we are primarily watching the enactment of a story. It is frequently a story with whose outlines we are already familiar. The story is basically sad in that the main character, the protagonist, is someone we admire and respect who nevertheless suffers greatly and may die in the end. The more we respect and admire the hero, the more we regret his or her lamentable passing. To augment our regret—to heighten our emotion and urge on our emotional and intellectual participation in the story—tragedians have a tendency to make their heroes as attractive and as high in social standing as possible. The protagonists may or may not be kings or queens or generals, but they must be persons of substance and stature, capable of inspiring our deep respect. In the ordinary course of affairs we would confidently expect these heroes to succeed in all their undertakings because they have all the personal qualities required for success. Usually they have been successful, prior to the events of the tragedy.

But tragedies emphatically do not encompass the ordinary course of affairs. The hero is usually a failure. Here is a problem, because we do not typically respect failure. We sympathize with it, we pity it, we may regret it. If the failure is not the hero's fault, if the hero is an unfortunate victim of circumstances beyond personal control, we naturally feel pity, even though tragedy is, finally, not pathetic. On the other hand, if the catastrophe is the hero's fault, we can hardly admire or respect the hero for making a terrible mistake or having a deep character flaw.

So we arrive at a paradox. To avoid mere pathos the tragedian must make the hero fully responsible for what happens; but how can the hero remain a hero if he or she is the cause of a disaster? In effect, the hero must be seen as someone who in extremely difficult circumstances acts reasonably, even virtuously, but whose action nevertheless triggers a sequence of events that ends in disaster. The hero commonly understands and takes full responsibility for what happens, bearing the brunt of the misfortune and suffering most deeply. But we do not blame the hero for what happened; in fact, we may well admire the hero more at the end of the story than at the beginning.

Tragic endings, I am arguing, are not avoidable events. They are not caused by the hero's stupidity or some other failure of character, and, most important of all in our present context, they do not flow from the hero's emotional disturbance, because tragic heroes do not have "personality disorders." I think tragic stories are possible only if we assume that there are situations, admittedly exceedingly rare, in which a good person acting honorably may bring painful misfortune on his or her own head. Although the hero, along with the audience, in retrospect may come to understand how and why the misfortune happened, we also understand that, given the hero's personality, the hero's choice of action was inevitable. The audience, without attempting to ameliorate or avoid the extremely painful events of the tragedy, are emotionally satisfied and at peace with what they have witnessed. This emotional satisfaction is fairly close to the catharsis that Aristotle says is the final effect of tragedy: a discharge of the pity and fear aroused by the events of the story.

This account of art and tragedy poses certain problems for psychoanalysis. To begin with, there is a greater gulf between tragedy and psychoanalysis than might appear to be the case. Psychoanalysis, as I have said, is in principle a general theory of human psychology and a distinctive form of psychotherapy. Tragedy, by contrast, is an art form, and a special, even unique art form at that. There are in fact no tragedies in real life; tragedies occur only in art. People like Achilles or Oedipus or Hamlet may exist in the real world; the extraordinary situations in which they find themselves could come to pass. But these people and situations are exceedingly unlikely to exist, and it is even more unlikely that in the actual unfolding of an unfortunate event there would be no accidental intrusion that would upset the delicate balance of forces that permits the tragedy to occur. In principle, tragedy is not impossible in life, just very unlikely.

Let me take one more step. Tragedies are like Picasso's *Guernica*. The painting is surely a brilliant imitation or likeness of a bombed town. But neither you nor I will ever see a real-life scene like that one. Tragedy, like Picasso's painting, is made to be seen, to be felt, to be appreciated by an audience. Even if, against all odds, a potentially tragic event should actually occur, there would be no witness, no audience for that event as there is for *Hamlet* or *King Lear*. The tragic hero has a complex role to play, being at one and the same time the primary cause or agent of the tragedy and its chief and ultimate victim. In the best tragedies the hero also comes to see and understand everything that has happened. But the one thing the tragic hero cannot do is be the spectator or audience to his or her own tragedy. The hero is simply too involved to be able to watch events with detachment. The same holds for any other person involved in the story, including even the psychoanalyst, who, though an observer, is a participant observer. There is no way except in an artwork to see and fully experience a tragedy.

Once we see that the experience of tragedy is an artistic—that is, fabricated—experience, not a real one, we can also see that the sequence of events that make up a tragedy could not actually occur, at least not the way they occur in tragedy. In a tragedy the audience come to understand that the events were fully caused and therefore happened by necessity. The necessity that links the elements of a tragedy into an organic whole is a crucial part of the experience of tragedy. Nothing that happens in the mundane world we live in is governed by that kind of necessity. Our world is a world of chance and contingency; everything that happens could have happened differently or need not have happened at all. Indeed, in making sense of our experience we have to accept what has already happened as absolutely given and unchangeable, but to accept that it *had* to happen would be to attempt to impose the terms and categories of art on the real world. To do that would be to try to turn ourselves into fictional characters created by ourselves. To be both the artist who creates and the hero who enacts the story is beyond our powers, except in the wonderful and unreal world of our dreams.

I need hardly dwell on the dangers and distortions attendant upon the attempt to impose the structural features of the dream world on the waking world of everyday reality. For a full and extraordinary analysis of the relation between dream, waking reality, and art, I cannot surpass the account given in Nietzsche's essay *The Birth of Tragedy,* the only work I know of that seriously challenges Aristotle's analysis of art and tragedy.

The necessity that governs the world of tragic action is reflected in the personality of the characters. Tragic heroes tend to be powerful, effective, admirable figures who most emphatically are not neurotic. The difficulties they find themselves in are real difficulties, not their projections on the world. Hamlet is not paranoid; Claudius really is trying to kill him. Nor is Hamlet enacting some sort of Oedipal drama with his mother; there is at least a possibility that she was adulterous and involved in the murder of Hamlet's father—she did marry her deceased husband's brother one month after she was widowed. The man she married seems to have usurped Hamlet's rightful claim to the throne and to be plotting against him by bribing his friends to be informers and using his beloved to entrap him. Add to that Hamlet's conversation with a ghost, whose existence is confirmed by several trustworthy observers but whose identity as either the benevolent spirit of his father or a malevolent devil remains unclear.

When Hamlet says, "The time is out of joint," he is neither exaggerating nor projecting. He is in considerable distress, but that is a perfectly realistic response to the situation in which he finds himself. In short, Hamlet does not seem to be in need of analysis. Discussion of the psychosexual origins of his problems seems to be largely beside the point. His problems are resolved at the climax of the play, but only at the terrible price of his own death, a price he is willing to pay.

Doesn't something in this tragic resolution evoke a profound ambivalence in the psychoanalytic tradition? On the one hand, in theory but even more in practice, psychoanalysis is committed to the resolution, or at least the understanding, of seemingly insoluble problems and the consequent relief of human suffering. Tragedy, in effect, narrows the hero's options for choice until, finally, none is left. Doesn't psychoanalysis as a therapy insist that there are always options, always better and worse choices to be made? Isn't there in the therapeutic process itself a built-in optimism of sorts that runs counter to the deep pessimism of tragedy? On the other hand, hasn't the psychoanalytic movement from its inception had a certain deep strain of pessimism, a sense of the sharp and permanent limitations of both its theory and its practice?

The very shape of a tragic action suggests that in certain extreme situations even the best humans acting morally may cause their own downfall, suffering, and death—but they can retain and even enhance their dignity and nobility until the very end. Tragedy suggests that the very best that humans can achieve as humans may occur only at the extreme of loss and defeat.

Whether or not this tragic view of the human condition is true, it seems to have a powerful attraction and repulsion for all of us. The ambivalence of psychoanalysis on this issue is uncomfortable; we would like to know the truth one way or the other. What tragedy takes for granted and presents with unequaled artistic power, psychoanalysis must take as a problem whose true answer must remain unknown.

14 Hume's "Of the Standard of Taste"
How Is the Canon Determined?

In an elegant little essay entitled "Of the Standard of Taste," David Hume has once and for all accurately stated and resolved the problem of aesthetic taste. His solution entails a solution of sorts to a related problem: What is a classic? It is a solution of sorts because he never explicitly defines the term *classic;* instead, he identifies and articulates the standard by which we can and do discern classics.

Although Hume's success in identifying the standard of taste resolves the problem of what a classic generically is, he does not list the canon of classic works. Rather, Hume shows us how to go about determining that canon, and, if we read the essay carefully and imaginatively, he shows us why the correct operation of taste and the accurate selection of the canon are of vital interest to us as educated and civilized human beings. The real thrust of Hume's essay, therefore, is not so much to show that there is a standard of taste as to demonstrate that the standard and its effective operation in the world are of immense importance.

Hume's essay is over two hundred years old; it is a marvelous piece of eighteenth-century prose littered with charming examples and displaying a quaint sensationalist psychology. It is also full of typical eighteenth-century prejudices. In other words, it is very much of its time and place, although, as I shall argue, it is also directly relevant to our time and place, and it will continue to be relevant to any historical culture that has the delicacy and the good sense to pay attention to it.

However, the thrust of much contemporary critical opinion is srongly opposed to Hume's views of artistic quality and aesthetic taste. Typical is Barbara

Hernstein Smith's book *Contingencies of Value,* which contains a ringing attack on what she takes to be the outdated, simpleminded absolutism of Hume's position, an attack launched in the name of a thoroughgoing contemporary and sophisticated relativism. I have two primary objections to Smith's essay. The Hume she attacks is not the Hume I intend to defend. Not Hume but Smith's reading of Hume is outdated, simplistic, and absolutist. Smith's view of Hume is a common one today, and all the more unfortunate for that. My other objection is that Smith's thoroughgoing relativism is not particularly modern. She presents her view as if it were a distinctive perspective of contemporary thinkers who have the advantage over earlier thinkers, like Hume, of being acquainted with such characteristic modern disciplines as analytic philosophy, cultural anthropology, and critical sociology. In fact, Smith's position is sophisticated in the precise etymological sense of the term in that it is essentially a contemporary restatement of the views on art and literature espoused by the sophists of ancient Greece. The original and, to my mind, most powerful statement of this position can be found in the remarks by the great sophist Protagoras in Plato's dialogue of the same name. (I refer to Protagoras' commentary on a poem by Simonides and his remarks on the role of the arts in the educational system and the cultural life of a community.)

The Hume essay is divided into six parts. The first contains the statement of the problem. In the second part, through a brief but effective philosophical analysis and an appeal to commonsense experience, Hume establishes compelling empirical evidence in support of the existence of a standard of taste. In the third part he takes up the defects and hindrances that prevent the standard of taste from operating effectively and in the process spells out the five fundamental features or skills that together constitute the true critic. The fourth part deals precisely with the empirical question of where and how one can locate such critics. In the fifth part Hume addresses two sources of variation in critical taste that do not undercut the existence of a natural standard. He concludes, in the last part, with a series of reflections on how questions of manners, morals, and opinions, both speculative and religious, should or should not affect the proper operation of taste.

Hume begins with the observation that we are all aware of the "great variety" of tastes in the world, no matter how narrow our experience or how uniform our education. Our initial response to this variety is to dismiss as barbarous whatever diverges widely from what we are used to. But we soon discover to our surprise that everyone feels as we do, that we are dismissed by others as contemptuously as we dismiss them. The discovery of variety leads then to an uncertainty about the adequacy of our own taste. Further reflection shows that there is even more variety in these matters than we might have initially believed. We all agree on a common vocabulary of general terms to use in expressing feelings. But we fail to agree when it comes to attaching these general terms to particulars. In "matters of opinion and science" the reverse is true: we may disagree about the general terms, but we can agree about particulars.

At this point Hume drops the discussion of taste and takes up morality. He argues that, at least for those who base morality on feeling rather than reason, the same general description holds: We agree on the general terms of moral praise and blame. We are all in favor of virtue and against vice, although we do not agree on whether particular acts are virtuous or vicious. To use a contemporary example: to co-conspirators the bomber of the U.S. Marine barracks in Beirut was a supremely courageous hero; to most Americans he was a despicable terrorist. According to Hume, it is true that courage is good and terrorism bad, but, says Hume, there is little point in making such an obvious assertion.

Hume suddenly and surprisingly concludes this introductory part by saying that "it is natural for us to seek a *Standard of Taste;* a rule by which the various sentiments of men may be reconciled; at least a decision afforded, confirming one sentiment, and condemning another." Why is it "natural" to seek a standard of taste? Why should we not simply live with the diversity of tastes? Notice that Hume does not say there is a standard; he merely insists that it is natural for us to seek one. Somehow, he thinks, we are committed to the search, whatever the outcome.

As I understand this first part, Hume takes it for granted that in matters of morality we cannot live comfortably with ethical relativity. For you to call heroism what I call terrorism is intolerable to me. Because we are dealing with sentiments, with feelings, moral judgment is an immediate, direct response to the situation. When you and I radically disagree in our moral judgments and thus I become uncertain about the rightness of my own judgment, I am put in an impossible emotional situation. At the very moment that I assert my moral judgment, my awareness that you disagree with me makes me doubt my judgment. I may be right or I may be wrong, but I cannot be both at the same time. I must at least attempt to escape this situation by finding a moral standard.

What is true of morality is equally true of taste. Moral matters do involve serious issues of action and responsibility; matters of taste do not, at least on the surface. But Hume's argument does not turn on practical consequences; the complex and contradictory feelings engendered in each of us by our awareness of the variety of tastes is what naturally impels us to seek a standard. To live with the variety of tastes without attempting either to reconcile or to decide among them is to deny the seriousness of our own feelings. To be alienated from our own gut responses may be very sophisticated, but it is not natural.

Having established the problem, Hume proceeds to search for a solution. He begins the second part by presenting a philosophical position that he calls skeptical, which denies in principle that a standard of taste can exist. Taste, according to this view, is a matter of sentiment, in distinction from matters of judgment and fact. "All sentiment is right," in this philosophy, but "all determinations of the understanding are not right." Understanding is about "real matters of fact," and disagreements can, at least in principle, be settled by recourse to facts.

But sentiment, or feeling, has no reference beyond itself. It does not, according to this skeptical view, assert anything about the object; it represents a response to the object. Consequently, each sentiment is what it is, and there are no grounds for pronouncing one right and another wrong. In this case, says Hume, common sense and philosophy agree that matters of taste cannot be disputed. But common sense flatly denies the skeptical position with regard to particular cases. It is one thing to assert that all tastes are equal and quite another to say that Neil Simon writes better than Shakespeare. People may say such things, but no one pays attention to them. In these cases, as Hume says, "the principle of the natural equality of tastes is totally forgot."

Here, Hume begins to talk about the "rules of composition," which he says are based not on reasoning or abstract principles but on experience. They are "general observations concerning what has been universally found to please in all countries and in all ages." These rules, which Hume never states or specifies, are based on the consensus that Shakespeare writes better than Neil Simon, and this consensus holds empirically even if the skeptical view of feelings—that is, the view that feeling has no reference beyond itself—is true. In effect, Hume has taken the strongest possible negative position about the very possibility of a standard of taste and shown that even if that position were theoretically true, there is strong empirical evidence to support a general human standard of taste, a standard based roughly on the proposition that we are all constituted more or less alike.

A common constitution, which seems to be the basis of the consensus of sentiment, requires for its proper operation no "exterior hindrance" or "internal disorder." Again, Hume never tries to describe the general human constitution. He is content to discern its operation in "the durable admiration which attends these works, that have survived all the caprices of mode and fashion, all the mistakes of ignorance and envy." Now, at last, we have arrived at the canon of the classics, those works that have supposedly transcended their own time and place to become great books.

This canon of classics is not Hume's standard of taste. It merely constitutes the best empirical evidence that such a standard exists. The standard itself, he says, is to be found "in each creature," where "there is a sound and a defective state; and the former alone can be supposed to afford us a true standard of taste and sentiment." In other words, the true and universal standard of taste would seem to be whatever pleases the person of good taste. The canon consists of the most pleasing works produced by human artists.

It is clear, as Smith points out with relish, that many problems are connected with the notion of a permanent canon of great works. I contend in response that Hume was fully aware of all the problems that Smith discerns and, further, that those problems were a major factor in his understanding of the operation of taste. I think it necessary first to acknowledge that we do have a canon of classics. I am prepared to admit that everything about that canon is problematic: which works belong and which should be excluded, whether the works in the canon change from age to age, what function, if any, a canon serves in our world, and so forth.

Prior to any consideration of these questions we need to be clear that such works as the *Iliad,* the *Oresteia,* Thucydides' *History, Oedipus Rex,* the *Aeneid, Hamlet,* and Keats' "Ode to Autumn" are all different from the bulk of poems, plays, and histories in our libraries. The cited works would seem to be classics, and they belong in the canon. Furthermore, more than literacy is required to read and appreciate these works. Like olives, they are an acquired taste. In the third part of his essay Hume spells out the skills and activities needed to enjoy these classics, these olives of the intellect and the imagination.

The true critic possesses five fundamental qualities, according to Hume: delicacy of imagination, practice, comparison, lack of prejudice, and good sense. The two crucial ones for my purposes are delicacy of imagination and lack of prejudice. Hume's account of delicacy of imagination is drawn entirely from a story in *Don Quixote* told by Sancho Panza.

> 'Tis with good reason, says SANCHO . . . that I pretend to have a judgment in wine: This is a quality hereditary in our family. Two of my kinsmen were once called to give their opinion of a hogshead, which was supposed to be excellent, being old and of a good vintage. One of them tastes it; considers it, and after mature reflection pronounces the wine to be good, were it not for a small taste of leather which he perceived in it. The other, after using the same precautions, gives also his verdict in favour of the wine; but with the reserve of a taste of iron, which he could easily distinguish. You cannot imagine how much they were both ridiculed for their judgment. But who laughed in the end? On emptying the hogshead, there was found at the bottom, an old key with a leathern thong tied to it.

The story, for all its brevity, is quite complex. Note first that delicacy is an analytic capacity: the capacity to taste something and distinguish all the ingredients in it. Second, like most human capacities, it is not equally distributed among us—some of us have a great deal of it, some of us very little. This may be natural, even hereditary, but it poses severe problems.

I am well aware, for example, that many people see much better than I can; they can recognize someone a hundred feet away and I cannot tell who it is until I am much closer. But delicacy of imagination is also a matter of perception, and if a friend tells me that the tomato sauce has too much oregano, and I with my dull palate can't even taste the oregano, how can I tell whether my friend is telling the truth or testing me because there's no oregano in the sauce at all?

Another problem with delicacy of imagination is that the "hogshead" of an artistic work can't be emptied to see what is at the bottom. If you don't perceive something, you don't, and no argument can substitute for direct perception, although we may come to accept our own shortness of sight or dullness of taste if the contrary testimony is strong enough. But the problems posed by the notion of delicacy are only beginning. In Sancho Panza's story his kinsmen were correct in opposing the multitude, but they also disagreed with each other. Delicacy, like any other human ability, is fallible, and no single instance of its operation is likely to be perfect; no one person is likely to detect every ingredient accurately.

Perhaps the greatest problem is that those with delicacy will always be greatly outnumbered by those who lack it. Given the likelihood that each expert is only partly right and is in disagreement with other experts, the multitude, who lack delicacy, have good reason to doubt the testimony of those who claim it. After all, if membership in the elite requires delicacy of imagination, many will pretend to have it. And why should we believe everyone who claims to have it? Sometimes the emperor doesn't have new clothes. Regardless of all these problems with delicacy, however, there is no reason to doubt that it is real and that some of us have a great deal more of it than others.

Hume is sensitive to these problems, and he concludes his discussion of delicacy of imagination by suggesting that it and taste are identical: "A quick and acute perception of beauty and deformity must be the perfection of our mental taste." But lest we become discouraged too easily, he immediately goes on to argue that we can "increase and improve this talent." It can reasonably be said that the remaining four qualities of the person with taste are essentially procedures to improve taste and, at least in part, compensate through education and training for the natural deficiency in delicacy from which most of us suffer to some extent.

First, we need to practice. Some of us may be able, through our natural abilities, to enjoy the beauty and perfection of *Oedipus Rex* the first time we read it, even if it is the first tragedy we have ever experienced. But most of us would find it helpful to read and see many tragedies so that we can distinguish those features of *Oedipus* which are more or less common to all tragedies from those unique features of that play which contribute to its extraordinary power and beauty. Given the subtlety and complexity of a work like *Oedipus,* it also usually helps to read or see it more than once. We are not likely to be able to grasp the whole and its details the first time around. But before dismissing these old saws as banal and superficial, we should remember that most of us were once unlettered. It was practice in Hume's sense that has enabled us to come to enjoy such initially forbidding works as *Oedipus Rex.*

The third activity of the true critic is comparison, for, says Hume, "by comparison alone we fix the epithets of praise or blame, and learn how to assign the due degree of each." Comparison is the natural extension of practice; it enables us to make judgments. For Hume judgment does not require explicit criteria or abstract principles. We do not need a critical theory in order to make an adequate aesthetic judgment, because we need only judge works against each other. But to do this effectively, the range of works compared must be as broad as possible. "A man," says Hume, "who has had opportunities of seeing, and examining and weighing the several performances, admired in different ages and nations, can alone rate the merits of a work exhibited to his view, and assign its proper rank among the productions of genius." In brief, to make a reasonable judgment of the musical value of the Beatles, it is not enough to listen to the Rolling Stones; one must also listen to Bach and Beethoven—and maybe Peking opera as well.

In order "more fully to execute this undertaking" the critic needs a fourth quality: "He must preserve his mind free from all prejudice." Every work, says Hume, "in order to produce its due effect on the mind, must be surveyed in a certain point of view." "A critic must place himself in the same situation as the audience in order to form a true judgment. . . . When any work is addressed to the public, though I should have a friendship or enmity with the author, I must depart from this particular situation; and considering myself as a man in general, forget if possible my individual being and my peculiar circumstances. A person influenced by prejudice complies not with this condition but obstinately maintains his natural position." A little later he says, about a critic who refuses to get rid of his prejudices, that "his sentiments are perverted; nor have the same beauties and blemishes the same influence upon him as if he had imposed a proper violence upon his imagination and had forgot himself for a moment." Hume's language in these statements on what it means to lack prejudice is remarkable. To lack prejudice means to consider myself as a man in general and to forget my individual being; to be influenced by prejudice is to maintain my natural position. To get rid of prejudice is to impose a proper violence on the imagination.

In these remarks, we can begin to see why taste is so rare and so hard to achieve. All of us are prejudiced both by our natural inclinations and by all of the manifold influences of our environment. We are all human, but we are always particular human beings living at a particular time in a particular place with the manners, morals, opinions, and beliefs proper to that time and place. I can no more escape being a twentieth-century American than Hume could avoid being an eighteenth-century Englishman. The particular circumstances of our cultural and historical context are given to us. I can no more choose to live in a prenuclear age than I can choose not to be a mammal; the one is as "natural" to me as the other. But, Hume argues, for taste to be effective we must do proper violence to ourselves, we must forget ourselves.

We can ask two questions about this process of freeing the mind from all prejudice: First, is it possible? Second, if it is possible, why should we bother? Hume is explicit about what it means to lack prejudice. It requires that, at least in our imagination, we stand in the position of the audience for which a work was intended. If the work was aimed at a particular audience, we must "have a regard to their particular genius, interest, opinions, passions, and prejudices" in the same way that the author of the piece did.

This kind of exercise of the imagination is limited primarily by one's knowledge and understanding of other times and places. Hume will later, in part VI of the essay, suggest certain moral limitations on such an imaginative exercise. But apart from that, there is no particular reason why we cannot in imagination temporarily substitute another set of prejudices for our own. To do so is an act of historical imagination; it is not yet an operation of taste.

The more peculiar and difficult situation occurs when a work is not addressed to a particular audience but to what Hume calls the public. The problem here is not to substitute one set of prejudices for another but to get rid of prejudice altogether. This is the real problem of taste. If getting rid of prejudice is not possible, there is no such thing as taste or a standard of taste, merely a plurality of tastes and a multiplicity of standards, each of which is essentially a set of prejudices. Hume's claim is that works of art, or at least some of them, are not addressed to particular audiences; they are addressed to the public, that is, to anyone, no matter where or when or under what cultural conditions that person lives. They are addressed not to this or that individual but to any and every human being, or, as Hume puts it, to a man in general.

Hume claims that each of us can stand in that position. Any of us can respond to a work not from this or that prejudiced point of view but from the perspective of a man or woman in general—a perspective devoid of the prejudice that always accompanies the actual situation of every particular human being. This is the crucial claim of the entire essay. What are the grounds, we may ask, for believing that it is possible?

I could make an argument about our generic human nature, but it would have to be based on a scientific account of human nature, and unfortunately, scientific accounts constantly change as new discoveries are made. Yesterday's science is even more outmoded and quaint than yesterday's fashion in clothes. Science is too unstable to provide a basis for taste.

The best evidence for the possible operation of taste is the taste evinced in the canon of classic works. After all, do we have to adopt the stance of a nineteenth-century Russian aristocrat or peasant to enjoy *War and Peace?* How much does any nonspecialist know about nineteenth-century Russia anyway? If our ignorance of nineteenth-century Russian life does not interfere with our pleasure in the novel, maybe our ignorance of archaic Greek culture will not interfere with our pleasure in an arcane and exotic work like the *Iliad.* Maybe both works are intended for "the public." You might argue that *War and Peace* and the *Iliad* belong to Western culture, but we can also read and enjoy the *Tale of Genji,* gaze with delight at a Song landscape or a Shang bronze, or appreciate a Balinese dance? Perhaps most extraordinary of all, is the powerful effect of such mysterious works of art as the Cro-Magnon cave paintings of Lascaux or Altamira, works of a people of whom we know nothing except that they were human and capable of perceiving and representing beauty.

Despite all the arguments of the relativists, historicists, and cultural anthropologists, great works of art persist across millennia and penetrate cultural boundaries as no other class of human artifact does. Scientific theories come and go, political and cultural institutions and customs change, and technologies develop or disappear. But great art endures.

The very range of art with which the twentieth century is familiar makes Hume's argument stronger than it was in the eighteenth century. The very diversity of the canon with which we are familiar enhances the notion that we can appreciate the canonical works only if we divest ourselves of particularity, of prejudice, and view them from the perspective of a man in general.

Following Hume's own practice, I do not insist that this argument in support of freeing the mind from prejudice is definitive. All I have done is to point out that the empirical evidence of our own experience with works of art from many times and places supports the notion that we can impose a proper violence upon ourselves, forget our individual being, and become, each of us, a man, a woman—a human—in general. Assuming, then, that there are reasonable grounds for believing that we can divest ourselves of prejudice, why should we bother, when it is neither natural nor easy?

Part of the answer is implicit in the previous argument. To free yourself from prejudice is to make available to yourself the best artistic works made by human beings. These works, from Homer and the Shang bronzes to Joyce and Picasso, are among the greatest sources of pleasure available to us as human beings. To remain prejudiced is to limit one's enjoyment of art to works with which we already have a natural, that is, prejudiced, affinity. Such works may indeed be a source of delight, but is it not evident that the products of any particular time and place are meager compared to the accumulated riches preserved in the canon? To acquire the discipline and education necessary to appreciate Homer, Lady Murasaki, and Chaucer takes considerable effort, but the pleasure they provide is surely worth it.

This is one argument in support of the kind of education in taste implicit in Hume's account of the true critic. A further argument cuts a good deal deeper and is, admittedly, only implicit in Hume's text. The existence of the canon of great works suggests, according to Hume, that despite the relative rarity of persons of taste in any particular society at any given time, there are *some* people in all times and places who have risen above the prejudices of their locale. These individuals, who are for the most part unknown and who are always outnumbered by their more or less tasteless contemporaries, constitute a concurrent majority in favor of the classics. They are the true elite of merit who sustain the canon.

The canon is important not only for the pleasure it provides but for another reason as well. The range of our human potentialities is only partly expressed in the limited conditions under which we live. Our natural, prejudiced condition is a limited and stunted condition. If we wish to understand ourselves, to know better, or at least attempt to know better, who and what we are, we need to transcend the particular situation in which we live. As Hume points out, science and speculative philosophy are subject to criticism and change, to prejudice and correction. Great art alone provides us with access to that general humanity which we all share, and to that small but select society of civilized men and women whose collective judgment constitutes the true standard of taste. What I am suggesting is that great art, according to Hume, is privileged in that, more than any other human endeavor, it provides us with such knowledge of ourselves as we are able to achieve. For true self-knowledge, we need the canon of classic works.

Two further implications of Hume's argument lend support to the notion that not only is it possible to exercise taste but we have a moral obligation to do so. If Hume's argument has merit, the canon has existed and continues to exist only because in each generation there are men and women of taste who transcend the prejudices of their own time and appreciate the great works of other times and places. That appreciation is what keeps those works alive and ensures their survival. The natural tendency is for all works to fade into obscurity and finally oblivion. It takes a special and continuing effort to see that ·this does not happen to those works whose continued existence both individually and collectively is so important to all of us.

We have good evidence that this process of ensuring persistence has not been uniformly successful. Think of the lost works of the great Greek play-wrights, for just one example. The canon is not only a genuine source of plea-sure and a possible source of wisdom; it is also a legacy, one that is available to us because others before us preserved it, a legacy that will be available to the generations to come only if we in our turn preserve it. When I say "preserve," I do not mean in the material sense in which well-made editions are carefully stored on library shelves. The preservation of the canon requires that it be ac-tively appreciated, understood, and discussed. Otherwise it may sit unread on that library shelf and go quietly out of print. The canon of great books handed down to us may not require piety, but it certainly requires active and contin-ued involvement.

This brings me to my last point. If works can disappear from the canon be-cause of ignorance, inattention, or sheer lack of taste, if the canon as a whole could disappear if a few generations failed to sustain it, then the question arises, How was the canon compiled in the first place? Or, more precisely, how do in-dividual works find their way into the canon? After all, every work was pro-duced at a particular time and place and was perceived by its initial audience as a contemporary work. Even Homer was once a contemporary poet, and the Il-iad was probably one of many contemporary epics about the age of the heroes.

I do not mean to suggest finding an answer to the question by undertaking the kind of historical research that traces the social, political, economic, and religious factors leading to the gradual emergence into classic status of a work like the Iliad. Such studies have a place, but I intend my question to focus at-tention on how books enter the canon. Like previous generations, we live in a time when there is a canon of classic works and a very large number of con-temporary works that are rivals for admission to the canon. I am not worried about lesser works that are praised beyond their merits. In a generation or two, when their timeliness wears out, they will be seen for what they are, and will then enter a deserved oblivion. Rather, I am concerned that we may fail to ap-preciate the truly great contemporary work and let it slip away. If the work is not read and reread, discussed by one person of taste and recommended to an-other, it may never emerge out of that welter of commercial promotion, hype, and literary politics that surrounds publication.

How can we recognize new great works? We can't, I believe, unless we are able to transcend the prejudices of our day and genuinely appreciate the clas-sic works of the canon. This conclusion brings Hume's argument full circle. The preservation of the canon of classic works of the past is the primary means by which we can do justice to the unique and unexpected contributions of our own age to the operation of good taste and the preservation of human civility.

PART III   EDUCATION AS DIALOGUE

15 Plato's *Protagoras*
Who Will Teach the Teachers?

Plato's *Protagoras* takes place in the house of Callias, who was immensely wealthy and spent more money retaining and entertaining sophists than anyone else. Protagoras is a sophist—a wise man who will, for a fee, impart his wisdom to others. It's been a long time since he visited Athens and explained why, despite the dangers implicit in geing a freethinking intellectual, he openly admitted his profession. Today nobody admits to the profession of sophist, and someone given to jumping to conclusions might take this to mean that the profession no longer exists. That person could hardly be more in error.

Today the profession of sophist flourishes as never before; only the name and the institutional pattern have changed. Protagoras along with his lesser colleagues Hippias and Prodicus traveled about from city to city, taking their old students with them and recruiting new ones. Today's sophists work together in large groups. Instead of traveling about to find students, they settle in one spot and let the students come to them. They are called professors, and they teach in universities.

No one professes to be a sophist today because the word has come to have a pejorative sense. A sophistical argument is a deceptive argument, a clever piece of fraudulent reasoning. Naturally no one openly admits to making a living by framing such arguments. But the term *sophist* did not originally have such a clear pejorative sense. In the Platonic *Dialogues,* particularly the *Gorgias* and the *Protagoras,* sophists are represented as men of eminence, learning, and dignity who expect and are accorded a great deal of respect. But even in the *Dialogues,* there is a slight undercurrent of uncertainty and doubt about the sophists. Hippocrates, for example, blushes with embarrassment when

Socrates draws from him the admission that if he studies with a sophist he will become a sophist himself. For all their apparent respectability the sophists were somehow unsavory, and the modern understanding of sophistry as deliberate intellectual fraud is not wholly lacking in Plato's *Dialogues*.

What exactly is the relation between these two conceptions of the sophist—the notion of a respectable person who professes wisdom and imparts that wisdom to others for a reasonable sum of money and the notion of a man or woman who lives by his or her wits, deceiving and defrauding others through specious arguments? The first conception is descriptive of a contemporary academic, the second of a cheap huckster. Is there a necessary connection between the two?

If Protagoras is the prototype of all college professors, Hippocrates is the quintessential college student: he is bright, eager for education, ambitious, impatient, good-natured, anxious, determined to settle for nothing less than the best, tactless, and ignorant. He is so ignorant that he is almost unaware of how little he understands. Hippocrates is prepared to rush off to Protagoras to get an education without having the slightest notion of what that entails. It takes considerable discussion with Socrates for him to become even dimly aware that some problems may be involved in what he is proposing to do. If a huckster and a charlatan lurks beneath Protagoras' paternal and wise exterior, that is Hippocrates' problem as well as Protagoras'.

The *Protagoras* is Socrates' account of a conversation with Protagoras about whether virtue can be taught. The conversation proceeds by fits and starts. It includes some of the worst arguments ever enshrined in a great piece of literature, as well as frequent digressions, and repeated squabbles; to cap it off, the debate ends inconclusively. Although the explicit philosophical problem under consideration is never resolved, the dramatic action of the dialogue is perfectly resolved. As an explicit investigation into the teachability of virtue, the *Protagoras* ends almost before it starts. As a dramatic account of the philosophical encounter between Socrates and Protagoras, the dialogue is a dramatic masterpiece with a defined and unified plot, a brilliant cast of characters, and all the other qualities associated with dramatic works of the first order. This dramatic work aims not at poetic pleasure, however, but at truth. Of course, the pursuit of truth has its own distinctive pleasure.

I shall examine one portion of the dialogue that is often puzzling from both a philosophical and a dramatic viewpoint: the long interlude on the poem of Simonides. The discussion of the poem takes up twelve of the seventy pages of the dialogue, and it sticks out like a sore thumb. It appears to be a long, complicated, silly, and irrelevant digression. Professor G. Vlastos thinks so little of the passage on Simonides' poem that he doesn't bother to mention it in his interesting fifty-page introductory essay on the dialogue. One might argue that the episode would be appropriate in the middle of a play like *Waiting for Godot,* where anything is likely to happen. But even Plato's sharpest critics have never quite accused him of writing for the theater of the absurd. Paul Shorey, another eminent scholar, admits that the passage "contains little or nothing that bears on the main argument," although he does think it has a point. "The one certain Platonic opinion [to be drawn from the digression on the poem of Simonides] is the conclusion that it is idle in discussions of this sort to invoke the testimony of poets who, being absent, cannot be cross-examined, and whose meaning will always be wrested to suit the purpose of the quoter."

Even if Shorey is right, it seems heavy-handed of Plato to devote twelve pages to a simple and irrelevant point. Another scholar, A. E. Taylor, thinks that the episode has little, if any, serious intent and is merely a kind of "humorous" or comic relief designed to break up a tedious string of arguments. These arguments, in Taylor's words, make "a severe demand on the reader's power of hard thinking." Thus, Vlastos ignores the episode; Shorey thinks it irrelevant; Taylor justifies it as comic relief. Their testimony is weighty, but if we accepted their views, we would be admitting that Plato is a second-rate writer both philosophically and dramatically. Before we admit that, perhaps we should look more closely at the context and substance of the digression.

How did Socrates and Protagoras ever come to discuss Simonides' poem in the first place? Protagoras introduces the poem into the discussion when he asks Socrates questions about it. The two men start discussing poetry in general and this poem in particular for no compelling reason. Therefore, if the entire passage is irrelevant to the main line of the argument, the fault seems to be Protagoras'—he is the one who changes the subject. But why does Protagoras start to question Socrates about it, and why does he change the subject? Just prior to the discussion of the poem Protagoras has refused to continue the discussion with Socrates because three times in a row Socrates has tripped him up in the argument. The assembled company, enjoying the show, want him to go on. Prodicus and Hippias, the other two sophists present, make barbed suggestions about how the discussion might be resumed. But Socrates rejects their advice and instead proposes that he and Protagoras reverse their roles of questioner and respondent. Thus Socrates supplies the form and Protagoras the content of the interlude on the poem of Simonides; they are jointly responsible for it.

The interlude thus appears to be a joint attempt by Socrates and Protagoras to reconstitute a discussion that has utterly broken down. But how could these two reasonable and intelligent men have allowed a polite and interesting discussion of the teachability of virtue to degenerate into an unpleasant and personal debate? On the surface at least, the responsibility for the breakdown seems to be Socrates'.

Earlier Protagoras asserted that the virtues are distinct from each other, and Socrates expressed some doubt about this. He articulated his doubt by directing a series of three arguments to Protagoras, the first demonstrating the absurdity of distinguishing piety and justice, the second doing the same for wisdom and self-control, and the third attempting to unite the first two arguments by showing the identity of self-control and justice. This third argument is never completed, for Protagoras breaks off the discussion. These arguments by Socrates are atrocious. It doesn't take an expert in logic to detect the fallacies, and we can hardly blame Protagoras for refusing to discuss the matter further.

Protagoras himself doesn't seem to resent Socrates' behavior at first. Socrates argues that if justice and piety are different, then justice must be impious and piety unjust. But there is a difference between saying piety is not justice and saying piety is unjust. To assert that democracy and economics are different is not to assert that economics is undemocratic or that democracy is uneconomical. The distinction is obvious, but surprisingly, Protagoras doesn't state it. He merely remarks: "This matter does not seem to be quite so simple, Socrates, that I can agree to the proposition that justice is pious and that piety is just, for there appears to be a difference between them. But what matter? If you please, I please; and let us assume, if you will, that justice is pious and that piety is just" (331e). It is clear from this comment that Protagoras doesn't resent Socrates' appalling logic because he is uninterested in the substance of the argument: if Socrates wants to identify piety and justice, that is all right with him; he is not going to quibble.

Socrates has different ideas about the argument, and he replies to Protagoras' complacent remark by saying: "Pardon me, I do not want this 'if you please' or 'if you like' sort of proposition to be put to the test, but I want you and me to be tested. I mean to say that the proposition will be best tested if you take the 'if' out of it" (331c). This answer marks the beginning of the end of the pleasant atmosphere at the house of Callias. With this remark Socrates has served notice that he will not allow Protagoras to argue hypothetically or indifferently; he must state and defend his own views. If Protagoras does not want to be made a fool before the distinguished audience, he must pay attention to the arguments. The bad arguments employed by Socrates thus serve a purpose: they force Protagoras either to argue seriously or to give up the argument altogether.

For a while Protagoras tries to avoid this choice. In the second argument he is bested, and during the third he breaks off as soon as he sees where Socrates is heading. On the surface, then, Socrates would seem to be guilty of bad manners. He deliberately employs bad arguments to embarrass Protagoras. But Socrates has a genuine and difficult problem: he wants to engage Protagoras in a serious discussion, whereas Protagoras wants to talk entertainingly, to present the audience with the appearance of a serious conversation without its substance.

How can Socrates persuade Protagoras to engage in a genuine dialogue? The answer is simple: fight fire with fire. If Protagoras will not talk seriously, neither will Socrates. If Protagoras wants to entertain the audience, Socrates will be entertaining. But instead of allowing Protagoras to show off his wisdom, he makes him look like a fool.

In this first set of arguments, Socrates picks the subject for discussion—the unity of the virtues—and Protagoras' indifferent attitude determines the superficial and fallacious quality of the arguments. As in the following interlude on Simonides' poem, *both* men are responsible for the argument. But we can see that the interlude on the poem not only reverses the roles of questioner and respondent but also reverses the responsibility for the form and the content of the discussion. The interlude on the poem of Simonides not only emerges out of the earlier arguments about the unity of the virtues but reverses these arguments. The interlude is not irrelevant or comic relief. It is tightly related to what precedes it.

The interlude is thus a formal inversion of the previous arguments in which Socrates and Protagoras exchange roles, each playing the part of the other. If we wish to understand the interlude, we must first understand the earlier, original roles of the two interlocutors. It is not enough to say that initially Socrates questions and Protagoras answers, that Socrates chooses the subject to be discussed and Protagoras the way that subject will be treated. These statements, though true, are too abstract. Why does Socrates question Protagoras, and why does he pick the unity of the virtues as the subject of his questions? Why does Protagoras answer the way he does, and why won't he argue seriously? These are the questions that we must consider if we want to grasp what is happening in the discussion of Simonides' poem. But to answer these new questions, we must inquire more fully into the character and position of Socrates and Protagoras, and this means that we must go back to the incidents preceding those initial three fallacious arguments on the unity of the virtues.

To understand Protagoras we must consider the scene in which he and Socrates meet and in which he reveals himself through his speech on the history of sophistry, his myth about the origins of man, his rational theory of punishment and his explanation of why eminent men often have undistinguished sons. That scene belongs to Protagoras. Socrates merely asks him leading questions in order to draw him out. If we want to understand what Socrates is up to, we must go back to the beginning of the dialogue, to the scene between Socrates and Hippocrates. While they wait for the sun to rise so there will be enough light to visit Protagoras, Socrates and Hippocrates talk about education.

The cream of sophisticated Athenian society has gathered at Callias' house early in the morning to hear the assembled sophists display their wisdom (or, in Socrates' less flattering terms, to watch them hawk their wares). Protagoras is the oldest and most eminent person there. In his explanation of why he prefers to speak in public rather than in private, he claims that many of the most famous and creative men in Greek history, among them the poet Simonides, were sophists. He asserts that these sophists disguised themselves as practitioners of other arts, such as poetry or music, for fear of arousing jealousy and hatred in the cities that they visited. The disguises were to no avail. The leading citizens were not fooled. Hence, says Protagoras, valor is the better part of discretion, and accordingly, he openly admits he is a sophist. His openness is not dictated by principle, or even by bravery, but by a calculating prudence. Honesty is the best policy, he says, because it pays. The trouble with such a defense is that if it doesn't pay, there is no reason to be honest.

In response to Socrates' question about what he does, Protagoras states that he teaches prudence in public and private affairs and the ability to act and to speak effectively in political matters. In sum, he claims to teach the art of politics and to make his students good citizens. Socrates expresses some doubt as to whether this art can be taught, giving two reasons. First, every citizen seems to have the political art already without having been taught it, which is not the case with the various specialized technical skills. Second, unlike other arts, politics apparently cannot be taught, since great politicians often have inept sons. The eminent political leaders obviously would have taught their sons the art of politics if they could have done so.

Protagoras answers these objections with his great speech. He offers to answer in the form of either a myth or a straight argument and ends up supplying both. Protagoras' myth is basically a parable. Compare it to Socrates' myth at the end of the *Republic* to see the difference between a true myth and a story that illustrates a theoretical position. Stripped of its poetic imagery, Protagoras' myth asserts that human life exists on three levels: the natural, the technical, and the moral/political.

On the natural level, where humankind is in direct competition with other species for survival, human beings are radically deficient, because they lack natural means of protection from the climate and the other animals. According to the myth, this is the fault of Epimetheus. The situation is partially remedied by the arts and fire—the technical order. The possession of the technical arts is secured by Prometheus' theft. These arts give human beings a "share in divinity."

The first thing humans do when they have the technical arts is to invent religion and language. They then start fabricating things to improve the quality of their life. Unfortunately the technical arts only enable humans to provide themselves with the means of life and to protect themselves against the forces of nature. Individuals, because of their relative physical weakness, are unable to contend with the brute animals, and therefore they come together and form communities for mutual protection. But without the art of government they cannot effectively work together, so they disperse again to their doom. Zeus, fearing their destruction, has Hermes bestow the virtues on all, for the community cannot exist if the civic virtues—justice, piety, and the rest—are distributed, like each of the technical arts, only among a few.

In Protagoras' myth the virtues are conceived in purely political or social terms. The technical arts are bodies of knowledge invented to cope directly with nature: the test of a shipbuilder's art is whether his ship floats and sails well. The virtues, by contrast, have as their aim the creation and maintenance of a communal life. If men with their technical skills can manage to live and work together, they can compete successfully with the other species. The virtues are what make communal life possible. The test of the virtues, as of the arts, is pragmatic—Do they work? Do they enable men to live and work together?

After presenting the myth Protagoras offers two further arguments in support of his view. He asserts that the end of rational punishment is improvement of the one punished and prevention of further crime by both the wrongdoer and those who see him punished. And he explains why good men often have sons lacking in virtue. Virtue, he points out, is taught not only by fathers but by everybody; apparently all citizens are constantly being educated in virtue by their fellow citizens. Some turn out better than others because they have more natural capacity for virtue. Similarly, although everyone is a teacher of virtue, some people have more natural capacity for teaching it than others, and Protagoras counts himself among these gifted teachers.

On the surface, Protagoras' speech is an elegant, beautifully organized and intelligent statement that more than answers Socrates' doubts and uncertainties. Protagoras presents himself as an enlightened, rational, undogmatic, progressive, modest, and thoroughly decent man. It is no accident that he has won adherents among modern readers of the dialogue, among them Vlastos and Bertrand Russell. But the appeal of Protagoras runs deeper than this, for he is the prototype not only of the modern academic but also of the modern liberal.

Like modern liberals, Protagoras believes in democratic civil rights, in technical and moral progress, in education as the rational, long-term solution for serious social problems. Like modern liberals, he is dubious of traditional beliefs, of overly consistent positions, of absolute ideas. In certain respects Protagoras is a pragmatist—he argues that the test of the technical arts is their success in coping with nature and that the test of the virtues is their success in creating the consensus necessary for the existence and effective functioning of the community. In other respects he is a cultural relativist, for the moral and civic virtues, as he understands them, have no necessary content. Justice is whatever the consensus of the community says it is, and the same holds for courage, piety, and the rest. Because the virtues have no fixed content, moral progress is possible. Whatever promotes the consensus of the community and thereby increases communal security and well-being effects progress in the moral order. On the other hand, there is no reason to suppose that what works for one community will work for another; each community defines the virtues in terms of its own particular social needs.

The Protagorean position is intelligent and strikingly similar to the modern liberal stance. But Protagoras is more than an ancient Greek version of a modern social scientist; he is, above all, a teacher of virtue. He has a theory, and he puts it into practice. If we contrast Protagoras to the other two sophists in the dialogue, Prodicus and Hippias, we can see his superiority. But they are not included in the dialogue simply to enhance his eminence. They also serve to define Protagoras' position by indicating its two extremes and locating him in the moderate middle.

Hippias is a typical social theorist—he distinguishes between nature and convention, and he is interested in the technical arts and sciences. To Hippias, politics is a subject for theoretical study. Prodicus, on the other hand, is interested in words and meanings; he can produce a term or a distinction to serve any purpose on any occasion. As Hippias is concerned primarily with the technical order, Prodicus is concerned almost exclusively with the moral order. But when the moral order is seen in isolation from the technical and natural orders, as it is with Prodicus, it becomes merely a matter of words. The moral order, according to Protagoras, is concerned with consensus, but consensus for a purpose. It achieves that consensus through language, through having a common meaning for the basic terms: justice, piety, self-control. When, as with Prodicus, the ultimate purpose of the moral order is ignored and its close connection to the technical order is not seen, the moral order is a purely verbal phenomenon, and wisdom becomes a matter of manipulating words. This is Prodicus' specialty.

Protagoras' sophism occupies the middle ground between the detached, theoretical views of Hippias and the mindless verbal manipulations of Prodicus. Like Hippias, Protagoras has a theory, but like Prodicus, he is interested in direct and immediate political action. His theory aims at practice, and his practical activity is informed with a theoretical understanding. By resolutely maintaining his position on this middle ground he avoids the obvious absurdities of the extreme views represented by Prodicus and Hippias. Protagoras is the great exponent of practical wisdom and effective action. He claims to understand these things and to be able to teach them to others.

Although Protagoras is a political relativist who finds one political regime as good as another so long as it works, he has, nevertheless, a certain bias in favor of democracy. Political virtue, he argues, must be distributed universally in a community in order for the community to exist. Only in a democracy—a community in which everybody participates in the political process—is this universal distribution given formal recognition. In addition to his other virtues, Protagoras has the final advantage for the modern liberal of advocating democracy. Plato has represented Protagoras and his position with precision, with fairness, and with intrinsic reasonableness. Protagoras is no straw man, set up to be knocked down.

But Protagoras *is* Socrates' opponent. If we are to understand their quarrel, we must also come to terms with Socrates. For this we must shift back one more scene, to that moment just before dawn when Socrates is awakened by Hippocrates. If Protagoras is shown off to advantage in his great speech, Socrates appears at his best in this beautiful little conversation with Hippocrates. Socrates' questions can, on occasion, be irritating, obtuse, unfair, confusing—but there is not one false note in his questions to Hippocrates. The enthusiastic young man has not thought through the implications of his intention to study under Protagoras. Socrates, with patience and gentleness, leads him to reflect on what he is about to do.

He does not tell Hippocrates anything very startling or new; he merely reminds him of some commonplaces with which he has long been familiar. The sophist is a vendor, a retailer of knowledge. Customers should be suspicious of people who, their noble statements of purpose notwithstanding, are trying to sell something. Socrates' questions about Protagoras are perfectly just, and they demand answers. Socrates asks, Does Protagoras deceive us "when he praises what he sells, like the dealers, wholesale or retail, who sell the food of the body, for they praise indiscriminately all their goods without knowing what is really beneficial or hurtful for the body . . . [and knowledge is more dangerous than food; for] but you cannot buy knowledge and carry it away in another vessel; when you have paid for it, you must receive it into your soul and go on your way, whether greatly harmed or greatly benefited" (313d–314b).

Socrates emerges from this scene with Hippocrates as a genuine friend. Socrates has acted purely in Hippocrates' own interest, reminding him of what is at stake for him in going to Protagoras. But he has done more than that. Hippocrates originally came to Socrates with a simple request: Introduce me to Protagoras so that I may become his pupil. Socrates, who is always polite and compliant, will carry out that request, as he makes clear in his first remarks to Protagoras. But out of their talk about the reasons for going to a sophist,

Socrates and Hippocrates arrive at a second task for Socrates to perform. For Hippocrates' benefit Socrates will examine Protagoras to see if he really understands his wares or if he praises everything he sells whether or not it is beneficial to the buyer.

After all, Protagoras makes no small assertion in his great speech. He claims that he can make Hippocrates a better man and citizen. If his claim is unfounded, the consequences for Hippocrates are not pleasant to contemplate. Socrates undertakes the examination of Protagoras in the interest of Hippocrates. If he handles Protagoras roughly, he has good grounds for doing so. If Protagoras' wisdom is genuine, he should be able to withstand Socrates' provocations.

When Socrates questions Protagoras about the nature of virtue, he has not picked a topic at random—virtue is what Protagoras publicly professes to teach. If he can't talk clearly and intelligently about virtue, his claim to wisdom is spurious. For the sake of Hippocrates, that spurious claim deserves to be publicly exposed. In his great speech Protagoras displays himself and his wisdom to advantage because he is selling himself. In the conversation with Hippocrates, Socrates subordinates his own interest to that of his young friend. The contrast between the two antagonists could hardly be more sharply drawn.

This account of the relationship between Socrates and Protagoras is accurate as far as it goes. But Socrates is more than one of the actors in the drama; he is also the narrator of the dialogue. The whole conversation with Protagoras is told by Socrates to an unnamed companion just after he has left the house of Callias. Socrates admits to his companion that he spent the morning in the company of his fair young friend Alcibiades, but that, strangely enough, he paid almost no attention to him because someone fairer, that is, someone wiser, was present. He is referring to Protagoras. Because he has no other engagement, Socrates agrees to recount his conversation with the great sophist, and the body of the dialogue follows.

Is Socrates ironic in this opening scene? He initially went to the house of Callias and examined Protagoras only for the sake of his innocent young friend. But long after Protagoras' shallow sophistication has been publicly exposed for the benefit of Hippocrates, Socrates stays to continue his talk with that wise old man. Why does Socrates do that? What is in it for him?

When Protagoras breaks off the conversation just prior to the interlude on the poem of Simonides, Socrates says, "I considered that there was no call upon me to continue the conversation" (315b). In other words, by that point in the dialogue Socrates has fulfilled his obligation to Hippocrates. But this implies that the rest of his conversation with Protagoras, that is, the whole interlude on Simonides and the final arguments on courage and the calculus of pleasure, are undertaken by Socrates in his own interests, not Hippocrates'. The last half of the dialogue takes place because Socrates himself wants to talk with Protagoras. What is it about Protagoras that interests, even fascinates, Socrates? Let us now look at the interlude on the poem of Simonides.

Socrates suggests that he and Protagoras exchange positions. Protagoras then states his view that skill in discussing and criticizing poetry is the principal part of education. By questioning Socrates about the poem of Simonides, Protagoras is testing the quality of Socrates' education, just as Socrates earlier tested Protagoras' claim to wisdom by asking him about virtue. Turn about is fair play. But Protagoras does more than this. He immediately produces an argument that traps Socrates in a contradiction. The argument turns out to be an exact parallel to the argument on wisdom and self-control with which Socrates had earlier caught him in a contradiction. Turn about is indeed fair play: Protagoras has not only taken on Socrates' role of questioner; he has also adopted Socrates' techniques, his style, his methods, and his mannerisms.

Protagoras thereby shows himself to be a much, much cleverer man than one might otherwise have suspected. He may not know a great deal about the virtues, and he may have been bested by Socrates in argument, but he learned something from Socrates in their first collision. His educability is exactly the quality of Protagoras that surprises and fascinates Socrates. Who would have thought that pompous, learned, self-advertising, glib old sophist still had the active intelligence, the wit, the suppleness to imitate Socrates sufficiently well to trap him with his own devices? Socrates reports that the assembled company "cheered and applauded" Protagoras' argument. And Socrates himself admits that "at first I felt giddy and faint, as if I had received a blow from the hand of an expert boxer" (339e). Protagoras, it turns out, is an expert fighter with arguments, and once he has shown Socrates his true expertise, the real battle between them is joined. Compliant as always, Socrates will fight on the ground chosen by his adversary. Since Protagoras has chosen to take on the role of Socrates, Socrates, by the rules of the game, must adopt the role of Protagoras, that is, he must in his turn employ the techniques, style, method, and mannerisms of the sophist.

But Socrates does more than expected; he reproduces not just one Protagorean argument but the whole of Protagoras' great speech, and he does it in the guise of an analysis and criticism of Simonides' poem. Socrates, too, is capable of counterpunching. His imitation of Protagoras is one of the cleverest and funniest parodies ever produced. Philosophy, as Plato understood it, is serious, but it is not necessarily solemn. Philosophy has its light moments and jokes.

Socrates' first move is to create a diversion to give himself time to plan his strategy. Protagoras, as we have seen several times, is a past master at creating diversions and changing subjects. In his first round of arguments with Socrates, he repeatedly attempted to avoid a direct confrontation of his ideas with

Socrates'. His technique was to interpose a third party or term between himself and Socrates. He appeals to the opinions of the multitude or accepts hypothetical positions for the sake of the argument, or, as in the present case, speculates about the views of a poet. But Socrates, too, can play that game, so without much difficulty he appeals to Prodicus and his distinctions.

Socrates begins by asking Prodicus to distinguish being from becoming. When Protagoras points out that the distinction makes Socrates' position worse, Socrates puts into Prodicus' mouth a ridiculous definition of the word *difficult*. Protagoras rebels; words are not infinitely malleable, and in this case, he argues, Simonides used the term in a perfectly conventional way. Socrates admits the absurdity of what he and Prodicus have been doing (although Prodicus doesn't). But Protagoras seems to grasp his basic point: No serious, intelligent discussion can ever take place between two people if one of them constantly drags in some third party who can be made to assert anything at all. By employing Protagoras' own device against him and by getting Protagoras himself to object to the device as absurd, Socrates has pushed Protagoras to reject one of his own fundamental tactics. By discreetly parodying Protagoras, Socrates is allowing Protagoras to see and to reject the absurdity of his own position and procedures. In effect, in the interpretation of the poem of Simonides, Socrates has undertaken the education of Protagoras. But this is only the beginning, for the diversion afforded by Prodicus has given Socrates the time he needs. He has worked out his full-scale imitation of Protagoras' great speech, disguised as an interpretation of Simonides' poem.

Socrates' critique of the poem of Simonides falls into four parts, beginning with an introductory account of the ancient, esoteric, and hitherto unknown philosophical tradition of Sparta and Crete. This provides, says Socrates, the historical background for the proper understanding of Simonides' poem. Second, Socrates argues that the poem is a secret refutation of Pittacus by Simonides within that esoteric philosophical tradition. This second portion of Socrates' account is in the form of an imaginary dialogue between Pittacus and Simonides on whether it is hard to be good or to become good. Third, Socrates continues his reconstruction of Simonides' position by considering the question of whom the force of circumstances overpowers. It cannot be the bad and the resourceless, for they are already helpless; therefore, he argues, only the skilled and the good can be overcome by circumstances. Socrates concludes his account by showing that Simonides understands that no one ever commits evil voluntarily. These are the four main sections of Socrates' venture into literary criticism. He starts with a wild and fantastic history and ends with an equally wild and fantastic grammatical analysis of Simonides' language. Strangely enough, this time Protagoras does not protest.

Socrates' treatment of the poem of Simonides poses some questions and problems for Protagoras, questions and problems that the old sophist must face seriously if he is to become educated. It would be rewarding, to begin with, for Protagoras to explore the obvious comic parallels between Socrates' absurd secret history of Spartan and Cretan philosophy and his own alleged secret history of sophism. What does Socrates' parody imply about the nature, value, and use of history in philosophical arguments? Is there any justification for concealment or privacy in genuine philosophical discourse, or should all philosophy occur in public?

Second, the meaning of Protagoras' myth of Epimetheus and Prometheus needs to be reconsidered in the light of Socrates' account of the quarrel between Pittacus and Simonides. Simonides, according to Socrates' account, tried to correct the oversight of Pittacus just as Prometheus tried to correct the error of Epimetheus. Does that apparently absurd quarrel about whether it is difficult to be or to become good shed any light on the meaning of progress and the role of the arts and virtues in relation to human nature?

In the third major section of his great speech Protagoras advanced an enlightened theory of rational punishment in which punishment was justified as a corrective and deterrent force. But if punishment is designed to make people good, and succeeds in doing so, then who can become bad and by what means? Here I suggest considering the third part of Socrates' critique, that seemingly silly passage in which Socrates asks, "Whom does the force of circumstances overpower?"

Finally, if virtue is teachable, as Protagoras asserts, there is the question of why good men often have bad sons. Protagoras argues in his speech that the education of the young and, in fact, of every citizen in a community is undertaken by every institution, every other citizen, and every law. If, despite this enormous and constant effort to make people virtuous, individuals achieve only the level of virtue or vice determined by their inborn nature, we might question the effectiveness of all this educational effort. In the last portion of Socrates' interpretation of Simonides' poem, Socrates argues pertinently that no one does evil voluntarily.

There are two noteworthy points about Socrates' procedure. First, he is polite and respectful to Protagoras. He disguises what he is doing so that no one but Protagoras among those present is aware of the deeper implications of his ludicrous attempts at literary criticism. Socrates thereby saves Protagoras from the embarrassment of an open, public critique. Is this, by any chance, a justifiable reason for concealment in philosophical discourse—a concealment, in this case, which takes place publicly in the presence of company? Second, Socrates undertakes to refute Protagoras from within, so to speak. He plays the role of Protagoras, and by playing it to the hilt he shows the sophist the real implications of his own position.

These two points about the way Socrates starts his attempt to educate Protagoras are of special importance to teachers and students. The major question both face is whether teachers are truly educable. There is no problem about students; we know they can learn, as we witness in Socrates' opening conversation with Hippocrates. But the professors, or sophists, are another matter altogether. Protagoras is obviously worth educating; the question is whether it can be done. The hopeful but modest answer of the dialogue seems to be: maybe. Professors can be educated, but only under certain conditions: they must be willing; they must be smart, like Protagoras; and they must be lucky enough to be taught by a Socrates.

In the absence of a Socrates, who can hope to succeed in teaching teachers? There is only one answer: the students. A problem remains: Hippocrates asked Socrates to examine Protagoras' worth as a teacher, but students today have no such recourse. They will have to examine their teachers themselves. This is not an easy task; they will have to be polite, and they will have to examine their teachers with methods of their teachers' choosing. I suggest that students prepare themselves for the task by rereading the *Protagoras,* by watching Socrates, and by thinking through the question of what virtue is and how it can be taught. If they do so, they will not only learn about philosophy; they will be actively engaging in it. Best of all, they may help the rest of us, teachers and students alike, to secure the real education that we are so reluctant to undertake but so desperately need.

16 Energizing the Classroom

The Structure of Teaching

Sometimes a teaching session fails. Student after student says, "I haven't read today's assignment yet," or "Were we supposed to read that?" or "I dunno," or "I just answered your question. Why are you attacking me by asking more questions?" Afterward, I try to understand why it failed: Did I talk too much? Was the assigned reading too hard? Did I start with the wrong question? Was I unclear in my assignment? Is this just one of those classes in which the chemistry between me and the students is no good? Did I teach unprepared and off the top of my head again? Did I take out my rotten mood on my students? The questions are endless and the answers inconclusive.

Since I have given up a better-paying administrative position to return to full-time teaching, I have been trying to formulate and reflect on a different and more fundamental question. Granted that teaching is sometimes exhilarating and fulfilling and sometimes frustrating and depressing, I have been trying to think about the activity itself. That is, what goes on in a classroom inhabited for a few hours a week by a group of students and a member of the faculty? Let us leave aside for the moment all questions about how teaching is done well or why it is so often done badly—in the language of the phenomenologists let us "bracket" these issues—and instead focus directly on what we do when we teach.

I want to begin with a number of anecdotes.

When I was five years old and in first grade, I had a teacher named Miss Goldberg. She was one of the most beautiful women I have ever known. Miss Goldberg was tall and slender. She had curly blond hair and a soft, sweet voice, and I was enchanted with her. Then, on the first day of class after the Christmas vacation, Miss Goldberg announced that she was no longer Miss Goldberg, that she had gotten married and was now Mrs. Something-or-Other. I don't remember her new, married name. But I do remember that from that moment on, first grade lost its charm for me. Fortunately, I had already learned to read in the first three months of school, so my schooling didn't suffer too much; but I did.

When I was thirteen or fourteen, I had a mathematics teacher who wanted the class to pay close attention to her and hated it when the students talked to each other while she was facing the blackboard writing out a proof or solving an equation. If she heard any whispering while her back was turned, she would whirl around and throw the blackboard eraser at the guilty party. Her fabulous reputation among us ninth graders was based on the excellence of her ear—she always heard a whisper—and the unerring accuracy of her arm. She had a very attentive classroom, although it was about equally divided between those who were silent for fear of being hit by a flying eraser and those who deliberately talked to provoke the action of that pitching arm.

In my first philosophy course in college I had another marvelous teacher. But he had his off days. Toward the end of the school year, we were discussing a particularly boring text. I don't remember the author or the text or the issue we were discussing, but it was a beautiful spring day, the class had not prepared very well, and the discussion was desultory. At one point the teacher asked a question, and a student eventually raised his hand and gave an answer. The teacher turned to another student and asked her what she thought of the answer. She replied that she thought it was wrong, and she gave another, quite different answer. There was a silence. It went on for a while, and everybody grew uneasy.

The teacher turned to the class. "Well?" he said in a questioning tone. More silence and uneasiness. What was he asking? What was he doing? What did he want? Suddenly he picked up his book and slammed it down hard on the table. "Damn it all," he said, "you've just heard two diametrically opposed answers to the same question. They can't both be right. At least one of them must be wrong. After all, it does make a difference!" For me, that last remark was like a bolt of lightning. He was right—it did make a difference. That may have been the moment at which I decided to study philosophy.

Sometime after that I took my first graduate seminar in philosophy. We spent the entire quarter going over, line by line, one of Plato's late dialogues, the *Parmenides*. The teacher was a refugee professor from Nazi Germany who spoke English slowly and with a thick accent. We struggled with that text week after week, and I became more and more confused. No interpretation that I tried worked. Some piece of the text didn't fit or posed an insoluble problem. At the last class of the quarter, the professor said that he would try to pull things together. He talked for two hours straight, working back and forth through the text, picking up and examining the different interpretations that we had read in the secondary literature or that we had devised ourselves. One by one, he showed why they failed, but he also showed in each case the initial insight that had made each one worth pursuing.

Gradually, by a kind of magic, a comprehensive and adequate interpretation of the dialogue emerged from his remarks, an interpretation that made use of all of the errors, confusions, false leads, and unresolved difficulties that we had encountered during the quarter. In the last five minutes of that class it all came together—not only what he had said during his lecture but more or less everything we all had said in our presentations during the course of the entire quarter. The virtuoso performance, delivered in halting, heavily accented English, was literally breathtaking. I remember to this day walking out of that classroom and leaning against the wall in the corridor to catch my breath. I had the distinct sense that that wonderful old man had just handed me, on a silver platter, a comprehensive vision of being. I felt as if I had just plumbed the depths of philosophy and seen the nature of things.

Do I need to add as a postscript to this story, that about five years later I went back to that dialogue in preparing for my doctoral qualifying exams and discovered that my old professor had been wrong, that his reading didn't work either? But that is another story, which doesn't belong here.

A few more stories. As a graduate student, I did a good deal of work in anthropology, primarily with one outstanding professor. This man, already an established figure in the field before the Second World War, was a prime mover in the process by which anthropology ceased to concern itself exclusively with small, preliterate, isolated communities and cultures—what we used to call primitive societies—and began to look at larger, more complex societies. I attended his seminar at which the first group of graduate students who had done fieldwork in India for a year came back to present reports of what they had found. These reports would, presumably, be the basis of their doctoral dissertations.

One session in particular I have never forgotten. A brilliant young graduate student described in detail the Indian village he had lived in and studied for a year. His presentation took about an hour. The second hour of the session was largely taken up with questions, criticisms, and comments by the other members of the seminar group. About five minutes before the end of the scheduled time, the professor, who had said almost nothing up to that point, cleared his throat and began to talk.

He first summarized the paper neatly and succinctly in about three brief sentences. Then he summarized the comments and criticisms of the other participants. Finally he announced that he himself had three comments to make.

In the first comment he restated his summary of the paper and ended with the remark: "All this I have heard before. It's probably true, but not very interesting." At that point about 90 percent of the paper that we had been discussing went down the drain. For his second comment he picked up on a small section of the paper that had not been commented on before, restated it, and concluded, "This I have not heard before, but frankly I don't believe it. I don't think it's true." It looked as if the remaining 10 percent of the paper had just been dismissed. I happened to glance at the face of the poor graduate student—author—it was gray, fallen, depressed. Then the professor made his third remark. He picked up a theme that the student had not made explicit in his paper, an idea whose elements were drawn from two or three different parts of the paper. He pulled these elements together, stated the idea in a sentence or two, and concluded, "This I have not heard before. I do not know if it is true or not. But if it is true, we will all have to rethink the nature of our discipline of cultural anthropology. I think [and here he turned to look directly at the student author, who was sitting next to him at the seminar table] we will have to look into the matter, and I am eager to hear what you have to say about it." The student whose report of a year's fieldwork had just been dismissed was ecstatic. He had just been handed, not merely the topic of his dissertation, but the core of his life's work as a professional anthropologist. And he had been treated as a peer by his dissertation supervisor.

Near the end of my career as a graduate student, a group of us who were working on our dissertations asked this same professor of anthropology if he would sponsor a small, private seminar in which we could each present our work in its early stages and profit from our mutual criticism. He agreed, and a group of eight of us met once a week in his office. We distributed the papers in advance so that the two hours of the seminar were completely devoted to the critique of that week's paper.

All of us were already on the faculty, most as teaching assistants, lecturers, instructors, or assistant professors. Besides the professor who sponsored the seminar, only one of the participants was a senior faculty member. He was a full professor from another department who had spent a year abroad and had written a long study on the community in which he had lived, which he planned to publish as a book. When we discussed each other's papers week by week, we tended to be kind, even gentle with each other, partly because we were all friends, partly because we each knew our own turn was coming. That is, we were all gentle except for the senior faculty member. Every session his criticisms were harsh, strident, even personal. Week after week he tore into us in turn.

On the next to last session a close friend of mine presented a long theoretical paper filled with abstract, formal distinctions. The writing was pedantic, the argument pompous. I was rather sharp in my comments, and, as usual, the critical professor could barely contain his contempt for this piece of graduate student pretentiousness. Surprisingly, the anthropology professor praised the effort and encouraged my friend to keep at the project he had undertaken.

The next week we discussed the draft of the village study done by the hypercritical professor. Naturally, we attacked him from every angle, but he smiled and lightly dismissed all our comments as trivial. The senior anthropologist began to talk. His language was formal, even ornate, and his manner excessively polite. But as he talked it became clear that he had serious and substantial criticisms of the draft. The author dismissed these remarks, too, and blithely said that since his training was not as an anthropologist, he didn't need to accept any of the methods or principles or criteria of the cultural anthropologist.

The anthropologist said, "I'm sorry you said that, because now I think you will have to hear in some detail what I think of your study." He reached into his desk, pulled out a thick sheaf of papers, and read what in all my experience as an academic was the single most devastating critique I have ever heard. He ended by saying, "I do not think you understand human beings or their communities. The people you describe are not real, and the village you have described does not exist. In the name of anthropology I beg you not to publish this book." I have often pondered with wonderment this professor who could be a gentle encourager one week and a ruthless buzz saw of a critic the next.

This next story occurred a few years ago, at a foundation workshop for liberal arts faculty from many different colleges and universities. I was conducting a seminar on movies, and the night before I had shown the great Marcel Ophuls documentary about the Nazi occupation of France, *The Sorrow and the Pity*. About fifteen attended the seminar—a random group of academics from different schools and disciplines.

A political scientist from Texas started the discussion. He was Dutch by birth, and he said he wanted to talk about the other side of what it meant to have fought in the Resistance. During the war, when he was a very little boy, his father, a hero of the Resistance, used to go out at night to lead his group in acts of sabotage against the German occupation. The Dutchman said that what he remembered was his mother's terror every night and her constant screaming at his father not to go out to get himself killed, leaving her a widow with small children to raise.

Across the table a drama teacher from California then talked about his childhood. He, too, had been a small child during the war, but his family was German, and his father had been in the German army in the conquest and occupation of France. He said that during the Ophuls' movie when there were shots of the German army parading in triumph through Paris, he looked to see if he could recognize his father's face in the ranks of marching soldiers. He said his father was involved in antipartisan campaigns in France and later in Holland. And then he said, "Our fathers may actually have tried to kill each other."

I was sufficiently moved by this to tell my own story about the Ophuls' documentary. At one point Ophuls describes an incident in which the Vichy French authorities rounded up about twelve hundred French Jewish children and tried to give them to the Nazis. The Nazis said they didn't want them, and while the Vichy and Nazi bureaucrats argued back and forth the children were kept in the local railroad station. Finally, the Nazis agreed to take them, so they were loaded onto a train, shipped to Auschwitz, and gassed. When my grandfather left Russia as a young man at the end of the last century, he first went to France, but after a year he decided to move to America. If he had chosen to stay in France, I very likely would have been one of those unfortunate children.

Another member of the seminar, a shy theologian from Minnesota responded by talking about the ironies of life. His wife, who was German and half Jewish, was also a child during the war. Near the end of the war the German authorities began to round up the remaining German Jews for shipment to the extermination camps. She and her sister were then living with their grandmother in Berlin, who knew that the the girls would soon be arrested. So the old woman sent them to some distant relatives who lived in the country. The grandmother was shortly arrested and killed, and the Berlin police sent the records of the girls to the police headquarters of Dresden, the city near where the girls were staying. When Dresden was obliterated in the worst firebombing of the European war, the police station and all its records were destroyed, and the Nazi authorities never caught up with the girls before the war ended.

With this fourth story the line separating a serious academic seminar discussion from a completely unexpected personal encounter was thoroughly blurred. When the class ended, the Dutch political scientist and the German drama teacher walked off together and spent the day, as I learned later, talking to each other about their fathers, a subject neither had talked about for over twenty years. That may have been the single most extraordinary class I ever attended. I wish I could take credit for it as a teacher.

All these anecdotes were deliberately chosen from my experience as a student rather than from my much longer career as a teacher. Teachers tend to forget what it was like to be a student. But each of us were students before we were teachers.

What I want to focus on for the bulk of my remarks is the teaching process. When there is talk of reforming education, of energizing the classroom, the focus is commonly on the curriculum: what we teach, what we do not teach, what we require, and what we leave to a student's choice. I have no quarrel with this concern. I enjoy a good knock-down-and-drag-out fight with my colleagues as much as anybody. In talking about teaching, however, I do not want to talk about curriculum beyond assuming that we are talking about a college classroom.

Recently there has been a good deal of interest in students and their intellectual and emotional development during the collegiate years. William Perry's work at the Harvard Study Center in articulating a set of sequential intellectual stages through which all college students are alleged to move is interesting and provocative, as is Lawrence Kohlberg's work in setting forth an analogous set of stages of moral development. Joseph Katz has described in detail the process of personality growth during the college years. The serious scholarly study of the development of college students can serve as a valuable and necessary corrective to the deeply ingrained tendency of academics to view problems of college education in formal curricular terms.

In addition to these research developments, there has been a general growth of interest in and sensitivity to a number of factors that powerfully affect, for better or worse, the education of students. I am thinking of such things as talent and personality, gender, class, and culture. Each of these factors is important in that they act as filters, as the mediating elements that block or facilitate, distort or enhance, the efforts of teachers. All teachers have experienced the intense frustration of trying to get through intellectually to a bright, talented student who is clinically depressed or paranoically suspicious. The feminist movement has taught us something valuable about the terrible price that we pay for the conscious and, even worse, unconscious gender stereotyping to which we are susceptible.

A student's economic class and ethnic background can profoundly limit and shape teachers' pedagogical efforts in ways they cannot control and often do not even perceive. On the other hand, the amazing diversities of personality and talent, gender, class, and ethnicity that increasingly characterize students are the very ground on which their most significant educational and personal developments are built. A great deal could be said about these mediating factors, and a great deal more about them of which we are ignorant. But I want to bracket them, too.

I don't want to talk about students any more than I want to talk about curriculum. I shall assume that we are discussing college students attending a reasonably serious educational institution. College students are in school because they want to be, not because they are required to be by law, as many high school students are. College students are in school and attending classes because they want something. The faculty have what they want. Students want what the faculty have so badly that they will do all kinds of strange, painful, unnatural things if that is what they have to do to get what the teachers have to offer. At the University of Chicago, for example, the students pay enormous sums of money, work long hours at their assigned schoolwork, and live well below the normally accepted poverty line for the privilege of being taught by me.

Instead of talking about curriculum or students and their development, I want to talk about what I think is the single most important element in higher education, the element that is most neglected in talk of education. I want to talk about the teachers and what we do.

In some respects institutions of higher education spend tremendous amounts of time thinking about faculty—about academic credentials, about research and publication, especially at reappointment and promotion time. I am not referring to these dimensions of teaching; they are all too familiar to us. I want to reflect, rather, on the teaching process itself, about what happens in a classroom when a teacher stands (or sits) before a group of students and conducts a class for an hour or so several times a week for a semester.

We all know that some students learn and some do not, or at least not very much. We all know that some of us seem to be better at getting students to learn than others, and we all know from bitter experience that sometimes we do our job well, but that too often we do not. If other teachers are like me and my colleagues at the University of Chicago, they regularly trade stories over coffee about how they made a point in a clever way, or smoothly handled a particularly difficult question, and so on. We rarely tell stories about how, being poorly prepared for yesterday's class, we completely confused the explanation of the central point of the lecture. Or how, no matter how many different ways we made a point, the students never quite seemed to grasp it. But again, I don't want to talk about these little victories and defeats that make up the daily life of a teacher. And I don't want to talk about the nuts and bolts advice that we can give each other to improve performance in the classroom. Advice and help are important, and most college faculties can do a great deal more than they usually do to help each other become more effective teachers.

What I want to ask instead is what we do in the classroom, all of us, no matter what our subject matter, regardless of whether we are teaching a lecture course with several hundred students or a seminar with only a few, whether it is an introductory course for first-year students or an advanced course for seniors. This question is rarely asked because we assume that the answer is obvious. What we do in the classroom is teach our subject, whatever that may be. We teach the students because we know the subject and they do not; we have knowledge and they are ignorant. Teaching is the process by which knowledge of the subject is transferred from the teacher to the student.

Obviously, teaching involves some such process as this, but what is not so obvious is what it is that the teacher knows that is transferred to the student. Teachers know a lot of things. They know lots and lots of facts. Historians know dates and names; chemists know many different chemical compounds and many formulas; anthropologists know many strange customs of many strange people, and so forth. This is the most superficial notion of the teacher's knowledge.

We are all familiar with the dreadful student who has committed gobs of facts to memory (or to a computer's data base) and who can spew them back on demand. Knowledge does involve the accumulation of independent bits and pieces of information. Teachers do have lots of information about their subject, and students frequently do not. And we do demand of our students that they become informed—the more informed the better. Students usually understand this demand and are usually prepared to spend time and energy learning the facts. They may complain that we ask too much, and we, since we have known the facts for so long that they are second nature, may forget how hard it is to absorb them in seemingly limitless quantities. Still, students tend to be curious about things, and young minds—most of them are young—do have an amazing capacity to absorb information.

The trouble with mere information, mere facts, is that by themselves, in the absence of an informing context, they are nearly useless. To read a dozen journal articles about a particular point and to learn all they have to say about it is a virtual waste of time if the student does not know that a later, thirteenth article describes an important new discovery that renders the previous twelve articles obsolete. To memorize the elements of the periodic table is an achievement, but a rather trivial one compared to understanding how and why nature should have arranged it that the fundamental elements are related in such a neat and orderly way.

Over and over as we teach the facts we try to get our students to see that the facts need to be ordered, to be arranged, to be put into some kind of context that renders them intelligible as a whole rather than keeping them isolated bits and pieces of information. Without such a context knowledge is chaotic, largely useless, and ultimately meaningless. If we want students to become learned, we must teach them more than the bare facts. We must teach them the contexts in which the facts become meaningful.

With this shift from the facts to their significance we encounter a new and quite different meaning for the activity of teaching, a meaning that our naturally curious students often have trouble grasping. If the facts have no significance without a context, then we can be said to teach the facts in order to get at their meaning, in order to understand their significance. Students frequently have trouble understanding this. Struggling to absorb the facts, they are often dismayed to discover that the facts are not the end but a means to the end.

There are lots of names for the things that give meaning or significance to facts. Depending on the field, they may be called theories or ideas or concepts or laws or hypotheses or points of view or—to use an old-fashioned term that

I rather favor—principles. To learn the periodic table does not require memorizing the particular facts contained within it but grasping the principle that organizes it. In studying the history of the Second World War, students are likely to become aware of many battles in every part of the world. Yet they will probably be asked to focus on relatively few of them. The battle of Stalingrad, for example, was, from the point of view of some historians, a turning point, perhaps the turning point of the whole war. To grasp its importance is to grasp something about the shape of the entire war.

Thus, to know a subject and to be able to teach it teachers must know its principles as well as its facts. But teaching principles is quite different from teaching facts. The desire for facts is essentially an expression of that natural curiosity inherent in all humans. But the need to find a principle that will order the facts is an expression of our natural desire for order, for coherence, for a patterned whole. Yet facts and principles are mutually dependent, for if the facts without a principle are meaningless and chaotic, then principles without facts are empty abstractions.

Students learn facts by committing them to memory. But how do they learn principles? To commit a principle or a theory to memory is to treat it like a fact. To be able to state a fact is, in a significant sense, to know it; to be able to state a theory or a principle is not necessarily to understand it in a significant way. To understand a theory, to grasp a principle, means being able to use it, to apply it. To put the matter differently, the nature of principles lies in their capacity to be employed. They are methods, procedures, ways of seeing and doing.

To learn a fact is to gain information; to learn a principle is to acquire a power, an ability, a capacity to organize facts, to link ideas, to think. When we teach facts, we expand the scope of our students' minds; when we teach a theory or a principle, we add a new power to their minds. The students can now do something they could not do before. They can organize facts into coherent wholes. More than that, they can now begin to look for relevant facts for themselves. They now have a principle of relevance that empowers them to decide for themselves what is and is not important, what is and is not relevant to the matter at hand. Learning the facts, committing them to memory, requires an active mind. Yet compared to the level of activity involved in learning a theory, the mind is practically inert while it memorizes.

No teacher teaches a single theory or only one method of procedure. During a semester-long course we commonly teach many principles, several theories, a variety of points of view. But these theories, interpretations, and hypotheses are not unconnected. They are normally related to each other as parts of a single discipline, be it physics, chemistry, history, or literature. We all profess some discipline or other. We may well be specialists in a branch of that discipline, but our training, our general expertise, is in that discipline as a whole. As we teach our students the procedures, methods, and points of view that compose our discipline, we are gradually teaching them the capacity to work in that discipline as physicists, chemists, historians, or humanists.

Every course in electricity and magnetism is also a course in physics. A course on the French Revolution is also a course in history. After a single course in the field or even a few, a student is not likely to be as knowledgeable as the professors, as sophisticated in the ways of the discipline. But the difference is one of degree, not of kind. If students have learned what we have to teach, they have at least begun to function for themselves within the discipline. To the extent that they, too, are practitioners of the discipline, they cease to be mere students. They have begun to be our colleagues.

As colleagues, even very junior colleagues, they naturally begin to do to us what we do with our colleagues all the time: judge us and the quality of our work in the field. This is a trying time for a teacher. The more successful we are in empowering our students to do what we can do, the higher will be the standards and the more grinding the scrutiny by which they judge us.

Once in a while, all of us teach a class on material with which we are not very well acquainted or bluff our way past a question to which we don't know the answer. On a bad day, we are tempted to chide a student for asking a stupid question, rather than admitting our ignorance to the class. Sometimes we even give in to that temptation. These are pedagogical sins, but minor ones: sins of a little laziness, a little sloppiness, a little ignorance. They are not the big sins of plagiarism, falsifying research, deliberately distorting the truth. How embarrassing it is to realize that the better our students, the more likely they are to see that we sometimes have succumbed to the temptation to sin.

So, we teach the facts of the matter, we teach our discipline, and, finally and inescapably, we teach by example; we become paradigms. Teaching, like every other significant human activity, has fundamental ethical and moral dimensions. The relationship between student and teacher is a moral one and carries with it an intrinsic moral code that cannot be violated except at the peril of education itself. Explicitly we teach students to have respect for the facts, that is, for the truth. Yet occasionally we fudge an answer to a question, thereby implicitly teaching that we don't really believe what we say. We can all supply plenty of examples from our own experience both as students and as teachers of the ways teachers, by their behavior, can significantly undercut and debilitate their own teaching. The reverse is also true: a teacher who understands and respects the ethical imperatives of teaching can have an extraordinary impact for good upon his or her students.

A classroom, then, is a place where teaching can occur, where professors can teach their subject. But that subject is always multidimensional and complexly structured. We teach the facts, we teach our discipline, and we teach the example of ourselves. In teaching the facts, we point students toward the truth; in teaching our discipline and thereby displaying the order and coherence of the world, we provide them with an experience of beauty; and in teaching by example, we inescapably present some lessons about the good.

Truth, beauty, and goodness were the three highest human values in ancient Greek philosophy, the fundamental and ultimate goals of human action and aspiration. Ultimately, then, these are what we teach, each of us in his or her own way. If we teach honestly with some awareness of the full human implications of what we are doing, how can our classrooms help but be places of passionate energy, places where teaching, of necessity, becomes a kind of love? And that is why I gave up a reasonably paid and important administrative position to return to teaching. How could money, power, and a personal secretary compete with the opportunity to teach?

PART IV   GLIMPSES OF PLATO'S ART

17 The Value of Failure
Structure and Argument in Republic, Book I

My text is book I of Plato's *Republic,* but my theme is failure—philosophical failure. Let me explain what I mean by failure in the context of philosophy and why we should bother to reflect on such a dismal topic. I begin with its opposite: success.

Kant, in his *Critique of Pure Reason,* claims that he has effected a Copernican revolution in philosophy, a revolution that will rescue science from Hume's skepticism and place it on solid ground, just as Copernicus, with the elegant simplicities of the heliocentric theory, had rescued astronomy from the endlessly proliferating complexities of the Ptolemaic system. More than a century before Kant, Descartes, perplexed and confused by the scholastic philosophy that he had learned in college, sought indubitable knowledge by engaging in the experiment of radical doubt. The experiment succeeded brilliantly with his discovery that, although it was possible to doubt anything and everything, he could not doubt his own existence without at the same time affirming it. He thus established, so he thought, a firm truth from which all the truths of mathematics and science could be derived.

Contemporary with Descartes, Thomas Hobbes, distressed by the disorder and insecurity caused by civil strife in England, argued, in his work *Leviathan,* that he had discovered and articulated the rational, scientific principles of a sound, stable, and satisfactory political order. About two millennia before that, when Aristotle undertook the study of first philosophy, that awesome science of metaphysics, he devoted the first three books of his treatise to the analysis of the profound problems implied in the very notion of such a science and to a detailed account of the unsuccessful attempts of his predecessors to establish it. After treating these difficulties and failures, he announced triumphantly at the beginning of book IV, "There is a [distinct] science, which investigates being as being. . . . And this is not the same as any of the so-called special sciences."

These claims by Kant, Descartes, Hobbes, and Aristotle are among the glorious moments in the long, distinguished history of Western philosophy. Later philosophers have questioned them, even rejected them, but no one seriously doubts the greatness of the achievements embodied in *The Critique of Pure Reason, The Meditations, Leviathan,* and the *Metaphysics.* These four books could almost stand as paradigms, each in its distinctive way, of what philosophers try to do—that is, state a problem and then think their way through to an adequate solution. These books are models of philosophical success.

Philosophy doesn't always work out that way. Fundamental philosophical problems are difficult to perceive and articulate, and genuine solutions are even harder to arrive at. Most of us, in fact, are content to live with the original muddle in which we normally find ourselves.

Some of us, not content with that, have undertaken the serious study of what the philosophers have said. We seek at least reasonable clarity on what the issues are and what those extraordinary thinkers have had to say about them. But few of us have been able to think our way through to a successful conclusion. The ones who do that are the true philosophers—Kant, Hobbes, Descartes, Aristotle. They, along with a handful of others, are the great ones whose works we study. Great philosophers are excessively rare—maybe one or two come along each century.

The problems with which philosophy deals are not specialized or arcane, at least in the muddled form in which we first encounter them. Problems on the frontiers of science, however, are frequently difficult to understand. The question, for example, of what holds the nucleus of the atom together concerns physicists, and I might have to study physics for years before I could even understand the question. But the problems of philosophy are not like that. They arise out of the stuff of everyday life. The *Metaphysics* of Aristotle is, indeed, a very difficult book, but the question of what is real and what is not is obvious to all of us. Similarly, Descartes' *Meditations* is complex and demanding, but we all can understand and share the desire to establish what we know, or what we think we know, on a sound footing free of doubt. So there would seem to be in philosophy a tension between the commonplace origin of the problems with which it deals, on the one hand, and the difficult, rarely achieved successes in resolving those problems, on the other hand.

Nor are the successes of the great philosophers necessarily accepted as such by their fellow philosophers. On the contrary, philosophers, in contrast to scientists, are notorious for their failure to make progress, to achieve agreement on anything, and to proceed from that agreement to attack further problems. Every seminal thinker starts all over again from scratch and frequently enough begins by displaying all the errors and inadequacies of philosophical predecessors.

So the history of philosophy is not a history of momentous successes but, rather, a history of apparent successes that turn out later to be failures. Over the centuries philosophers and nonphilosophers alike have frequently been scandalized by this state of affairs. They have called for reform, heroic efforts, or despairing abandonment of the whole enterprise as hopeless. What I find fascinating is that after two and a half millennia of struggling with the fundamental problems of the discipline, most philosophers still feel that they must either overcome the problem of failure or abandon the enterprise of searching for answers. Nobody seems prepared to live with failure as the natural condition of philosophy. Nobody even seems very much interested in philosophical failure as such, except to try to avoid or overcome it.

This lack of interest in failure pervades the entire history of Western philosophy. Furthermore, most efforts to philosophize are failures, but philosophers never record those failures. We have no classic philosophical treatises that start with a clear analysis of a fundamental problem and then, after five hundred pages of profound and difficult analysis and argument, conclude by admitting that there is no solution to this problem. All the great books of the philosophical tradition present themselves as successful. Such confident affirmations stand in sharp contrast to the overwhelming evidence, both of the tradition itself and of the actual experience of most of us who have tried to engage in philosophy.

There is an exception to the general rule. There is one philosopher who seems to have been aware of the predominance of failure over success in the philosophical enterprise, and he undertook to record cases of philosophical failure. I am referring to Plato. His *Dialogues* stand at the very beginning of the Western tradition of philosophy, and Alfred North Whitehead, in one of his most famous epigrams, says that the entire tradition of European philosophy consists of a series of footnotes to Plato. By that he means that the tradition of Western thought largely consists of elaborations and expansions of ideas and philosophical intuitions found in Plato. But one of the most conspicuous features of the *Dialogues,* that most of the philosophical arguments are failures to find solutions, has never been taken up, reflected on, or replicated by later philosophers. Plato remains the first and only philosopher to record serious efforts at philosophical speculation that ended in failure. And he did it over and over again.

Scholars and philosophers have long noticed this embarrassing fact, and they have, almost without exception, explained it away. The failed dialogues are labeled "inconclusive," as if the standard invitation of Socrates at the end of each to try once more was ever taken up by Euthyphro or Meno, as if the result would have been any different if someone did so. Some scholars classify the failed dialogues as "youthful" works, written by Plato before he had made up his mind about the problem being discussed. They argue that these failed dialogues record an early stage in the development of Plato's thought, and they do not see them as pointing to a significant fact about the nature of philosophy. Others suggest that these problems have no answers. By this they mean that philosophy itself doesn't work or that the answers don't matter; what counts is the pure activity of thinking and talking. Why a serious person would continue for a lifetime to talk (like Socrates) or to write (like Plato) about problems that are insoluble is hard to fathom. In what follows I propose to discuss philosophical failure. I don't want to avoid it, deny it, explain it away, or use it as an excuse for despair.

Although Plato wrote many dialogues that end in failure, he did write one dialogue that early on appears to end in failure but starts up again after book I with a direct challenge to that failure, constructs a massive, even epic, argument, and then ends with an apparently triumphant and successful resolution to the problem. I am referring to the *Republic,* book I, which ends after Socrates has shown Cephalus, Polemarchus, and Thrasymachus that their diverse views of justice are all inadequate. It looks so much like one of the so-called inconclusive or youthful dialogues that some scholars have said that it was written to stand alone.

I agree that book I of the *Republic* is very like many of the short, failed conversations of Socrates. But I suggest that the rest of the dialogue, books II–X, are intended to show us the magnificently successful conversation that lurks in the aftermath of a serious failure if one responds to the failure adequately. I suggest that every failed dialogue of Plato's has an implied sequel, an unrealized equivalent of books II–X of the *Republic,* although Plato, an economical writer, has given us only this one example of how to deal with failure. I propose to look at book I to see if we can discover why the conversation there fails and then to look at books II–X to see what we might learn from that failure.

Book I breaks down into four parts. First is the dramatic scene in which Socrates and Glaucon, returning to Athens after seeing the festival of Bendis, meet Polemarchus, Adeimantus, and some others and go with them to Cephalus' house. Second is the brief, charming conversation of Socrates and Cephalus in which the topic of justice is introduced and Cephalus leaves after acknowledging that his barely articulated notion of justice is not adequate. Third is the more substantial conversation between Socrates and Polemarchus, Cephalus' son, in which Socrates first gets Polemarchus to develop something like a formal definition of justice and then subjects that definition to a systematic cross-examination, after which Polemarchus admits that his definition is thoroughly untenable. The fourth and last part of book I, Socrates' argument with the sophist Thrasymachus, is by far the longest and most complicated part, taking up about two-thirds of book I and involving at least three different statements by Thrasymachus of his account of justice—all of them refuted by Socrates. At the beginning of book II, Glaucon and Adeimantus, the older half-brothers of Plato, initiate the successful argument of the dialogue by expressing their dissatisfaction with Socrates' refutation of Thrasymachus. They insist that Socrates give an adequate account of justice, and to ensure that he does so, they each openly defend Thrasymachus' final and most radical position by making an impassioned and powerful argument in favor of injustice.

Now let me provide more detail. In the opening scene of book I, as Socrates and Glaucon are returning to Athens, Socrates is physically restrained by Polemarchus' slave boy, more or less at the order of his master. In the conversation that follows, Glaucon three times answers a question directed at Socrates, thereby minding Socrates' business. Polemarchus tries to persuade Socrates to come to his home with him and other friends by more or less promising Socrates that he will be given dinner and will see a torch race on horseback later in the evening. Since they talk all night, Polemarchus' double commitment to dinner and a torch race is not kept; that is, the promise of what they will do turns out to be untrue, and the obligation that he accepted in return for Socrates' company is not fulfilled. In brief, Polemarchus neither tells the truth nor pays his debt to Socrates. On a second reading, we see that the deeds of the opening scene anticipate the speeches of the *Republic* about justice.

Polemarchus, who views himself as Socrates' friend, opens the conversation with Socrates with a lighthearted but explicit threat of violence when he insists that because they are outnumbered, Socrates and Glaucon must either come home with him or fight against heavy odds. That is, he treats Socrates as if he were an enemy, someone subject to coercion, rather than a friend to be helped. Finally, then, when Socrates attempts to avoid the two alternatives posed by Polemarchus—either fight against heavy odds (and probably lose) or give in to threatened coercion—by suggesting a third alternative, that he, Socrates, might persuade Polemarchus to let them go, Polemarchus asks in response, "Could you really persuade, if we don't listen?" (327d). It is after this exchange that Polemarchus, at the gentle suggestion of Adeimantus, undertakes to persuade Socrates to stay by making his double promise of dinner and a torch race. Thus, Polemarchus gets Socrates to come home with him by abandoning his own strategy of coercion, actual and threatened, and by adopting Socrates' strategy of persuasion—that is, he gets his way by giving up the traditional prerogative of the strong and instead employing the traditional tactics of the weak: coercion is abandoned for persuasion.

In the rest of book I, Cephalus identifies justice with telling the truth and paying one's debts, Polemarchus defines it as helping friends and harming enemies, and Thrasymachus says that justice is the interest of the stronger. In book IV, Socrates himself defines justice as minding one's own business. So the opening scene of book I is filled with violations of justice as that term is explicitly defined by the participants in the later discussion.

The three accounts of justice that constitute the bulk of book I are, indeed, all failures, but the brief opening scene surely suggests that at least part of the failure is due to the failure by the individuals who present the definitions to understand the implications of what they themselves say and do. But the opening episode is not just a random series of small acts of apparent injustice, either. The conversation is carefully ordered. It displays a developing pattern that begins with the slave boy restraining Socrates by grabbing his cloak and concludes with a remark of Socrates as they all go off together to the house of Cephalus, "Well, if it is so resolved, that's how we must act" (328b). The scene thus moves from simple necessity to complete freedom. It moves from Socrates coerced— enslaved by the slave boy—to the unanimous and unforced agreement of a group of friends to spend the evening together. They freely unite into a congenial group to share their leisure time in the pleasurable activities of eating, talking, and observing a spectacle.

Socrates and his now expanded group of friends soon arrive at the house of Cephalus. There they discover Thrasymachus the sophist surrounded by a large group and, sitting off by himself, Cephalus, the aged father of Polemarchus. Socrates sits with Cephalus, and the conversation that ensues, though brief and hardly an argument in the conventional sense, is nevertheless charming, thoroughly in character, and deeply significant for book I and indeed the whole of the *Republic*.

It is in the context of this discussion that the theme of justice first emerges explicitly in the dialogue, and it is worth noting how this occurs. In answer to Socrates' question about old age, Cephalus says it is not so bad, at least for decent men of good character like himself. Playing a gentle devil's advocate, Socrates suggests that it may be Cephalus' wealth, not his character, that makes old age manageable. Cephalus agrees that money helps, but insists it is not the whole story.

Socrates, who is himself proverbially poverty-stricken, asks Cephalus to name the greatest good his wealth has provided. In response Cephalus beautifully describes how, when the end of life is imminent, the traditional stories of an afterlife with a final judgment, stories scorned in youth, begin to appear to be possibly true. In the face of that frightening possibility, says Cephalus, "the possession of money contributes a great deal to not having to cheat or lie to any man against one's will, and moreover, to not having to depart for that other place frightened because one owes some sacrifice to a god, or money to a human being" (331b).

But, says Socrates, if a friend gave you a weapon to hold and then, in an obviously deranged state, demanded it back, you wouldn't return it, would you? Of course not, says Cephalus. So then, says Socrates, "speaking the truth and giving back what one takes isn't the definition of justice." When Cephalus unhesitatingly agrees, his son Polemarchus leaps to his defense, and with a laugh Cephalus leaves for the sacrifices (331b–d).

The long conversation with Polemarchus that follows is a real argument that breaks into several distinct parts. First, Socrates gets Polemarchus to explain what he means by "paying one's debts," and as he explains, Polemarchus shifts from his father's understanding of justice to the poet Simonides' view and finally to his own, namely, that justice is helping friends and harming enemies.

In the ensuing cross-examination Socrates questions, first, what the just man does and, second, who friends and enemies are. In answer to the first question it turns out that besides helping friends in war, the just man is mainly useful for taking care of things, mostly money, when there is no use for it. Justice, however, is useless when money and other things are useful. Furthermore, in order to help friends in war and take care of their money, the just man has to know how to protect them and their money from enemies and thieves; that is, he has to be a kind of thief himself.

With respect to the identification of friends and enemies, Socrates points out that if we are friends of a bad person and enemies of a good person, Polemarchus' definition would require us to help the bad and hurt the good. Polemarchus, horrified at this, redefines his terms to make good people friends and bad people enemies. But Socrates then gets him to acknowledge that since harming someone makes the injured person worse, and justice is good, to harm someone is to make that person unjust, making it the function of the just man to promote injustice. Again, Polemarchus is horrified, and he and Socrates conclude that justice cannot mean helping friends and harming enemies, for it cannot be the nature of justice to make anyone unjust (336a).

At this point Thrasymachus, who has been growing restless, breaks into the discussion and takes over the argument from Polemarchus. The ensuing debate with Socrates, which goes to the end of book I, basically falls into three parts, each of which is initiated with a different interpretation by Thrasymachus of his basic definition of justice as the interest of the stronger. Before he gives his definition, however, Thrasymachus attacks Socrates as hypocritical and as attempting to win honor by questioning others rather than risking attack by giving his own answers.

Thrasymachus refuses to give his account of justice unless Socrates pays for it. When Glaucon offers to pay for Socrates, Thrasymachus presents his definition. After some prodding by Socrates, he explains that by the stronger he means the rulers of communities, and by the weaker he means the ordinary, law-abiding citizens. The interest of the stronger, he asserts, is embodied in the law of the community, the law that the rulers pass and enforce in their own interest, so that the citizens are constrained by the law to do what is to the interest of their rulers. Socrates proceeds to question this cynical, realist view of justice. He points out that if the rulers make a mistake and pass a law that is not to their own advantage, the subjects would therefore be constrained by the law to do what is not to the interest of the rulers, but this would be just, because they would be obeying the law.

Before Thrasymachus can respond, Polemarchus breaks in to affirm Socrates' conclusion that in this case, it would be just to do what is against the interest of the stronger. Then Cleitophon, one of those sitting around Thrasymachus before Socrates and his friends arrived, comes to Thrasymachus' defense. For a brief interlude Polemarchus and Cleitophon argue, the one restating the Socratic argument, the other defending the position of Thrasymachus. Cleitophon says that Thrasymachus meant that justice is what the stronger think or believe is in their interest. Thrasymachus, however, disdainfully rejects Cleitophon's help, which would rescue him from the immediate problem posed by Socrates' argument but only by weakening his overall position. Instead, Thrasymachus restates his position by asserting that the stronger never make a mistake, at least insofar as they are stronger. In effect, he now has redefined the stronger to mean those who know what their true interest is and can enact it as law. Thrasymachus, in this second version of his position, defines justice as the art of knowing how to bring about what is in one's interest. This art is the art of political rule.

Socrates examines this new definition by exploring the general features of an art or craft. Every art, he shows, is devised to provide what is advantageous or to the interest of someone or something—medicine, for example, serves the interest of the body, not that of the doctor. The doctor in the strict sense is not a moneymaker but someone who cares for the sick. This means, however, that each art exercises its power in the interest of the weaker instead of in the interest of the stronger.

At this point Thrasymachus breaks into a harangue in which he likens the rulers of cities to shepherds with their flocks. The rulers, he says, regard their cities the way shepherds regard their flocks, as a source of food, clothing, and revenue. The laws that rulers pass, enforce, and persuade their subjects to obey are always in the interest of the rulers. Thus the rulers require that their subjects obey the law, which is in the rulers' interest. But they reserve for themselves the right to do anything they want. They demand that their subjects act justly—that is, according to the law—but they themselves are free to act with complete injustice. Human happiness, he says, is complete tyranny, the art of doing whatever you want, the art of perfect injustice.

With this speech Thrasymachus has, at last, fully revealed his position. He is an immoralist who praises injustice and thinks it stronger and better than justice. Before examining this version of Thrasymachus' understanding of justice, Socrates goes back to the notion of the perfect art as the skill of caring for the interests of what the art deals with rather than the interests of the practitioner. The result, he says, is that shepherds who practice their art work for the good of the sheep, and rulers rule for the sake of their subjects. This means, he says, that no one wishes to rule voluntarily because it is against his own interest. Rulers demand wages, he says. The rulers of cities, he continues, must be paid with money or honor or a penalty for not ruling, or they will refuse to rule. They must practice the wage earner's art in addition to shepherding, or medicine, or ruling, if they are to be persuaded to work for the good of someone else. Glaucon interrupts to ask about this third kind of wage, the penalty for not ruling. Avoiding the penalty, Socrates explains, is the wage that the best people earn for ruling; it is simply the privilege of not being ruled by others worse than oneself.

Socrates then confronts what he says is Thrasymachus' true position: that injustice is better than justice, especially when it is perfect injustice, presumably the injustice of the tyrant. This is a difficult position to attack, he admits, because Thrasymachus now treats injustice, not justice, as the virtue, as what is to be praised and desired. He asserts that the unjust man is prudent, wise, and good and that the unjust man thus claims to deserve getting the better of everyone. The just man is an innocent fool who takes only what is his due and does not try to get the better of other just men, only of those who are unjust. Socrates now shows that those who are wise and learned in some area of knowledge try to overcome only those who are ignorant, not other knowledgeable men. But the ignorant try to overcome, to outdo, both those who are knowledgeable and those who are ignorant. Thus the man who aspires to overcome everyone, the unjust man, is not wise and good but foolish and ignorant, whereas the just man is revealed as wise and good. Thrasymachus resists the argument and has to be dragged along. Socrates notes that Thrasymachus sweats heavily and, at the point where his position seems to have been refuted, blushes as well. Socrates, always the gentleman, suggests the blush is because of the summer heat, not profound embarrassment at being bested. At any rate, Thrasymachus no longer resists Socrates' arguments and docilely agrees to a long list of conclusions, all of which seem to reaffirm the conventional moral view that he had originally rejected.

These are the conclusions: Injustice produces faction and quarrels, while justice produces harmony and unanimity. Injustice renders cities and individuals impotent; it makes the unjust man an enemy to himself, to just men, and finally to the gods. Virtue, or excellence, on the other hand, is the ability of anything to function well. Justice is the excellence of the soul, the function of which is to live and to rule well, and injustice is the vice; so the just man will live well and be happy, and the unjust man will live badly and be wretched.

Thus, concludes Socrates, justice, not injustice, is in the interest of all of us. "Let that," says Thrasymachus, "be the fill of your banquet at the festival of Bendis, Socrates." "I owe it to you, Thrasymachus," replies Socrates, "since you have grown gentle and have left off being hard on me. However, I have not had a fine banquet, but it's my fault, not yours. So long as I do not know what the just is, I shall hardly know whether it is a virtue or not and whether the one who has it is unhappy or happy" (354b). And so book I ends, with Socrates admitting, after he has reduced Thrasymachus to embarrassed silence, that the sophist may be right after all.

Book I, then, seems to be a failure on all counts. Neither Cephalus', Polemarchus', nor Thrasymachus' views of justice can withstand the withering force of the Socratic cross-examination. Even Socrates is not satisfied, because although he has demonstrated the inability of the three interlocutors to successfully defend their views, he himself is not convinced that they are wrong. In the absence of an adequate account of what justice is, he says, he does not even know that Thrasymachus' radically immoral view is wrong. In the face of this uncertainty and perplexity, can we learn anything from book I? Can anything be salvaged from the general disorder and sense of failure?

Let me take a clue from my remarks about the opening scene of the dialogue, when Polemarchus first confronts Socrates. There is, as I pointed out, a good deal of injustice in the behavior of Polemarchus toward Socrates. Overall, the scene has a pattern, a structure, which is illuminating in itself and suggestive for an understanding of the entire *Republic*. In examining Socrates' conversations with Cephalus, Polemarchus, and Thrasymachus, I want to look at the individual arguments and to reflect on the overall pattern of the discussion.

The three conversations with Socrates are disturbing because the arguments he uses do not always seem valid or sound. Readers are frequently irritated by Socrates' slippery, even sophistical arguments. I have to admit that the arguments he directs at his interlocutors leave much to be desired. Indeed, not a single argument in book I is entirely free of some logical fallacy or defect. Some objection can always be made, some distinction drawn, some further inference teased out. Although the interlocutor does not do these things, the reader could. As always, Plato himself shows his readers how to do it within the dialogue itself.

Remember that in the conversation with Polemarchus, Socrates refutes the argument that justice is helping friends and harming enemies. But people sometimes make mistakes, so if enemies are actually good and just, and not bad and unjust, those who are good and just are justly harmed. Polemarchus is a decent young man who wants to be just—that is, to help his friends and harm his enemies—but he cannot accept this conclusion. In his perplexity he goes back to the premises of his position, admits that they were faulty, and proposes to correct them. Instead of defining a friend simply as one who seems to be good, he now proposes that a friend is someone who both seems and is good; someone who seems good but is not good is not a friend. This redefinition permits Polemarchus to escape the moral dilemma of having to assert that under some circumstances it is just to harm someone who has done nothing unjust. We, Plato's readers, are always free, like Polemarchus, to object to Socrates' arguments and to suggest changes that would enable us to escape unwanted consequences. We can do this whenever we catch Socrates in one of his tricky arguments. But once we start to argue in this way, we may find ourselves on a very slippery slope.

Here, for example, note what might happen when Polemarchus redefines friends. Although he never quite figures out the implications himself, it is clear that in trying to escape a moral dilemma he has opened up a Pandora's box of profound problems. In redefining friends as those who are in fact good, Polemarchus is now committed to discovering who the good are. Friendship has now become a problematic question of what we know rather than an obvious one of what we feel. More than that, to know who the good are further implies that one knows what the good itself is. Those who have read the whole *Republic* know that the most difficult point of the argument of the entire dialogue is the passage at the end of book VI where Socrates attempts to define the Good with a definition that entails nothing less than a comprehensive account of the structure of being itself.

Yes, Socrates' arguments leave much to be desired, and yes, we can, with some effort, see the deficiencies in those arguments and attempt to correct them. But that is only the beginning, for further problems emerge that need to be thought through. Those further problems are grist for Socrates' mill. Let us look at three of the arguments in book I, one from each of the interlocutors.

The degree to which we commonly do not think through the implications of our own position is perhaps most powerfully illustrated by Cephalus in book I. Consider Cephalus' reply to Socrates' question about the greatest good that he has received from his wealth. Cephalus starts by saying that his view will not be persuasive to many people; presumably only those persons of good character, like himself, who do not rail at old age will appreciate it. When a man grows old, he says, and faces the prospect of dying, he feels fear; perhaps those stories about punishments in the afterlife for misdeeds done here, stories that he used to laugh at in his youth, are true. Reflecting on this possibility, an old man is beset with fear and misgiving. He examines his life to see if he has done anything wrong. If he has done nothing wrong, then he has "sweet hope," as Pindar put it. The value of money, concludes Cephalus, is that it enables us to pay our debts—that is, to be just.

It is hard, when reading Cephalus' account of the best use of money, not to remember that Socrates was poor. Later in book I, when Thrasymachus refuses to tell the company what justice is unless he is paid in cash up front, Socrates pleads poverty, and Glaucon has to pay for him. If Cephalus is right about the real and best use of money, is Socrates thereby condemned to a life of injustice?

Before I answer, let me look more closely at the implications of what Cephalus says. Cephalus' fear of injustice has two parts: first, he doesn't want to cheat or lie to any man against his will, and, second, he doesn't want to die frightened because he owes some sacrifice to a god, or money to a human being. These apparently distinct possibilities are two aspects of the same situation. If you should die owing a god some sacrifice or a man some money, you have cheated or lied, for in contracting a money debt or an obligation to sacrifice, you have agreed—that is, promised—to pay back the money or make the sacrifice. By dying you have made it impossible to do so. Being a decent person, you probably didn't intend to die before you met your obligations. But that only means that you broke your promise—lied and cheated—against your will, not deliberately. The implication is clear: If you want to go to that other place without being in debt to god or man, even unwillingly, then you had better never borrow any money, and you had better make your obligatory sacrifices immediately, because you may die at any time.

But the argument has a further implication. If a friend in need comes to you for money, you, as a decent person in possession of some wealth, give it to him. But then either you or your friend may die before repayment. Thus by lending the money you have inadvertently caused your friend to break his promise, that is, to be unjust. Is it not obvious, as Polemarchus says a little later, that to make someone else unjust is itself unjust? The only fully logical and coherent solution to Cephalus' desire to go to that other place without cheating or lying or being in debt to god or man, even unwillingly, is the exact opposite of what he explicitly says. The solution is not to have any money at all— "neither a borrower nor a lender be." All this follows from the simple, unexamined assumption that one must pay back incurred debts, an assumption that Cephalus himself immediately rejects when he agrees that he would not return a weapon to a deranged friend.

But this leads to the further thought that we may commit injustice unintentionally in more ways than one. What if, for example, being ignorant of what justice is or what justice requires of us, we act in violation of it? If ignorance can lead to injustice, are we not impelled to at least attempt to replace our ignorance with knowledge?

So what does Cephalus do? Does he stay and talk to Socrates? Does he take advantage of the opportunity to talk to his friend and to find out about the one thing that obsesses him—the terrifying fear that he has been unintentionally unjust now that he is very close to the end of his life? Not at all. Unaware of the implications of his own position, he goes back to the sacrifices from which he has just come, hoping against hope that his wealth can compensate for his possibly misspent life.

In the conversation with Polemarchus, we confront step by step arguments rather than simple statements of belief. After defining justice as the art of helping friends and harming enemies, Polemarchus agrees that though useful in war, this art seems to be useless in peace except in money matters when money is not being used and thus needs to be kept safe. That is, he agrees with Socrates, that *justice is useful when money is useless, and vice versa*. Poor Polemarchus! He breaks into the discussion in order to defend his father's position against Socrates' attack, and within five minutes he affirms a conclusion that directly contravenes his father's major assertion about the relation of money and justice.

At the next step in the argument, Socrates apparently demonstrates, to Polemarchus' horror, that the art of justice is the art of thievery and that the just man is a thief. This conclusion precisely states the true position of Thrasymachus near the end of book I. The argument therefore carries the suggestion that long before Thrasymachus breaks into the conversation and steals the argument, Socrates knows what his views are and is preparing to deal with them.

The argument that Socrates makes to reach his conclusion—the just man is a thief—seems dubious at best. Socrates uses three examples, all supposedly analogous to the art of justice. He cites the boxer, who knows how to strike blows and is therefore good at warding them off; the doctor, who can guard against disease and is therefore also good at producing it; and the commander, who can guard an army and therefore is good at stealing the enemy's plans. The general conclusion is that a person who is good at keeping something is also good at stealing it. The specific conclusion is that the just man who is skilled at guarding money is also good at stealing it. The just man thus appears to be a kind of thief, and justice seems to be an art of stealing—for the benefit of friends and the harm of enemies, to be sure. Polemarchus, appalled, refuses to accept this conclusion but admits that he no longer knows what he meant originally, although he still thinks that justice is helping friends and harming enemies.

Of the three analogous examples Socrates uses, the first and the third, the boxer and the commander, are straightforward enough, although Socrates seems to misconstrue them for the purposes of his argument. Properly speaking, there is no distinct art of striking blows or guarding an army. There *is* an art of boxing and an art of leading men in war. A skilled boxer knows how to strike blows, and that very knowledge implies a knowledge of how to block them. The same is true of a military commander: to know how to guard men is the other side of knowing how to get around guards. The main point, however, is that it is an essential part of the boxer's and the general's skills to do both things: you can't be a skilled general unless you both guard your own army and successfully attack the enemy. And to be a skilled boxer requires that you both hit your opponent and prevent him from hitting you.

The second example, however, the case of the doctor, is qualitatively different from the other two. Socrates seems to include preventing disease as well as curing it within the art of medicine. Polemarchus accepts this without question, apparently forgetting that a minute earlier he had agreed that medicine was useless when people were not sick. The inclusion of prevention as well as cure in the art of medicine requires that we reexamine that earlier argument, where it was implicitly denied. This phenomenon, in which a later argument develops a point that requires a revision or at least a review of an earlier argument, happens over and over again in the *Republic*.

The art of medicine, on the one hand, and the arts of boxing and military command, on the other, are significantly different. It is no part of the doctor's art to give people diseases or to keep them sick. A doctor presumably has the knowledge to do so, but this would be a complete perversion of the medical art. The doctor might unintentionally make someone sick or fail to effect a cure, but in that case, the doctor would simply be incompetent, lacking full control of his art. If he intentionally uses his skill to make someone ill or to keep her so, it would be proper to call him a bad man, unjust.

This example of the doctor, then, displays something essential about the relation between justice and the special arts. Medicine is not a neutral body of knowledge about sickness and health: it is the art of preventing and healing illness. Apparently, then, when medicine is known and practiced as it should be, it is just. A doctor is not someone with a particular skill who may or may not be just; to be a skilled physician is necessarily to be just in the practice of the art.

Are there situations in which a doctor should use his art to make someone ill or to prevent him from getting better? In this all too possible case, what is at stake is not a problem for the art of medicine but a question of what is and is not just. So, the examples of the boxer and the general are much better supports for the notion that justice is a kind of thievery than is the example of the doctor. But they are not analogous to justice in this case, and the example of the doctor is.

The medical example does not support well the notion that the just man is a kind of thief except in the very limited sense of a potential thief. The knowledge of how to do something is part of the art. But sometimes the normal practice of the art forbids its being done. On the other hand, justice can entail protecting some things and attacking others, protecting the innocent, for example, and attacking law breakers and thieves. In such instances, the art of justice (if it is an art) might well require a thorough and practical knowledge of how law-breakers and thieves act, so that they can be either thwarted or caught and punished afterward.

In sum, the apparently ridiculous argument in which Socrates shows Polemarchus that the just man is a thief is interesting, suggestive, complex, and far less absurd than it appears at first glance. Interestingly, it strongly suggests that Thrasymachus is wrong when he argues a little later that the just man is a naive, ignorant, manipulable fool. But Thrasymachus discovers his error when he confidently attacks Socrates under the mistaken impression that as a just defender of justice, Socrates is no match for Thrasymachus' unscrupulous willingness to fight dirty in order to win. Socrates turns out to be far tougher, more skilled, and perhaps even more unscrupulous in argument than the wily sophist.

The first substantial argument between Socrates and Thrasymachus is short and to the point.

"While I, too, agree," says Socrates, "that the just is something of advantage, you add to it and assert that it's the advantage of the stronger, and I don't know whether it's so."

"Go ahead and consider," he said.

"That's what I'm going to do," I said. "Now, tell me: don't you say, though, that it's also just to obey the rulers?"

"I do."

"Are the rulers in their several cities infallible, or are they such as to make mistakes too?"

"By all means," he said, "they certainly are such as to make mistakes too."

"When they put their hand to setting down laws, do they set some down correctly and some incorrectly?"

"I suppose so."

"Is that law correct which sets down what is advantageous for themselves, and that one incorrect which sets down what is disadvantageous?—Or how do you mean it?"

"As you say."

"But whatever the rulers set down must be done by those who are ruled, and this is the just?"

"Of course."

"Then, according to your argument, it's just to do not only what is advantageous for the stronger but also the opposite, what is disadvantageous."

"What do you mean?" he said.

(339b–d)

The whole tone of this argument, which is typical of the Thrasymachus section, is different from the tone of discussions with Cephalus and Polemarchus. With Cephalus, Socrates seems less interested in developing formal arguments than in eliciting Cephalus' views on a number of issues. Even when he challenges Cephalus' implicit account of justice, Socrates seems to take for granted that Cephalus would agree that it is wrong to return a weapon to a deranged friend. With Polemarchus, Socrates' questions and arguments seem designed less to refute than to display to that passionate and unsophisticated young man the ambiguities and confusions in his own understanding of what he has asserted. With Thrasymachus, Socrates seems out to frame arguments designed to refute Thrasymachus, and so cleverly that Thrasymachus will not see in advance where Socrates is heading. Thrasymachus himself makes it clear from the moment he enters the conversation that he intends to dispute Socrates, to refute him, and to replace him as the central figure in the conversation. In effect, Socrates responds in kind to this challenge.

Socrates' first question in the argument is whether it is just to obey the rulers. Thrasymachus must agree because he has identified the just with the lawful. Although he asserts that justice is the interest of the stronger, from the point of view of the weaker, justice is whatever the stronger—that is, the rulers who make and enforce the laws—say it is. This first question of Socrates thus brings out an ambiguity in Thrasymachus' position. Justice is two things, related but distinct. From the point of view of the weaker, to do as you are told by the stronger, that is, the rulers, is just. From the point of view of the stronger, justice is the power to tell the weaker to do things that are for the advantage of the stronger. To be just, therefore, the stronger must know and do what it is to their advantage to do.

Socrates does not use the term "stronger"; he uses "ruler." He has not accepted Thrasymachus' identification of the stronger with the rulers. This first assertion of Socrates, that it is just to obey the rulers, is never challenged, questioned, or even discussed further by either Socrates or Thrasymachus. It is, on its face, a perfectly commonplace statement, one that everybody would accept. It is the sine qua non of political life and of all serious political discourse. The difficulties arise when we attempt to identify the rulers that we should obey. This is the point at which most discussions of political legitimacy, authority, and justice begin. Thrasymachus seems to hold that for the weak—that is, the subjects—obeying the rulers exhausts the content of justice. Socrates seems to hold that obeying one's rulers is just, but this does not necessarily mean simply doing what one is told to do.

We know that Socrates at least twice in his own life flatly refused to do as he was told—once when he would not go along with the majority in the Athenian council in illegally indicting the admirals of the battle of Arginusae and once when he did not obey the order of the thirty tyrants to arrest Leon of Salamis. In the *Apology* he makes it abundantly clear that even if ordered by the city to refrain from philosophizing, he would not obey. But that it might sometimes be just to disobey the law is apparently not an option for Thrasymachus. From his position, the behavior of the weak is unproblematic. It is just for them to obey the law even if the law is itself unjust. Thus, this first serious argument directed by Socrates against Thrasymachus reveals that Socrates not only is more skilled in argument but is more radical in his understanding of justice. The Socratic argument trips up Thrasymachus because despite his immoralism, cynicism, and unscrupulousness, he firmly holds to the conventional view that to obey the law is always just. By contrast, Socrates is prepared to consider a more radical conception of justice that transcends the law and might, on occasion, violate it.

The three arguments that we have considered are very different from one another, but each represents a philosophical failure. In each case, beyond the inadequacy of the conclusion (as in the case of Cephalus) or the argument (Polemarchus) or the initial premise (Thrasymachus), we were able to discover a number of new and surprising possibilities. Cephalus' speech about the good use of money requires us to think seriously about our felt obligation to tell the truth and pay our debts to man and god—in other words, to reflect on our own lived experience. Socrates' argument with Polemarchus that the just man is a thief requires us to watch the details of the argument. We need to scrutinize the examples to see if they exemplify what they are supposed to, to see if the analogies hold. We have to study the conclusion to see what it really means. In other words, we must pay attention to the details and structure of the argument to determine what is and is not valid in it. Finally, Socrates' refutation of Thrasymachus' view that justice is the interest of the stronger leads to a first, provisional examination of the otherwise unquestioned assumption that to be just is simply to obey the law.

We could fairly conclude that whether or not the particular arguments fail, we, the readers, cannot fail to learn something deeply serious from their study about how to participate in philosophy. But what about the subject of book I, the nature of justice? Are we as much in the dark about that at the end of book I as at the beginning? To answer this question, we need to shift from looking at particular arguments to the pattern of book I as a whole.

Book I moves from speaker to speaker. Cephalus says justice is to tell the truth and pay debts, Polemarchus says it is to help friends and harm enemies, and Thrasymachus says it is the interest of the stronger. In each definition there are two major undefined terms or pairs of terms: "truth" and "debt" for Cephalus, "friends/enemies" and "helping/harming" for Polemarchus, and "interest" and "strength" for Thrasymachus.

Polemarchus tries to help Cephalus by redefining debt to mean helping and harming rather than a specific sum of money, and in the process he shifts the locus of justice from the individual human being, where Cephalus places it, to interpersonal relationships. Cephalus speaks of individuals as just or unjust in character. Polemarchus speaks of acting justly or unjustly toward others. As for Cephalus' concern for the truth, Polemarchus ignores it.

Thrasymachus then redefines what is helpful or harmful to mean what is in one's own interest or against it, and he ignores Polemarchus' concern with friends and enemies. In the process he shifts the locus of justice again, this time from interpersonal relationships to the political, to the relationship between the rulers and subjects in a community.

In each case, the shift in the locus of justice arises initially from a difficulty in the previous speaker's understanding of justice. Thus, Cephalus is centrally concerned with whether or not an individual is just. But that very concern leads to difficulty with a friend. Polemarchus' concern with interpersonal relationships leads to the conclusion that we should never harm anyone. This conclusion, if taken seriously, would make all war unjust and would make it impossible for any community to defend itself. Such a conclusion enrages Thrasymachus, whose concern for self-interest is expressed in political—that is, communal—terms. But Thrasymachus' central and exclusive focus on the political meaning of justice and its locus in the city-state leads finally to the image of the perfectly unjust man, at war with everyone, including himself, and therefore wretched in the extreme. And there we are, at the end of book I, back to the concern of Cephalus with the quality of the life of the individual.

Structurally, then, in terms of content, book I is circular; each definition of justice tries to restrict justice to a particular area—the individual, interpersonal relationships, or the city-state. But then each notion of justice meets a difficulty precisely where it needs to expand beyond the restriction. Because the movement is circular, at the end of book I we can say that despite the differences all three definitions of justice suffer from the same fundamental weakness: each unsuccessfully attempts to limit justice to one specific area of human life.

The problem with each definition is not that it is wrong but that it is only partially right. A full and adequate account of justice would have to see it as essential to the individual, to relationsships with others, and to the life of the community. Thus, when Socrates presents his own account of justice in books II–IX, he does so by explicitly locating it in both the individual and the city-state.

But what about interpersonal relationships? If Socrates' account does justice to Cephalus and Thrasymachus, what about Polemarchus and his desire to help his friends? At what is perhaps the crucial turning point of the entire dialogue, the moment at the beginning of book V when Socrates has finished his account of justice and is about to begin an account of the various forms of injustice—at that moment Polemarchus, who has been sitting quietly, leans forward and whispers something to Adeimantus. When Socrates asks what they are talking about, he is told that Polemarchus wants to know what Socrates meant earlier when he said that the guardians of the just city, being friends, would have all things in common including their women and children.

After some attempts to avoid the question, Socrates succumbs to the joint demand of everyone, including Thrasymachus, and he launches into his account of the three waves of paradox—the equality of the sexes, the community of women and children, and, finally, the philosopher-king. This digression takes up books V, VI, and VII—the philosophical heart of the dialogue. I suggest that it is in those three central books, which are primarily concerned with philosophy, that Socrates treats the crucial, Polemarchian dimension of justice expressed through relationships with friends.

So although each definition of justice in book I is, by itself, inadequate, there is good reason to think that the three definitions may succeed as an integrated whole. I have mentioned in passing that the position of each of the three interlocutors is grounded in and yet vulnerable to a different aspect of philosophical reflection. Thus Cephalus starts from experience and is vulnerable to an appeal to experience. Polemarchus uses argument like a weapon to defend his father and is peculiarly vulnerable to arguments that appear to refute him. Thrasymachus begins from a fundamental political principle, but because he has not grasped it adequately, he has trouble defending it in the face of Socrates' cross-examination. I suggest that long experience, valid argument, and comprehensive principles are not mutually exclusive grounds for philosophy but three necessary aspects of any philosophical enterprise.

The succession of interlocutors suggests a historical sequence of the generations. Thus, old Cephalus with his moderate relation to the moneymaking of his grandfather and the profligacy of his father seems the veritable incarnation of the traditional ancestral order. His young, passionate son Polemarchus is expressly described as his heir—that is, as a member of the next generation, which is taking over. Thrasymachus, who is already in the house talking to Polemarchus' younger brothers when Socrates and his friends arrive, has a certain sinister quality as the immoral, unrestrained, cynical wave of the future.

What is scary about this view of the history of Athens is that Cephalus is no longer a competent defender of the tradition, if he ever was. Polemarchus is a very nice young man but hardly capable of withstanding the unscrupulous Thrasymachus. But even Thrasymachus, by far the smartest, most sophisticated, and most philosophically talented of the interlocutors in book I, is ultimately revealed as incapable of making an intellectually viable defense of the claims of the city-state on the lives of its citizens. If Cephalus, Polemarchus, and Thrasymachus are the immediate past, the imminent present, and the looming future of Athens, then the city-state is in a bad way, and the role of Socrates in the life of Athens, as well as in this dialogue, takes on considerable significance.

But this historical perspective suggests still another dimension to the sequence of the three interlocutors. The three conversations grow longer and longer; it is apparently increasingly difficult for Socrates to uncover the inherent weakness of each succeeding view. Cephalus' position collapses with a single question, but Polemarchus requires a series of arguments systematically exploring and demolishing the several parts of his definition. Thrasymachus is the toughest of all to defeat. He has at least two fallback positions, each stronger than the one before it. Socrates himself acknowledges that the final and real position of Thrasymachus is difficult to refute. But, disturbingly, if the interlocutors are increasingly difficult to refute, each position is, by implication, better than the one before it—that is, truer.

But in the sequence from Cephalus to Polemarchus to Thrasymachus, the positions move from the fully conventional and morally decent to the less conventionally acceptable and more morally questionable. Does this mean that the conventional morality of Cephalus is superficial and untrue and the radical immorality of Thrasymachus is philosophically sounder? Does it, perhaps, suggest that the fourth account of justice in the dialogue, the account given by Socrates himself, beginning in book II, is both the best account of justice and the most radically unconventional, so unconventional that even Thrasymachus looks rather traditional by comparison?

Mention of Socrates' unconventionality is a reminder of one of his most idiosyncratic qualities: his proverbial poverty. He never has any money. His poverty becomes significant in book I when he needs Glaucon to pay Thrasymachus for him. But money is not just a dramatic detail in book I; it is a major element in all three accounts of justice—a problematic element. Justice was introduced into the dialogue explicitly by Cephalus, who said that money was useful because it permitted its possessor to be just. By contrast, his son Polemarchus accepts the Socratic conclusion that justice and money are mutually exclusive, that where money is useless, justice is useful, and where money is useful, justice is useless. Finally, Thrasymachus makes it very clear that justice, in the form of the laws passed by the rulers in their own interest, is the best way to acquire money. So the relation of justice and money in book I is thoroughly problematic—does one use money to secure justice? Does one use justice to secure money? Or are they mutually exclusive?

Let me mention one more contrasting set of terms. For Cephalus justice is a *hexis*—"a settled state of character formed by habituation"—much like moral virtue as Aristotle understands it. For Polemarchus, by contrast, justice is a *techne*, "an art or technique by which the individual who has it is empowered to do something." Finally, for Thrasymachus justice is "a body of knowledge," the subject of a theoretical science that constitutes the basis for the rational behavior of rulers who understand how to acquire and to exercise political power.

I could go on almost indefinitely showing the luminous structure of book I—the ways the sequence of the interlocutors and their arguments compare and contrast with each other so that the problem of justice gradually emerges in all its complexity. The foregoing is sufficient, however; we can see how powerful that structure is. In sum, book I, both in its specific arguments and in the sequence and interrelations of the interlocutors, provides a perfect introduction to the serious argument that begins in book II with Glaucon and Adeimantus' challenge to Socrates.

In isolation, book I is indeed a failure, for at the end, Socrates says he remains ignorant of the nature of justice. But as an introduction to the extraordinary discussion in books II–X, book I leaves nothing to be desired. It encourages us to reflect seriously on our own experience. It trains us to follow arguments, and it develops our capacity to grasp principles. Book I displays the range of questions that need to be considered in investigating justice, and it shows what is at stake in that investigation. What more could one ask of an introduction?

Is book I, then, turned from an inconclusive failure as an independent dialogue into a remarkable success as an introduction to the *Republic*? Does Plato, like all the great thinkers that follow him, write only successes? My answer must be somewhat equivocal. Yes, book I of the *Republic* is a successful introduction to the rest of the *Republic*. It can teach us how to read the main argument, and it displays in a preliminary form all the topics, concepts, problems, and phenomena that an adequate understanding of justice entail.

Book I also does at least one more thing. In introducing the *Republic* it also, and of necessity, introduces the enterprise of philosophy. Philosophy becomes an explicit theme in the *Republic*, in books V, VI, and VII, through the figure of the philosopher-king who is to bring about the realization of the just city. In the discussion of the education of the philosopher-king, Socrates introduces the notion of the idea of the Good, which he calls the "greatest study" of these future rulers, greater even than justice, and the end point of their studies.

At the end of book VI and the beginning of book VII, Socrates presents a metaphorical account of the idea of the Good. I want to make only one point about the passage. In the third part of the so-called simile of light, the parable of the cave, Socrates describes the education of a philosopher as a journey up and out of imprisonment in a dimly lit cave. The high point of that journey into the clear light of day comes when the former prisoner, after seeing the real things in the real world outside the cave, turns to the source of light—the sun, which Socrates explicitly identifies as the Good. At that culminating moment the philosopher understands reality and achieves wisdom. Unfortunately, as we all know and as Socrates fails to mention in the passage, the sun is too bright to look at directly. It will blind you if you try.

But if looking at the sun, the Good, will blind the seeker of light, the completion of philosophy, the consummation of wisdom that would come with full knowledge of the Good, is beyond human capacity. Philosophy, the love and desire for wisdom, never becomes *sophia,* "wisdom." We may become wiser, but we never become wise. The highest human activity, philosophy, remains the desire for wisdom; it never achieves it. It begins, and ends, with awareness of our fundamental ignorance. Philosophy itself is necessarily a failure.

Insofar as book I introduces us to failure, shows us what failure can do, and shows us what failure means, it not only prepares us to read the *Republic* but serves as an introduction to the discipline of philosophy. It prepares us for the failure that Socrates thinks makes life worth living.

18 Knowing, Being, and the Community
The Divided Line and the Cave in Republic, *Books VI and VII*

Plato's *Republic* is far more like Shakespeare's *Hamlet* than like Aristotle's *Ethics*. In discussing the figure of the divided line and the parable of the cave, we must consider them primarily not as one argument in a long series of arguments but as two poetic images in a series of images, as elements of one highly dramatic episode in an extremely complex dramatic plot.

Every drama tells a story. *Hamlet,* according to some critics, is the tragic story of a man who couldn't make up his mind; and Conrad's *Heart of Darkness* is Marlow's account of his journey up the Congo River and back again. What is the story of the *Republic?*

Ostensibly, it is the story of how Socrates and his young friend Glaucon went to the Piraeus, the port of Athens, to see a new religious festival, met some old friends there, and after a little friendly arm-twisting stayed on for a visit and spent the night talking. While this description is accurate, it hardly does justice to the plot of the *Republic*. Perhaps we should ask what they talk about. But that answer does not help much either, for there is very little in the course of that three-hundred-page conversation that they do not talk about. Does the conversation have a single theme, a thread that runs through and binds together the subjects touched on? The title of the work suggests that it is concerned with politics, with the structure and purpose of human communities, and with the structure and purpose of the best possible human community in particular.

Yet politics explicitly enters the discussion only in the second of the ten books of the *Republic*. There, after Socrates is challenged by Glaucon and Adeimantus to set forth the real nature of justice and injustice and to prove that the just life is intrinsically best, Socrates responds to their challenge and begins his exposition by establishing an analogy between the city and the individual so that by considering the city first, the discussants may more easily perceive the nature of justice. Politics, or the city, or the just city, is brought into the discussion only as an illustration, as a heuristic device with which Socrates can help his earnest young friends see the true nature of justice.

This analogy between the city and the individual is overtly maintained throughout the *Republic*. The bulk of the pages in books II–IX are concerned with political matters. Yet unless you believe that the major theme of a work is the one with the most space devoted to it, I think you must admit that politics is not the central theme of the *Republic*. If not politics, what? The next obvious answer is justice. Politics is introduced only to elucidate the nature of justice, and the concern with justice does, admittedly, run through the entire work. But at the beginning of the *Republic,* in Socrates' short discussion with old Cephalus, in which the problem of justice first emerged, justice itself was brought into the discussion when Cephalus was talking to Socrates about the advantages of having lots of money. And money, in turn, became a topic of conversation within the context of Cephalus' remarks about the condition of extreme old age. At this point, we are practically back at the moment at which Socrates and his friends arrived at the house of Cephalus, and we still have not been able to determine the true theme of the *Republic*. We have stumbled, however, on a pattern of organization. For my present purpose of describing the context of the divided line, this pattern is what is important.

The *Republic* is structured like a nest of Chinese boxes. We start with one box—the nature of extreme old age—and when that box is opened, we discover another box within it, the advantages of money. When that box is opened, there is a third—the nature of justice. The pattern has become clear, but when that third box—justice—is opened, at the urging of Glaucon and Adeimantus in book II, we discover that, instead of coming to the innermost box, we have been gaining experience for what is to come.

Within the box of justice, Socrates tells his friends, there are two smaller boxes, one labeled "the city" and the other "the individual." To know what justice is, we must examine the contents of both boxes. Luckily, according to Socrates, they both contain the same things. The only difference is that the city is a bigger box with bigger things in it. Thus its contents are easier to see than the otherwise identical contents of the "individual" box. The remainder of book II and the whole of books III and IV consist of peeking first into the big box of the city and then into the smaller box of the individual. By the end of book IV, justice itself has been discovered, and it only remains to describe the various forms of injustice in cities and individuals and then to show how justice is intrinsically superior to injustice in both cases—or so it seems.

At the beginning of book V, as Socrates is about to start on the last and easiest part of his task, he is interrupted by Adeimantus, who has been egged on by Polemarchus. Polemarchus, the son of Cephalus, in book I defined justice as helping one's friends and harming one's enemies. His primary difficulty in that early argument was that he didn't know who his friends were and had no idea of how to go about helping them. In the course of describing the education of the guardians of the just city, near the beginning of book IV, Socrates said that they would be reasonable men and friends and, as such, would hold all things in common, including their wives and children. At the time, this intriguing little remark was passed over, but at the start of book V it is clear that Polemarchus, who is deeply concerned about how friends should act toward one another, has been brooding about it, and he now wants some explanation before Socrates goes on to other issues. The result of his modest request for further information is a digression from the main line of the argument—a digression that consists of the whole of books V, VI, and VII, one-third of the entire work. Book VIII begins where Socrates attempted to begin book V, with the description of the four forms of injustice in cities and individuals.

What has happened is that Polemarchus, either by accident or through the very subtle needling of Socrates, has stumbled onto another Chinese box. Inside this box Socrates reveals three more boxes, which he calls the three waves of paradox. The first two, the equality of the sexes and the community of women and children, are examined rather quickly, but a problem remains— namely, how to bring about these two rather shocking and unconventional institutions in an actual city. The answer is the third paradox of the philosopher-king, the means by which the just city described in books II, III, and IV is to be realized.

But within this third paradox is still another box to be opened, labeled "philosophy." Defining the philosopher and describing his role in the just city takes up the remainder of book V and the whole of books VI and VII. After describing the philosopher in book V and arguing that he is fit to rule at the beginning of book VI, Socrates says that it only remains to discuss "in what way and as a result of what studies these preservers of the regime will form a part of our city and at what ages they will severally take up each study." Thus, the bulk of books VI and VII concerns the education of the philosopher-kings.

The content of a philosophical education is itself dealt with in two parts: first, what Socrates calls the "highest studies" is discussed, and then a specific curriculum of five sciences plus dialectic is spelled out. The description of the highest studies begins with an exposition of the idea of the Good in book VI, goes on to the figure of the divided line, and ends with the parable of the cave at the beginning of book VII.

We have finally arrived at the immediate context of the figure of the divided line and the cave: they are the last two parts of a three-part discussion of the highest studies undertaken by future philosopher-kings if they are to develop into the kind of men and women who can bring the just city into existence and maintain it. The entire digression consisting of books V, VI, and VII is a box located in the center of the *Republic*. Within that large central box, there are the paradox boxes. Within the third paradox box is the philosophy box, and within that box is the education-of-philosophers box. Within that box is the highest-studies box of the philosopher-to-be. In that one we find two more boxes, one of them containing the images of the sun and the Good, the divided line, and the cave, and the second, a discussion of the specific curriculum of the sciences to be learned by the future philosophers. That scientific curriculum is determined in its scope and purpose by the images of the sun and the Good, the divided line, and the cave.

These images occur at the very center of the *Republic*. They are the innermost box of the entire structure. When we reach these three images, we have penetrated to the dramatic and formal center of the work. From that point on, we begin to work out from that center through all the larger enclosing boxes opened on our way in. But—and this is the crucial thing to see—the contents of these enclosing boxes will look very different in light of the contents of the innermost box.

I cannot stop even here. To be precise, I must say that the three images of the sun and the Good, the divided line, and the cave are not all at the same level. The image of the divided line is the authentic and final center of the *Republic*. The analogy of the sun and the Good prepares the way for the figure of the divided line, and the parable of the cave is an application of the principles articulated in the divided-line figure to the political and psychological life of man. Apparently, then, when we talk about the divided line, we shall be discussing the first or highest principles enunciated in the *Republic,* and when we move on to the cave, we will be considering the political implications of the line.

Let me make this point more clearly. In the first six books of the *Republic,* up to the description of the divided line, Socrates and his interlocutors make an enormous number of distinctions, definitions, and decisions. For example, they distinguish the three parts of the individual soul and the city, they define justice and the other virtues, and they decide to purge their model city of improper poetry.

In every single one of those distinctions, definitions, and decisions, however, the discussants do not know what they are doing or whether they are right, for they are working from opinion and not from knowledge. Furthermore, they are themselves working toward knowledge as they make these distinctions and definitions. Whether the definitions and distinctions made on the way to knowledge are correct or not can be decided only when knowledge has been attained, and then all the steps leading toward it can and must be re-examined in the light of that knowledge.

The divided line is the closest approximation to an explicit statement of first principles that can be found in the dialogue, and ultimately it is in terms of that figure, or the principles that it embodies, that everything preceding it must be reconsidered. In effect, this brief account of the context of the divided line and the cave has resulted in a complete reversal of the purpose with which it began. I started by arguing that we could not understand the two figures except within the context of the entire *Republic*. But it is now clear that we must seek to understand the entire *Republic* in terms of the line and the cave.

THE DIVIDED LINE (509E–514A)

The figure of the divided line is preceded by Socrates' description of the idea of the Good. Socrates begins his discussion of the Good by suddenly and rather sharply criticizing the earlier conversation on the tripartite nature of the soul and the four cardinal virtues as imprecise and sloppy. The argument that he and his friends followed took the shorter and easier way, he says, but a person who is to be a guardian must take the longer and surer way, or "he will never come to the goal of the greatest study and the one which is most fitting for him." And, Socrates continues, the "greatest study is not justice, but the idea of the Good by reference to which just things and all the rest become useful and beneficial" (504d–505b).

Glaucon cannot resist such tempting bait; he insists that Socrates give an account of this object in relation to which even justice is reduced to a derivative and secondary status. Although Socrates refuses to give a literal account of the Good, he does agree to describe it analogically through a comparison with the sun. Regardless of the apparently loose and hyperbolic language, Socrates presents an extraordinarily precise and exhaustive definition of the Good. The analogy depends on the previously established distinction between being and becoming, between things perceived by reason and things perceived through the senses. The conclusion of the analogical argument is that as the sun is the cause of everything in the realm of becoming, so the Good is the cause of everything in the realm of being. This is accurate as far as it goes.

The difficulty arises when we ask exactly what the realm of being is that is ruled over by the Good. The realm of being includes within itself the realm of becoming. That is to say, the things of the ordinary world about us, the things perceived through our senses, are, in one respect, distinct and different in kind from the intelligible realities in the realm of being. But in another respect, the things of the ordinary, sensible world also have a kind of being, even though they are mutable, even though they come into existence and pass away. Thus when Socrates argues that the Good is the cause of all things in the realm of being, he is actually asserting that the Good is the cause of everything—of the eternal, unchanging things grasped by the intelligence and of the impermanent, changing things known through the senses. But if this is true, the analogy between the sun and the Good no longer holds, because there would appear to be no distinct realm over which the sun rules.

To make this point perfectly clear, Socrates argues that it is not the sun that makes the flowers grow but the Good. You will object to this as absurd. And so it is, unless Socrates can prove otherwise—which is what he tries to do through the figure of the divided line.

Let me sum up this rather technical discussion: In making the analogy between the sun and the Good, Socrates is asserting that the Good is related to the realm of being as the sun is related to the realm of becoming. He thus presupposes the separate existence of the two realms. But the content of the realm of being turns out to be all-inclusive; there is not and cannot be any other realm beyond being, and the so-called realm of becoming is a part of being. To assert all-inclusion does not prove it; Socrates must show us how becoming can be a part of being. This he does by way of the figure of the divided line.

The passage in which Socrates describes the figure to Glaucon is one of the most vexed in philosophical literature; commentators have been arguing about its meaning for 2,400 years. Three aspects of the figure must be taken into account in any serious attempt to interpret it. Ignoring or distorting one or more of these aspects means misconstruing the meaning of the figure to some extent. The three aspects are in themselves quite simple; the difficulty comes in trying to include all three in one interpretation.

First, Socrates divides the single line into four segments (see my diagram). Whatever each segment may represent, symbolize, or contain, it must be seen as one part of a continuous line without any gaps. Second, he gives the line two distinct sides, one representing the various "kinds and realms" of things and the other the different "conditions in the soul" corresponding to each of these realms. Third, Socrates is very careful to establish a complex proportional relation between the several segments of the line. The line is divided into two unequal portions, and each of these is further bifurcated according to the same ratio. Keeping these three simple points in mind—the unity and wholeness of the line, the two correlative sides, and the precise proportional relations of the segments—we can investigate the significance of the image as a whole.

Because the line is a single, though complex figure, it cannot be understood bit by bit but must be grasped comprehensively. Yet, paradoxically, the best way to do this is to begin with a part of of the line. I propose to begin with the lower half, the large segment representing the whole "visible realm." This segment is divided into two smaller segments. My reasons for starting there is that

THE GOOD

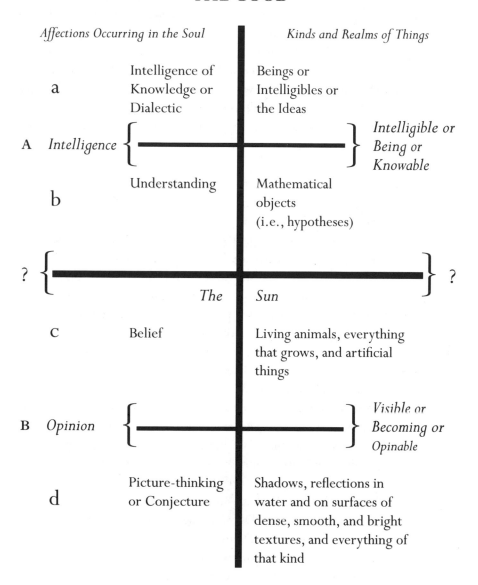

| Affections Occurring in the Soul | | Kinds and Realms of Things |

a — Intelligence of Knowledge or Dialectic — Beings or Intelligibles or the Ideas

A Intelligence } { ——————— } Intelligible or Being or Knowable

b — Understanding — Mathematical objects (i.e., hypotheses)

? { ——————— } ?

The | *Sun*

c — Belief — Living animals, everything that grows, and artificial things

B Opinion { ——————— } Visible or Becoming or Opinable

d — Picture-thinking or Conjecture — Shadows, reflections in water and on surfaces of dense, smooth, and bright textures, and everything of that kind

1. The line is a single, unbroken line divided into four unequal segments.
2. The line has two distinct sides, one representing "kinds and realms of things;" the other the "affections occurring in the soul."
3. The several segments of the line are proportionally related as follows: A = a + b, and B = c + d, and A : B :: a : b :: c : d and A : a :: B : c.

The figure of the divided line

the things included in the lower segments or levels are much more familiar to us than the rather mysterious entities in the two higher segments. We should therefore find it easier to understand relation between the lower segments, and once we have grasped that relation, the rest should follow, because the ratio between the two lower segments is identical both to the ratio between the two higher segments and to the ratio between the two major segments of the line. In effect, the relation between visible images and their originals, on the two lower segments, can serve as a perfect model for the relation between the mathematical entities of the third level and those mysterious entities called ideas, on the fourth and highest level.

At the very bottom level are images such as "shadows and reflections in water and in mirrors . . . and all things of this kind" (510a). Corresponding to these images is the condition of the soul that Socrates calls "conjecture." On the level above the images are the "things" that the images resemble, "the animals about us, everything that grows and the whole class of artificial things," and correlative to these is the condition of the soul called "belief" (510a). Considered together, these two kinds of things—sensible images and their originals—constitute the realm of the visible, or, more properly, the realm of becoming. Corresponding to this single large realm is the single condition of the soul known as "opinion." As belief is clearer than conjecture, so the sensible originals of the second level are truer than their sensible images on the first level.

But what is a sensible image and how is it related to its original? Socrates gives shadows and reflections in water and mirrors as examples of images, but he indicates that there are many other images beyond these. What are they? If a shadow or a reflection is an image, why not a drawing or photograph? They, too, are images. But why restrict ourselves to visual images? When someone imitates the voice of another person, isn't that also an image? Surely a recording of a symphony orchestra is as much an image of its sound as a photograph would be of its visual appearance. Does an image need to be a directly perceivable likeness of its original? Can't an image achieve its likeness indirectly, through the medium of words? A painting or a recording may be considered images of a person, but so can a verbal description of what he or she looks like or says. In sum, any sensible perception of something as a likeness of some other sensible thing is the perception of an image.

Keeping this definition in mind, we can now describe the relation between images and their originals. We can say that an image is sharply different from its original, because the original is simply what it appears to be, whereas the image, by its very nature, appears to be something other than itself—namely, the original. Yet the difference between an image and its original is not absolute; to be an image at all, the image must be like its original. There is also a sense in which images and originals are absolutely the same as each other, for although they are distinct kinds of things, they are both perceived through the senses and are equally things that come to be.

We can now see why Socrates separates images from the things they resemble and why he asserts that each is perceived by a distinct condition of the soul. Compared with their originals, images manifest a peculiarly shifting and uncertain nature. A man, a tree, or any other sensible thing has a relatively fixed and ascertainable character. But the images of that thing range all the way from accurate likenesses to vague and misleading representations to serious distortions. The images themselves provide no substantial grounds for determining whether or in what respects they are reliable representations.

The truth of an image, that is, its accuracy, can be known only when it is held up to its original. To see and hear a statesman is a direct experience of something. If he is seen and heard on television or heard over the radio, he is already being perceived through images. A verbatim reprint of his speech is further removed from the original, and an edited account in an opposition newspaper is even more so. As the distance between the image and the original increases, the likelihood of distortion grows. At the farthest extreme are images so unlike their originals that they can almost—but never quite—be said to be images of nothing. The propaganda reports of battles that were never fought or of victories that were not won, the public reputation for virtue of a venal, selfish man—such images are sufficiently real in themselves to affect the lives of individuals and communities, but the originals of which they are images are very different from their representations.

By insisting on a sharp distinction between things and their images Socrates does not mean to imply simply that the former are clearly known and the latter less so. Knowledge of things gained through direct sensory perception is not without its own difficulties. There is, for example, an enormous difference between seeing a friend on the other side of the street and seeing him on the other side of the table. Yet the difficulties posed by the variation in clarity with direct sense perception of things are minor compared to the inescapable ambiguities attendant on a knowledge of things solely through their images.

The difference between the two kinds of knowledge may be described as a difference in degree, symbolized on the line by the placement of things and images: sensible originals are higher on the scale of clarity and truth than their images. But the difference between images and originals is also sharply qualitative, symbolized by their placement on different segments of the line. When the perceiver no longer confronts things directly but knows them only through the radically uncertain and dubious medium of images, he no longer "believes" what he sees but can only "conjecture" about it.

Although the difference between things and images is unequivocal, this does not mean that the status of every visible thing is fixed once and for all as either an image or an original. On the contrary, the exact opposite is the case. By the same token, seeing or hearing something directly does not mean that it is necessarily perceived as an object of belief rather than as an object of conjecture. An old school chum of your father's may see you as a chip off the old block—that is, as an image of your father. You may see a building as a structure of steel, concrete, and glass, but a student of modern design may see it as an image expressing the unique genius of the architect who designed it. On the other hand, the apparently insubstantial shadow or reflection of a tree may be seen—by an artist or poet or physicist, for example—not as an image of something else but as a thing in its own right, a thing to be painted, written about, and studied. Hence the status of a perceived object, whether as an image or as an original, depends on the context in which it is perceived; insofar as it is capable of being an object of sense perception, it may be perceived in either mode.

The distinction between images and the things that they resemble divides the realm of becoming into two related kinds of things without assigning once and for all the many things that become to one or the other of these modes. In fact, all the objects belonging to the realm of becoming are always simultaneously in both modes. If an individual or a painting may be perceived either as an original or as an image of something else, then it must be fully known as both an original and an image, for neither mode by itself exhausts the full becoming of the thing. Therefore, nothing that becomes is either an image or an original; whatever becomes is always both. Just as a single scale of truth connects sensible images and originals, these two kinds of things which together constitute the objects of opinion must be understood to exist simultaneously along the entire scale represented by the first two segments of the divided line.

So far, we can say that the lower half of the divided line illustrates by means of a figure the form or structure of the realm of the sun, a realm variously called the realm of becoming, of the visible, or of the opinable. Socrates subdivides this realm in three interrelated ways: into souls that perceive and objects that are perceived; into the generic modes of objects—sensible originals and their images—and the correlative conditions of the soul by which these different modes are correspondingly perceived; and into degrees of truth within each sensible object and a corresponding gradation of clarity in the perceptions of the soul.

In elucidating the lower half of the line I have concentrated on the meaning of the term *image*. I have said that images are (1) different in kind from their originals, (2) like their originals, (3) absolutely the same as their originals, (4) perceived in the same way as the originals, (5) perceived in a completely different way from the originals, (6) found along a single continuous, graded scale of truth with the originals, and so on. If the contradictions, real or only apparent, in all these statements bother you and at the same time seem inescapable, then you are on your way to grasping what Socrates means by image.

More important for my present purposes, the meaning of the term *image* cannot be understood in abstraction or isolation from all the other terms associated with the lower half of the divided line. To understand this one term, you must understand all of the others and their manifold interrelations. Then you can begin to see that all of the terms have an extraordinarily flexible, almost fluid quality that allows them to take on an almost infinite variety of special meanings in diverse contexts. Yet each term has a single, unvarying core meaning from which all the special meanings derive. The same is true of the terms used in the rest of the figure.

Let us now consider the line as a whole. The relation between sensible images and their originals is identical with the relation between becoming and being. This means that the sensible things of this world, the things that come into being and pass away, the things that we touch and see, the things that we manipulate and that manipulate us, the things that we love and hate—all these, including ourselves, are images or likenesses of something else. The originals of which the things of our sensible world are images are not themselves sensible. Rather, they are intelligible: they are known not through the senses but through the intellect, and they do not come into being and pass away. To put it somewhat differently, they do not exist as temporal entities; they exist beyond time. They are not immortal in the sense that they exist forever; instead, they exist outside time altogether—they are eternal. These are the qualities of the originals, of which the world that presents itself to our senses is merely an image.

If these are the qualities of the intelligible realities, what are the realities themselves, those mysterious, remote entities called the beings? The answer is that they are neither remote nor mysterious; we are perfectly familiar with them. Let me give two brief examples. Think of first-grade arithmetic textbooks. "Johnny has two apples and Jane has two apples. How many apples do they both have?" When we answered "four apples," we were at that moment perceiving an intelligible entity: two apples and two apples makes four apples because two and two makes four. But we cannot see numbers and their necessary eternal interrelations with our eyes or feel them with our hands; we can know them only with our intelligence. Furthermore, the numerical relation between Johnny's apples and Jane's apples is merely an example—in Socrates' language, an image—of an eternal reality. And we know this because the textbook was obviously talking not about apples but about numbers.

For my second example, let me take someone I admire intensely, Washington or Lincoln or Gandhi—the name doesn't matter. The person is someone of whom we can say, "There is a great human being." Now think of someone at the other end of the scale—Hitler or Stalin at their worst moments. Those are people of whom we can say, "They were monsters." Such statements imply that we know what a human being is and that some individuals fit our notion more exactly than others; that is, some are better images and some worse.

But this idea of matching human beings with an image of a human being further implies that all human beings of flesh and blood are indeed images of the human or an idea of the human that is not a creature of flesh and blood but an eternal, intelligible entity. We will never shake hands with that eternal human being, but the people with whom we do shake hands are what they are by virtue of their relation to that entity. I am well aware that this rough description of the things that are, of the beings located by Socrates in the upper half of the divided line, is grossly inadequate and open to many objections. Plato was aware of it, too, and he wrote an entire dialogue, the *Parmenides,* in which Socrates, the creator of the theory of ideas, is cross-examined and reduced to silence as effectively as Thrasymachus is in book I of the *Republic*. But that is another story. For my purposes it is enough to show that Socrates is not talking nonsense when he speaks of being in distinction to becoming and relates the two by saying that the beings are the originals of which the sensible, mutable things are the images.

In asserting that the things of the sensible world are images of intelligible realities, Socrates is not reducing them to insignificance or denying their reality. On the contrary, he is specifying precisely what their significance is and what degree of reality they can achieve. Things of the sensible world are necessarily vague and less knowable than their intelligible originals, just as the shadow of a tree is vaguer and less knowable than the tree.

At the same time, the sensible things are images; they are what they are by virtue of their likeness to their originals. This means that they always reflect their originals. We can learn something about trees from looking at their shadows, and we can learn a great deal about a man from a good portrait of him. Similarly, we can learn much about the intelligible realities from sensible things, but here we must be careful. As a clever but unscrupulous painter may represent a weak, vapid man as having a strong, noble personality, so Hitler and Stalin may not be the best images to study in order to improve our understanding of the nature of man. Yet we must not simply ignore them. Just as we can see a thing only when we have seen the whole range of images of it, our understanding of human nature is inadequate if it cannot comprehend the worse as well as the better instances of it.

These last remarks suggest that there is in the realm of being, as in the realm of becoming, a scale of truth and clarity. As our sensible perceptions may be more or less clear, so may our understanding, and as the sensible things themselves vary in their intrinsic truth, so may the intelligible things. The upper part of the line, the part that symbolizes the realm of being, is, like the lower part, subdivided into two segments. The relation between these subsegments exhibits precisely the same generic characteristics as the relation between the things that *become* and the things that *are* on the two major portions of the line.

Again, how are we to understand this distinction within the realm of the intelligible? On this third level, says Socrates, are the entities with which mathematics deals, entities that seem self-evident but are not. For over two thousand years it seemed obvious that one and only one parallel line could be drawn through a point outside a line. When Lobachevski and Riemann raised doubts, it suddenly became apparent that the postulate was not necessarily true. This is the kind of intelligible entity that exists on the third level.

Euclid's axioms are one example; another is Freud's structural model of the human psyche. Unfortunately for both Euclid and Freud, their accounts of spatial figures and the human psyche, for all their brilliance and intelligibility, are not the last word. Riemann stands as a challenge to Euclid, as Marx, with his economic interpretation of human motivation, stands as a challenge to Freud. This does not mean that Euclid and Freud were wrong. It means only that the intelligible entities that they described do not represent the full truth—they are images of it. Both Euclid and Freud tell us something about spatial figures and human beings, respectively, but neither of them tells us the whole truth any more than the most perfect portrait of a man can tell the whole truth about him. The intelligible entities of the third level, the entities perceived by the understanding, are hypotheses—general statements in terms of which we attempt to understand the physical, sensible realities of the world.

Euclid, Riemann, Freud, and Marx were brilliant formulators of hypotheses, but the entities of the third level are not limited to scientific examples. Whenever in a discussion of politics, for example, someone says, "Oh, well, you know that all politicians are crooks," and proceeds to explain the particular case by reference to this remark, the speaker is no less a hypothesizer than Euclid or Riemann. The hypothesis may be less precise and less true than Euclid's, but the difference is one of degree, not of kind. All general statements that purport to explain phenomena, from the vaguest remarks made during a conversation over a cup of coffee to Einstein's unified field theory, are expressive of the intelligible entities of the third level of the line.

Most scientists and many modern philosophers stop here. For them, hypothetical thought is the peak mental activity and is understood primarily in relation to the sensible things of the physical world. Socrates recognizes the importance of hypotheses as explanations of the physical world, but he insists that explanation is not their primary significance. Rather, they are important as intelligible images of the intelligible originals.

On the fourth level, says Socrates, are the intelligible originals of which these third-level entities are images. The "ideas" are the originals not only for the level immediately below but for all sensible things. Thus the ideas of the fourth level are the ultimate originals; everything else is either directly or indirectly an image of them. This means that nothing that exists can be understood until the ideas are understood.

In spite of the enormous explanatory power of hypotheses, many diverse hypotheses may be associated with the same physical realities. These hypotheses cannot be reconciled merely by reference to the sensible things that they purport to explain. Their reconciliation can occur only by reference to a higher reality of which they are images. Behind Freud's and Marx's partial images of human nature there is human nature itself. Behind all the theories of aestheticians about why beautiful things are beautiful there is the idea of beauty itself. Such ideas, according to Socrates, are the ultimate originals. They are, admittedly, somewhat mysterious, and Socrates does not say much about them—largely, I think, because talking about them is so difficult. Experientially, however, I think his meaning is clear.

The ideas are not remote entities accessible only through the ecstatic vision of a mystic. On the contrary, we have constant and direct experience of the ideas even if we are not aware of it. If someone asks whether two and two is four, we answer yes. If our questioner then asks why that is true and what truth itself is, we might have considerable difficulty responding. But our difficulty in answering these further questions does not mean that we have no knowledge of the idea of truth. It means only that our knowledge is partial, inadequate, and vague. Similarly with beauty. If we have ever been in love, we know what beauty is—we have seen that ultimate intelligible reality manifest in the person we love. And so it is with that most mysterious idea of all—the idea of the Good. When we assert that cheating on exams is not good, or that honesty is good even if impractical, we, no matter how dimly, already have some direct experience and knowledge of the idea of the Good.

The line with its inner articulations is a figurative account of reality, as seen from the perspective of knowledge. It provides an exhaustive classification of the several kinds of being and their correlative states of knowledge. Each kind of being has an intrinsic nature, which is integrated into the whole structure in such a way as to determine and be determined by each of the others and by the whole structure. Thus the sensible images of the lowest level have their own essential reality, but this reality implies and is implied by all the other kinds of being found on the line. Hence the many interrelations of the parts of the line are as intrinsic to each of the parts as are the individual natures of those parts.

The structure represented by the line is all-inclusive. Everything that is, along with every correlative act of knowledge, must be understood to occur within the framework of the line and to be conditioned by it. Even the figure of the line and the understanding of it must be grasped within this context. When Socrates is talking to Glaucon, he seems to be describing a rather simple geometric figure constructed according to a ratio. In effect, he presents a verbal image of a geometric figure. It is clear from the beginning that the visible figure referred to is itself only an image of something else that is not visible but that is intelligible.

One may draw the figure, but only in the form of a rough sketch. The lengths of the segments cannot be drawn in the correct proportion to each other. That is, there is no real-world geometric figure that corresponds to Socrates' account. The figure cannot be drawn without making the second and third segments of equal length, and this would violate the sense of the whole figure. In other words, the line is not ultimately capable of mathematical formulation. Socrates' use of geometry is only metaphorical.

The figure of the line points to a set of relations that transcends mathematics. The full meaning of the line can be grasped only on the fourth level of reason, not by the hypothetical understanding proper to the third level. The geometry of the divided line is as much an image of its intelligible reality as Socrates' verbal description is an image of its visual form.

The line, therefore, is visible and intelligible; it may be understood as both an object of opinion and an object of intelligence. And as an instance of each of these two major kinds of being, it may be seen in either or both of their constitutive subcategories. As an object of knowledge, the divided line, like all other things, is simultaneously an object of opinion and intelligence, of conjecture, belief, understanding, and reason. It exists simultaneously on all levels. What is true of it is true of everything else that is. The divided line is nothing less than an account of the nature or structure of reality.

What, finally, does this account of the structure of reality mean for understanding the *Republic?* Let me suggest only two of its staggering implications. Consider first the relation of justice to wisdom. Earlier, justice was established as the chief virtue, governing the order and interrelations of wisdom, temperance, and courage. But now it appears that reality is apprehended not through justice but through wisdom; wisdom can no longer be thought of as subordinate to justice, for justice itself depends on wisdom. Thus, the entire philosophical psychology and system of virtue of the earlier books need to be radically revised.

Second, consider the figure of the philosopher-king, the person through whom the just city is to be realized. The philosopher is defined as the person who has studied and grasped the idea of the Good. In some sense, all of us already have some knowledge of the Good; we would not be human if we didn't. But we are not all capable of being philosopher-kings, for our knowledge of the Good, though real, is partial and inadequate. The philosopher is the one whose knowledge of the Good is complete. But is perfect knowledge possible? Can anyone know anything completely? Can any object of knowledge be known perfectly? Think of a tree, a chair, another person. As a sensible thing, it presents itself as an object of vision, but only a fool would assert that it is possible to see everything that is potentially visible about it. No matter how carefully we look at anything visible, there is always more to be seen.

According to the proportions of the line, the same thing is true of the objects of intelligence with respect to our reason. The Good is, indeed, always visible to all people. Some see it more clearly and more fully than others—but as there is no one who fails utterly to see it, so there is and can be no one who sees it fully and perfectly. This means that there can only be "seekers after wisdom," never people who are wise. And this, in turn, means that there can never be a fully just city or a fully just individual.

But if the just city and the just person are beyond the possibility of realization, what are we to make of the bulk of the *Republic,* which seems to depend precisely on the assumption that both individuals and cities can be perfectly just? Clearly, Plato saw this implication of the divided line, and I think he hoped that his readers would see it as well. If we accept the challenge that he presents to us, and seek to resolve the problem for ourselves, we will begin to understand what that philosophical education in the highest studies is like; we will understand it because we will be engaged in the search for wisdom. But what does the search for wisdom entail? The question leads to the parable of the cave.

THE PARABLE OF THE CAVE (514A–517A)

The parable of the cave may be broken into three parts. First, Socrates describes the geography of the cave and the activities of the various groups that inhabit it. Second, he describes what happens if a prisoner is released and journeys out of the cave and then returns. Finally, he sums up the parable and interprets part of its symbolism and significance in terms of the earlier analogy of the sun and the Good and the figure of the divided line.

The cave is a deep, wide hole slanting downward into the earth. The entranceway is presumably steep and twisting, so that little, if any, light from the sun penetrates to the far end of the cave. Within the cave, close to the entrance, is a fire that serves to illuminate the cave. Past the fire is a wall, and on the side of the wall toward the fire there is a rampart along which a small group of men walk back and forth. These men are holding up models of natural objects—animals, plants, rocks—and as they walk back and forth they speak.

On the other side of the wall, still farther from the entrance, is a bench on which a large number of people sit; they are chained so they cannot turn around and see either the men walking along the rampart or the fire beyond. These prisoners are also talking to each other, but their major attention is focused on the far wall of the cave, for on that wall are reflected the shadows of the models carried by the men walking on the rampart. The shadows are cast by the fire. The far wall of the cave not only serves as a screen for the shadows cast by the models but also reflects the voices of the men carrying those models.

The prisoners sitting on the bench, chained there since childhood, can see only the shadows and hear only the echoes. They can speak to each other, but apparently they cannot directly see either their neighbors or themselves. Apparently—and this point is difficult to determine—the prisoners can see only their own and their neighbors' shadows as these, too, are cast on the wall before them. Thus the prisoners know themselves and each other only through shadows; they know about other things only through the shadows of artificial images and through the echoes that reach them. When they talk, they talk only of the shadows, and when they assign names to things, they naturally assign them to the shadows and echoes. In effect, they consider the shadows to be reality. Note how the structure of the cave is based on the figure of the divided line, in that it contains a complex series of images, images of images, images of images of images, and so forth.

Earlier, in book II, there is another cave. Speaking in defense of injustice, Glaucon tells the story of Gyges, the ancestor of King Croesus of Lydia. Gyges was a shepherd who, after a storm, found in a cave that had opened in the earth a golden ring that conferred the power of invisibility upon him. Glaucon does not continue with the story of Gyges, but those who have read Herodotus will remember that although Gyges was the trusted confidant of his king, he assassinated the king, took the king's beautiful wife as his own, and founded his own dynasty. Gyges, in brief, is the embodiment of the unjust man, the tyrant. Book IX of the *Republic* contains Socrates' full analysis of this kind of man.

What interests me in Glaucon's story of Gyges is that Gyges goes down into a cave to find the secret of invisibility, a secret that confers upon him the power to be completely unjust without danger of punishment. As I understand it, the parable of the cave in book VII is the exact opposite of this story. In the parable of the cave the journey starts in the cave, proceeds up and out, and ends with a return to it, rather than the other way around. In Glaucon's tale the journey culminates with the traveler possessing the power to commit perfect injustice, whereas in Socrates' parable the story ends with the suggestion that the prisoners in the cave are likely to kill the returned traveler.

One major element in Glaucon's story is not explicitly mentioned in Socrates' parable: the power of invisibility. Glaucon's story is a kind of fantasy. Socrates' parable, on the other hand, is not impossible; he himself says that the details of the cave can be applied to human life as we ordinarily understand it. But—and this is the interesting thing—if we look closely into the details of the parable, we discover that the traveler who has returned to the bench and taken his place again among the other prisoners has discovered the secret of invisibility for himself. His secret is very different from Gyges', because it is based on justice rather than injustice, but the secret does confer the power of invisibility upon him.

I have discussed the relation between the cave and the myth of Gyges in book II and Socrates' parable here in book V in order to confirm that I was serious earlier when I described the *Republic* as a dramatic work. The connection between these two passages is based not on argument but on images.

The parable follows the divided line. We have seen that the line is an account of the degrees of knowledge and ignorance. The cave translates that abstract account into terms with immediate human significance. To put it somewhat differently: the figure of the divided line contains a theory of knowledge, and the parable of the cave describes the consequences of that theory for the education of the human soul as it progresses, or may progress, from ignorance to knowledge. If the parable of the cave is a description of the journey of the human soul from ignorance to knowledge, from a concern with appearances to a concern with reality, then what is the meaning of the carefully worked-out details of the fire, the rampart with the men walking back and forth, the chained prisoners with their talk about the shadows on the wall, and so forth? Nothing in the figure of the divided line explains the presence of all these details. Socrates says that the prisoners are like ourselves, but what does he mean by that? And who are the men walking along the rampart holding up images? These questions, I believe, can be answered only by thinking of the entire parable within the context of the discussion of politics that took place in books II, III and IV. But—and this qualification is important—that discussion of politics is now to be seen in the light of the principles of truth and knowledge set forth in the figure of the divided line. The prisoners seated on the bench can be thought of as the citizens of a state, or, as it is called in the *Republic,* a city. These citizen-prisoners are not symbolic of any particular kind of city, good or bad; they represent the body of citizens of any possible political community. The wall with the rampart on it, the wall behind them, represents the wall that surrounded every major Greek community and, metaphorically, the arbitrary and limited area of land that each community incorporates as its own.

In the attempt to construct the just city in books II, III, and IV, Glaucon, Adeimantus, and Socrates based their city on human nature and the human condition, deliberately refusing to accept any institution, custom, or law based on tradition rather than on reason. But now, in the parable, the limits of the city are determined by a wall—a man-made thing—rather than by a natural boundary. I interpret this to mean that Socrates is here denying the very possibility of there ever being a city based purely on nature and reason. That is to say, every human community must include essential elements based on tradition, opinion, or convention; and the completely just city cannot exist in this world. It can exist, if at all, only as a pattern "laid up in heaven," a pattern that may be discernible in thought but that cannot be actualized. The men walking back and forth on the rampart of the wall, holding up the images of natural things, are the legislators of the city—using the term *legislator* in a very broad sense. The citizens of the community, according to the parable, do not and cannot look directly at reality; they can see only the shadows of reality, or, more precisely, the shadows of imitations of reality. Those imitations are the products, the artistic products, if you wish, of the legislators.

In the United States, for example, the basic form of the community is given by the Declaration of Independence and the Constitution. What is just and unjust is basically determined by those products of the founding fathers. Within the United States substantive political and legal debate about basic laws and institutions is based not directly on abstract notions of justice but on the interpretation of justice found in the artifacts produced by our founding fathers and on the work of the generations of legislators, judges, and executives who have continued to build the artifices upon which the community is based. But the human beings on the rampart behind the wall are more than legislators in this narrow sense; they are all those whose products provide the citizens with an understanding of reality. Historians present interpretations, that is, images, of the past, and those images give form and significance to our lives in the present. We cannot look directly at our past; we can do so only through the eyes of a historian; more precisely, we can see the past only as it is reflected in the image of the past that the historian presents.

Perhaps the most important group of image makers are those much-maligned human beings who go by the name of artists, for they, above all others, present us with images of the human, that is, with images of ourselves. Homer, Dante, Shakespeare, Michelangelo, Rembrandt, Frank Lloyd Wright—they, too, are among the legislators of our community, and perhaps the most important ones, because even the specialized images of justice and equity constructed by legislators in the narrow sense may well be based on the general images of man created by the artists.

Every community is given its characteristic form by its legislators. The kinship between communities is based on the possession of one or more legislators in common. Shakespeare legislates for the entire English-speaking world, Homer for the whole of Western civilization. The parable of the cave contains a complete theory of sociology and history implicit in the conception of politics that is the basis of the parable.

So far I have been describing legislators and their images in neutral terms, but there may be vast differences in the quality of the images. Legislators provide the models whose shadows are taken as reality by the citizens of the community. But the models are not pure constructs; they are themselves imitations of the true realities found outside the cave. The models made by the legislators may be good or bad—that is, accurate or inaccurate—representations of the realities. The difference in accuracy, I suggest, is precisely the factor that determines the value and worth, or, in Plato's terms, the justice, of each community. A community based on inaccurate or distorted models will necessarily be an unjust and distorted community. We can now see why Socrates spends so much time in books II and III chastising and reforming the poets. Poets may be unaware of the enormously significant role that they play in the life of the community, and may inflict confusion and misunderstanding by sheer accident or personal whim. Socrates' harshness toward the poets in the early books of the *Republic* is based not on his contempt for poetry and its power but rather on his profound awareness of the tremendous effect that poets have on the entire life of the community. The poets are too important to be left alone.

These two of the three major elements in the parable of the cave—the prisoners on the bench and the men walking on the rampart—have political implications, some of which I have suggested. I shall not discuss the third major element—the fire that illuminates the cave. Even the barest sketch of the meaning of this element requires a very complex philosophical discussion of the relation between being and becoming. So let me turn now to the next portion of the parable—the journey of the released prisoner.

The prisoner, released from his chains, turns around for the first time only to be blinded by the light of the fire. He is confused and unhappy and wants to return to his old position. If my interpretation so far is correct, his response is perfectly intelligible, for the release and turning around of the prisoner amount to his discovery that his own society, his values, even his sense of reality, are nothing less than a sham, a puppet show created not by the gods or some other divine agency but by fellow human beings. He discovers that what he had always thought was true and good and beautiful is nothing more than what some other men think is true, good, and beautiful.

The journey of the prisoner is metaphorical; the prisoner himself goes nowhere. His soul journeys from ignorance to knowledge while the body stays where it is. If we think of the prisoners on the bench as the citizens of a community, this means that when one of them is released, turned around, and set upon his journey to the real world outside, only his soul is affected: his body remains on the bench. That is, the released prisoner continues to live in his community, sleeping, eating, talking, going about his daily business of getting an education or earning a living. And this in turn means that unless the released prisoner freely chooses to tell his fellow citizens what his soul is doing, none of them will be aware that he has undertaken a great and perilous journey. This is the true secret of invisibility. The released prisoner can make the most important journey of which human beings are capable in complete privacy, without those about him having even a hint that he is engaged in a search.

The shock of the released prisoner upon discovering that his grasp of reality has been socially conditioned is understandable; the stability, security, and solidity that he has always known has vanished, and his comfortable world has been replaced by a world in which everything is relative, nothing is fixed. He realizes that he has been a fool whose ideas, beliefs, and values have been produced by the manipulations of other men.

In connection with the journey of the released prisoner, three final points bear mentioning. The first has to do with his ascent out of the cave, the second with his attitude when he is living in the upper world of reality, and the third with the significance of the journey for the conception of justice developed earlier in books II–IV. These points are closely related. In regard to the first point, I wish only to observe that for the prisoner to get out of the cave, he must go past the wall with the rampart on which the legislators are walking. Because the prisoner's soul and not his body undertakes the journey, we might think of the crossing of the wall as a transcending, by the soul, of the limitations inevitably placed upon it by its membership in a community. That is, in the journey of the soul from ignorance to knowledge, the soul must transcend the realm of politics and community life altogether. This can only mean that the soul that transcends its own community no longer accepts the values, beliefs, and conception of reality on which that community is based. From the point of view of the community, such a soul is a terrible danger—remember what the Athenians finally did to Socrates. This apparently simple point can be pushed much further. If it is necessary, for example, to transcend the realm of politics in order to see unreflected, undistorted reality, human communities by their very nature must be in some respect opposed to truth; they cannot exist except in the realm of shadows and images, which are necessarily distorted. That is, human communities cannot exist or sustain themselves without the aid of lies, distortions, subterfuges.

Beyond the problem of the community's "noble lie" is the much greater problem of the relation between philosophy and politics. This problem is at the heart of the *Republic,* and Socrates seems to have conceived the institution of the philosopher-king to bridge the gap between the two realms. From what he says about philosophy and politics it is clear that they need each other in order to fulfill themselves. Cities, Socrates says, will never be just until they are ruled by philosophers; on the other hand, potential philosophers, unless they live in a just city, are likely to be corrupted by their communities and thus will fail to develop their true philosophical capabilities. But if what I have said about the parable of the cave is correct, the disjunction between philosophy and politics is much deeper than the earlier discussions might suggest. If philosophy by its nature is concerned with the truth, and politics by its nature requires the lie, the marriage of the two in the figure of the philosopher-king needs to be reconsidered.

The second point about the journey of the released prisoner has to do with his attitude toward his former life when he is out of the cave. Socrates says that the former prisoner who lives in the upper world will congratulate himself on his good fortune in escaping from the cave and will remember with pity his former comrades who are still prisoners. The thought of returning to the cave will be abhorrent to him, so much so that, with Homer, he will say, "Better to be the poor servant of a poor master." This passage is from the *Odyssey*, book XI, and it is spoken by Achilles when Odysseus visits him in Hades. Achilles says that he would rather be a "serf on the land of a poor and portionless man than rule over all the dead who have come to naught."

At the beginning of book III of the *Republic*, when Socrates undertakes to purge Greek poetry of those passages that express sentiments unfit for the ears of youth—the first obnoxious passage that he mentions, which serves as the paradigm of improper poetry, is this passage from the *Odyssey*. Yet here in the parable of the cave, when Socrates wants to present the feelings of the person who has escaped from the cave, the person whose soul has beheld ultimate reality, he turns to this same Homeric passage. The contrast between the two uses of the passage could hardly be more extreme. Plato, I believe, was too careful an author not to realize what he had done. I therefore suggest that by employing that passage to express the feelings of the philosopher at the moment when he has at last realized his deepest desire, Socrates undercuts and thus renders dubious the entire discussion of poetry in the earlier books of the *Republic*. Like the noble lie and the figure of the philosopher-king, the attack on poetry needs to be reconsidered. As the parable of the cave implies that the marriage of philosophy and politics is much more difficult than the earlier books might imply, so, too, it implies that poetry and philosophy might be much closer to each other and in less conflict than the explicit attacks on poetry and the poet suggest.

My last point about the parable of the cave is very simple, but its consequences are far from simple, for they require a complete reconsideration and rethinking of the first six books of the *Republic*. The parable of the cave contains a symbolic account of both the nature of the community and the movement of the human soul in its journey from ignorance to knowledge. In the way Socrates treats these two subjects in the parable, he fundamentally denies that an individual human soul and the political community are analogous. The individual and the community may well be alike or similar in certain respects. But in the most crucial respect—in their relations to truth and reality—they are fundamentally different. The individual human soul is in some sense fettered by its relation to a community, and as the journey of the released prisoner makes clear, the soul must break its chains, must transcend the community, in order to achieve the knowledge of reality that it naturally desires and that it needs in order to fulfill its own nature. The ignorant soul is a maimed soul, incomplete, unhappy, and lacking in virtue. The community, on the other hand, lives necessarily in the cave; it may be better or worse depending on the wisdom of its legislators, but it can never escape from the cave—only the individual soul can do that. The individual human soul can, and in a sense must, live both in the cave and outside it, but human communities are restricted to the cave. The individual soul needs the truth, the community needs the lie.

This radical difference between the individual soul and the community means that the entire analysis of justice based on the analogy between the two is in some fundamental sense defective. I do not mean to imply that one should throw out everything said in the first six books of the *Republic*. Quite the contrary. We should consider the contradictions or, better, the tensions between the parable of the cave and the earlier books as a problem to be solved, a problem posed by Plato to aid our philosophical education.

19 The Ancient Quarrel

Socrates' Critique of Poetry in Republic, *Book X*

The discussions of art and poetry in Plato's *Dialogues,* particularly the *Republic,* are the oldest systematic treatment of art and poetry in the Western philosophical tradition. Aesthetics and poetics, as we understand these branches of philosophy, begin with these discussions. Yet, with very few exceptions, the opinions expressed and positions developed about art in the *Republic* have been rejected and repudiated by every major philosopher who has reflected on these matters. A large body of scholarly literature now exists to explain how Plato could possibly have held those views. Put simply, it seems that Plato rejects all art and poetry as untrue and morally corrupting—a position that has scandalized philosophers, artists, critics, and ordinary readers from Aristotle down to the present. But the Platonic rejection of art and poetry is paradoxical, for Plato was himself a consummate artist; the *Republic,* the dialogue that contains the critique of poetry, is a poetic masterpiece.

My purpose is to make sense of this scandal and paradox. More particularly, I will examine two closely related passages in book X of the *Republic:* the myth of Er, with which the dialogue concludes, and the critique of poetry, which occurs a few pages earlier.

THE MYTH OF ER

The myth of Er, which Socrates tells as the conclusion of his discussion with Glaucon, Adeimantus, and the others at the house of Cephalus, purports to be an account of the experiences of Er, a man who died in battle and came to life again twelve days later, just before his body was to be burnt on a funeral pyre.

Er's story breaks into three distinct parts: the postmortem judgment of the souls, the vision of the cosmos, and the souls' choice of their next life.

In the first part of the myth Er describes a scene at a "mysterious place" where the souls of all who have just died go to receive judgment. Those who led a just life are rewarded with a thousand years of happiness in the heavens; those who were unjust are punished with a similar period of torment beneath the earth. In addition to the steady arrival, judgment, and departure of the newly dead, there is also a constant stream of other souls who have either completed their thousand-year sojourn above or beneath the earth or have never been born into the body of a living creature. These other souls mingle with the newly dead for several days, exchanging experiences, until they depart on a journey.

At the moment of departure, the souls must pass through an opening that will not allow egress to any who have sunk into "incurable wickedness." These most wretched souls, many of whom were tyrants on earth during their last life, are seized by devilish creatures and thrown into Tartarus, presumably to suffer eternal torments. This first portion of the myth bears a striking resemblance to many Christian accounts of the Last Judgment. I mention the resemblance only as a warning: Plato lived four centuries before Jesus, and although Christianity may have a great deal to do with Plato, Plato has nothing to do with Christianity.

The second portion of the myth describes a five-day journey of the souls, which ends with their arrival at a place where they are privileged to have a comprehensive vision of the cosmos. Er gives a confusing account of the spatiotemporal universe, likening it to a complicated spindle with concentric revolving spheres of different thicknesses and colors, all moving at different speeds. I shall not discuss the significance of the numerical relations among the spheres—partly because it would be too technical but largely because I am very uncertain of their meaning myself. For those who are interested, I recommend the analysis of R. S. Brumbaugh in his book *Plato's Mathematical Imagination*. Brumbaugh may or may not be right in his interpretation of this portion of the myth, but he is certainly right in his insistence that the mathematical details are significant. I will have more to say later about the general significance of this portion of the myth.

The third and final portion of the myth, and the conclusion of the entire *Republic*, describes the process by which the souls choose the next life they are to lead. To begin with, they pick lots that determine the order of their choice. Then they wander, one by one, among a very large number of slips placed on the ground, each of which has an entire life written on it. After each has freely chosen a life, the choice is ratified by the three Fates. Then comes a journey over the dry and barren plain of Lethe, or Oblivion, after which each soul drinks from the River of Forgetfulness. At midnight on the twelfth day after the souls' arrival at the original place of judgment, when all have gone to sleep, there is thunder and an earthquake, and like shooting stars the souls are carried up and away to the places and times of their appointed births. Er reports that he suddenly awoke and found himself on the funeral pyre at dawn. Socrates ends the dialogue with an injunction to Glaucon to take the story seriously.

I would like to raise three questions in connection with the story: Why is it in the dialogue at all, and why, more particularly, is it at the end of the dialogue? What is the story really about? And why is it told in the form of a myth? Although each question concerns the whole myth, in exploring each I shall emphasize a different portion of the story.

The myth of Er ends with Er's awakening on his funeral pyre at dawn, and the dialogue ends a moment later, when Socrates tells Glaucon that if they all take seriously what has been said, "we shall fare well." We can imagine the group of discussants at the house of Cephalus standing up, stretching after their long conversation, and going about their business.

Socrates and Glaucon originally went to the house of Cephalus on the promise that they would have dinner and spend the evening watching a relay race on horseback, with torches being passed from hand to hand. In fact, they never sat down to dinner, and they never saw the torch race, but they were treated to a marvelously rich three-course feast of discourse in book I, and they did have a chance to see, and participate, in an even better competition as Glaucon and Adeimantus, two brilliant young men, passed the conversation back and forth.

Given the length of the work, it is not far-fetched to imagine that the discussion takes all night and, like the myth of Er, ends at dawn, suggesting faintly but clearly a correspondence between the dialogue and the myth of Er. The *Republic* begins in the evening, at the end of one day, and ends at the beginning of the next day; similarly, the myth begins at the end of a person's life and ends at the beginning of the person's next life.

There is another peculiar connection between the beginning and end of the dialogue. The *Republic* begins with a trip by Glaucon and Socrates to the Piraeus to witness a religious festival. The discussion of justice is initiated in the short conversation that Socrates has with old Cephalus. The religious festival is a celebration by the community of its beliefs about divinity and the world. When Cephalus leaves the discussion of justice to participate in the ritual, he is turning away from the search for knowledge and reentering the realm of common belief. In dramatic terms, the opening pages of the *Republic* suggest strongly that there is an opposition, a tension, between the beliefs, the accepted opinions, of a community and the uncompromising quest for truth represented by the activity of the philosopher. This is a common theme in Plato's works.

Plato is too good a philosopher and much too good an artist to make such an important point in the *Republic* only indirectly through the dramatic situation. Thus, in book V, when Socrates defines the philosopher, he does so by opposing the figure of the philosopher to the man of belief or opinion. In effect, Socrates there defines his own way of life by contrasting it to the kind of life most vividly represented in the *Republic* by Cephalus. Despite the friendliness and respect that Socrates and Cephalus show for each other at the beginning of the dialogue, they are in radical disagreement.

For more substantial confirmation of their difference, think of the second wave of paradox, also discussed in book V. When Socrates explains what he means by the need for the guardians of the just city to share their women and children, he makes it clear that women and children are examples of private property. What he is really arguing for is a situation in which the guardians do not possess private property, because it is incompatible with the requirement that the guardians be perfectly just and harmonious. In crude terms, Socrates is asserting that money and justice are antithetical—one cannot have both.

Socrates is not the first person in the dialogue to discuss the relation between justice and property. The issue of justice arose in book I, when Socrates asked Cephalus what he thought was the greatest good that came from the possession of money and property. Cephalus' answer was striking. He said that money enables a man to be just. This is in diametrical opposition to Socrates' own account of the relation of money and justice in book V. If we had only the first five books of the *Republic,* we might think that we had discovered something significant about Plato's conception of philosophy and its relation to common opinion when we saw this deep opposition between the two ways of life represented by Socrates and Cephalus. It would be significant, but only half the truth. From the whole *Republic,* we know that in the myth of Er, Socrates tells a story that in its first portion is remarkably like the kind of story about the afterlife that Cephalus refers to in book I when he talks about the fears of an old man facing death. That is, Socrates, in his exposition of justice in books II–IX, seems radically to reject everything Cephalus stands for. But at the very end of the discussion in book X, Socrates partly returns to the position of Cephalus and affirms the central belief of the old man, the belief in a postmortem judgment of individual lives with attendant rewards and punishments.

The *Republic* is unquestionably one of the most unconventional, even anticonventional, books ever written. Yet the radical, unconventional analysis of justice in books II–IX is framed by passages at the beginning and the end that seem to affirm the very beliefs rejected in the body of the work. Here, then, is the basis of an answer of sorts to the question of why the myth of Er is in the *Republic* and at the very end of the work.

On the basis of book I and the subsequent expositions of justice in books II–IX, Cephalus can be seen as the exponent of a decent, common, but limited and wrongheaded, notion of justice. He and everything he stands for need to be rejected, to be transcended, if the true nature of justice is to become manifest. Furthermore, book I as a whole is a dead end. Cephalus', Polemarchus', and Thrasymachus' conceptions of justice are all shown to be deficient in clarifying the nature of justice. Not until book II, when Glaucon and Adeimantus challenge Socrates to present an adequate defense of the intrinsic value of justice, does the serious discussion seem to begin. Socrates answers the challenge in books II–IX. By the end of book IX these two bright young men are willing to accept his account of the intrinsic superiority of the just over the unjust life.

The *Republic,* however, does not end with book IX; it continues in book X with a reconsideration of poetry, then with a discussion of the immortality of the soul, and finally with the myth of Er. Book X can be seen as an appendix to the main argument, a gathering-up of loose ends from the preceding nine books. The corollary assumption is that Plato was a sloppy writer who could not fit everything he wanted to say into his main argument.

In a somewhat more sophisticated view, book X is conceived as analogous to book I, with its brief discussions with Cephalus, Polemarchus, and Thrasymachus, in which the whole range of problems connected with justice are spread before the reader. In terms of any conclusions about justice, book I is wholly inadequate, but as an introduction to a discussion of justice, it is well-nigh perfect. Balancing book I, then, book X can be seen as the conclusion of the *Republic*. It does not complete the formal argument—that is finished in book IX. But it does complete the discussion of justice and treats those subjects that are not strictly a part of the argument but are necessary to a full understanding of justice.

Because Socrates' demonstration of the intrinsic superiority of justice over injustice in books II–IX does not exhaust the subject of justice, he insists on prolonging the discussion past the conclusion into book X. What are these subjects that require further discussion? They are to be found, I believe, in book I, for that is where the problem of justice is initially explored. The poetic and dramatic hints of a connection between Cephalus and the myth of Er, between the very beginning and the very end of the dialogue, imply that Cephalus' remarks include something about justice that was not adequately treated in books II–IX but that requires some comment.

Cephalus' view of justice as "truthfulness and paying one's debts" (331c) is disposed of very quickly by Socrates in book I. In the central books of the *Republic,* Cephalus' whole way of life is treated as the strongest possible contrast to the true way to live. What, then, in Cephalus' remarks leads Socrates to reconsider in the myth of Er the views of the old man?

In the first place there is Cephalus' conception of the locus of justice. Polemarchus defines justice as "helping friends and harming enemies" (332d), and in so doing he locates justice in the realm of interpersonal relations. Thrasymachus, on the other hand, defines justice as "the interest of the stronger" (338c). When he explains that he conceives of the stronger as rulers and the weaker as subjects, it is evident that he considers justice to be primarily a political principle. In the body of the *Republic,* Socrates gives full weight to these two dimensions of justice—the interpersonal and the political.

In spite of their importance, both these dimensions of justice are derivative. Neither quite touches the heart of the matter. In the deepest sense, justice, as Socrates expounds it in books II–IX, is primarily a quality inherent in the individual human soul. Of the three interlocutors in book I, only Cephalus saw and gave expression to this most significant aspect of justice. Within the central argument of the *Republic,* there is already some indication that Cephalus is not to be dismissed so easily. He may be wrongheaded and confused, his whole way of life may stand in the sharpest contrast to the philosophical endeavor of Socrates and his young friends, but Cephalus in his brief remarks is closer to the true character of justice than either Polemarchus or Thrasymachus is. Of the three he alone speaks of individual persons, rather than their relationships with other persons or their communities, as just or unjust. In light of the first nine books of the *Republic,* Cephalus is ambiguous. He is hopelessly wrong, and he must leave the scene before a serious analysis of justice can take place. He is also closer to the truth as Socrates sees it than anyone else in the dialogue.

A second theme in Cephalus' remarks in book I is not given its due in books II–IX. As an old man approaching the end of his life, Cephalus is deeply concerned about what will happen to him after death. In more general terms Cephalus is concerned with human destiny—the meaning and significance of the whole life of a human being. But in another sense Cephalus is not concerned with knowledge. In the face of his own impending death he has no time to sit around talking about the meaning of life—that is the privilege of young people. Cephalus is up against the brute fact of his own mortality, and that fact requires action, not words. So it is that Cephalus leaves the conversation almost immediately to go back to the sacrifice.

Socrates and the others stay and talk all night. At dawn Socrates ends the conversation by telling the myth of Er. In effect, Socrates tells Glaucon and the others that old Cephalus was right. Whether they like it or not, they do have a destiny. Some day each of them will be judged on the justice or injustice of his life. In preparation for that moment talking about justice is not sufficient; what they all need to do is live a just life.

If we pay attention to the myth as a statement about human destiny, a statement made at the end of a long and complex analysis of the nature of justice, perhaps, as Socrates says, "we too shall fare well." But what specifically does the myth tell us about human destiny? Two crucial moments in the experience of the souls are the postmortem judgment with its rewards and punishments and the choice of the next life. In the first of these moments the soul is completely passive. Apparently there is no formal court procedure by which souls may defend themselves, seeking to lighten their sentences or escape punishment altogether. Each seems to be judged by impersonal, objective standards. What counts is the state of the soul at the moment of death, a state determined by the soul's whole life on earth. The choice of the next life, in contrast, is almost completely free except for a certain ambiguous element of chance. Necessity enters the picture only after the choice has been made, when the three Fates ratify the soul's decision.

Separating the two crucial moments in the story—of a foregone judgment of the past and a free choice of the future—is the peculiar episode in which Er describes the vision of the cosmos. Why is the vision included in the myth, and what purpose does it serve? What relevance does it have to the general theme of the myth, the theme of human destiny? Before I attempt to sketch out my tentative answer to these questions, I need to make three points.

The first has to do with the relation of the myth to Cephalus. I have argued that in the scene of postmortem judgment, Socrates returns to the position of Cephalus and affirms the old man's belief in the reality of human destiny. Cephalus himself, however, is concerned with only a part of human destiny—that is, with judgment and the following reward or punishment. When Socrates continues the myth past final judgment, he seems to imply that Cephalus' view of destiny is limited and partial. When Er leaves the place of judgment and journeys to where he sees the cosmos and watches the souls choose their next life, the myth takes up aspects of destiny that are completely beyond Cephalus' horizon.

If there is a parallel between the myth and the *Republic,* as I suggested earlier, we must seek the counterparts to the last two sections of the myth in the main body of the dialogue. The myth, like the dialogue, begins in the realm of common opinion with a story of postmortem judgment. Like the dialogue, it soon leaves that realm. The parallel thus suggests that a part of human destiny, final judgment of and payment for the deeds of a lifetime, is visible to the man of belief or common opinion but that other aspects of human destiny, perhaps much more important, are perceptible only to those who have engaged in philosophy.

The second point that I want to make about the vision of the cosmos is necessitated by a misinterpretation common to modern discussions of the myth. Although there is no sanction for it in the text, some modern commentators have said that what Er sees is not the cosmos but a working scale model. The reason for this peculiar misreading is that Er describes a series of revolving concentric bands of light as if he were looking down at the cosmos from above. This, say the modern commentators, is impossible, because the cosmos in the myth consists of a series of concentric spheres. If Er were looking at it, he would see only the outer surface of the outermost sphere, so what he describes must be a cutaway model, something like the transparent working models of automobile engines that can be seen at science fairs or on television commercials. This reading of Er's vision of the cosmos makes a kind of rough and literal sense out of the passage. But it does so, as we will see shortly, by undermining the significance of the myth.

This brings me to the third point about Er's vision. If I am correct in taking Er's account as a vision of the physical universe, the whole account needs to be translated. It takes only a moment's reflection to realize that Er's description, whether of the universe or a model of the universe, cannot be understood as it is literally presented by Socrates. Er and the other figures in the myth are not living persons, each with a body and a soul. They are disembodied souls. Even if we temporarily put aside our natural skepticism about the possibility of disembodied souls, it is obvious that if they exist, they could not see and hear and talk as we do. If Er and the other souls "see" the cosmos, they do not see it with the eye of the body but must see it with the eye of the soul. The myth is essentially metaphoric in its terminology. It uses the language of ordinary sense experience to describe an experience that is neither ordinary nor sensible.

This is not the first time in the dialogue that Socrates has employed the language of sense experience to describe what is essentially non-sensual. I am referring to the simile of light at the end of book VI and the beginning of book VII. The simile of light has three parts: the analogy of the sun and the Good, the figure of the divided line, and the parable of the cave. Socrates' language is metaphoric in all three parts. The idea of the Good is not really like the sun in any literal sense, nor is the structure of reality adequately described by a geometrical figure, nor is the education of the soul literally comparable to a physical journey from a murky cave to the sunlight outside.

The literal, sensual terminology of the simile of light requires translation into non-sensual, intelligible concepts; no one would seriously think of taking it literally. Similarly, the whole myth of Er requires such translation. Using the metaphoric language of the simile of light, if we say that Er sees the cosmos with the eye of his soul, the apparent contradictions disappear. The inconsistencies in the myth are not indications of Socrates' inability to construct a coherent story but deliberate devices that he utilizes to point the way to an understanding of the myth.

We have now, I think, sufficient background to attempt an answer to the question of why the vision of the cosmos is included in the myth. The vision immediately precedes the choice of the next life. It sets the stage, and provides the context for, that choice. The physical universe, the cosmos, is the place where the souls will lead the life they choose. But when they make their choice, they are not in the cosmos; they are outside it, looking in.

What does it mean to be outside the cosmos? The cosmos, after all, is the entire spatiotemporal universe. There can be no literal place outside the cosmos. Here again the simile of light is instructive, for it is based on the distinction between being and becoming. The cosmos is nothing else than the realm of becoming. To be outside the cosmos is not to be in another place but in another realm, the realm of being. By including Er's description of the cosmos in the story, Socrates makes it clear that each soul's choice of the life that it will lead is not made at a particular time and place; it is made outside time and space altogether. It is made in the realm of being, not becoming.

Without going into the ramifications and implications of this transtemporal choice, it seems to me that a full understanding of Er's vision of the cosmos, and of the relation of that vision to the souls' choice of the next life, depends on a prior understanding of the simile of light. It is in that simile that Socrates spells out his conception of being and becoming and their relation to each other. Yet we must not assume that the simile of light is a statement of Socrates' ultimate metaphysical principles and the myth of Er merely an application of those principles to the problem of human destiny.

Socrates introduces the simile of light for the benefit of Glaucon and Adeimantus, primarily as the basis for deciding the relative merits of the just and unjust life. Within the argument of the *Republic,* the simile of light is Socrates' major statement of first principles. It is also the structural center of that argument. That is, in books II–IX, Socrates is not only spelling out the nature of justice and the just city but also gradually leading his interlocutors toward first principles, the principles governing the whole of reality.

After he states those first principles at the end of book VI and the beginning of book VII, the discussion consists largely of the application of those principles to various problems connected with justice. In book IX that discussion comes to a triumphant conclusion when the tyrannical and philosophical lives are compared in terms of the principles, and the life of philosophy is seen to be intrinsically superior. Thus, the statement of first principles in the simile of light is adequate to meet the challenge of Glaucon and Adeimantus. But there is no reason to assume that it is also adequate to resolve the larger problem of human destiny posed by Cephalus.

On the contrary, I would suggest that the myth of Er implies the need for a reconsideration of the statement of principles made in the simile of light. The accounts of being and becoming given in the simile of light and the myth of Er differ in their perspectives. In the simile of light, being is always seen from the perspective of becoming. The idea of the Good is described by analogy with the sun. The relation between the sensible objects on the two lower levels of the divided line is used to illustrate the relation between the purely intelligible objects of the two upper levels. In the parable of the cave, the whole course of human life is treated as a journey from ignorance to knowledge—that is, from becoming to being. In the myth of Er, on the other hand, this perspective is exactly reversed: the disembodied souls look at becoming from the perspective of being. If the differences in perspective complement each other, there is nevertheless a crucial difference between them. For a purely intellectual problem, a problem of knowledge, the perspective afforded by the simile of light is adequate.

In book II, Glaucon and Adeimantus are explicit in explaining that they are decent young men who have no intention of leading unjust lives. What they want from Socrates is the confirming knowledge that their opinion that they should be just is correct. At the moment of choice, therefore, the moment at which any one of us determines our own fate for better or worse, opinion and belief will not do; what we require is the certainty of knowledge. This brings me to the third and final portion of the myth, the description of how the souls choose their future life.

Except for the workings of pure chance in the fall of lots that determine the order of choice, each soul is completely free to choose any life. This freedom carries its own burden; because each soul is free to choose as he wishes, he is completely responsible for his choice.

Socrates insists that the element of chance is real, but he seems to go out of his way to minimize its significance. Er reports that the first soul to choose, the luckiest, makes the worst possible choice: he chooses the life of a tyrant who is fated to devour his own children. Odysseus, whose lot is last and thus unluckiest, chooses a life of quiet obscurity. This, given the nature of the world, may be the best possible choice, for it provides Odysseus in his next life with the opportunity to lead a life of philosophy.

It would appear from Er's account that every human being is predestined for a specific fate before his or her life begins. This is what the myth seems to say, but in this portion of the myth, as well as in the others, the details need to be translated. The transcosmic context in which the choice occurs indicates that the choice of one's life does not take place at a particular moment but is transtemporal, a choice made out of time altogether. The choice, then, does not literally take place before birth. To speak of it as prenatal, as Er does, is to speak metaphorically. But if it does not occur at any given time, when does it take place? The answer is that, as an eternal choice, it is being made all the time.

Every moment of our life, the myth says, is a moment of choice in which we freely determine our own fates. It is true that we are time-bound creatures. We are born at a particular moment, we live for a limited time, then we die. But this temporal dimension of our existence is not exhaustive. We do live in the realm of becoming, but our lives are essentially oriented to the realm of being. The choices that we are constantly making about the kind of life that we want to live determine our being, not our becoming. What happens to us in five minutes, or tomorrow, or next year, or at the end of our life belongs to the temporal dimension of our existence. What happens to us is not a matter of personal choice. What we choose, and choose freely, according to the myth, is the kind of person we will be.

We make this choice continually throughout our life. Each choice that we make, and we make choices at every moment of our life, determines the range of possibilities open to us at the next moment. Cephalus freely chooses to leave the discussion in order to attend the sacrifice, thus cutting himself off from the possibility of hearing Socrates' account of the nature of being given in the simile of light and the final statement about human destiny given in the myth of Er. The others stay to talk, to listen, and to learn. Among other things they learn that Cephalus was right in his concern with fate. But in his implicit and perhaps unknowing rejection of philosophy Cephalus also turns his back on the one path by which human beings can at least hope to determine their own fate intelligently.

The last question that I want to take up concerns the form of the myth. If I have been right up to this point in my very sketchy interpretation, then I think it can fairly be asked why Socrates does not come right out and say what he thinks about human destiny. Why does he choose to express himself metaphorically through a myth? One part of the answer to this question can be seen if one addresses it, not to the myth, but to the simile of light.

The conception of being expressed through the simile of light is stated metaphorically because there is no other way to state it. The realm of ideas is eternal and immutable, in contrast to the realm of becoming, where everything is transient and undergoing constant change. All the transient, mutable things that become are images or reflections of the eternal ideas. They are signposts pointing to the ideas.

Language—the words and sounds and conceptions that we use in communicating with each other—is no less transient and mutable than anything else in this world of becoming. Language can be used to point to that other world of eternal being, but it cannot literally express the nature of that world. Thus, according to Socrates' conception of being, discourse about the ultimate nature of things can never be literal. It must always be metaphoric at best. But this quality is not unique to discourse—all becoming is a metaphor of being.

It is a mark of Socrates' intellectual integrity that he never tries to deceive his interlocutors by presenting them with an apparently literal account of being. What is not yet clear is why the understanding of the human condition embodied in the myth of Er is presented in mythical or poetic form. To grasp fully the myth of Er, therefore, we need to consider its poetic form, as well as its philosophical content. Since Socrates himself prefaces the myth of Er with his systematic critique of poetry at the beginning of book X, it seems reasonable that we now consider that earlier passage.

THE CRITIQUE OF POETRY

After the great digression of books V, VI, and VII, in which the nature of philosophy and the requirements of an adequate philosophical education for the guardians are set forth, Socrates turns in books VIII and IX to the gradual decline of the just city and the just individual through political and personal injustice. By the end of book IX he has described the forms of injustice and developed three distinct arguments, each of which seems to prove conclusively that tyranny, the ultimate form of injustice, is intrinsically inferior to justice.

At this point Socrates has answered triumphantly the challenge of Glaucon and Adeimantus presented at the beginning of book II. Readers assume that the dialogue will end here, and yet, surprisingly, it continues for another book. Socrates begins book X by unexpectedly asserting that he and his interlocutors were entirely right in their earlier description of the organization of a good city—especially in the matter of poetry, which is discussed in books II and III. He goes on to develop a new and even more devastating critique of poetry than he made in those earlier books.

In books II and III, the argument concludes with the observation that poetry is too important to be left in the hands of the poets and that the poetry of Homer and the other traditional poets requires very careful censoring of objectionable passages so that it is suitable for the proper education of the young. In book X Socrates is not so gentle. All imitative poetry is deceptive and corrupting, he says, and it is banished from the just city. What follows is a short and thoroughly inadequate proof of the immortality of the soul. He finally concludes by telling the myth of Er. There it turns out that after death, whether or not the just life is its own reward, and the unjust life its own punishment, those who have been good will enjoy the delights of heaven, and those who have been evil will suffer the torments of fire and brimstone.

The discussion of poetry in book X seems, then, to be arbitrarily tacked onto the dialogue after the main argument is concluded, along with an unconvincing proof of the soul's immortality and a myth of the afterlife that seems to undercut the whole argument of books II–IX. If arguments, like people, were judged by the company they keep, the attack on poetry in book X would not be considered very respectable.

But let us look more closely at what Socrates says about poetry before we dismiss his argument. The passage breaks into three main parts. First comes an analysis of the nature of imitation, based roughly on the theory of ideas developed in book VI in the image of the divided line. Socrates says that the original things, the real things—that is, ideas—are made by God. The ideas are replicated by human craftsmen, and the imitations in turn are replicated by artists. The artist emerges from this first section of the argument as a producer of imitations, a craftsman like other craftsmen, with one crucial difference: whereas the carpenter who makes a bed out of wood imitates the true and real bed made by God, the artist imitates the bed made by the carpenter. But in doing so he doesn't make a bed that a person can actually sleep on. He produces only the appearance of the carpenter's bed. Thus it is not the imitative character of art that is damning but its being at two removes from reality. Artists create phantasms.

Socrates turns from works of art to their makers and takes up the claim that poets or artists "know all arts and all things human that relate to virtue and vice and things divine. For a good poet, people say, if he is to make a beautiful poem on his subject, must do so with knowledge of that subject, or fail altogether" (598e). Socrates argues that if the poet really knew all arts and things human, he would produce examples himself rather than merely celebrate the deeds of others. After all, he says, what inventions are credited to Homer? For what city was he a lawmaker? What battles did he win? If he knew as much as people claim he did, then during his lifetime people would have fought to have him live in their cities rather than let him wander homeless around Greece.

Socrates asks what art, if any, Homer did possess. He argues that for every object there are three distinct arts: the art of the user, the art of the maker, and the art of the imitator. The horseman, for example, knows about bridles and how to use them; that is his art. The bridle maker doesn't have firsthand knowledge, but on the basis of information and directions given him by the horseman, he knows just enough to make a bridle. His knowledge of bridles, being secondhand, should properly be called opinion. Finally, there is the artist who imitates the bridle made by the bridle maker. He doesn't have the "opinion" of the maker, much less the "knowledge" of the rider. In fact, this imitator doesn't know anything significant about bridles except what they look like.

Having reduced artists to utter ignoramuses, Socrates then turns his attention to the audience and asks about the effect of art on them. Here he relies on the tripartite analysis of the soul set forth in books II, III, and IV. Art, he says, appeals to the lowest element in the soul, the passions, which are governed by pleasure and pain; and art appeals to this beggarly part of ourselves because it deals primarily with people and events that are essentially passionate. A reasonable man, if he suffered some terrible misfortune, would not weep and wail; he would control his passions and bear his suffering with moderation and decency. Tragic heroes, however, are not reasonable men; they beat their breasts and publicly declaim their misery in a way prudent men would be ashamed to let themselves do. But art does not appeal only to these lower, passionate elements in our souls. Socrates argues that by looking at works of art and vicariously indulging our wretched passions, we strengthen the passions at the expense of the higher and more reasonable parts of the soul. As a consequence, when we are faced with situations that call for self-control, moderation, and prudence, we find it more difficult to restrain ourselves than if we had not so indulged.

Having utterly demolished poetry, Socrates sums up the argument. Up to this point he has been irritatingly aggressive, dogmatic and sanctimonious. Strangely, in his summary he suddenly becomes defensive, apologetic, and uncertain. He says:

> Let this, then, be our defense now that we have recurred to the subject of poetry, that it was only to be expected that we should expel poetry from the city, such being her nature. The argument compelled us. And let us tell poetry also, in case she should accuse us of brutality and boorishness, that there is an ancient quarrel between poetry and philosophy. . . . Nevertheless, let us also state that if the pleasure-producing and imitative poetry has any arguments to show that she is in her right place in a well-governed city, we shall be very glad to welcome her back again. We are highly conscious of the charm she exercises upon us. But all the same it would be impious to betray what we believe to be the truth. Is that not so, friend? Do not you feel her magic charm, especially when she speaks with Homer's lips?
>
> (607B–D)

What are we to make of this conclusion? After deliberately and arbitrarily reintroducing the subject of poetry and attacking it as despicable from every possible point of view, Socrates ends by tacitly admitting that he has been brutal and boorish. He admits that he personally doesn't dislike poetry; it was the argument that compelled him to say those disparaging things. Nor is he convinced that his argument has been cogent. Not only is he willing to listen to any counterargument but he invites those who disagree with his position to step forward.

Let us step forward—not to defend poetry but to question Socrates. What follows are some questions that we might put to him: Socrates, we are confused. We thought the conversation ended in book IX when you showed that justice is intrinsically better than injustice. If you had to continue the discussion, why did you bother to take up an issue that had already been discussed at great length in books II and III? If you wanted to reconsider one of the subjects treated earlier, surely poetry was a strange choice, for many other topics touched on during the conversation were not so fully treated and deserve further consideration. But if you had to talk about poetry a second time, surely you could have spoken more reasonably and more convincingly? If you felt compelled to say those dreadful things about poetry, why do you suggest so clearly at the end of your remarks that you don't believe them yourself and that you think a good deal more can be said about poetry? If there is a genuine quarrel between philosophy and poetry, surely you can describe it for us more adequately than you have.

These, I think, are some of the questions to ask of Socrates. Let us begin with the first and most massive: Why is book X in general, and the second discussion of poetry in particular, included in the *Republic* at all? To find an answer, we must turn briefly back to book IX. At the very end of the book, at the conclusion of the discussion of justice, Glaucon says to Socrates: "You are speaking of the city whose foundation we have been describing, which has its being in words; for there is no spot on earth, I imagine, where it actually exists" (592a). Socrates replies: "No, but perhaps it is laid up in heaven as a pattern for him who wills to see, and seeing to found a city in himself. For whether it exists anywhere or ever will exist, is no matter" (592b). With this one remark, Socrates admits openly that the perfect city that he and his interlocutors have been describing does not exist in this world and never can exist—and its lack of existence doesn't matter.

If the just city does not and cannot exist in this world, why have Socrates and his friends been talking all night about the various institutions and devices to be employed in founding and maintaining the city? Socrates himself indirectly explains. During the discussion of poetry in book X, where he rejects the claim that artists are wise men who know and can do all things, he says: "Now, do you suppose that if any man could make both the object of imitation and the image, that he would trouble to set himself down to the manufacture of images, and would put this power in the forefront of his life as his best possession"? (599a). Glaucon replies, "Not I," and Socrates continues: "But, I imagine, if he had true knowledge of those things he also imitates, he would be much more zealous in the doing than in the imitation of them, and he would try to leave many beautiful deeds as memorials behind him. He would much rather be the hero whose praises are sung, than the poet who sings them" (599b).

The contempt in Socrates' voice is unmistakable. But is not Socrates himself in almost exactly the position of the poets whom he seems to despise? Hasn't he spent an entire night singing the praises of the just city and the just man to Glaucon and Adeimantus? Where are the cities that Socrates has founded, the institutions that he has established? Perhaps more than any man who ever lived, Socrates spent his time talking rather than doing. But, you may object, Socrates cannot be blamed for not founding the just city, for in this world that city can exist only in words. That is exactly my point: Socrates has been a poet during his long conversation with Glaucon and Adeimantus, the conversation that constitutes the *Republic*.

The discussion of poetry in book X thus reflects back on the entire discussion of justice in books II–IX and puts that discussion in its proper context. But the discovery that Socrates has been a poet during his long discourse on justice does not solve any problems; instead, it raises a host of unexpected difficulties. Are we now to say that Socrates' objections to poetry, poets, and the effect of poetry apply to his own poetic account of justice? Surely that cannot be. In the first place, Socrates has carefully avoided the faults with which he charges Homer and the other poets. He has not produced an imitation of an imitation. The city that he has described is not an imitation of any earthly city but an imitation in words of the ideal city, which, like the ideal bed imitated by the carpenter, is the one and only true city.

Second, the discussion of poetry substantiates Socrates' claim to wisdom, such as it is. Glaucon and Adeimantus challenged him to present an adequate defense of the intrinsic superiority of justice over injustice, and he has done so to their satisfaction. I have not said that Socrates' defense of justice is perfectly adequate. Step by step Socrates developed his conception of the just city and the just individual, and Glaucon and Adeimantus were free to object or disagree with him at any point. As we know, they exercise their right to disagree many times during the discussion. Each time Socrates is equal to the challenge; each time he is able to show them that his view is reasonable. There are also many, many places in the *Republic* where Glaucon and Adeimantus could have objected but didn't. Socrates has shown himself willing to undergo the critical cross-examination that he subjects others to in order to test the validity of their ideas. To this extent, then, Socrates' claim to wisdom, unlike the claim made for the traditional poets, is valid.

Finally, Socrates' poetry has precisely the opposite effect of the poetry of Homer and of the tragedians. Socrates does not appeal to the lower part of our souls, our passions. His appeal throughout is to our reason. Furthermore, by shocking and irritating us, he seeks to engage us in active reasoning. We must therefore deliberately suppress our baser emotions and meet Socrates mind to mind if we are to converse with him. The result of a sensitive reading of the *Republic* is the exact opposite of the result of a sensitive reading of the *Iliad* or

Oedipus Rex. We leave the *Iliad* or the tragedies, according to Socrates, with stronger passions and a weaker reason, but we leave the *Republic* with a good deal of training in controlling our emotions and exercising our reason. This is true whether or not we end up agreeing with Socrates.

Thus the first result of asking why Socrates reintroduces the subject of poetry in book X is the discovery that Socrates himself has been a poet in his long discourse on justice in books II–IX. We have also discovered that as a poet, Socrates has avoided the snares that entangle the traditional poets. If he is a poet, he is not an ignorant and irresponsible one like Homer. He is a philosophical poet attempting to imitate in words, not the mutable, transient things of this world of becoming, but the eternal, intelligible things of the other world of being.

But if Socrates has been revealed as a poet, and a good one to boot, his status as a philosopher, at least as a good one, is now open to doubt. For the plain fact is that Socrates' own account of poetry in book X does not cover his own case. All poetry, according to his argument, is bad. There is not and cannot be good poetry or a wise poet.

Has Socrates saved his reputation as a poet only to lose what for him must be his much more significant reputation as a philosopher? Again, as we might expect by now, the answer is no. The ironic, slippery little man has only to remind us of his concluding remark to the attack on poetry. There he admitted that he had been brutal and boorish toward poetry. He acknowledged that he was unconvinced by the argument that he had presented and that poetry exercised an enormous attraction for him. This remark, which was so puzzling when we first looked at it, now begins to make some sense.

It would appear that the attack on poetry in book X is in fact defective, not because it is false but because it is only partly true. What seemed to be an attack on all poetry was, we now see, an attack on part of poetry. Socrates' own performance as a poet in books II–IX forces us to revise his explicit conclusions about poetry. Now it appears that two kinds of poetry stand in diametric opposition—the old, traditional, bad kind, represented most fully by the poems of Homer, and the new, philosophical, good kind, represented most fully by Socrates' conversations and, of course, Plato's *Dialogues.*

At this point in the argument all our problems seem to be solved. We know why the attack on poetry is included in book X. We have seen that the contradiction in tone between the argument and its concluding statement can be resolved. We have arrived at what seems to be a consistent position concerning poetry. But we have stumbled onto a new problem, which promises to be far more significant and difficult than anything yet encountered. I am referring to the question of the true relation between poetry and philosophy.

Socrates, you will remember, mentioned in his concluding statement that there is an ancient quarrel between poetry and philosophy. This remark now needs to be modified to bring it into line with our new understanding of poetry. The quarrel, it would seem, is not between two distinct activities, poetry and philosophy, but between two parts of one activity—poetry. The quarrel is not between Socrates the philosopher and Homer the poet but between Socrates the good or philosophical poet and Homer the bad or ignorant poet.

This conclusion implies that the true relation between poetry and philosophy is exactly the opposite of almost everything explicitly said about the two in the course of the *Republic.* All through the *Republic,* it has been assumed that philosophy, the search for wisdom, is the generic, all-inclusive term. Poetry, along with every other significant human activity, could be either assimilated to philosophy, made philosophically respectable, so to speak, or dispensed with. Now it appears that poetry, not philosophy, is the master term, that philosophy is not a distinct activity but a qualifying term. A person can be a philosophical or an unphilosophical poet, but that is the only choice. This conclusion shakes the whole foundation of the argument of the *Republic;* even more shocking, it implies that Socrates has covertly—certainly not openly—gone over to the enemy. He and Homer are practitioners of the same art. His quarrel with Homer is not over whether imitative poetry should be practiced but over how it should be practiced.

If you think that I have overstated the case in these last remarks, let me remind you of the context of the second discussion of poetry. Coming as it does at the beginning of book X, it not only reflects back on and illuminates the entire discussion of justice in books II–IX but also serves as a preparation, introduction, and justification for the myth of Er, which concludes book X and the entire *Republic.* I have already discussed the context of the myth. For our present purposes a few things need to be repeated. It is, in the first place, Socrates' final statement in the *Republic* of the meaning and nature of human destiny. As such, it is the true ending of his account of justice. Second, far from undercutting Socrates' earlier argument that justice is intrinsically better than injustice, the myth restates, reaffirms, and reinforces that argument. It may be a myth, but it is not for that reason any less philosophical than the explicitly argumentative parts of the *Republic.* Third, and most important for the quarrel between philosophy and poetry, the telling of the myth constitutes an implicit admission on Socrates' part that when he wants to talk about the things that are most important to him, he must say them in the form of a myth—that is, a story. But telling stories is, after all, what the traditional poets traditionally do. In the discussion of poetry at the beginning of book X, Socrates implicitly admits that he has been a poet in his earlier conversation with Glaucon and Adeimantus—a philosophical poet to be sure, but still a poet. At the end of book X, when he tells the myth of Er, he goes one step further and implicitly admits the full extent of his kinship with Homer.

The myth, as I argued earlier, is told from the perspective of being. It implies on the part of the speaker a complete knowledge of the nature of reality. Yet the possession of such knowledge, as we have seen, is beyond the capacity of humans. The highest and best kind of life is based on philosophy, the desire and search for wisdom. But it is one thing to search for wisdom, another to possess it. The simile of light makes it clear that no human can ever possess full and perfect knowledge of the Good. That being the case, every human necessarily lives according to opinion. In the final analysis, it is fair to say that Socrates is wiser than old Cephalus, but the difference between them is only a matter of degree, not of kind.

Socrates uses a myth to give his account of destiny because ultimately his account is merely probable; he does not know if it is true. This does not mean that in telling the myth Socrates abandons philosophy. As I have tried to argue, the content of the myth is an affirmation of the validity of each person's search for wisdom. That mythical affirmation, however, is no more than an opinion. Socrates believes that philosophy, the search for wisdom, is valid. But because he himself is ignorant, as he always admits, he can't be sure of its validity.

To state his belief adequately he has recourse to the traditional devices of imaginative poetry. When he talks about poetry, he is critical and contemptuous. But when he talks about what is most important to him, he pays the poets the highest compliment he can. He tells the myth of Er, thereby becoming a traditional poet himself. This destiny is indeed strange and poetically just: Socrates, the brutal and boorish critic of traditional poetry becomes a traditional poet.

But even if the myth of Er is a poetic work, Socrates could easily defend himself against the charge of being a traditional poet by admitting it and then pointing out that the stories he tells are designed to express a philosophical argument. But with this admission the cat is out of the bag. If the stories that Socrates tells are to be taken as poetic expressions of a philosophical truth, why can't the same thing be said for traditional poetry? If Socrates can claim to be a traditional poet who nevertheless is a philosopher, why can't Homer make the same claim? If Socrates can unite the apparently irreconcilable elements of traditional poetry and philosophy in his stories, can we be certain that Homer did not do so also? To answer these questions, we must turn back to Socrates' attack on the poet's claim to wisdom.

Let me note that the terms of our analysis have again shifted. We started with the explicit opposition of philosophy to poetry. The examination of Socrates' behavior in books II–IX led us to reformulate that opposition. The quarrel turned out to be between the philosophical poetry produced by

Socrates and the nonphilosophical traditional poetry produced by poets like Homer. Our brief review of the myth of Er forced us to change again and say that the quarrel is between traditional poets like Socrates who are wise, or at least lovers of wisdom, and traditional poets like Homer, who are ignorant.

In asking whether Homer is as ignorant as Socrates says he is, we will not be asking about Socrates but about the traditional poets. We have already asked whether Socrates the philosopher is a poet, and if so, what kind of poet. We discovered that he is a poet, and, in fact, a traditional poet like Homer. Now we must look at the other side. We must ask whether Homer the poet is not also a philosopher, and, if so, what kind of philosopher.

The first thing to be said about Socrates' attack on Homer's wisdom is that it is shoddy. He says to Glaucon: "We must examine tragedy, and Homer its leader, since people tell us that tragedians know all arts and all things human that relate to virtue and vice and things divine. For a good poet, they say, if he is to make a beautiful poem on his subject, must do so with knowledge of that subject, or fail altogether." This claim to knowledge is made not by the poets themselves but by other people on their behalf. I can almost hear Homer saying, "I can protect myself against my enemies, but save me from my friends!" Let us ask: Would Homer or any serious poet claim to understand fully the things that he writes about? This is a loaded question, for the answer depends entirely on what is meant by "the things the poet writes about." Socrates explicitly interprets the term in its most simpleminded sense. If Homer writes about the Trojan War, this means that he claims to have knowledge of military tactics and strategy. If he writes about Odysseus sailing home, he claims to understand seamanship. Since the *Iliad* and the *Odyssey* cover just about the whole range of human activities, Homer would be claiming to be a universal genius. As Socrates shows very easily, the claim is absurd.

But is Homer claiming such extensive wisdom? Does he or any poet claim to understand fully this or that technical human activity? Is military strategy or sailing his subject? The answer is no. What, then, does the poet claim to understand, or, to put it more objectively, what subject does he treat in his poetry? Socrates himself supplies the answer in the next section of the argument where he is talking about the effects of poetry. He says to Glaucon: "Imitation, we say, imitates men acting compulsorily or voluntarily, thinking that in the event they have done well or ill, and throughout either feeling pain or rejoicing. Is there anything else besides that?" (603c). Glaucon answers, "Nothing." Here, I think, is a fully adequate statement of what the poet claims to know. He understands human actions, passions, and thoughts, not as they relate to technical activities but as human phenomena in themselves.

Homer does not claim either to understand or to render the art of generalship. But to know what it feels like to serve under a stupid, incompetent, selfish general, we can read Homer's account of how Achilles responds to Agamemnon in book I of the *Iliad*. Homer may not fully understand the techniques of man-to-man fighting. But to know what it means to face a hated enemy in a fight to the finish, we need only look at his account of the climactic battle between Achilles and Hector. Human actions and feelings are what the poet treats in his poems and what he thereby claims to understand.

Is this claim justified? On the surface, it seems fully justified, particularly for the great poets. It is, in fact, the measure of the great poet. Socrates' admission that he is deeply moved by Homer would seem to imply that he, too, accepts the claim. With regard to the human significance of the human phenomena, then, we all agree that the poets' claim to knowledge and wisdom is justified by the immediate emotional assent that we give to their imitations.

How far does the claim extend, and how significant is the poet's wisdom? Homer, through his representation of Achilles and Briseis, makes it clear, for example, that he understands what it means for a man to be forcibly separated from a woman he loves. Through his account of Achilles' mourning for Patroklos, Homer shows that he understands what it means to lose one's dearest friend. Through his account of the battle between Achilles and Hector, he shows what it means to hate a man and seek revenge.

Ultimately, however, the *Iliad* is not a collection of little but true vignettes about this or that aspect of life; it is a unified story of the wrath of Achilles from the moment of its inception in a petty quarrel with Agamemnon through its manifold developments to the climactic moment when Achilles and Priam meet face to face over the body of Hector and Achilles' anger is purged. Yet the *Iliad* is even more than that. As a result of his anger and his withdrawal from the Greek army, Achilles is forced to reconsider the significance of his life. His anger is not a fixed emotion. As the situation grows and deepens, so does his emotional response to it.

At its deepest level, Achilles' anger is directed at his own finite, mortal condition. He is angry because he is human and because all humans must die. When his anger is purged in his meeting with Priam, it is purged at all levels. He is no longer angry with the Trojans, no longer angry with Agamemnon, no longer angry with Hector, and, most important of all, no longer angry that he is human. He accepts his impending, inevitable death and is at peace with it and himself. As a whole, then, the *Iliad*, by virtue of the emotional assent we give to the human significance of that story, claims no small thing—the *Iliad* claims to tell the truth about the meaning of the human condition, and Homer thereby claims to understand human destiny.

Precisely what does Homer say about human destiny? To put it briefly and unfairly, he claims through the story he tells that a human is a time-bound, predestined creature. Human beings are born into the world for a limited time, and then they die and are no more. There is nothing much that we can do about our mortality or any of the particular things that happen to us. Human wisdom, to the extent it exists, consists only in coming to terms with our human condition. The possibility of a true human dignity based on the full awareness that we do not control our own destinies is the only solace offered by Homer. His picture of life is not comforting, but it is noble.

The *Iliad* thus presents us with a profoundly tragic vision of human life, but a vision that makes sense of and even exalts the human phenomena as we know them directly from the experience of our own life. This vision is what Homer renders in the *Iliad*. It is the true basis of his claim to wisdom. It is this vision that moves us so deeply when we read the *Iliad*.

Now we can fairly ask Socrates if he dares to call this vision a mere phantasm, if Homer is devoid of wisdom, and if his vision can possibly be corrupting. The Socratic answer is a resounding yes. The entire *Republic,* culminating in the myth of Er, is a monumental effort to refute Homer.

Homer's error lies in thinking that he has the whole truth. Although man is a temporal thing, is born, lives for a time, and dies, he is not, according to Socrates, a fully predestined, time-bound creature. On the contrary, man may live in the realm of time, the realm of becoming. But the meaning of his life and his destiny are oriented to a transtemporal reality. Reality includes being as well as becoming, according to Socrates, and it is each man's relation to being that determines the significance of his life.

What determines a man's fate is not the temporal sequence of events but the transtemporal movement of the human soul from ignorance to knowledge, from becoming to being. A man, as a physical creature, may well be a helpless, passive pawn of the forces of this world. But each man can choose freely whether he lives in swinish ignorance or seeks to understand his true nature. Since the only thing that matters in the end is a man's relative ignorance or wisdom, to this extent each man does determine his own fate. Not a noble acceptance of human impotence in the face of an inevitable death, but philosophy, the desire and the search for genuine wisdom, is the highest possibility for man, according to Socrates.

This is the Socratic answer to Homer. It is given its sharpest statement in the myth of Er, but a full understanding of Socrates' position requires that we grasp the *Republic* as a whole. From Socrates' point of view, Homer's vision, for all its intrinsic truth and nobility, is a phantasm, for Homer ignores reason, the part of the human soul that orders the psyche and is itself oriented to being. Homer himself is profoundly ignorant because he thinks that the temporal realm, the realm of becoming, is the only reality. Finally, Homer is radically corrupting precisely because he makes such a marvelously convincing case for his view. To the degree that we are emotionally convinced by Homer, we deny the possibility of philosophy. We affirm with him that becoming, not being, is the ultimate reality.

Homer is not the only thinker who denies the reality of being and insists that becoming is all there is. An entire school of thinkers, the sophists, advocated exactly this view. But Thrasymachus is a weak exponent of the sophistic position. To see that position in all its power we must go to its finest spokesmen, the traditional poets, and finally to the first and greatest sophist of them all—Homer. Sophistry, the affirmation of the ultimate reality of becoming, can receive its full due only in imitative poetry, in stories that present a temporal sequence of events and claim that the temporal sequence has significance. Only in imitative poetry is this basic premise of sophistry built into the very structure of the argument.

We have come full circle; we can say with Socrates that there is indeed an ancient quarrel between philosophy and poetry, and a present and future quarrel as well. The grounds of the quarrel, now apparent, are not trivial, shoddy, or absurd. They touch the heart of both poetry and philosophy. Yet the quarrel is peculiarly one-sided, for the poets have no interest in it; they ignore philosophy and go about their business of presenting human reality as they see it. Philosophers, on the other hand, do not and cannot ignore the poets except at the peril of the philosophical endeavor, for the poets are the great enemies. They are the ones to overcome if the philosophical way of life is to have any meaning.

As Socrates and Plato realize, the poets have the weight of human experience on their side. Their account of reality is immediately persuasive to everyone, whereas philosophers must constantly struggle to make their case, even to themselves. The poets, furthermore, claim wisdom, and the philosophers claim only to be seeking wisdom—they admit their own ignorance. True philosophers even recognize that they cannot even attempt to make their case without becoming poets themselves.

If philosophy deliberately picks a quarrel with poetry, it does so knowing that its opponent has everything in its favor. Thus, philosophy cannot do without Homer and the other poets, for the poets present with immense power the eternal problems that make philosophy possible and necessary. Here, then, is our response to Socrates' invitation to step forward in defense of poetry and its inclusion in the just city: we admit the validity of his charges against poetry but add that without poetry philosophy itself would be trivial, if not altogether impossible.

20 Dialogue and Dialectic

The Limitations on Human Wisdom

Plato's *Dialogues* occupy a peculiar position in the Western philosophical tradition. On the one hand, they are the earliest complete set of philosophical writings that has come down to us. Occurring as they do so close to the dawn of philosophical thought, the *Dialogues* still retain much of the freshness, delight, and sense of discovery that often mark the first stages of a great intellectual adventure. In the *Dialogues,* philosophy is not yet a recognized profession; there are no learned professors of philosophy and no earnest graduate students, no carefully defined and well-established schools and isms; and the discipline itself has not been sufficiently institutionalized to take its place among the well-established and respectable professional disciplines. Philosophy, as Plato represents it in the *Dialogues,* is completely open: anyone can participate in the quest for wisdom—old or young, foolish or wise, naive or sophisticated—and the quester can address any interesting question or problem without worrying about trespassing on the preserves of another discipline. Any theory, any proposition, no matter how half-baked, can be investigated with the utmost seriousness, and no one ever suggests in the *Dialogues* that the person who raises an issue should read all the books and technical articles on the problem before attempting to work out a solution. This sense of the openness of philosophy has given the *Dialogues* the reputation of being the perfect text for introducing philosophy to beginners.

Yet the *Dialogues* have been and remain of great interest to professional philosophers of the first rank. The study of philosophy in the Western tradition may well begin with Plato, but it never seems to leave him behind. Starting with the first generation after him—with Aristotle—philosophers have been praising Plato for his magnificent insights while at the same time they undertake to refute him, showing that his system is unclear, his arguments weak, and his conclusions fallacious. This ambivalent attitude toward Plato is as prevalent today as ever, to wit, such diverse thinkers as Martin Heidegger, Alfred North Whitehead, and the modern linguistic analysts.

It would not be far-fetched to suggest that the *Dialogues* play a role in our philosophical tradition similar to that assigned to Socrates within the dramatic world of the *Dialogues* themselves. In Chapter 1, I referred to four striking images of Socrates. He likens himself to a gadfly in the *Apology* because he insists on asking simple and obvious questions, which, unfortunately, no one can answer. In the *Theaetetus* he speaks of himself as a philosophical midwife, one who, though barren of ideas himself, is able to help others bring their ideas to birth. Meno, speaking for all those who, thinking they have the answers to Socrates' questions, have the misfortune to fall into his hands, likens Socrates to a stingray, which numbs and paralyzes everything it touches. A fourth image of Socrates, in the *Symposium,* applies even better to Plato's writings than these three and expresses perfectly the major theme to which I shall direct my remarks. I refer to Alcibiades' comparison of Socrates to the little figurines of Marsyas, the semidivine satyr, that can be bought in the shops of Athens. These images, like Socrates, are outwardly grotesque, but they are cleverly hinged, and opening them, one finds images of the divine within. Socrates, continues Alcibiades, is like Marsyas not only in appearance but also in person. Socrates, too, enchants and charms men, not with a flute but with words, words that seem obvious, even trivial, but conceal beauty and even divinity.

As with the commonplace figurines of Marsyas, Socrates offers more than meets the eye. But Alcibiades is right in suggesting that it is one thing to catch a momentary glimpse of the beauties concealed within Socrates' words and quite another to see those divine images revealed in all their purity and power. He is also right in hinting that much of Socrates' attraction lies precisely in his ability to provide those momentary glimpses with their promise of future revelations. Surely, much of the appeal of the *Dialogues,* both for beginners and for mature thinkers, is based on that ability. Plato's *Dialogues* hold out to the reader the promise of knowledge, of insight, of wisdom. The promise is never made openly, but it lurks just beneath the surface of the discussion, enticing the reader to look a little closer, to think a little harder. But, like Alcibiades in his relationship with Socrates, the reader is always frustrated by the dialogue, for it fails to deliver on its promise: the true nature of justice and other virtues is never quite revealed, the secret of successful rhetoric remains hidden, the immortality of the soul is never firmly established.

A multitude of reasons are given for this failure of the *Dialogues*. Some scholars argue that Plato had no final answers to these problems, that he merely explored the questions and suggested a variety of possible solutions. Others assert that Plato believed that he had answers but could not adequately demonstrate them. Still others insist that the failure is the reader's, not Plato's, and that if we look long enough and hard enough, the *Dialogues* will reveal their treasures. All of these views have something to recommend them, but each is insufficient by itself. My own conception of Plato's writing and thought is that for Plato, too, there are no final or complete answers to any humanly significant questions. Philosophy for Plato means the desire for wisdom, and the search for wisdom constitutes the supreme human activity. Yet we can never achieve wisdom, at least not the wisdom of the gods, if they exist at all.

If Plato denies that man can ever become fully wise, his *Dialogues* do hold out the possibility of a lesser kind of wisdom that *is* humanly attainable. The mark of this lesser wisdom is an acute sense of the radical limitations of human understanding. I propose, therefore, to discuss Plato's philosophy, not by examining his answers to various problems, but by indicating the ways his answers are limited and problematic. That is to say, I shall try to articulate Plato's philosophy through a consideration of several problems that the *Dialogues* do not resolve because of the intrinsic limitations of human wisdom.

The most obvious limitation of Plato's philosophy can be seen in his use of the dialogue form. Philosophers have always argued for the superiority of the philosophical life, for the unalloyed happiness that comes to those who devote themselves to the search for knowledge. By adopting the dialogue form, Plato has been able to portray this life concretely. By dramatizing the life and death of Socrates, the *Dialogues* depict the philosophical existence better than any argument or description. The delight that Socrates takes in disinterested conversation, the eagerness with which he takes up all questions and seeks for answers wherever the argument may lead, and the unwavering conviction with which he faces his trial and execution present an unparalleled picture of the claims of the philosophical life. The historical Socrates may have been a unique figure, and the Socrates portrayed in the *Dialogues* may be, in large part, a creation of Plato's imagination, but as long as the *Dialogues* are read, our conception of human greatness must include the quiet life of the philosopher as well as the more passionate lives of the tragic hero, the creative artist, the all-conquering general, and the dedicated statesman.

To praise Plato for the artistic genius with which he has rendered the philosophical life is, at best, a backhanded compliment. It implies that philosophy, as he understood it, is incapable of making its own case, that it needs the help of art. I do not mean that the *Dialogues* are to be understood as philosophy with a sugarcoating of drama. Plato was far too suspicious of art itself and had too much poetic and philosophical integrity to practice a cheap combination of the two. Plato did not refrain from writing straightforward philosophical treatises because he felt that dramas would be more palatable and more rhetorically effective to a general audience. He wrote the *Dialogues* as dramas because he had no other way to make his case.

In a famous passage in the *Seventh Letter,* Plato attacks those who have written or will write about his philosophy. He says that philosophy is unlike all other subjects and disciplines in that it cannot be put into words. He implies that putting it into words would, in any case, do no good, because philosophy cannot be taught to anyone, only learned. Philosophy, he says, "comes from constant association with the subject itself and constant living with it; it is like a light which is kindled from a leaping flame in the soul of the knower and then supports itself."

Thus philosophy is intrinsically incommunicable for Plato, and the *Dialogues,* whatever else they may be, cannot be viewed in any simple sense as expressive of Plato's own philosophy. When a man writes a philosophical treatise, he necessarily assumes that he knows what he is talking about and that he can teach what he knows to his reader. By writing dialogues Plato avoids both assumptions. He himself is never present in the *Dialogues,* so he never talks directly to his readers. Only his characters talk, and they never speak directly to readers but only to each other. Plato remains invisible behind the facade of his dramas, and it is useless for readers to try to penetrate that facade to grasp the philosophical opinions and beliefs of the author.

Some have argued that Plato adopted the dialogue form in order to stimulate readers to engage in the kind of intensive and prolonged thought that might generate that self-sustaining spark of philosophy in their souls. The *Dialogues* can quite adequately be seen as a set of texts for a home study course entitled "How to Teach Yourself Philosophy." But writing about learning to love wisdom presents its own problems. Plato's adoption of the dialogue form implies that wisdom is radically incapable of being communicated from one person to another.

Plato does not enjoy a reputation among philosophers for being a moderate or cautious thinker. Yet in his entire career as a writer, a career that probably lasted for more than fifty years, only once, so far as we know, did he depart from the dialogue form to write in his own person, unequivocally stating his opinions directly to the reader. That exception is his collection of thirteen letters.

Much more could be said about the formal characteristics of Plato's writings in relation to his conception of philosophy. I think, however, these few general remarks are sufficient to show that Plato's refusal to express himself openly on philosophical issues by writing treatises is not based on personal idiosyncrasy, nor on esoteric doctrine, nor on an inability to come to firm conclusions. It derives directly from his awareness of his human limitations as a writer, a teacher, and a thinker.

If we accept the notion that the dialogue form of writing was self-imposed by Plato because of his belief in the incommunicability of philosophy, we might naturally ask why philosophy, perhaps alone among human activities, should be mute. Plato is not unique among philosophers in insisting on this point. Some have said that wisdom is achieved through a mystical experience of union with God or some other transcendent reality. Others have spoken of philosophy as culminating in contemplation, in that silent and solitary activity in which the soul at last stands face to face with the objects of its search and sees them as they are. Still others, especially in recent times, have argued that wisdom, if it is possible to attain, is accessible only through action, through the engagement of the whole person in the formless, unpredictable, but fully real world in which we live.

Plato's reason for denying that philosophy can be put into words has elements of mysticism, of contemplation, and of existential commitment. But it is not based primarily on any one of these three. It derives, rather, from his understanding of the human condition and of the place of philosophy in the world. We must, therefore, go beyond the purely formal characteristics of his writings and look more closely at the substance of his dramas.

I have said that the *Dialogues* are not philosophy because, according to Plato, philosophy cannot be expressed in words. Yet the *Dialogues* are deeply philosophical in content and intention. I suggest that the *Dialogues* can most accurately be viewed as imitations of philosophy, dramatic representations of the search for wisdom. The *Dialogues* show who may participate in this search and under what conditions, how the search begins, what it involves, the direction it takes, and so forth. Considered in this way, the *Dialogues* do not so much tell Plato's answers to the problems of politics, ethics, psychology, epistemology, and cosmology as show in images what it means to ask these questions and to look for answers. The *Dialogues* may not be philosophy as Plato understood it, but they do provide glimpses of what he thought the search for wisdom was like.

From this point of view, the most striking aspect of Plato's dramas is the degree to which he has anchored the abstract speculations of the participants in reality. The speakers themselves are not cardboard figures. The character of a man always corresponds to the opinions that he expresses in the *Dialogues*. That correspondence, however, is never perfect or exhaustive. The man is always bigger, richer in possibilities, and more interesting than his explicit statements.

Old Cephalus is present at the beginning of the *Republic* for only a few pages, during the course of which he makes some suggestive remarks about old age, money, and the way a man ought to live. Those remarks do far more than provide a starting point for the subsequent discussion of justice. They establish Cephalus as a three-dimensional character. His presence is felt throughout the dialogue, not only when the conversation explicitly takes up questions relating to money, old age, and businessmen but throughout the discussion of justice. Cephalus, more through his personality than through his few remarks, suggests that justice, in addition to having political and interpersonal dimensions, is concerned with the inner health and ultimate fate of the individual human soul. Socrates' prolonged conversation with Glaucon and Adeimantus, two talented and thoughtful young men, gives shape and substance to the analysis of justice in the *Republic*. But that analysis would have been very different if it had been initiated by anyone other than the old Cephalus. What is true of Cephalus holds for all the speakers in the *Dialogues*. Every character has an effect on the subject, scope, direction, and outcome of the conversation in which he participates.

Plato further concretizes his dialogues by giving them settings. They take place early in the morning in the house of Callias, one of the richest men in Athens, or in prison on the day when Socrates is to be executed, or on the grassy, secluded banks of a stream outside the city walls. To sense the degree to which the setting affects the substance of a dialogue, we need only compare the *Phaedrus* with the *Symposium*. Both dialogues are about love, both are initiated by Phaedrus, and both reach their high point in a speech by Socrates in praise of love. Yet these dialogues by no means cover the same ground, and both stand in sharp contrast to the *Lysis*, which is also about love. A sophisticated dinner party celebrating the victory of a tragic poet is very different from a leisurely walk in the country taken by two friends. They are as different as the myth of the surreptitious begetting of love during the birthday party of Aphrodite is from the mythical journey of the soul to the place "beyond the heavens." There is no myth in the *Lysis*, but then the crowded courtyard of a school for adolescent boys hardly seems appropriate for that sort of conversation, apart from the innocence and naïveté of Lysis and his friends.

The specificity of character and setting in the *Dialogues* is not an artistic embellishment but an essential part of Plato's art and his conception of philosophy. The search for wisdom, as it is depicted in the *Dialogues*, may begin almost anywhere and under almost any circumstances. It may start casually with a chance encounter, as in the *Republic* and the *Phaedrus*, and only gradually take on an air of urgency and seriousness. It may, as in the *Crito*, begin with the consideration of a practical situation that requires a hard choice between two mutually exclusive courses of action. (In this case, Socrates can either commit injustice by escaping from prison or suffer it by being executed for a crime of which he is not guilty.) Or, as in the *Phaedo,* which describes Socrates' execution, it may start from a situation in which the outcome is perfectly clear but in which the human significance of that outcome is uncertain.

The precise circumstances and persons in any given dialogue are less important for my present purposes than the general fact that there are always several people involved and they are always in some particular problematic situation. The dramatic action of each dialogue has as its natural terminus the resolution of the problem faced by the participants—a terminus that may or may not be achieved. Theaetetus, for example, is a budding scientist; his whole life is bound up with the acquisition of knowledge. When he and Socrates discuss the nature of knowledge, they are investigating the fundamental issue of Theaetetus' vocation. Until Theaetetus is personally satisfied that he knows what knowledge is—within the context of the dialogue this means until he can withstand Socrates' friendly but relentless cross-examination—his life will remain problematic.

The need for wisdom thus emerges from the concrete phenomena of life as they are revealed and rendered dubious by the clash of conflicting opinions. Wisdom itself is achieved, if it ever is, when the opinions no longer conflict either with each other or with the phenomena. In sum, the search for wisdom is dramatically represented by Plato as a historically conditioned, communal enterprise of several individuals.

For Plato, philosophy cannot be written because there are no standard problems of philosophy that can be considered in abstraction from the individuals concerned and the situations in which they find themselves. There is, for Plato, no such thing as the problem of knowledge, which is the special subject matter of that branch of philosophy called epistemology. Knowledge is a problem for those who are in some way concerned with it. But because people are real individuals and not mere types, and because each person is in a unique existential situation, everyone has unique problems.

Theaetetus is concerned with knowledge, but so are Simmias and Cebes, so is Meno, so is Protagoras, so are Glaucon and Adeimantus. Precisely because they are dealing with the problem of knowledge from different points of view and in different contexts, the problem itself is different for each. If the problems are different, so are the solutions. What is satisfactory to Glaucon and Adeimantus would not necessarily be so to Theaetetus or Meno or anyone else.

In contrast, a philosophical treatise by its very nature purports to give valid answers to general problems. Plato, by the dramatic character of his writings, denies the reality of these general problems. What disturbs the author of a treatise may not disturb the reader; if by some chance both author and reader are bothered by the same problem, the solution that satisfies the author may not satisfy, or may be misunderstood by, the reader.

Near the end of the *Phaedrus* Socrates describes the difficulties of an author, who, ideally, should follow his written works about as they circulate through the world so that he can answer the questions of readers and clarify their confusions. In philosophy there is no substitute for the direct, personal relationship of two or more individuals engaged in conversation.

If this description of philosophy as a form of conversation accounts for Plato's refusal to write philosophical treatises, it does not explain his insistence on the incommunicability of wisdom. On the contrary, the identification of philosophy with conversation—the fact that Socrates, who devoted his life to the search for wisdom, spent his time talking to others, or, as his victims might put it, interrogating them—suggests that Socrates has something to learn from his interlocutors, just as they have a good deal to learn from him.

One can learn without being taught. This possibility makes conversation—dialogue—the human activity most suited to the growth of wisdom in the soul. The greatest block to learning is our ignorance of our own ignorance, our failure to realize, or to admit that we do not understand or even perceive, the problems we face. The block can be removed most effectively in a free, intimate conversation in which any participant can raise objections, demand clarification, or request further information.

Even so, the success of such a conversation is dubious at best, and in recognition of this likely lack of success, a large proportion of Plato's works end inconclusively, if not in outright failure. Some, such as the *Ion* and *Euthyphro,* end this way because the interlocutors do not perceive the magnitude of their own ignorance. In others, such as the *Protagoras,* the interlocutors seem to be aware of their difficulties but prefer not to continue the discussion for personal or professional reasons. In still others, such as the *Theaetetus,* the interlocutors have both the intelligence to grasp the problem and the desire to find a solution, but they run out of ideas with which to continue the conversation.

The failure to communicate wisdom in a discussion depends on much more than the personal limitations of the participants, however. It is, finally, an intrinsic limitation on discourse itself. Every dialogue starts with a particular group of men and a problem special to them, and they proceed to search for an adequate solution to that problem. The problem is always specific, but the search for a solution always seems to move away from concrete issues into realms of higher and higher abstraction. Thus the simple question of what the sophist Protagoras will teach Hippocrates is transformed almost immediately into a general discussion of the nature of virtue. This tendency of a Platonic dialogue to expand the scope of inquiry and to generate larger and larger abstractions is annoying to those whose taste in drama runs to neatly plotted stories, and in philosophy, to carefully developed sequential arguments.

The disorder and lack of unity so apparent in the *Dialogues* are, however, merely apparent. Few, if any, writers have created works as tightly structured as Plato's *Dialogues*. The difficulty for us lies in perceiving the unity. To do that, the surface disorder of a dialogue must be understood in terms of its dramatic context. The context, in turn, includes the full range of intellectual issues embedded in the problem facing the interlocutors. The scope of that problem can be defined only by the man or men who face it. Normally, the problem is central to the discussant's life. As the discussion continues, everything relevant to the conduct of his life naturally becomes a topic of conversation. Any attempt to limit the scope of the discussion in advance would be arbitrary and would preclude the possibility of discovering a genuine solution.

The movement toward higher abstraction and greater generality parallels the tendency of every dialogue to become all-inclusive in content. Because each conversation is generated and dominated by a single existential problem, the significance of the problem is constantly enlarged as more and more topics are seen to be included within it. Every dialogue is, in principle, holistic in content and integral in structure. Put simply, this means that every dialogue is potentially an entire philosophical system, that the solution to any single significant existential issue necessarily involves the solution to all problems.

The cure for Charmides' recurrent headache requires an investigation of the health of the soul—that is, of temperance, and thus of virtue in general; but virtue involves knowledge, and knowledge is ultimately concerned with being. There is undoubtedly a certain amount of drollery in the way Socrates moves from a slight headache to the deepest problem of philosophy. But then there is more than a touch of absurdity in the human condition itself, and every dialogue has a strain of humor.

The point is that the participants, whether they know it or not, are always seeking for a vision of the whole of things, one comprehensive insight into the nature of reality. The concrete situation from which they begin and which they hope to resolve is always unique, but the grounds on which it may be resolved—that is, the wisdom they seek—are always the same. This in itself poses no particular problem—until one looks at the character of that insight. Then it becomes clear that whatever Plato thinks is the goal of philosophy, that thing is not subject to discursive reasoning. It cannot be grasped bit by bit, one point after another. The wisdom that is sought is a knowledge of the whole. Although that whole is articulated into parts, each part can be understood only within the context of the whole.

Here is the real basis for the incommunicability of wisdom. True discourse requires a dialogue in which each point is taken up, examined, and agreed to by the participants in the inquiry before the next point is raised. Not only is this procedure the only way by which the closed-mindedness and ignorance of the inquirers can be overcome, but it is unavoidable. Human discourse, like all other human activities, takes place in time and is therefore necessarily discursive.

But this necessary commitment to the dialogue also means that the goal of the inquiry can never be adequately articulated because that goal is nondiscursive. It has no first step that can be examined and satisfactorily established before moving on to the next. The validity and meaning of each part are derived from the relation of the part to the whole. Thus, for Plato, wisdom is never partial in the sense that the possessor knows some things and not others. Wisdom is knowledge of the whole. A man may be more or less wise depending on the adequacy of his grasp of the whole, but until he sees the whole of being, any claim that he makes to wisdom is mere folly or deliberate fraud.

The gap between the means and the end of philosophy, between discursive conversation and a comprehensive grasp of reality is, in one sense, unbridgeable. It is a limitation that someone of intermediate wisdom recognizes and accepts. Yet for Plato, who in his *Dialogues* is attempting to show what philosophy is like, this limitation is also a challenge. To show the full limitation of human discourse, he has to provide at least a glimpse of the end, a vision of the whole—not once, but many times. It is to be found, among other places, in what scholars are fond of calling the myths of Plato.

The Platonic myths have been subjected to an immense amount of comment, criticism, and analysis. I do not wish to enter into the controversies about whether Plato believed in an immortal soul, postmortem judgment, and a life after death, whether he thought the universe was eternal or created. All such controversies miss the real point of the myths. They are not meant to present Plato's personal beliefs and convictions on these unknowable matters but to provide the interlocutors in a dialogue with a momentary glimpse of the whole of being.

The myth is not the only device by which Socrates, or the other leaders of discussions, can achieve this end in the *Dialogues*. The myth is appropriate in some contexts but not in others. In the center of the *Republic,* for example, when the time has come to present Glaucon and Adeimantus with an insight into being, Socrates employs not a myth but an immensely complicated and extended image, which is often called the simile of light.

The whole that is dimly perceivable in the myths and the other nondiscursive passages in the *Dialogues* is not primarily cosmological; it is ontological. The wisdom sought by philosophers is not based on exhaustive knowledge of the universe and everything in it. It is not equivalent to a complete scientific understanding of the many aspects of the world. It is instead based on knowledge of one thing—on being; and being, in this emphatic sense, is present as a whole in everything that exists. Any problem, any topic, is as good a starting point for the investigation of being as any other.

In the *Phaedrus,* Socrates gives his great second speech on love to counter Phaedrus' misunderstanding of his first speech. In this second speech he proposes to tell the truth about love, and he casts his account in the form of a myth, likening the soul to a chariot drawn by two horses. For my present purposes two general points will suffice. First, love is defined in that myth as the movement of the human soul—a movement motivated by the overwhelming desire for beauty. In the myth of the *Phaedrus* love is the starting point from which to approach being, and a full understanding of love is identical with a full understanding of being.

In books VI and VII of the *Republic,* however, Socrates is not concerned with love but with the knowledge that the philosopher-kings must have in order to exercise their function as rulers of the just city. Through the related figures of the sun and the Good, the divided line, and the cave, Socrates sketches what these guardians need to know. What they require, he says, is a knowledge of the idea of the Good. But by the time he finishes his figurative account of the Good, it is nothing less than the principle of reality, and to know it is equivalent to possessing comprehensive knowledge of being. Thus, in the simile of light, being is seen not as an object of love but as an object of knowledge, and the articulation of being is set forth in terms of the knower and the known, not the lover and the beloved.

I have mentioned these two quite different but equally complete accounts of being in the *Dialogues* for two related reasons: first, to emphasize the holistic and integral character of each dialogue, the degree to which every true conversation can, in its own way and in its own terms, approach the understanding that is the goal of philosophy, and second, to emphasize that even here, at moments of wordless insight, Plato has indicated the limitations of achievable wisdom. The flash of comprehension that may come at the climax of a serious philosophical discussion is genuine enough. But it is not the end of the search, only the beginning. The fact that Plato could, in the different dialogues, present many different accounts of being implies that no one of them is fully adequate. It is possible and valid to see being as the object of love, but it is equally possible and valid to see it as, among other things, the object of knowledge. In each case, being itself looks different; as the human perspective shifts, so does the appearance of the object. The claim that each myth presents the whole truth is thus undercut by the identical claim on behalf of every other myth. The Platonic myths do provide us with glimpses of the true nature of things, but no more than glimpses.

One last limitation in the search for wisdom requires comment. All the nondiscursive portions of the *Dialogues* implicitly claim to offer some insight into reality. In every case that claim, and, in fact, the entire conception of philosophy depicted in the *Dialogues,* is based on a single notion, the so-called theory of ideas or forms. Yet as every commentator from Aristotle on has complained, Plato never gave a satisfactory account of the theory. I will not presume to do in a few paragraphs what Plato never attempted. But I think I can indicate briefly why he never tried to do so and what the implications of his reticence are.

The forms, or ideas, are usually described both with reference to things and in contrast to them. Things exist in time and space; as such, they are mutable—they come to be and they pass away. In contrast, the forms exist beyond time and space. They are eternal and immutable; they do not become, they are. Yet if the many things of this world of becoming are totally different from the forms in the world of being, the two worlds are not unrelated. The things in the world of becoming are what they are by virtue of their participation in or imitation of forms. A work of art is beautiful because of its participation in the form of beauty. Just men, just cities, and just acts are just through their relation to the form of justice. Thus the forms serve as the ground of moral and aesthetic values, as the basis for all predication of general terms, as factors determining the character of things in the world of becoming, and so forth.

When the theory is stated in this bald and simplistic form, it is easy to demolish utterly with a dozen unanswerable objections. Later philosophers often wonder why Plato himself didn't see the flaws. He did see them, of course; and to the constant embarrassment of opponents of the theory of forms, as well as simpleminded Platonists, he went so far as to devote the first half of an entire dialogue, the *Parmenides,* to all the standard objections to the theory. The joke of the *Parmenides* is that Socrates, for the only time in all of Plato's writings, is represented as a bright young man who has recently discovered the theory of forms and is pleased with his own intelligence. Parmenides, an old and experienced philosopher, is interested in Socrates' theory and questions him about it. Socrates expounds his conception of the forms in much the way I have just done, and Parmenides, with great kindness and tact, proceeds to cut Socrates down to size as Socrates himself does to his interlocutors in most of the other *Dialogues*.

The classical objection to the theory of ideas, and the one that Parmenides employs with the greatest effect against Socrates, is that sharply distinguishing the forms from the things makes it impossible to establish any relation between them. Socrates, like many of the young men whom he later questions, responds to the attack on his views with exactly the wrong strategy. Instead of holding his ground and strengthening his position by reexamining it, he retreats in confusion. His major error seems to lie in not separating enough the transcendent forms from the mutable things of this world. It appears that the theory of forms can become viable only if one rigorously distinguishes forms and things and resolutely rejects any attempt to treat forms as if they were things. Parmenides does exactly this for Socrates in the latter part of the dialogue: he shows him how to talk about forms without treating them as if they were things.

The consequences of such a de-reification of the forms are extraordinary and startling, and difficult to understand. In general terms, there emerges the outlines of a logic of being. As Kurt Riezler once described it to me, this logic is analogous to the relation between the axiomatic system of space of a geometry and all the particular geometrical figures in that space. The logic or geometry of being that the theory of forms expresses is not perfectly analogous to the axioms of Euclidian geometry, for there are many other geometries besides Euclid's. The theory of forms is analogous to the attempt to formulate an axiomatic system for all possible geometries. Thus the theory of forms is an attempt to articulate the axioms or principles that govern all phenomena—those that are, those that might be, those that should be. Ideally, the theory cannot fail to be exemplified by every phenomenon, including philosophy, which is the perennial human attempt to articulate the theory.

Plato's reticence about the crucial conception of this entire philosophy is now more understandable. In attempting to talk about the forms, language breaks down. Language is built to articulate the world of mutable things, not the necessary axioms governing the eternal structure of that world. In attempting to talk about the forms, we are in the impossible position of trying to employ discourse to articulate the necessary preconditions of discourse itself.

Thus, full and direct knowledge of the forms is, for Plato, beyond the limits of human understanding. The theory of forms must always remain a theory, a hypothesis framed by a fallible human mind. Philosophy is the movement of the human soul toward a direct and immediate perception of the forms. Since human beings are mortal creatures bound to the world of becoming, they can never know whether or not there is anything eternal to perceive.

The only alternative to the theory of forms for Plato was Sophism, the assertion that there is no being, only becoming, that human life has no essential meaning or direction. Plato constantly fought Sophism in all its forms, but that in itself is tantamount to an admission on his part that it might be true.

Even if the theory of forms is true, and knowledge of them is available to human beings, knowledge, or wisdom, would not constitute an infallible guide to action. Perfect knowledge of the forms would involve a full understanding of the intelligible necessities governing the world. Everything that comes to be must conform to the unbreakable and eternal structure of being at every moment of its existence.

But the world in which we live is not wholly intelligible; it is also and necessarily contingent and accidental. Hence the structure of being does not and cannot determine the particular things that occur. For example, everything that becomes must eventually pass away—this seems unquestionable. The human craving for immortality is not simply a desire to overcome the limitations of the human condition. It is a desire for what is ontologically impossible. Yet if our mortality is determined by the very nature of being, when we die and, even more important, how we die are not. The particularities of existence are contingent. This is, I think, the ultimate limitation of wisdom: the insight that we seek and that we can never quite achieve is primarily a knowledge that the things of this world, including ourselves, are absolutely unknowable.

At each level—from the artistic form of Plato's writings, to the character of a philosophical conversation, to the nondiscursive accounts of being in the *Dialogues,* and finally to the core of philosophical thought, the theory of forms—Plato took considerable pains to indicate the narrow and modest boundaries within which human understanding must operate. As we penetrate deeper and deeper into his thought, the same unresolved problems constantly reappear. They remain unresolved, but we gradually comes to understand why that is so. At each step along the way Plato insists that we can go no further and simultaneously invites us to take the next step.

The reader who shares the foolish hope of Alcibiades that the ironic satyr figurine will one day open wide and reveal its hidden treasures is bound to be disappointed. The half-revealing, half-concealing glimpses of the truth are all there is to see. The full understanding and acceptance of this hard fact are the beginning and the end of human wisdom and moderation. Plato failed to write philosophy in a conventional manner and to produce a conventional system of philosophy not because he saw too little but because he saw so much.

References

Adler, Mortimer, ed. 1952. *The Great Ideas: A Syntopicon of Great Books of the Western World*. 2 vols. Chicago: William Benton; Encyclopedia Britannia.

Arendt, Hannah. 1958. *The Human Condition*. Chicago: University of Chicago Press.

Aristotle. 1941. *The Basic Works of Aristotle*. Ed. Richard McKeon. New York: Random House.

Brumbaugh, R. S. 1954. *Plato's Mathematical Imagination*. Bloomington: Indiana University Press.

Cicero, Marcus Tullius. 1989. *Tusculan Disputations*. Trans. J. E. King, ed. J. P. Gould et al. The Loeb Classical Library. Cambridge: Harvard University Press.

Confucius. 1861. *Confucian Analects*. Vol. 1 of *The Chinese Classics*. Trans. J. Legge. London: Trübner.

————. 1960. *Confucian Analects*. Vol. 1 of *The Chinese Classics*. Trans. J. Legge. 3d ed. Hong Kong: Hong Kong University Press.

Conrad, J. 1946. Author's Note to *Youth, Heart of Darkness, and The End of the Tether*. London: J. M. Dent and Sons.

————. 1963. "The Congo Diary." In *Heart of Darkness,* ed. R. Kimbrough. New York: W. W. Norton.

————. 1963. Extracts from Correspondence, January 16–June 18, 1890. In *Heart of Darkness,* ed. R. Kimbrough. New York: W. W. Norton.

————. 1963. *Heart of Darkness*. Ed. R. Kimbrough. New York: W. W. Norton.

Du Fu. *See* Tu Fu

Herodotus. 1987. *The History*. Trans. D. Grene. Chicago: University of Chicago Press.

Homer. 1951. *The Iliad of Homer*. Trans. R. Lattimore. Chicago: University of Chicago Press.

————. 1991. *The Odyssey of Homer*. Trans. R. Lattimore. New York: HarperPerennial.

James, H. 1966. "Loose Baggy Monsters." In *War and Peace,* ed. G. Gibain. New York: W. W. Norton. First published as the preface to *The Tragic Muse* (New York: Charles Scribner's Sons, 1908).

Katz, Joseph, and Mildred Henry. 1988. *Turning Professors into Teachers*. New York: Macmillan.

Kohlberg, Lawrence. 1984. *The Psychology of Moral Development*. San Francisco: Harper and Row.

Lerner, Ralph, and Muhsin Mahdi, eds., with the collaboration of Ernest L. Fortin. 1963. *Medieval Political Philosophy: A Sourcebook*. New York: Free Press of Glencoe.

Li Po [Li Bai]. 1911. "Thoughts in a Tranquil Night." In *A Lute of Jade*, trans. L. Cranmer-Byng. 2d ed. London: Butler and Tanner.

————. 1978. "In the Quiet Night." In *The Chinese Translations*, trans. W. Bynner from the texts of Kiang Kang-hu, ed. J. Kraft. New York: Farrar, Straus, Giroux.

Parry, Milman. 1971. *The Making of Homeric Verse: The Collected Papers of Milman Parry*. Ed. Adam Parry. Oxford: Oxford University Press.

Perry, W. 1970. *Forms of Intellectual and Ethical Development in the College Years*. New York: Holt, Rinehart and Winston.

Plato. 1914. *Phaedrus*. Trans. H. N. Fowler, ed. G. P. Goold et al. The Loeb Classical Library. Cambridge: Harvard University Press.

————. 1924. *Laches*. Trans. W. R. M. Lamb, ed. G. P. Goold et al. The Loeb Classical Library. Cambridge: Harvard University Press.

————. 1956. *Protagoras*. Trans. B. Jowett, rev. M. Ostwald, ed. G. Vlastos. New York: Macmillan.

————. 1961. *Plato: The Collected Dialogues*. Ed. E. Hamilton and H. Cairns. Princeton: Princeton University Press.

————. 1968. *The Republic of Plato*. Trans. A. Bloom. New York: Basic Books.

Shelley, M. 1983. *Frankenstein, or The Modern Prometheus*. 3d ed. Reprint, New York: Penguin Books.

Shorey, Paul. *What Plato Said*. Chicago: University of Chicago Press, 1934.

Sinaiko, Herman L. 1965. *Love, Knowledge and Discourse in Plato: Dialogue and Dialectic in Phaedrus, Republic, Parmenides*. Chicago: University of Chicago Press.

Smith, B. H. 1988. *Contingencies of Value: Alternative Perspectives for Critical Theory*. Cambridge: Harvard University Press.

Taylor, A. E. 1948. *Plato: The Man and His Work*. 5th ed. London: Methuen.

Tolstoi, L. 1966. *War and Peace*. Ed. G. Gibain. The Maude Translation. New York: W. W. Norton.

Tu Fu [Du Fu]. 1969. "A Night at the Apartment." In *Tu Fu: China's Greatest Poet*, trans. W. Hung. New York: Russell and Russell.

————. 1978. "Night in the Watch-Tower." In *The Chinese Translations*, trans. W. Bynner from the texts of Kiang Kang-hu, ed. J. Kraft. New York: Farrar, Straus, Giroux.

Unger, Douglas. 1992. "Trying to Break Away." In *An Unsentimental Education: Writers and Chicago*, ed. Mary McQuade. Chicago: University of Chicago Press.

Whitehead, Alfred North. 1933. *Adventures of Ideas*. New York: Macmillan.

Yeats, W. B. 1928. "Among School Children." In *The Collected Works of W. B. Yeats*, vol. 1: *The Poems*, ed. Richard J. Finneran. New York: Macmillan.

————. Yeats, W. B. 1954. Letter to Olivia Shakespear, September 24, 1926. In *The Letters of W. B. Yeats*, ed. A. Wade. London: Rupert Hart-Davis.